BUSINESS
SHORTCUTS

WordPerfect® for Windows™ Business Shortcuts

Sams

Revised by Jean Jacobson

SAMS

A Division of Prentice Hall Computer Publishing
11711 North College, Carmel, Indiana 46032 USA

Publisher	*Richard Swadley*
Associate Publisher	*Marie Butler-Knight*
Managing Editor	*Elizabeth Keaffaber*
Development Editor	*Faithe Wempen*
Manuscript Editor	*Lisa Hoffman*
Editorial Assistants	*Martha Norris, Hilary Adams*
Cover Design	*Tim Amrhein*
Designer	*Michele Laseau*
Indexer	*John Sleeva*
Production Team	*Jeff Baker, Paula Carroll, Christine Cook, Mark Enochs, Brook Farling, Joelynn Gifford, Dennis Clay Hager, Debbie Hanna, Audra Hershman, Carrie Keesling, Bob LaRoche, Laurie Lee, David McKenna, Matthew Morrill, Barry Pruett, Linda Quigley, Joe Ramon, Linda Seifert, Dennis Sheehan, Suzanne Tully, Jeff Valler, Mary Beth Wakefield, Corinne Walls, Kelli Widdifield, Lisa Wilson, Phil Worthington, Christine Young*

Special thanks to Avon Murphy for assuring the technical accuracy of this book.

CONTENTS

CONTENTS by FEATURE

CONTINUED

CONTENTS by FEATURE

PREFACE

You may have purchased WordPerfect for Windows for your office, based on WordPerfect's well-deserved reputation as one of the most powerful word processing packages on the market. But having that power and knowing how to apply it are two different things. Although several books on the market explain WordPerfect for Windows features, few tell you how to use the program to perform a particular task. And those books often waste your time by leading you through examples that you'll never use.

This book is different. It provides you with concrete, practical applications, *on disk*, that you can use right out of the package. You can open these templates in WordPerfect for Windows and use them immediately. Each chapter tells you how to use the application in its present form. As you work through the chapter, you learn how to customize the application for your own use. In other words, you learn how to use WordPerfect's many powerful features in the context of a practical application.

The *Business Shortcuts* series is designed with the business person in mind. You'll find easily accessible, step-by-step instructions that tell you what to do and what you can expect. You'll also find Beginner's Tips, which provide a little more detail, and Business Shortcuts, which help you save time with the program or application. And, most importantly, you'll find practical applications that you can use every day.

If you bought WordPerfect for Windows, you've taken the first step toward improving the quality of your work and increasing efficiency in your office. From writing letters to developing proposals, from putting together a company newsletter to creating letters for mass mailings, WordPerfect for Windows is there, offering every tool and feature you need to create high-quality work efficiently.

But even if you already know how to use WordPerfect's many features, it may not be clear how those features can be applied to real projects, and real needs that arise in an office. That's where *WordPerfect for Windows Business Shortcuts* comes in. This book, together with the many applications and macros that are included on disk, provide twenty-two applications that you can use to make office life easier. In addition, these applications provide concrete examples of how features can be used to accomplish real tasks.

About This Book

WordPerfect for Windows Business Shortcuts contains 20 chapters, each explaining one or more applications on the disk that accompanies this book. On the inside front cover is a list of the applications you'll find on disk, along with the main WordPerfect for Windows feature used in creating the application. At the end of each chapter is an example of the application explained in the chapter.

Each chapter contains at least four sections. The first paragraph of the chapter explains the application and tells how the application is useful in a business setting. The section *About the Application* briefly explains how the application was created. *Opening the Application* tells you the file name of the application, so you know which file you need to open in WordPerfect for Windows. For more information about opening a file, see Chapter 1. The fourth and longest section, *Customizing the Application*, provides step-by-step instructions on how to use the application and customize it for your use. A few chapters have additional sections that explain related WordPerfect for Windows features. Throughout each chapter, you'll see the following icons:

 The Beginner's Tip icon flags information that may be useful to someone who is learning to use WordPerfect. Advanced users can skip these tips.

The Business Shortcut icon flags tips that reveal faster ways of performing tasks. The icon also flags business tips and ideas that may increase the quality or efficiency of your work.

WordPerfect for Windows Business Shortcuts also contains several appendixes that explain how to install and set up WordPerfect for Windows, how to navigate in Windows, how to manage files in WordPerfect, and more. A tear-out Quick Reference card is included, providing you with a list of common features and the keystrokes or menu commands you need to enter to use those features.

Using This Book

If you just purchased WordPerfect for Windows and you need to install it on your hard disk, refer to Appendixes A and C. These appendixes explain how to install WordPerfect for Windows and set it up for your system.

If WordPerfect for Windows is the first Windows application you have used, review Appendix B, "Windows Primer," for information about using Windows menus, dialog boxes, and windows. If you are new to WordPerfect for Windows, you should next read Chapter 1, "WordPerfect for Windows Basics." This chapter explains how to start WordPerfect, exit the program, use the menu system and keyboard commands, open and save files, and perform other basic tasks. If you're an experienced user, you can skip Appendix B and Chapter 1.

Once you're comfortable with the basics, turn to the Table of Contents. This table provides a list of the applications and the page number where the chapter starts. Following the Table of Contents is a *jump table* that provides a table of contents by feature. To learn about a particular feature instead of about an application, refer to this table to find where the information is located.

Most important, explore all WordPerfect for Windows features and see how they can apply to the various applications. Don't be limited by the major feature used to create a particular application. WordPerfect for Windows provides you with many powerful tools. If you learn to take advantage of them, your work will be faster, easier, and more enjoyable.

Using the Disk That Accompanies This Book

At the back of this book is a 5.25" 360K disk that contains all the applications, macros, and styles mentioned in this book. Specific directions for using each template, macro, and style are contained in the chapter that focuses on that particular application. However, you should know some general information about the files on this disk before you start using them:

- Each template contained on the disk has the extension .APP. For example, the letterhead application is named LETTER.APP. Each macro contained on disk has the extension .WCM. And the style file used for the résumé application is named RESUME.STY.

- Many of the templates consist of the structure of the application without specific content. This allows you to enter your information without having to delete what is already there.

- All of the templates are WordPerfect files. In order to use them you must be in WordPerfect.

Before you use the applications, you should make a copy of the applications disk, as explained in the following steps. You can then use the copy. That way, if anything happens to the copy, you still have the original disk to fall back on.

Making Backup Copies with a Single Drive

1. Insert the original applications disk into the floppy drive (drive A).

2. Type **diskcopy a: a:** and press Enter. A prompt appears, asking you to insert the Source diskette into drive A and press Enter.

3. Since you already inserted the source diskette in step 1, just press Enter. DOS starts to copy the files from the disk to your computer's memory. When you need to switch disks, a prompt will appear on screen.

4. When the Insert Target Disk prompt appears, replace the applications disk with the blank, formatted disk, and press Enter. DOS copies the files from your computer's memory to the disk in drive A. A prompt will appear telling you when the copying is complete.

5. Remove the disk from drive A, and label it *WP Windows Business Shortcuts*.

6. Store the original disk in a safe place that's free from heat and moisture. Use the copy you just made to copy the files onto your hard drive or to retrieve the files from your floppy drive.

Making Backup Copies with Two Drives

1. Insert the original applications disk into drive A. Drive A is usually the top or left drive.

2. Insert a blank formatted disk in drive B. Drive B is usually the bottom or right drive.

3. Type **copy a:*.* b:** and press Enter. DOS starts to copy the files from the applications disk to the blank, formatted disk. When all the files are copied from A to B, a prompt indicates that the process is complete.

4. Store the original disk in a safe place that's free from heat and moisture. Use the copy you just made to copy the files onto your hard drive or to retrieve the files from your floppy drive.

You can now use your copy of the applications disk, or you can copy the files to your hard drive. If you plan on opening the application files directly from the disk you just created, refer to Chapter 1 to determine how to open a file. If you plan on opening files from your hard disk, you must first copy the files from the floppy disk into the correct directory on your hard drive. You must copy the files into the correct directory, so that WordPerfect knows where the files are located (refer to Appendix C).

The following instructions assume you already have WordPerfect for Windows installed on your hard drive. If the program is not installed, turn to Appendix A, and install the program now.

Copying the .APP Files to Your Hard Drive

1. Start WordPerfect for Windows, as explained in Chapter 1.

2. Select File/File Manager. (You can select this is several ways. One way is the following: Press the Alt key, type **f**, and then type **f** again.). The File Manager window appears.

3. Select File/Create Directory (you can select it with the mouse or by pressing Ctrl+T). The Create Directory dialog box appears.

4. Type *drive:\directory\apps* to create a subdirectory under the directory that holds your WordPerfect for Windows files. For example, if you installed WordPerfect for Windows in C:\WPWIN, type **c:\wpwin\apps**.

5. Select Create by pressing Alt+C or by clicking on it. WordPerfect creates the directory. (If a directory of the same name already exists, WordPerfect displays a message that it cannot create the directory because it already exists. In that case, press Esc to return to the previous dialog box and type a new directory path.)

6. Insert your copy of the applications disk in drive A.

7. Select File/Copy (you can select it by pressing Ctrl+C). The Copy File(s) dialog box appears.

8. Go to the File(s) to Copy text box by pressing Alt+I or by clicking in the text box.

9. Type `a:*.app`.

10. Go to the To text box by pressing Alt+T, or by clicking in the text box.

11. Type the path for the directory you created in step 4, for example, `c:\wpwin\apps`.

12. Select Copy by pressing Alt+C or by clicking on it. The Copy Directory/File(s) dialog box appears.

13. Select Files in Directory Only by pressing Alt+F or by clicking on it. WordPerfect copies the selected files to the APPS directory.

Stay in the File Manager window to copy the other files from the applications disk to the required directories on your hard disk.

Copying the .WCM Files to Your Hard Drive

1. Select File/Create Directory (you can select it with the mouse or by pressing Ctrl+T). The Create Directory dialog box appears.

2. Type *drive:\directory\macros* to create a subdirectory under the directory that holds your WordPerfect for Windows files. For example, if you installed WordPerfect for Windows in C:\WPWIN, type `c:\wpwin\macros`.

3. Select Create by pressing Alt+C or by clicking on it. WordPerfect creates the directory. If a directory of the same name already exists, WordPerfect displays a message that it cannot create the directory because it exists. In that case, press Esc twice to close the dialog boxes.

4. Insert your copy of the applications disk in drive A.

5. Select File/Copy (you can select it by pressing Ctrl+C). The Copy File(s) dialog box appears.

6. Go to the File(s) to Copy text box by pressing Alt+I or by clicking in the text box.

7. Type `a:*.wcm`.

8. Go to the To text box by pressing Alt+T, or by clicking in the text box.

9. Type the path for the directory you created in step 2, for example, `c:\wpwin\macros`.

10. Select **C**opy by pressing Alt+C or by clicking on it. The Copy Directory/File(s) dialog box appears.

11. Select **F**iles in Directory Only by pressing Alt+F or by clicking on it. WordPerfect copies the selected files to the APPS directory.

 Copying RESUME.STY to Your Hard Drive

1. Select **F**ile/**C**reate Directory (you can select it with the mouse or by pressing Ctrl+T). The Create Directory dialog box appears.

2. Type *drive:\directory\styles* to create a subdirectory under the directory that holds your WordPerfect for Windows files. For example, if you installed WordPerfect for Windows in C:\WPWIN, type `c:\wpwin\styles`.

3. Select **C**reate by pressing Alt+C or by clicking on it. WordPerfect creates the directory. If a directory of the same name already exists, WordPerfect displays a message that it cannot create the directory because it exists. In that case, press Esc twice to close the dialog boxes.

4. Insert your copy of the applications disk in drive A.

5. Select **F**ile/**C**opy (you can select it by pressing Ctrl+C). The Copy File(s) dialog box appears.

6. Go to the **F**ile(s) to Copy text box by pressing Alt+I or by clicking in the text box.

7. Type `a:*.sty`.

8. Go to the **T**o text box by pressing Alt+T, or by clicking in the text box.

9. Type the path for the directory you created in step 2, for example, `c:\wpwin\styles`.

10. Select **C**opy by pressing Alt+C or by clicking on it. The Copy Directory/File(s) dialog box appears.

11. Select **F**iles in Directory Only by pressing Alt+F or by clicking on it. WordPerfect copies the selected files to the APPS directory.

Formatting Applications for Your Printer

The applications are formatted for a QMS-PS810 printer. If you try to print the applications *as is*, you might run into problems. To avoid these problems, set up WordPerfect for Windows so that the applications are automatically formatted for your printer when you open the application.

Formatting Files for the Default Printer

1. Start WordPerfect for Windows, as explained in Chapter 1.

2. Select **File/Preferences/Environment**. (You can select it by pressing the Alt key, typing **f**, typing **e**, and then typing **e** again.)

3. Select the **F**ormat Retrieved Documents for Default Printer check box by clicking on it or by pressing Alt+F.

4. Press the Enter key to save the change and close the dialog box.

Trademarks

All known trademarks and service marks mentioned in this book are listed below. In addition, terms suspected of being trademarks or service marks have been appropriately capitalized. SAMS cannot attest to the accuracy of this information. Use of a term in this book should not be regarded as affecting the validity of any trademark or service mark.

WordPerfect is a registered trademark of WordPerfect Corporation.

Button Bar is a trademark of WordPerfect Corporation.

Microsoft is a registered trademark of Microsoft Corporation.

Windows is a trademark of Microsoft Corporation.

QMS and QMS-PS are registered trademarks of QMS, Inc.

PostScript is a registered trademark of Adobe Systems, Inc.

Helvetica and Palatino are registered trademarks of Linotype.

ITC Bookman is a registered trademark of International Typeface Corporation.

AT A GLANCE

Start WordPerfect for Windows

1. Start Windows.

2. Double-click on the WordPerfect icon.

Use mouse to select from menus

1. Click on the menu name.

2. Click on the menu selection.

Use keyboard to select from menus

1. Press Alt.

2. Type underlined letter in menu name.

3. Type underlined letter in menu selection.

Reveal format codes

1. Select View/Reveal Codes or press Alt+F3.

Scroll through document

1. Press Page Up or Page Down key, or drag scroll box in scroll bar.

Use mouse to select text

1. Place cursor at the beginning of text you want to select.

2. Press and hold the mouse button while dragging the mouse pointer to the end of text you want to select.

3. Release the mouse button.

Use keyboard to select text

1. Place cursor at the beginning of text you want to select.

2. Press F8 or hold down the Shift key.

3. Use cursor movement keys to move cursor to the end of text you want to select.

4. If you used the Shift key in step 2, release it.

5. If you used F8 in step 2, you can deselect EXT by pressing F8 again.

Copy text

1. Select the text you want to copy.

2. Select Edit/Copy, or press Ctrl+Insert.

3. Move the cursor where you want to insert the copy.

4. Select Edit/Paste, or press Shift+Insert.

Move text

1. Select the text you want to move.

2. Select Edit/Cut, or press Shift+Delete.

3. Move the cursor where you want to insert the text.

4. Select Edit/Paste, or press Shift+Insert.

Undo your last edit

Select Edit/Undo or press Alt+Backspace.

BUSINESS
SHORTCUTS

WordPerfect for Windows Basics

If you already know how to create, save, and move files, move the cursor, and use the mouse in WordPerfect for Windows, you might want to skip to the chapter that explains the template you want to use. If WordPerfect for Windows is your first Windows program, you might want to first review Appendix B, "Windows Primer." That appendix explains Windows basics: selecting from menus, entering information in dialog boxes, and moving and resizing windows. If you're familiar with Windows but new to WordPerfect for Windows, you can work through this chapter to learn the basics of WordPerfect.

Starting WordPerfect for Windows

If you have not already installed WordPerfect for Windows, go to Appendix A and follow the installation instructions. You cannot directly copy the WordPerfect for Windows program files to your hard disk. You must install the files using the Installation program. If you've already installed the program files on your hard disk, you're ready to start the program.

Starting the WordPerfect for Windows Program

1. Type **WIN** at the DOS prompt to start the Windows program. The Program Manager window appears, displaying icons or windows such as Main and Accessories. (See Figure 1.1.)

   There may be one or more program groups open within the Program Manager window. If the WordPerfect program group is open, skip to Step 3.

You can also start Windows from the DOSSHELL program. See your DOS manual for details.

A *program group* is a window within the Program Manager that contains program icons. Windows comes with several program groups: Main, Accessories, Games, and so on. Software installation programs often create other program groups. By default the WordPerfect for Windows installation program creates one called WordPerfect, where all your WordPerfect for Windows program icons reside (unless you move them).

2. If the WordPerfect program group window is not already open, double-click on the label of the WordPerfect icon at the bottom of the Program Manager window. The WordPerfect program group window appears, displaying icons for the WordPerfect for Windows program, the File Manager, the Speller, and the Thesaurus. (See Figure 1.2).

   You can also select the WordPerfect icon from the keyboard. Hold down the Ctrl key and press the F6 key until the label of the Word-Perfect icon is highlighted. Press Enter.

3. Double-click on the label of the WordPerfect program icon to start the program. (Figure 1.2 shows the WordPerfect program icon.) Or, from the keyboard, press the arrow keys until the label of the WordPerfect program icon is highlighted. Press Enter.

   The first time you start WordPerfect for Windows, it displays a message asking you to enter your license number. Type your license number and press Enter.

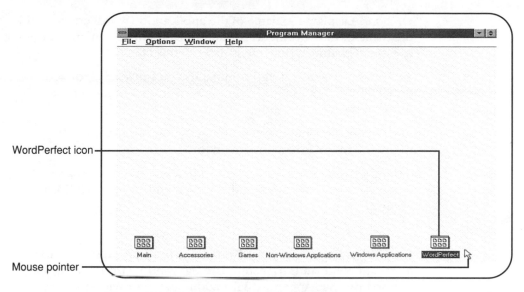

WordPerfect icon

Mouse pointer

Figure 1.1   Program Manager window.

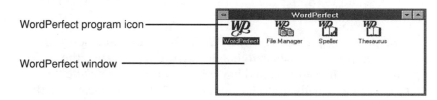

WordPerfect program icon

WordPerfect window

Figure 1.2   WordPerfect window displaying the program icon.

If you purchased WordPerfect for Windows as a new program (rather than as an upgrade), your license number is on a certificate inside the box containing the program disks. If you purchased WordPerfect for Windows as an upgrade from an older version, use the license number that belongs to the older version. (An older version's license number typically is shown on a card inside the original reference manual.)

The Opening WordPerfect Window

When you start WordPerfect for Windows, you see the opening window shown in Figure 1.3. The window is the WordPerfect application window, which has the following components:

- *Title bar:* Displays the name of the application (WordPerfect) and the name of the document. For additional information on the title bar, see "Creating a Document" later in this chapter.

- *Menu bar:* Lists menus and commands you can select. For additional information, see "Selecting WordPerfect Commands" later in this chapter.

- *Button Bar:* Provides shortcuts for selecting commands. See Chapter 2 for additional information.

Beginner's Tip

The Button Bar may not be displayed when you start the program. If not, you can turn it on through the View menu, as you will learn in Chapter 2.

- *WordPerfect and document Control-menu boxes:* Allow you to use keyboard commands to manipulate the window (move it, close it, and so on). (See Appendix B for additional information.)

- *Minimize and Restore buttons:* Allow you to use the mouse to minimize and maximize the size of windows. (See Appendix B for additional information.)

- *Mouse pointer (if a mouse is installed):* Provides a mouse-controlled pointer to select items. Inside the typing area, the pointer looks like an I-shaped bar called an *I-beam*. Outside the typing area, it usually looks like an arrow. (With some features, the pointer changes to a special symbol related to the feature.)

- *Typing area:* The blank area in the center of the window, where you enter your text. For additional information, see "Creating a Document" later in this chapter.

- *Cursor:* A vertical bar indicating the insertion point for text. For additional information, see "Creating a Document" and "The Status Bar" later in this chapter.

- *Scroll bar:* Allows you to scroll backward and forward through the document. If a document is wider than the screen, a horizontal scroll bar allows you to scroll side to side. For additional information, see "Moving Within a Document" later in this chapter.

- *Reveal Codes bars:* Allow you to display a window that reveals the format codes in the document. For additional information, see "Revealing Format Codes" later in this chapter.

- *Status bar:* Displays information about the default font, page number, cursor position, highlighted menu items, and the status of tasks under way. For additional information, see "The Status Bar" later in this chapter.

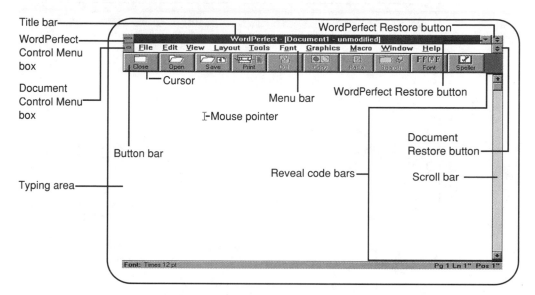

Figure 1.3   Opening window in WordPerfect for Windows.

The Title Bar

The title bar contains the application name (WordPerfect) and the document name. In a newly created document, the title is simply "Document 1." You give the document a more descriptive name when you save it. See "Saving a Document" later in this chapter.

If you reduce the size of the document window from its maximum size (see Appendix B), the WordPerfect application window title bar displays only "WordPerfect." The smaller document window has a separate title bar showing only the document name.

The Status Bar

The status bar is the shaded bar across the bottom of the WordPerfect window. When WordPerfect for Windows starts, the status bar displays the default font, the page number, the cursor's vertical position, (that is, the line

7

position), and horizontal position (see Figure 1.4). As you work in a document, the status bar also displays helpful messages about menu items or tasks under way.

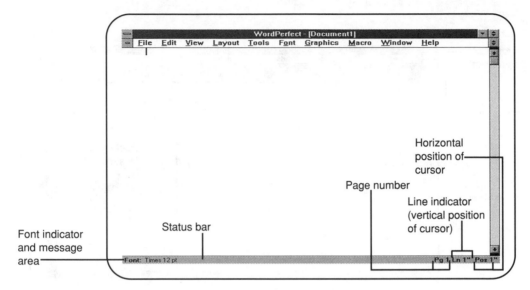

Figure 1.4   The status bar.

The Font Indicator

The font at the cursor position is displayed at the left side of the status bar. For an example, refer to Figure 1.4.

The Page Number

The page number appears at the right side of the status bar, as shown in Figure 1.4. It is the page on which the cursor rests. Note that this is not necessarily the page displayed in the window. If you use the scroll bar to scroll the document, for example, the cursor remains in its original position and the page number does not change as you scroll. (See "Moving Within a Document" later in this chapter.)

WordPerfect considers the displayed page to be the current page. If you ask WordPerfect to print the current page, for example, the displayed page will be printed whether the cursor is on the page or not.

The Line Indicator

The line indicator appears at the right side of the status bar, as shown in Figure 1.4. It displays the position of the line containing the cursor. As you enter lines of text, the line position changes. When you first use WordPerfect for Windows, the line position is expressed in inches from the top of the page. You can change the unit of measure to be centimeters, points, or 1,200ths of an inch. (See "Display" in Appendix C for information on display settings.)

The Position Indicator

The position indicator also appears at the right side of the status bar, as shown in Figure 1.4. It displays the horizontal position of the cursor. Like the line position indicator, it initially is expressed in inches, but you can change the unit of measure to points, centimeters, or 1,200ths of an inch. (See "Display" in Appendix C for information on display settings.)

Messages

WordPerfect also uses the status bar to display brief messages. They can include the status of tasks under way (for example, generating a table of contents), or a description of the currently highlighted menu item. The status bar thus provides a convenient way to obtain a description of any menu command: Select a menu, use the arrow keys to highlight the command, and then view the description in the status bar. If you highlight New in the File menu, for example, WordPerfect displays the following message in the status bar: `Create a new document in a new window.`

Using WordPerfect Features

As are all Windows programs, WordPerfect for Windows is menu-driven—that is, you select WordPerfect features from menus. To select the features, you can use the menu bar in the WordPerfect window or you can use *accelerator* keys, special keys or key combinations that let you quickly select menu options. To display the menu shown in Figure 1.5, for example, you can select either Columns from the Layout menu, or press Alt+Shift+F9 (Columns). Reviewing the following descriptions of each method might help you decide which method you prefer.

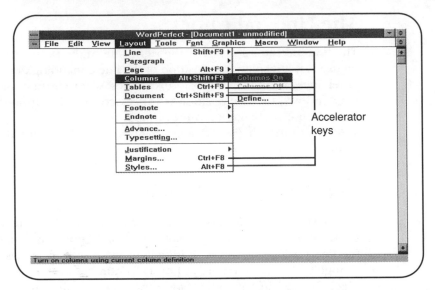

***Figure 1.5   Menu that appears when you press Alt+Shift+F9 or select
Columns from the Layout menu.***

The Menu Bar

Menus are an easy way to view and select options. With the menu bar, you
can use menus to select nearly all WordPerfect features. The main Word-
Perfect window menu bar is shown in Figure 1.6. It lists the names of the
following menus, which you can display and then use to select options:

- *File:* Use to create, print, save, organize, view, and search files, or
  open one or more files. Also use to set defaults for WordPerfect and
  for documents.

- *Edit:* Use to move, copy, search, replace, and select text, or convert
  text to upper- or lowercase. Also use to link a WordPerfect document with another Windows application, go to a different position,
  reverse the last edit, and restore any of the last three deletions.

- *View:* Use to display or hide the following: the Ruler showing tab
  and margin settings, the Button Bar, the Reveal Codes screen,
  graphics, and comments. Also use to create and modify a Button
  Bar and to switch between draft and regular viewing modes.

- *Layout:* Use to change line and page formats in text and to create
  columns, tables, footnotes, endnotes, and styles.

- *Tools:* Use to check spelling; look up synonyms in the thesaurus; enter the current date or a date code; change the date format; create an outline; automatically number paragraphs; sort text; merge documents; create lists, cross-references, and tables of contents and authorities; create a master document from several documents; link with a spreadsheet; and create line drawings.

- *Font:* Use to select fonts; change the text size and text appearance (for example, bold, italic, redline, strikeout); create superscripts and subscripts; and create characters from the WordPerfect character sets.

- *Graphics:* Use to create figures; text, table, and user boxes; equations; and graphic lines.

- *Macro:* Use to create and run macros and to assign frequently used macros to the Macro menu.

- *Window:* Use to arrange the display of two or more document windows and to switch between document windows.

- *Help:* Use to obtain help on WordPerfect and its functions, commands, keystrokes, menus, and terms.

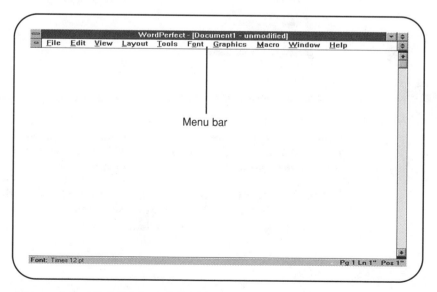

Figure 1.6   The WordPerfect menu bar.

Information on viewing the menus and selecting options from them is given later in this section. But first, let's look at some important menu characteristics.

Menu Characteristics

When you select a menu name from the WordPerfect menu bar, the menu appears below the name, as illustrated in Figure 1.7. The menu is a list of items that you can select. In viewing a menu, keep in mind the following:

- Some menu items are followed by a right-pointing arrowhead, such as the Preferences option on the File menu, as shown in Figure 1.7. If you select such an item, WordPerfect displays a *cascading* menu, offering a list of additional, more specific options, as shown in Figure 1.8.

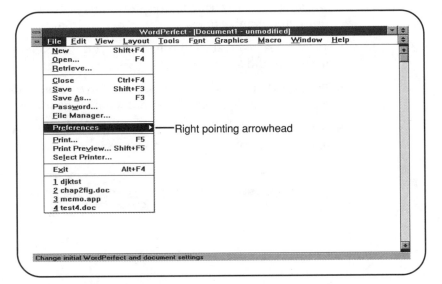

Figure 1.7   The File menu. Notice that the Preferences option is followed by a right-pointing arrowhead, which indicates a cascading menu will appear if you select Preferences.

- Some menu items are followed by an ellipsis (...), as illustrated in Figure 1.9. If you select one of these items, WordPerfect displays a *dialog box*, such as the Font dialog box shown in Figure 1.10. Use the dialog box to provide WordPerfect with information it needs to execute the option. (For information on dialog boxes, see Appendix B.)

- If an item is not followed by an arrowhead or an ellipsis, selecting the item executes a function or command.

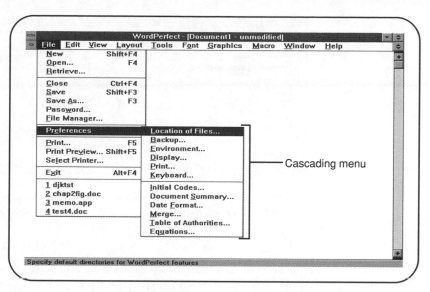

Figure 1.8   The cascading menu that appears when you select Preferences on the File menu.

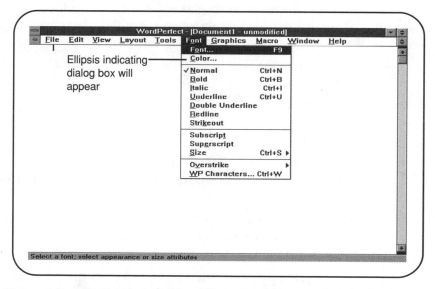

Figure 1.9   The Font menu. The ellipsis (...) following the options Font, Color, and WP Characters indicates a dialog box will appear if you select one of those options.

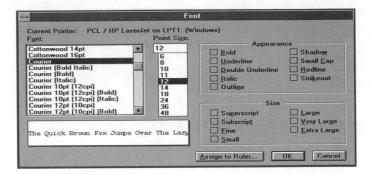

Figure 1.10   Dialog boxes, such as the Font dialog box, appear when WordPerfect needs additional information before it can execute an option.

- Some selections toggle between turning a feature on and off. If the Reveal Codes screen isn't displayed, for example, selecting Reveal Codes from the View menu turns the display on. If you select Reveal Codes again, WordPerfect turns the display off. On menus, you can tell if a feature is on or off by looking for a check mark or diamond preceding its name. A check mark or diamond means the feature is on, as shown in Figure 1.11. No check mark or diamond means the feature is off.

- If a menu item is dimmed, it is unavailable to you. On the Edit menu, for example, Cut is dim unless you have selected text, as shown in Figure 1.12.

Selecting from Menus

To use menus, first select a menu from the menu bar and then select an option from the menu. You can use the mouse or the keyboard to make your selections.

- *Using the mouse:* Click on the name of the menu you want to display, and then click on the menu option. (Mouse techniques, such as "click," are described in Appendix B.)

- *Using the keyboard:* Press Alt to enter the menu bar. Display a menu by typing the underlined character in the menu name, or by pressing the Right and Left Arrow keys to highlight the menu name, and then pressing Enter. Select an option from the menu by typing the underlined character in the option name, or by pressing the arrow keys to highlight the option, and then pressing Enter.

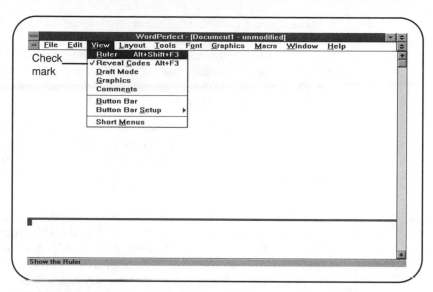

Figure 1.11 *The check mark preceding Reveal Codes indicates that feature is turned on—that is, the Reveal Codes screen is being displayed.*

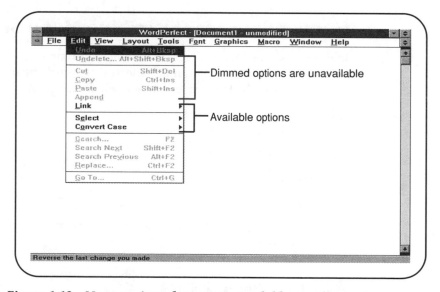

Figure 1.12 *Menu options that aren't available are dimmed.*

As mentioned earlier, if the menu option has an arrow to the right of it, selecting the option opens a cascading menu. Select from the cascading menu to execute a command. If the menu option is followed by an ellipsis, selecting the option opens a dialog box that must be completed before WordPerfect can execute the command. (For information about completing dialog boxes, see Appendix B.)

To leave a menu without executing a command, move the mouse pointer off the menu bar and click the mouse button, or press the Alt key or the Esc key. Pressing the Alt key returns you to the typing area. Pressing the Esc key returns you to the previous menu or, if you are at the main menu bar, to the typing area.

Shortcut

To move through a series of cascading menus quickly, place the mouse pointer on the initial menu you need to open on the menu bar and hold down the mouse button. Drag the mouse pointer through the cascading menus until you reach the menu item you want. Release the mouse button to select the item. To leave a menu without selecting an item, just drag the mouse pointer off the menu bar and menus and then release the mouse button.

Conventions for Describing Menu Selections

In this book, when we want you to use the menu bar to select an option, you will see the menu items you must select, listed sequentially and separated by a forward slash. The instruction for selecting Save **As**, for example, will be:

Select **File**/Save **As**.

This means that you should:

1. Select **File** from the menu bar.

2. Then select Save **As** from the **File** menu.

The bold letters are the letters you can type to select the item. You also can use the mouse.

Accelerator Keys

As mentioned earlier, many Windows-based programs offer accelerator keys, which are function keys or special key combinations that allow you to bypass the layers of menus to execute a function or command immediately. The accelerator keys appear to the right of command and function names in menus, as illustrated in Figure 1.13.

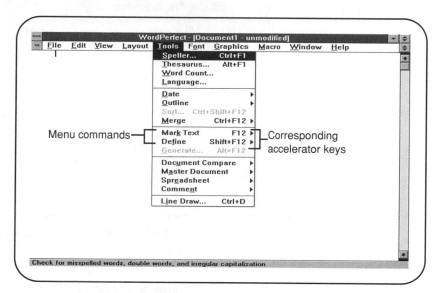

Figure 1.13   Menus list the accelerator keys across from the corresponding menu options.

Using accelerator keys usually requires fewer keystrokes than selecting from the menu bar using Alt plus the required letters. It is also faster than using a mouse, which requires that your fingers leave the keyboard. The disadvantage is that you must learn the keyboard commands. With frequent use, however, this is not difficult.

WordPerfect for Windows Function Keys

In many cases, you can select a WordPerfect command by pressing one of the function keys (F1, F2, F3, and so on) alone or combined with the Alt, Shift, and Ctrl keys. The default keyboard in WordPerfect for Windows is compatible with the Common User Access (CUA) keyboard. This means the default function key combinations are similar to ones used in other Windows applications. This is a great sanity saver if you use other Windows applications—your brain won't have to juggle two or more sets of keystroke sequences as you switch between applications.

A two-sided plastic template that fits over the function keys should accompany the disks and documentation in your WordPerfect for Windows package. You can use the template to help you remember which key combinations you press to use a feature. One side of the template is for the CUA-compatible keyboard. The other side is for the WordPerfect 5.1 DOS-type keyboard, described later in this section.

Figures 1.14 and 1.15 show an on-screen version of the CUA-compatible keyboard template. You can view the template by following these steps:

1. Select **Help/Keyboard**.

2. In the Help: Keyboard area, select CUA Keyboard Template. To use the keyboard to select it, press Tab and Shift+Tab until you highlight CUA Keyboard Template. Press Enter. To use the mouse, place the mouse pointer (which looks like a hand) on the selection and click the mouse button.

3. If the Help window is too small to show the full keyboard template, use the scroll bars to view the rest of the template or select the Maximize button in the Help window (see Figure 1.14). To restore the Help window to its original size, select the Restore button (see Figure 1.15). (For information on these buttons, see Appendix B.)

4. To exit the Help window, press Alt+F4, or select **File/Exit** from the Help window menu bar.

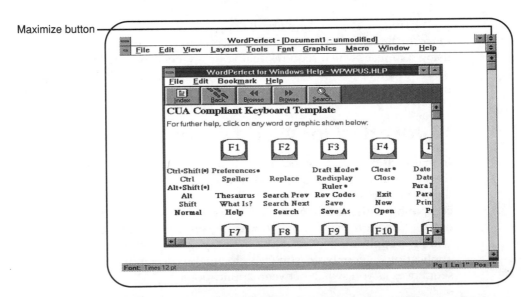

Figure 1.14   Template for the CUA-compatible keyboard, as shown in a small window. View other portions of the template by using the scroll bars or selecting the Maximize button.

Restore button—

| | F1 | F2 | F3 | F4 | F5 | F6 |

WordPerfect for Windows Help - WPWPUS.HLP

File   Edit   Bookmark   Help

Index   Back   Browse   Browse   Search...

CUA Compliant Keyboard Template

For further help, click on any word or graphic shown below:

	F1	F2	F3	F4	F5	F6
Ctrl+Shift [•]	Preferences•		Draft Mode•	Clear•	Date Code•	Prev Doc•
Ctrl	Speller	Replace	Redisplay	Close	Date Text	Next Doc
Alt+Shift [•]			Ruler •		Para Define•	PrvWindow•
Alt	Thesaurus	Search Prev	Rev Codes	Exit	Para Num	Nxt Window
Shift	What Is?	Search Next	Save	New	Print Prev	Prev Pane
Normal	Help	Search	Save As	Open	Print	Next Pane

	F7	F8	F9	F10	F11	F12
Ctrl+Shift [•]	Dbl Indent •		Document•	Macro Stop•	Vert Line•	Sort•
Ctrl	Hang Indnt	Margins	Tables	Macro Rec	Horiz Line	Merge
Alt+Shift [•]	Dec Tab •	SpecCodes•	Columns•		Txt Box Ed •	
Alt	Flush Right	Styles	Page	Macro Play	Txt Box Crt	Generate
Shift	Center	Select Cell	Line		Figure Edit	Define
Normal	Indent	Select	Font	Menu Bar	Fig Retrieve	Mark Text

Figure 1.15   The full template for the CUA-compatible keyboard. To return the window to its original size, select the Restore button.

When you use function keys to select a feature, WordPerfect often displays a menu or dialog box. To finish selecting such a feature, you must provide WordPerfect with additional information, which you select from the menu or enter in the dialog box. For more information about dialog boxes, see Appendix B.

WordPerfect 5.1 for DOS Function Keys

If you have used WordPerfect 5.1 for DOS and would like to continue using those keyboard commands, you can change to a keyboard layout that is similar to the WordPerfect 5.1 for DOS keyboard. With this keyboard, most function key and keystroke commands are identical to those used in WordPerfect for DOS.

> ⊘   In dialog boxes, you can use only CUA keystrokes.

To select the WordPerfect 5.1 DOS-type keyboard, follow these steps.

Selecting the WordPerfect 5.1 for DOS Keyboard

1. Select File/Preferences, or press Ctrl+Shift+F1 (Preferences). A cascading menu appears.

2. Select Keyboard. The Keyboard dialog box appears.

3. Choose Select. The Select Keyboard dialog box appears.

4. Use Tab and Shift+Tab to go to the Files list.

5. Choose wpdos51.wwk, either by using the arrow keys to highlight it and then pressing Enter, or by double-clicking on it. (You also can click once on it and then choose Select). The Keyboard dialog box reappears.

6. Select OK.

The keyboard template for the WordPerfect 5.1 for DOS keyboard is on one side of the plastic template that accompanied your WordPerfect for Windows package. To view the template on screen, follow these steps.

Viewing the WordPerfect 5.1 for DOS Keyboard Template

1. Select Help/Keyboard.

2. In the Help: Keyboard area, select DOS Keyboard Template. To use the keyboard to select it, press Tab and Shift+Tab until you highlight DOS Keyboard Template. Press Enter. To use the mouse, place the mouse pointer (which looks like a hand) on the selection and click the mouse button.

3. To exit the Help window, press Alt+F4, or select Exit from the Help window File menu.

For additional information about keyboard templates, see "WordPerfect for Windows Function Keys" earlier in this section.

Keystroke Shortcuts

In addition to the function key combinations, WordPerfect for Windows provides shortcut keystrokes for commonly used commands. These keystrokes combine Ctrl, Shift, and Alt with the Backspace, Shift, Insert, Delete, and character keys. For example, you can press Ctrl+P to print the full document in the current window. To view a list of these keystroke commands, follow these steps.

Viewing a List of Keystroke Shortcuts

1. Select **Help/Keyboard**. The Help: Keyboard area, shown in Figure 1.16, appears.

2. Select the underlined category of key combinations you want to view. (Press Tab and Shift+Tab until you highlight the category and then press Enter, or place the mouse pointer on the category and click the mouse button.) To view Ctrl+key combinations, for example, select Ctrl+key keystrokes. A list such as the one shown in Figure 1.17 appears.

3. To exit the Help window, press Alt+F4, or select **E**xit from the Help window **F**ile menu.

Categories
of key
combinations

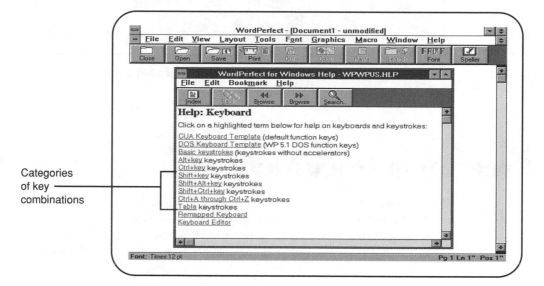

Figure 1.16   The Help: Keyboard area.

You can print any of the Help facility's lists, templates, and explanations by selecting **P**rint Topic from the Help window **F**ile menu. Because the Help feature uses Windows printer drivers, you must have first set up the Windows printer driver for your printer. See your Windows manual for directions.

The command shortcuts also appear to the right of option names in menus. For an example, refer back to Figure 1.13.

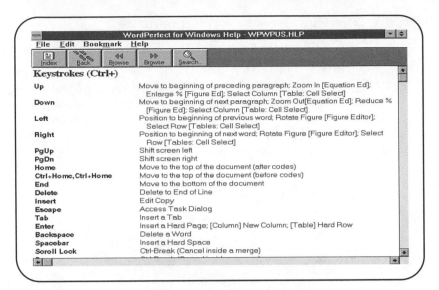

Figure 1.17 *You can view lists of Ctrl, Alt, and Shift key combinations. This figure shows the list of Ctrl+key keystrokes.*

Creating a Document

When you start WordPerfect for Windows, the typing area is blank. You can create a new document by entering text, formatting it as necessary. Formatting can be as simple as changing left and right margins or as complex as using automated features such as cross-references and paragraph numbering.

Entering Text

Enter text by typing from the keyboard. The text appears in the typing area to the right of the cursor (not the mouse pointer), so make sure the cursor is in the proper location before you type. (See "Moving Within a Document" later in this chapter for information about moving the cursor.)

As you type, you'll notice that you don't have to press Enter at the end of each line. WordPerfect automatically *wraps* the words from one line to the next. The only time you must press Enter, and the only time you *should* press Enter, is at the end of a paragraph.

Revealing the Format Codes

If you change the text format, WordPerfect enters format codes that specify the new format. Making "Yes!" boldface, for example, causes WordPerfect to insert the following codes in the text:

```
[Bold On]Yes![Bold Off]
```

The first code in the pair indicates bold is turned on and the second code indicates that bold is turned off. Text between the codes is bold. Text outside the codes is not.

The format codes are normally invisible, but you can display them by selecting the Reveal Codes feature. This can be an important tool for troubleshooting format problems and for modifying format. (See "Deleting Format Codes" later in this chapter.)

To display the Reveal Codes screen, you can use the following methods:

- Accelerator key method: Press Alt+F3 (Reveal Codes).

- Menu method: Select View/Reveal Codes. A check mark appears next to the option when it is selected.

- Reveal Codes bar method: Place the mouse pointer on the Reveal Codes bar and drag the bar up or down the scroll bar. (For the location of the Reveal Codes bar, refer back to Figure 1.3.) Notice that the mouse pointer changes to a double-headed arrow when it's on the Reveal Codes bar (see Figure 1.18).

Figure 1.18 illustrates a Reveal Codes screen for a simple document. Notice that the text in the screen appears in a monofont regardless of the fonts you have selected. The codes indicate the changes in font and other formatting. Also notice that the cursor position is indicated by the highlight in the screen. The vertical bar denoting the insertion point in the main window does not appear in the Reveal Codes screen.

To size the screen, drag the Reveal Codes bar up or down the scroll bar. To hide the screen, press Alt+F3 again or reselect View/Reveal Codes (the check mark by the option name will disappear). You can also drag the Reveal Codes bar until the Reveal Codes screen disappears.

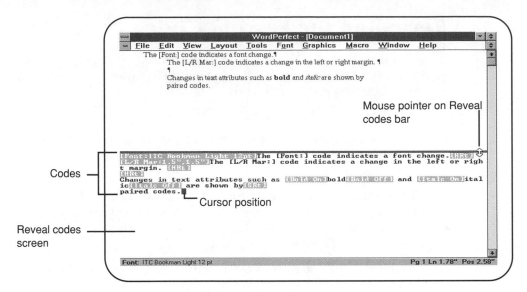

Figure 1.18   You can reveal format, graphics, and other WordPerfect codes by displaying the Reveal Codes screen.

Moving Within a Document

You can use the mouse or the keyboard to move through a document. The major difference between the methods is that the mouse lets you scroll through a document without affecting the cursor location. If you use the keyboard, on the other hand, the cursor always moves to the new location.

Moving Using a Mouse

To use a mouse to scroll through a document, use the scroll bar to the right of the typing area (see Figure 1.19). Notice that the scroll bar has three components: an Up Arrow at the top of the scroll bar, a Down Arrow at the bottom of the scroll bar, and a box within the scroll bar. You can use the mouse and scroll bar as follows:

- To scroll a few lines, place the mouse pointer on the up or Down Arrow in the scroll bar and click the mouse button.

- To scroll one window, place the mouse pointer in the scroll bar above or below the scroll box and click the mouse.

- To scroll continuously, place the mouse pointer on the Up or Down Arrow and press and hold the mouse button. Release the button to stop scrolling.

- To scroll to an approximate location, place the mouse pointer on the scroll box and drag the box up or down the scroll bar. The position of the box relative to the scroll bar reflects the position of the viewing area relative to the document. To view text that is about one-quarter through a document, for example, drag the scroll box one-quarter of the way down the scroll bar.

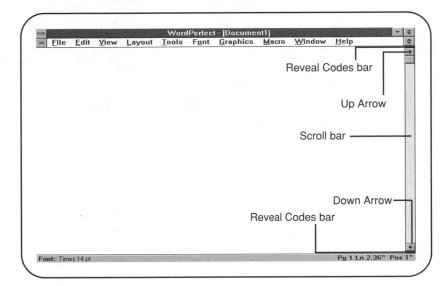

Figure 1.19 *The Scroll bar.*

As mentioned earlier, when you use the scroll bar to view a document, the cursor location does not change. For example, if the cursor is on page one and you use the scroll bar to display page five, the cursor remains on page one. WordPerfect considers the displayed page to be the current page. If you ask WordPerfect to print the current page, for example, the displayed page will be printed whether the cursor is on the page or not.

Using the mouse to move the cursor

1. If necessary, scroll to the text where you want to place the cursor.

2. In the typing area, place the mouse pointer where you want the cursor.

3. Click the mouse button.

Moving Using the Keyboard

You can also move through a document by typing commands from the keyboard, as shown in Table 1.1. When you use the keyboard commands, the cursor always moves to the new location.

Table 1.1   Cursor Movement Keys

To Move	Press
Left or right one character	Left or Right Arrow key
One word left or right	Ctrl+Left Arrow or Ctrl+Right Arrow key
To the beginning of the line, *after* any format codes	Home
To the beginning of the line, *before* any format codes	Home Home
To the end of the line	End
Up or down one line	Up or Down Arrow key
Up or down one paragraph	Ctrl+Up Arrow or Ctrl+Down Arrow key
Up or down one screen	Page Up or Page Down
To the top or bottom of the current page	Alt+Home or Alt+End
Up or down one page	Alt+Page Up or Alt+Page Down
To the beginning of the document, *after* any format codes	Ctrl+Home
To the beginning of the document, *before* any format codes	Ctrl+Home Ctrl+Home
To the end of the document	Ctrl+End

Not all of these key combinations apply to tables and columns. See Chapter 6 for information about moving the cursor in tables and Chapter 11 for columns.

Editing Text

This section describes basic editing techniques: selecting text to edit, inserting, deleting, copying and moving text, and most importantly, undoing your last edit. More advanced techniques, such as editing graphics or changing font characteristics, are described in later chapters where they are used in applications.

Selecting Text to Edit

Editing often involves changing a block of text. To select the block you want to edit, you can use either a mouse or the keyboard.

Using a Mouse to Select Text

1. Place the mouse pointer at the beginning of the text you want to select.

2. Press and hold the mouse button.

3. Move the mouse pointer to the end of the text you want to select. As you move the mouse pointer, the selected text is highlighted (see Figure 1.20), and the status bar indicates what you are selecting.

4. Release the mouse button.

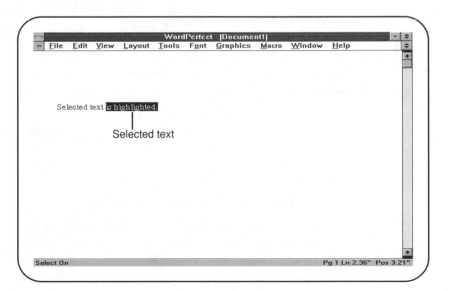

Figure 1.20   Selected text is highlighted.

Table 1.2 shows some mouse shortcuts for selecting text.

Table 1.2   Mouse Shortcuts for Selecting Text

To select	*Do this*
A word, including the space after the word	Place the mouse pointer on the word and double-click the mouse button.
A sentence, including the space after the period	Place the mouse pointer anywhere in the sentence and click the mouse button three times.
A paragraph, including any space after the paragraph	Place the mouse pointer anywhere in the paragraph and click the mouse button four times.
Text and codes from the cursor to the I-beam mouse pointer	Place the cursor at the beginning of the text block and the mouse pointer at the end of the block. Press and hold the Shift key while clicking the mouse button.

If you have used the mouse to select text, you can deselect the text in two ways: by clicking the mouse button while the mouse pointer is in the typing area, or by pressing any of the cursor movement keys (for example, the Left Arrow key).

Shortcut

To use the mouse to select text in the Reveal Codes screen, place the cursor at the beginning of the text block and place the I-beam mouse pointer at the end of the block. Press and hold the Shift key while clicking the mouse button. The [Select] code will appear at the beginning of the block. (For information on the Reveal Codes screen, see "Revealing the Format Codes" earlier in this chapter.)

You can select a text block from the keyboard in two ways: by using the Select function key, which is F8, or by using the Shift key. These text selection methods work both in the regular typing area and in the Reveal Codes screen. (For information on the Reveal Codes screen, see "Revealing the Format Codes" earlier in this chapter.)

Using the Select Function Key to Select Text

1. Use the cursor movement keys (or the mouse) to move the cursor immediately before the first character in the text block. (See Table 1.1 for the cursor movement keys.)

2. Press F8 (Select). The status bar indicates that you are in Select mode.

3. Move the cursor to the end of the text block. As you move the cursor, the selected text is highlighted. (Refer back to Figure 1.20.)

With this technique, you deselect text by pressing F8 again.

The Select feature provides the greatest flexibility in selecting text. It allows you to use the Search feature to select text between the cursor and a specific text or code string. With Select, you can also select text by just typing a character, such as a period. WordPerfect will select the text between the cursor and the first instance of the character.

Using the Shift key to Select Text

1. Use the cursor movement keys (or the mouse) to move the cursor immediately before the first character in the text block. (See Table 1.1 for the cursor movement keys.)

2. Press and hold the Shift key.

3. Use the cursor movement keys to move the cursor to the end of the text block. As you move the cursor, the selected text is highlighted (refer back to Figure 1.20), and the status bar indicates that you are selecting.

4. Release the Shift key.

To select a paragraph, for example, move the cursor to the beginning of the paragraph, press and hold the Shift key, press Ctrl+Down Arrow, and then release the Shift key.

Notice that this method is similar to using a mouse. Instead of pressing and holding the mouse button as you move the cursor, however, you press and hold the Shift key while moving the cursor. As with the mouse technique, you can deselect the text by pressing any cursor movement key or by clicking the mouse when the mouse pointer is in the typing area.

If you are a speed typist, the keyboard methods are usually faster than the mouse method because your fingers do not have to leave the keyboard.

Inserting Text

You insert new text by moving the cursor where you want the text inserted, and then typing the new text. You can type in insert mode or in typeover mode; pressing the Insert key toggles between the two modes. In insert mode, new text is inserted within the original text at the location of the cursor. In typeover mode, new text overwrites the original text to the right of the cursor. (In the Reveal Codes screen, the highlighted character or code is deleted.)

If you aren't sure which typing mode is current, check the status bar. If you are in typeover mode, the status bar displays "Typeover." If you are in insert mode, the status bar has no special message.

Deleting Text

To delete a single character, press the Backspace key or the Delete key. Pressing the Backspace key deletes the character to the left of the cursor. Pressing the Delete key deletes the character to the right of the cursor. You can delete a word by pressing Ctrl+Backspace, and a line by pressing Ctrl+Delete.

To delete a block of text, select the block, (see "Selecting Text to Edit"), and press the Backspace or Delete key. You can also select a block and type new text; the selected text is replaced by the new text.

Shortcut

You can use the Cut command to delete text and store it temporarily. See "Moving Text" later in this section for additional information on the Cut command.

Restoring Deleted Text

1. Move the cursor where you want to insert the restored text.

2. Select Edit/Undelete. (You can also select Undelete by pressing Alt+Shift+Backspace.) Your last deletion appears and is highlighted on screen. The Undelete dialog box also appears.

Note: If the Undelete dialog box overlaps the highlighted text, you can move the dialog box: Place the mouse pointer in the title bar of the dialog box, press and hold the mouse button, drag the box to a new location, and release the mouse button. (See Appendix B for more information, including using the keyboard to move dialog boxes.)

3. To display the previous two deletions, select **Previous** or **Next** from the dialog box.

4. When the deletion you want to restore is displayed, select **Restore** from the dialog box.

You cannot use U**n**delete to restore text and codes you deleted with the Cu**t** command. Use the **P**aste command instead. (See "Moving Text" later in this section, for additional information).

Copying Text

To copy text, you use the **C**opy and **P**aste commands. The text you copied remains in a temporary storage area, called the *Clipboard*. The Clipboard retains the text until you use the **C**opy or **C**ut command again or until you exit WordPerfect. You can paste the Clipboard contents at many locations.

Copying Text

1. Select the text you want to copy.

2. Select **E**dit/**C**opy, or press Ctrl+Insert. The text is copied to the Clipboard.

3. Move the cursor where you want to insert the Clipboard contents.

4. Select **E**dit/**P**aste, or press Shift+Insert. WordPerfect inserts, or *pastes*, the Clipboard contents at the cursor location and moves the cursor to the end of the pasted text.

Beginner's Tip

You can paste Clipboard contents almost anywhere in a WordPerfect document, including headers, footers, footnotes, columns, and text boxes. You also can paste between WordPerfect documents and to and from other Windows applications.

Shortcut

You can use the Appen**d** command to add several text blocks to the Clipboard without replacing previous Clipboard contents. The text you append is inserted at the end of the Clipboard contents. To append text, select it, and then select Appen**d** from the **E**dit menu. (You cannot use Appen**d** to add tabular columns or rectangles, which are another type of column selection. You also cannot use Appen**d** if the Clipboard contains tabular columns or rectangles.)

31

Moving Text

To move text, you use the **Cut** and **Paste** commands. As with the **Copy** command, the text you cut remains on the Clipboard until you use the **Copy** or **Cut** command again or until you exit WordPerfect. You can paste the Clipboard contents at many locations.

Moving Text

1. Select the text you want to move.

2. Select **Edit/Cut**, or press Shift+Delete. The text is deleted from the document and stored temporarily on the Clipboard.

3. Move the cursor where you want to insert the Clipboard contents.

4. Select **Edit/Paste**, or press Shift+Insert. WordPerfect inserts, or *pastes*, the Clipboard contents at the cursor location and moves the cursor to the end of the pasted text.

Editing Format Codes

To edit format codes, you need to display them first in the Reveal Codes screen. (See "Revealing Format Codes" earlier in this chapter.) Then you can edit them as you would any text. You also can use **Un**delete to restore deleted codes.

If you use the **Cut** and **Copy** command to move and copy text that contains format codes, the codes within the text block are moved and copied as well. This is true regardless of whether the Reveal Codes screen is displayed.

Undoing Your Last Edit

WordPerfect has a feature that can give you new life: Undo. It allows you to reverse your last edit in most cases, whether the edit be deletion of a single character or the moving a large section of text including graphics and tables. Undo cannot reverse actions such as saving and printing a document, which are not edits.

Other examples of edits it cannot reverse are the following: merges; sorts; generation of lists; tables of contents; master documents; and so forth; conversion of tabular columns to tables; retrieval of new stylesheets; edits to figures; and most actions entered by macros.

To use Undo, select **Edit/Undo**, or press Alt+Backspace. To reverse Undo, select it again.

If you used Backspace or Delete to delete text and have since typed new text or otherwise edited the document, you cannot use **Undo** to restore the deleted text, but you might be able to use **Undelete**. Refer back to "Deleting Text" for additional information.

Saving a Document

As you type a document, what you type is stored only in your computer's RAM, an electronic storage location. If you turn off your computer, or if you experience a power outage, the document is gone. To save your document for future use, you must save the document to disk, your computer's magnetic storage location.

Whenever you save a document, WordPerfect saves it in a file on the default drive and directory. You can change the default by selecting **File/Preferences**, or pressing Ctrl+Shift+F1, and then selecting **Location of Files**. This displays the Location of Files dialog box, which lets you change the default directory for your document files. You can override this default directory when saving a file by typing a *directory path* before the file name. A path tells WordPerfect the drive and directory where you want to save the file. For example, if you want to save a file called SAMPLE.DOC to the C:\WPWIN\FILES directory, you would type `c:\wpwin\files\sample.doc`.

Saving a Document for the First Time

1. Make sure that the document you want to save is the one that's displayed on screen.

2. Press F3 (Save As), or select **File/Save As**. You can also press Shift+F3 (Save) or select **File/Save**. WordPerfect displays the Save As dialog box, as shown in Figure 1.21.

3. In the Save **As** text box, enter a name for the document. (You can type the name or select the name from the file list.) If you don't want the document saved in the current directory listed in the Save As dialog box, type the full path name. File names must follow DOS

rules. Eight letters may be used with a period and a three-letter extension. For example: **schedule.mem** or **sam.ltr**. The name cannot include any of the following symbols:

```
* ? < > : ; = [ ] / \ " + , ~ [space]
```

4. Select **S**ave. When WordPerfect has finished saving, the name of the file appears in the document window title bar.

The complete path for the specific file appears as well. For example, if you are saving this file in a directory named ANNUAL, then the title bar would read

```
c:\annual\schedule.mem
```

If WordPerfect displays a dialog box with the question

```
Replace c:\schedule.mem?
```

you have already saved this file once under the name you just entered, and WordPerfect is prompting you to determine if you want to save the contents of the current file using the same name. If you select **Yes**, the file on screen overwrites (replaces) the version on disk. If you select **No**, the Save As dialog box reappears.

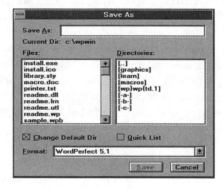

Figure 1.21   The Save As dialog box.

When you're naming files, use a name that is descriptive but as unique as possible. For example, don't assign the file name LETTER or LETTER1 to save a letter. Without retrieving and examining that file, it will be difficult to know what it contains. Instead, save the letter under the name of the recipient, with the extension .LTR, such as GREENWLD.LTR or LENI.LTR. The same holds true for reports (use the extension.RPT), memos (use the extension .MEM), and so on.

Saving a Document under the Same Name

As you edit a document, you probably will want to periodically save the changes. To do this, you can use the Save As feature described in the preceding section. A faster way is to use the Save feature. When you select the Save feature (by pressing Shift+F3 or by selecting **File/Save**), the document in the window is saved under the name shown in the document window title block, replacing the earlier version of the same name. With the Save feature, WordPerfect does not ask you to confirm that you want to replace the previous version.

Saving a File under a Different Name

It is sometimes valuable to save a file under a different name. For example, you may want to copy a file so you can change it without changing the original. To copy a file, select **File/Save As**, or press F3 (Save As), to display the Save As dialog box. In the Save **As** text box, type a different name for the file and then press Enter.

When to Save

How often should you save a file? WordPerfect offers a Timed Document Backup feature that automatically saves your file at specified intervals to protect your changes. (See Appendix B for information on how to use this feature.)

But, even though WordPerfect automatically saves your changes, you should get in the habit of saving your changes using **File/Save As**, or F3 (Save As), to save for the first time. Use **File/Save**, or Shift+F3 (Save), to save every time thereafter. Save often enough so that if there is a breakdown or power failure, you lose little work. For most people, that's probably about every 15 to 30 minutes.

Opening a File

To work on a file that you've saved to disk, you must open the file in the WordPerfect window. If another document is already open, WordPerfect opens the file into a second window, without closing the old document window. For information about working with more than one document window open, see Appendix B.

Opening an Existing Document

1. Select File/Open, or press F4 (Open). The Open File dialog box appears.

2. In the Filename text box, enter the name of the file you want to open. (You can type the name or select the name from the Files list.) If the file is not in the current directory, type a complete path to the drive and directory that contains the file. For example, type `c:\wpwin\files\sample.doc`.

3. Select Open.

If you enter an incorrect path or if WordPerfect cannot find the file, it displays the following message in a dialog box:

```
File not found: [the name you entered]
```

There are two reasons why you might get this message. First, you may have typed an incorrect path, that is, the file you want to open is not where you think it is. Second, you may have mistyped the directory or file name. If you receive this error message, check the path and file name you typed. If it matches what you intended to type, then select File/File Manager and use it to search for and open the file. (See Appendix D for information about File Manager.)

In the Open dialog box, you can list files in different directories by typing the directory name in the Filename text box and then selecting Open. The file list in the dialog box will display the names of files in the new directory. You also can list directories by deselecting Quick List. The list box will then show the subdirectories and the parent directory, denoted by [..]. To list the files in one of these directories, double on the directory name and select Open.

The last four files you saved are listed in the File menu. You can quickly open any of them by selecting them from that menu.

You also can open a new window. This allows you to create a new document without closing the current document.

Opening a New Window

1. Select File/New, or press Shift+F4 (New). WordPerfect opens a new window, ready for you to create a new document.

2. Create the new document as you would any WordPerfect document.

   You can use **Retrieve** to retrieve another document into the document that's displayed on screen. For example, if you're creating a report on screen and you want to use a table that you've already created and saved to disk, you can retrieve the table into the report.

Retrieving a File into Another File

1. Open the document into which you want to place the second document.

2. Place the cursor in the exact position of document #1 where you want the next document inserted.

3. Select File/**Retrieve**. WordPerfect displays the Retrieve dialog box.

4. In the Filename text box, enter the name of the file you want to retrieve. (You can type the name or select the name from the file list.) If the file you want to retrieve is not in the current directory, type a complete path to the drive and directory that contains the file. For example, type **c:\wpwin\files\sample.doc**.

5. Select **Retrieve**. A message appears, asking if you want to insert the file into the current document.

6. Select **Yes** to confirm. WordPerfect retrieves the specified document at the cursor location.

Closing a Window

To close a document window without leaving WordPerfect, select File/Close, or press Ctrl+F4 (Close). If you have modified the document since it was last saved, WordPerfect displays a dialog box asking whether you want to save the changes. Select one of the following:

- **Yes** to save the changes. If you have previously saved the file (that is, so that it has a file name), WordPerfect displays a dialog box asking you to confirm that you want to save the file under that name. Select **Yes** to confirm that you do. If you have never before saved the document (that is, so that it doesn't have a file name), WordPerfect displays the Save As dialog box. Enter a file name and select **S**ave. (See "Saving a Document" for additional information on this dialog box.)

- **N**o to close the window without saving the changes.

- Cancel to return to the document window without taking any action.

Printing

The printing process is managed by a *printer driver*, a file that controls printer operation. Most Windows-based programs do not supply their own printer driver; they simply use the printer driver already installed for Windows. This allows the fonts and features you have installed for Windows to be available for every Windows application that you run.

WordPerfect for Windows allows you to use Windows printer drivers, but it also provides its *own* drivers, which offer advantages not available with the Windows drivers. For example, printing with WordPerfect printer drivers allows you to use both portrait and landscape letters on the same page. Also, the printing process is faster. You can switch back and forth between the WordPerfect and Windows drivers freely, but you cannot use both simultaneously.

If you're not sure whether you have installed a Windows printer driver, return to the Windows program manager window, open the Main program group, open the Control Panel program group within it, and then double-click on the Printers icon. The Printers dialog box appears. If there is no printer listed under Installed **P**rinters, consult your Windows documentation to learn how to add a printer.

When you install WordPerfect, it copies an .ALL file containing information about all WordPerfect printer drivers. When you add a printer, as described later in this section, WordPerfect extracts information from the .ALL file to create the WordPerfect printer driver file for the printer. This file has the extension .PRS.

Whether you choose a WordPerfect or a Windows printer driver, WordPerfect's Print feature allows you to send a document to the printer and then continue working in WordPerfect or Windows while the document prints. You don't have to wait for your printer to finish. To allow this background printing, WordPerfect uses the Windows Print Manager. If you did not install the Print Manager when you installed Windows, you cannot print in the background while working on a document—while the document is printing, your computer will be unavailable to you.

Selecting a Printer Driver and Printer

To choose a WordPerfect or Windows printer driver and select a printer, select File/Select Printer. This displays the Select Printer dialog box, shown in Figures 1.22 and 1.23.

To change printer drivers, select the WordPerfect or the Windows option button. If you select WordPerfect, the dialog box appears as shown in Figure 1.22. If you select Windows, it appears as shown in Figure 1.23. Although the dialog boxes are somewhat different, the procedure for selecting a printer is the same for both.

Figure 1.22   The Select Printer dialog box for WordPerfect printer drivers.

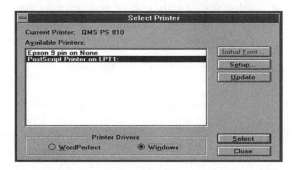

Figure 1.23   The Select Printer dialog box for Windows printer drivers.

Selecting a Printer

1. Go to the Available Printers list box by clicking in it, or by pressing Alt+V. Notice that the currently selected printer is named in the Current Printer field above the list box.

2. Highlight the name of the printer you want to select and then choose Select. You can also select the printer by double-clicking on the printer name.

If you are using WordPerfect printer drivers and the printer you want is not listed, you can add it to the list as follows: (For information about adding a printer in Windows, see your Windows manual.)

Adding a Printer (WordPerfect Printer Driver)

1. In the Select Printer dialog box, select Add. The Add Printer dialog box appears, as shown in Figure 1.24.

2. To list all printers supported by WordPerfect, select Additional Printers (*.all). To list only those for which you've already created a .PRS file, select Printer Files (*.prs). (If you selected a printer when you installed WordPerfect or previously added a printer, you created a .PRS file for that printer.)

   WordPerfect looks for the .ALL and .PRS files in the directory named at the top of the dialog box. If you copied them to a different directory, change directories before performing Step 2. To change directories, select Change and then enter the directory path for the .PRS and .ALL files.

3. Go to the Available Printers list box by clicking in it, or by pressing Alt+V.

4. Highlight the name of the printer you want to add and then choose Add. You can also add the printer by double-clicking on the printer name. When you select the printer name, the Copy Printer dialog box appears, displaying a suggested file name.

5. Select OK to accept the file name, or edit the file name and then select OK.

You can obtain information about a printer in both the Select Printer and Add Printer dialog boxes. Highlight the printer name in the Available Printers list box and then select Info.

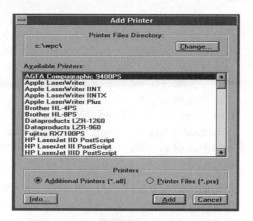

Figure 1.24   The Add Printer dialog box.

Printing a WordPerfect Document

Once you've decided on a printer driver and printer, you can print your documents. Select **File/Print**, or press F5 (Print), to display the Print dialog box, as shown in Figure 1.25. The Print dialog box offers the following options:

> *Options:* Choose the document or document selection you want to print. Select **Full Document** to print the document currently open. To print the page currently displayed in the window, select **Current Page**. To print a block of text, highlight the text before displaying the Print dialog box, and then select **Selected Text**. Select **Multiple Pages** to print noncontiguous pages or a range of pages. Select **Document on Disk** to print a closed document.
>
> If you select **Multiple Pages** or **Document on Disk**, selecting **Print** displays a dialog box. In this dialog box, enter a range of pages, and for **Document on Disk**, the name of the file you want to print.
>
> To specify noncontiguous pages, separate the page numbers with a comma or space: for example, **1 5 7** or **1,5,7**. To specify a range, separate the beginning and ending page numbers with a hyphen: for example, **1-7**. To print from page *X* through the end of the document, enter the page number followed by a hyphen: for example, **7-**. You can also use this dialog box to specify printing only odd or even pages and printing the document summary.

Copies: This group of options lets you specify how many copies to print and whether or not to collate them. Enter the number of copies in the **Number** of Copies text box. To collate the copies, select the Generated **By** pop-up list button and then select **WordPerfect** from the pop-up list. WordPerfect will create the number of copies and then send them, collated, to the printer. If you select **Printer** from the Generated **By** pop-up list, WordPerfect generates only one copy of the document and the printer prints the number of copies you specify. In this case the copies are not collated.

Document Settings: Use the Binding **Offset** option to specify the amount of space you need to allot for the binding. The printed text will be shifted the amount you specify from the left margin (on odd-numbered pages), or the right margin (on even-numbered pages). Select the **Graphics** Quality and **Text** Quality buttons to specify the print quality or to suppress printing graphics on text.

Windows Print Drivers: If you are using a Windows printer driver, select the Fast Graphics Printing check box to increase the printing speed for graphics. This should not affect the graphics quality. If graphics are not printing correctly, however, try deselecting **Fast** Graphics Printing.

Select: The current printer is named at the left of this button. To select a different printer, choose **Select**. This displays the Select Printer dialog box. Follow the directions given earlier in this section to select a printer.

Initialize Printer: If you are using a WordPerfect printer driver and want to download fonts to your printer, select this button after you turn on your printer and before you begin printing.

Print: Select this button to begin printing. If you selected **Multiple** Pages or **Document** on Disk, selecting **Print** displays a dialog box. Fill in the dialog box,(see "Options" above), and then begin printing by selecting **Print** in the dialog box.

 When you save a document, its print settings are saved with it.

If you use the same print options for most documents, you can make those options the default settings in the Print dialog box. Select **File/ Preferences/Print** to display the Print Settings dialog box, select the options you want as defaults, and then select OK (see Figure 1.25). (For details, see Appendix C, under "Print.") In the Print dialog box, you can override the default settings simply by selecting a different setting.

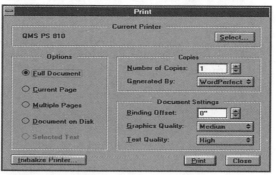

Figure 1.25   The Print dialog box.

Printing a Document

1. Select **File/Print**, or press F5 (Print). The Print dialog box appears.

2. Select the printing options.

3. Select **Print**. If you selected **Multiple Pages** or **Document on Disk**, selecting **Print** displays a dialog box. Fill in the dialog box, and then begin printing by selecting **Print** in the dialog box.

You can quickly print the current document by pressing Ctrl+P. This prints the full document according to the current settings in the Print dialog box.

Help!

WordPerfect has an excellent on-line Help program that provides you with information about using WordPerfect features. The Help program offers two kinds of help. One kind is an encyclopedia-style help, including an index, a glossary, and descriptions of features. The other is context-sensitive help, presenting information about the feature you are currently using.

The Help Menu

To display the Help menu, select **Help** from the menu bar. The **Help** menu, as shown in Figure 1.26, has the following options:

- **Index:** Displays an alphabetical list of Help topics.

- **Keyboard:** Lets you view templates of function key commands for the CUA and WordPerfect 5.1 for DOS keyboards. Also lets you display list of shortcut keystroke commands.

- **How Do I:** Explains how to perform the most common tasks—for example, setting tabs.

- **Glossary:** Displays definitions of terms used in the Help program.

- **Using Help:** Explains the Help program.

- **What Is:** Lets you obtain context-sensitive help.

- **About WordPerfect:** Displays the WordPerfect for Windows version and release date and your license number.

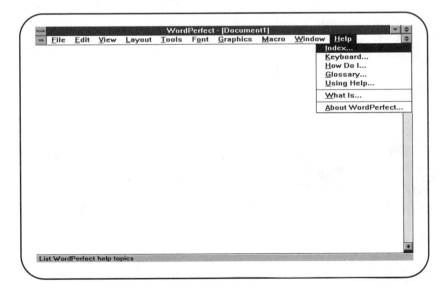

Figure 1.26   The Help menu.

If you ever call WordPerfect support for assistance, they might need to know the release date of your copy of WordPerfect for Windows. You can use the About WordPerfect selection to obtain this information.

Selecting from the **Help** menu is the same as selecting from other menu bar menus.

Selecting from the Help menu

1. Select **Help** from the menu bar. The **Help** menu appears, as shown in Figure 1.26.

2. Select the Help option you want. The Help window appears, displaying the Help information.

3. To exit the Help window at any time, press Alt+F4 (Exit), or select **File/Exit** from the Help window menu bar.

Notice that the Help feature has its own window with its own menu bar, as shown in Figure 1.27. You can display the menus in the menu bar to display additional Help options. Select these options as you do any menu options.

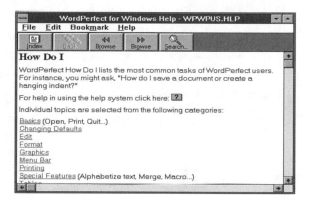

Figure 1.27   Example of a Help window.

Context-Sensitive Help

When you're working on a document and aren't sure how to use a WordPerfect feature, you can use the What Is feature to ask WordPerfect "What is this?"

To use this Help feature, select **Help/What Is** or press Shift+F1 (Help: What Is?). A question mark by the mouse pointer indicates you are now in What Is mode, as shown in Figure 1.28. In this mode, you can obtain information about a feature simply by pointing at it and clicking, or by pressing the keystroke combination for it. For help on menu items, drag the mouse pointer to the menu item or press the keystroke shortcut for that item. When you select a feature, WordPerfect displays the Help window for the feature and leaves the What Is mode.

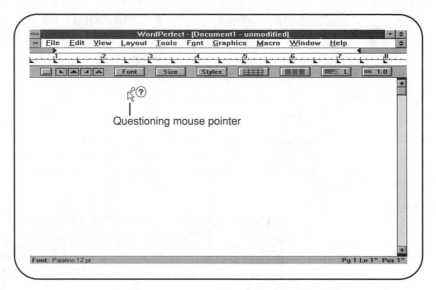

Figure 1.28   When you are in What Is mode, a question mark appears next to the mouse pointer.

Exiting WordPerfect

Once you are finished with a document and ready to end your current WordPerfect session, you need to exit WordPerfect. It is important that you exit WordPerfect properly. Do not exit by turning off the power to your computer.

To exit WordPerfect, select **File/Exit**, or press Alt+F4 (Exit). If you have modified the document since it was last saved, WordPerfect displays a dialog box asking whether you want to save the changes. Select one of the following:

- **Yes** to save the changes. If you have previously saved the file (that is, so that it has a file name), WordPerfect displays a dialog box asking you to confirm that you want to save the file under that name. Select **Yes** to confirm that you do. If you have never before saved the document (that is, so that it doesn't have file name),

WordPerfect displays the Save As dialog box. Enter a file name and select **Save**. (See "Saving a Document" for additional information on this dialog box.)

- **No** to exit WordPerfect without saving the changes.

- **Cancel** to return to the document window without taking any action.

Summary

That's the basics of using WordPerfect for Windows. The rest of this book includes descriptions of business applications and accompanying templates in WordPerfect for Windows that allow you to use the applications quickly and easily in your own business activities.

Set left and right margins

1. Select **Layout/Margins** or press Ctrl+F8.

2. Enter margin settings, and then select OK.

Center page

1. Select **Layout/Page** or press Alt+F9.

2. Select **Center Page**.

Change justification

1. Select **Layout/Justification** and then **Left**, **Right**, **Center**, or **Full**.

   or

2. Press Ctrl+L (left), Ctrl+R (right), Ctrl+J (center), or Ctrl+F (full).

Center text

1. Place the cursor at the *beginning* of the line.

2. Select **Layout/Line/Center** or press Shift+F7.

Change line spacing

1. Select **Layout/Line/Spacing**, or press Shift+F9 and type **s**.

2. Enter the line spacing and then select OK.

Enter tab settings

1. Select **Layout/Line/Tab** Set or press Shift+F9 and type **t**.

2. Enter tab settings and then press Enter or select OK.

View Ruler

1. Select **View/Ruler** or press Alt+Shift+F3.

Insert date

   Text: Select **Tools/Date/Text** or press Ctrl+F5.

   Code: Select **Tools/Date/Code** or press Ctrl+Shift+F5.

Change date format

1. Select **File/Preferences/Date Format** or press Ctrl+Shift+F1 and type **f**.

2. Select **Predefined Dates**, **Dates Codes**, or **Time Codes**.

3. Select the date and time codes or the predefined format.

4. Select OK.

Change Auto Code Placement

1. Select **File/Preferences/Environment**, or press Ctrl+Shift+F1 and type **e**.

2. Select Auto Code **Placement** and then select OK.

Create Button Bar

1. Select **View/Button Bar Setup/New**.

2. Select menu functions for the Button Bar.

3. Select OK. A dialog box appears.

4. Enter a file name (and directory path, if desired) and then select **Save**.

BUSINESS SHORTCUTS

Meeting Memo

A memo is a simple, direct communication between members of an organization. It is less formal than a letter, but more formal than a note passed between colleagues. Since the memo is a printed document, it is a record of the interaction, documenting that the information was passed from one person to the other. In this chapter, you will learn how to customize a memo by changing some common format settings.

About the Application

The memo application, shown at the end of this chapter, is a basic Word-Perfect document. It consists of very little text, formatted with some of the more common WordPerfect formatting features. The top and bottom margins are WordPerfect's default settings of 1", and the left and right margins are set to 1.5". The text is fully justified to make it flush with both the left and right margins. The title is centered. The date is inserted using WordPerfect's Date feature. And tab stops are at 0.5" intervals, WordPerfect's default setting. In this chapter, you will learn how to set all of these options.

This chapter also introduces you to the *Button Bar,* one of the most powerful features WordPerfect for Windows offers. From a Button Bar you can quickly select the functions and macros you use most frequently. In this chapter, you will learn how to use the default Button Bar, create your own Button Bars, and customize individual buttons. Assigning macros to Button Bars is discussed in Chapter 12.

Opening the Application

To customize the memo application for your own use, you must first open
the file called *MEMO.APP* (use **File/Open**). If you're not sure how to open
a file, refer to Chapter 1. When WordPerfect opens the file, it formats the
document for the printer that you installed, so your memo application may
look a little different from the one shown in this chapter.

You can set up WordPerfect so that it doesn't automatically format a
document for your printer (see Appendix C, under "Environment"). In
that case, WordPerfect looks for the original printer's .PRS file when it
retrieves the document. If it can't find the file, it displays a message to
that effect and then formats it for the installed printer.

Customizing the Application

You change most of the formatting options for this application by using the
Layout menu, shown in Figure 2.1. The menu lets you change several settings that affect the appearance of your document, including the left and
right margins, line spacing, justification, and tab settings. To view the Layout
menu, select Layout from the menu bar.

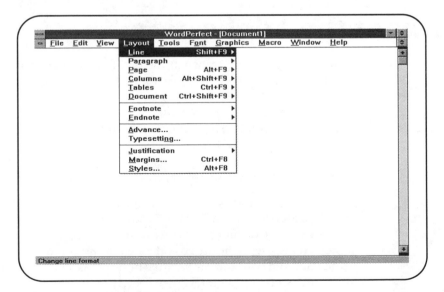

Figure 2.1   The Layout menu.

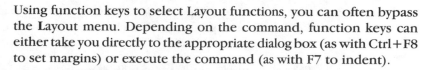

Using function keys to select Layout functions, you can often bypass the Layout menu. Depending on the command, function keys can either take you directly to the appropriate dialog box (as with Ctrl+F8 to set margins) or execute the command (as with F7 to indent).

Whenever you change a default setting to change the appearance of your lines, WordPerfect inserts in your document a hidden code that changes the formatting for all text that follows. If you want the change to affect the entire document, make sure the cursor is at the beginning of the document when you change the format setting. To return the document to the previous format setting, you must enter another code in the document where you want the setting to change back. See "Revealing Formatting Codes" in Chapter 1 for additional information.

Later in this chapter, we'll introduce the WordPerfect Ruler, which you can use to set many formatting options. The Ruler allows you to view margin and tab settings in the document and drag them to new locations. You can also use it to specify certain other format settings, such as justification. But first, let's learn to set the margins using the menu.

Setting Left and Right Margins

Whenever you create a document, WordPerfect assumes you want to set the left and right margins to 1". (To learn how to change this default, see Appendix C.) Short documents, such as the MEMO.APP file, may look more substantial with larger margins. Since the memo application was so brief, we decided to increase the margin settings to 1.5" to improve its appearance. When you have a long document, decrease the margins so you can fit more text on the page.

Changing Left and Right Margins

1. Place the cursor anywhere in the paragraph where you want the new margins to begin. (If you have turned off the Auto Code Placement function, place the cursor exactly where you want the margins to begin; see "Automatic Code Placement" later in this chapter.) If setting the margins for the entire document, place the cursor at the top of the document.

2. Select Layout/Margins or press Ctrl+F8 (Margins). The Margins dialog box appears. The cursor is in the Left text box.

3. In the **Left** text box, type the setting you want for the left margin. (The default unit of measure is inches; see Appendix C to learn how to change the default.)

4. Press Tab to move to the **Right** text box.

5. Type the setting you want for the right margin.

6. Select OK to close the dialog box and save the new settings.

WordPerfect inserts a [L/R Mar:] code at the beginning of the paragraph containing the cursor, replacing any existing [L/R Mar:] code at that location (see "Automatic Code Placement," later in this chapter). All lines from this point until the next [L/R Mar:] code are formatted according to the new settings.

To check your margin settings, select View/**R**uler or press Alt+Shift+F3 (Ruler). Look at the bar at the top of the Ruler, shown in Figure 2.2. The right and left arrowheads indicate the left and right margins. For more on the Ruler, see "Using the Ruler to Change Formatting" later in this chapter.

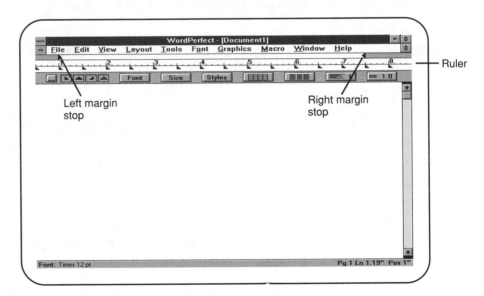

Figure 2.2   The Ruler indicates margin settings.

Centering a Page

If you create a brief memo, you might want to vertically center the memo between the top and bottom margins, so the memo won't appear top-heavy. You could set the top and bottom margins, as you did the right and left, but there is an easier way. WordPerfect offers a page centering feature that centers your page automatically. To use it, follow these directions:

Centering a Page

1. Place the cursor anywhere on the memo page. (If you have turned off the Auto Code Placement function, place the cursor at the top of the page; see "Automatic Code Placement" later in this chapter.)

2. Select **Layout/Page** or press Alt+F9 (Page).

3. Select **Center Page**. WordPerfect returns you to the window and inserts the [Center Pg] code at the top of the page (see "Automatic Code Placement" later in this chapter).

Want to check the placement of the [Center Pg] code? Press Alt+F3 (Reveal Codes) or select **View/Reveal Codes**. The Reveal Codes area appears at the bottom of the window. In that area, you can see the [Center Pg] code you just entered. If you want to delete the code, highlight it and press Delete.

Justifying Text

Justification controls the position of the line in relation to the left and right margins, as shown in Figure 2.3. *Left-justified* text, the default setting, is flush against the left margin and has a ragged right margin. *Right-justified* text is flush against the right margin and has a ragged left margin. *Centered* text is centered between the two margins. And *fully justified* text is spread out to be flush with both margins.

The effects of some formatting features, such as full justification, may not appear on-screen. To see the effect of the change, either print the document or use the Print Preview function to see how the document will appear in print. To preview a document, move the cursor to the page you want to view, select **File/Print Preview** or press Shift+F5 (Print Preview). You cannot edit the document in the Print Preview window. To close the window, select **File/Close** or press Ctrl+F4 (Close).

In the memo application, the text is fully justified. This gives the memo a neat professional look. But be careful. If your memo has a narrow column of text, the space between the letters and words might appear exaggerated. In that case, change to left justification.

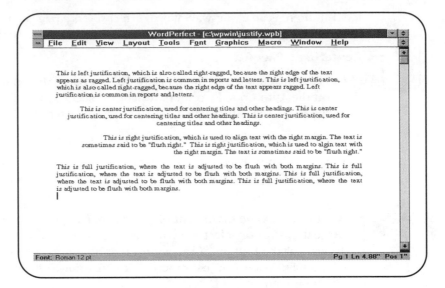

Figure 2.3   Justification options.

Changing Justification

1. Place the cursor anywhere in the paragraph where you want the new justification to begin. (If you have turned off the Auto Code Placement function, place the cursor exactly where you want the justification to begin; see "Automatic Code Placement" later in this chapter.) To have the justification affect the entire document, place the cursor at the top of the document.

2. Complete one of the following steps, depending on the type of justification you want:

   Left justification: Select **L**ayout/**J**ustification/**L**eft or press Ctrl+L.

   Right justification: Select **L**ayout/**J**ustification/**R**ight or press Ctrl+R.

   Center justification: Select **L**ayout/**J**ustification/**C**enter or press Ctrl+J.

   Full justification: Select **L**ayout/**J**ustification/**F**ull or press Ctrl+F.

WordPerfect returns you to the window and inserts a [Just:] code at the beginning of the paragraph containing the cursor, replacing any existing [Just:] code at that location (see "Automatic Code Placement" later in this chapter). Text from this point on is formatted according to the justification option you selected.

If you're not sure how your printer handles fully justified text, retrieve the file called *PRINTER.TST.* This file should be in the directory that contains your WordPerfect for Windows program files (for example, C:\WPWIN). Select File/Print or press F5 (Print), and then select Full Document. The resulting printout will illustrate what your printer can and cannot handle.

Centering Text

Centered at the top of the memo application is the word *Memo.* You can center any word or line in either of two ways: as you type the text or after you type it.

Centering Text as You Type It

1. Place the cursor at the beginning of the line. If the cursor is more than one space from the left margin, text will be centered over the cursor location, not between the margins.

2. Select **L**ayout/**L**ine/**C**enter or press Shift+F7 (Center). WordPerfect enters the [Center] code, and the cursor moves to the center of the line.

3. Type the text you want centered. As you type, the letters shift so that the line remains centered.

4. Press Enter to end the line of text.

Centering Existing Text

1. Move the cursor to the beginning of the line. If the cursor is more than one space from the left margin, text will be centered over the cursor location, not between the margins.

2. Select **L**ayout/**L**ine/**C**enter or press Shift+F7 (Center). WordPerfect inserts the [Center] code and centers the line.

The fastest way to center more than one line of text is to select the block of text you want to center, and then select **Layout/Line/Center** or press Shift+F7. WordPerfect inserts a [Just:Center] code before the text block; after the text block, WordPerfect inserts a [Just:] code restoring the original justification. For information about selecting text, refer to Chapter 1, under "Selecting Text to Edit."

To center a heading in a right-justified document, select the heading and then select **Layout/Line/Center** or press Shift+F7. Make sure that you select the heading before you perform the operation. Otherwise, the line remains right-justified.

Changing Line Spacing

By default, WordPerfect single-spaces lines of text, leaving enough extra space between lines so the letters do not run together. With single-spacing, the distance from baseline to baseline is one line height, where a line height is normally 2 points greater than the point size for the font—for example, a 12-point font has a 14-point line height.

If you change the line spacing to something other than 1 (single), WordPerfect determines the new distance from baseline to baseline by multiplying the line height by the line spacing setting you enter. For example, if you're using a 12-point font (and therefore have a 14-point line height), and you enter a line spacing setting of 2 (double-spacing), the distance from baseline to baseline is twice the line height, or 28 points.

You can change the line spacing for a complete document or for a section of a document. For example, in the memo shown at the end of the chapter, line spacing is set at 2 for the numbered list. It is then reset to 1 (single spacing) for the list of names. Figure 2.4 shows the effects of various line spacing settings.

You can set line spacing to a number less than one (such as 0.5), but your text will look cramped, and it may even overlap. As a general rule, enter a setting that's one or greater.

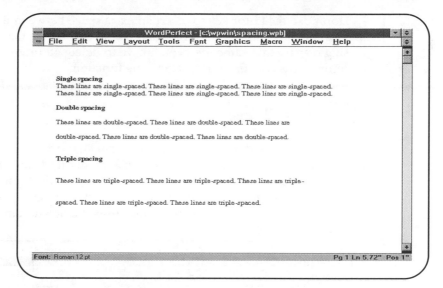

Single spacing
These lines are single-spaced. These lines are single-spaced. These lines are single-spaced. These lines are single-spaced. These lines are single-spaced. These lines are single-spaced.

Double spacing

These lines are double-spaced. These lines are double-spaced. These lines are

double-spaced. These lines are double-spaced. These lines are double-spaced.

Triple spacing

These lines are triple-spaced. These lines are triple-spaced. These lines are triple-

spaced. These lines are triple-spaced. These lines are triple-spaced.

Figure 2.4   Line spacing in WordPerfect for Windows.

Changing Line Spacing

1. Move the cursor anywhere in the paragraph where you want the new line spacing to begin. (If you have turned off the Auto Code Placement function, place the cursor exactly where you want the line spacing to begin; see "Automatic Code Placement" later in this chapter.) To have the new setting affect the entire document, move the cursor to the top of the document.

2. Select Layout/Line/Spacing, or press Shift+F9 (Line) and type **s**. The Line Spacing dialog box appears.

3. In the Spacing text box, type a number (for example, type **2** for double-spacing or **1.5** for one-and-one-half spacing). You also can change line spacing by selecting the incrementing buttons.

4. Select OK. WordPerfect returns you to the window and inserts the [Ln Spacing] code at the beginning of the paragraph containing the cursor, replacing any existing [Ln Spacing] code at that location (see "Automatic Code Placement" later in this chapter). This code affects all subsequent text up to the next [Ln Spacing] code.

Shortcut

Don't use the Enter key to insert an extra space between lines to give the appearance of double-spaced text. If you ever have to single-space that same text, you'll have to delete all those hard returns. Instead, use the Line Spacing function.

Setting Tabs

Tabs are useful for aligning text in columns. In Figure 2.5, for example, tabs are used to align text for the committee assignments. By default, WordPerfect sets left-aligned tab stops at 0.5" intervals. (See Appendix C for information on changing the default.) Left-aligned means the text is aligned flush left with the tab stop. The memo application uses the default tab settings.

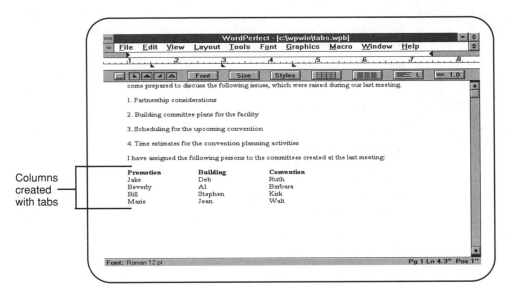

Columns created with tabs

Figure 2.5   Tab stop settings used to align text in columns.

Use the Ruler to see where your tab stops are set. To display the Ruler, select **View/R**uler or press Alt+Shift+F3 (Ruler). The tab ruler displays a set of small triangles that represent the tab stops; the shape of the triangle denotes the type of tab stop, as shown in Figure 2.6. For more information about the Ruler, see "Using the Ruler to Change Formatting" later in this chapter.

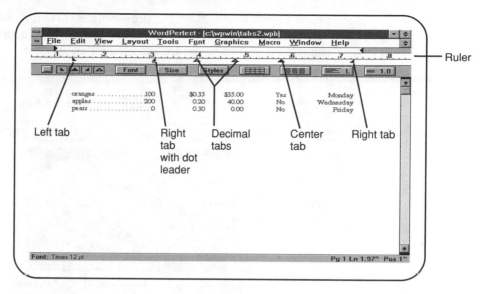

Figure 2.6   The Ruler shows current tab settings.

You can change the position and type of tab stops at any time, at any point in the document. For example, Figure 2.5 begins with the default settings, but changes to tab stops spaced 1.5" apart just before the list of committee assignments. When you change the tab stop settings, WordPerfect inserts a [Tab Set:] code at the beginning of the paragraph containing the cursor (unless you turned off the Auto Code Placement feature; see "Automatic Code Placement," later in this chapter). This changes the tab stop settings for all tabs until the next [Tab Set:] code.

If the tab stop settings are too close for the text to fit, WordPerfect will not move things for you. Instead, words will overlap.

Changing Tab Settings

1. Move the cursor anywhere in the paragraph where you want the new tab settings to begin. (If you have turned off the Auto Code Placement function, place the cursor exactly where you want the tab settings to begin; see "Automatic Code Placement," later in this chapter.) To have the new settings affect the entire document, move the cursor to the top of the document.

2. Select **Layout/Line/Tab** Set, or press Shift+F9 (Line) and type **t**. The Tab Set dialog box appears (see Figure 2.7). Current tab settings are shown in the list below the **P**osition box.

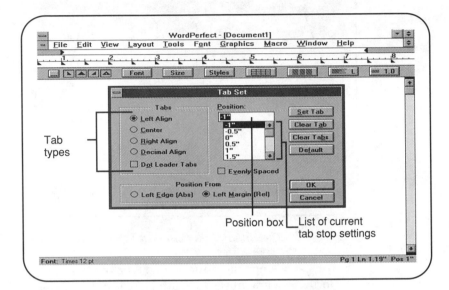

Figure 2.7   The Tab Set dialog box.

3. Select Left **E**dge (Abs) or Left **M**argin (Rel). If you select Left **E**dge, tabs are measured from the left edge of the page. If you select Left **M**argin, tabs are measured from the left margin; if the margin changes, the tabs shift so they are the specified distance from the new margin.

Tabs measured from the edge of the page are sometimes called *absolute* tabs; and tabs measured from the margin, *relative* tabs.

4. Complete one or more of the actions in Table 2.1 to modify your tab settings.

5. Press Enter or select OK to return to the window. WordPerfect inserts the [Tab Set:] code at the beginning of the paragraph containing the cursor (see "Automatic Code Placement," later in this chapter).

Table 2.1   Changing tab settings using menus

Desired Result	Steps
Clear all tab stops	Select Clear Tabs.
Add a tab stop	Type the tab stop position in the Position box.
	Select the type of tab (for example, Left Align).
	If desired, select Dot Leader Tabs to include a dot leader.
	Select Set Tab.
Change the type of an existing tab	Select the tab setting from the list.
	Select the tab type.
	Select Set Tab.
Delete tab	Select the tab setting from the list.
	Select Clear Tab.
Use the default tab settings	Select Default.
Select evenly spaced tabs	Clear all tab settings.
	Select Evenly Spaced.
	In the Position box, type the position for the first tab stop.
	In the Repeat Every text box, type the number of spaces you want between each tab.
	Select the tab type.
	Select Set Tab.

Figure 2.8 illustrates the four types of tabs that can be set using the Tab Set function.

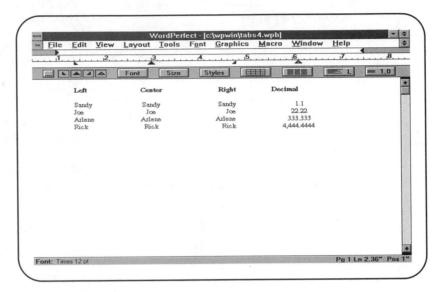

Figure 2.8   Examples of the four types of tabs.

Using Decimal Tabs

Decimal tabs are especially useful for aligning columns of numbers around decimal points. If your memo includes a list of sales figures, for example, you can use a decimal tab to align the figures around a decimal point. You can do this in either of two ways.

The first way is to set a decimal tab as explained above. You then press the Tab key to move the cursor to that decimal tab stop. As you type the numbers before the decimal point, the numbers are inserted to the left of the cursor, and the cursor remains stationary. The decimal point is inserted at the cursor location, and any numbers you type after the decimal point are inserted to the right of the decimal point.

The second way is to use decimal tabs without setting a decimal tab stop. Instead of pressing Tab to move the cursor to the next tab stop, press Alt+Shift+F7 (Decimal Tab). WordPerfect inserts a [HdDecTab] code at the cursor position, and moves the cursor to the next tab stop. No matter what type of tab stop it is, WordPerfect treats it as a decimal tab stop and aligns the text accordingly.

Although decimal tabs are most useful for aligning columns of numbers, you can also use decimal tabs to align text around a specific decimal/align character. For example, you can align text on each side of a colon by telling WordPerfect to use the colon as the decimal/align character. Try it in the memo application.

Aligning Text around a Colon

1. Move the cursor to the top of the memo application.

2. Select Layout/Line/Special Codes, or press Alt+Shift+F8 (Special Codes). The Insert Special Codes dialog box appears.

3. Select Decimal Align Character with the mouse or by pressing Alt-G. The margins on the Decimal Align Character option indicates it is selected.

4. Press Tab to move to the text box next to Decimal Align Character. (You can use the mouse to select the text box by clicking in the box.)

5. Type : (a colon).

6. Select **Insert**. WordPerfect inserts a [Decml/Algn Char] code at the cursor location.

7. Move the cursor to the S in September and press Alt+Shift+F7 (Decimal Tab). This moves the date to the next tab stop and makes the tab stop a decimal tab. (Because the tab stop is now a decimal tab, the date appears to the left of the tab stop; this is fixed in the next step.)

8. Type **Date:** and press the space bar. Date is inserted to the left of the tab stop; the colon is inserted at the tab stop; and the space and date move to the right of the tab stop.

9. Move the cursor to the T in To: and press Alt+Shift+F7 (Decimal Tab). WordPerfect aligns the colon after To directly under the colon that follows Date.

10. Move the cursor to the F in From: and press Alt+Shift+F7 (Decimal Tab). WordPerfect aligns the colon after From directly under the colons above it.

11. To return to using the period as the decimal align character, repeat Steps 2 through 6, but in Step 5 type a period (instead of a colon). WordPerfect inserts the [Decml/Algn Char] code at the cursor location.

Using the Ruler to Change Formatting

Earlier in this chapter you learned to view the margin and tab settings by displaying the Ruler. If you have a mouse, you can also use the Ruler to change margins, tabs, and other format settings. To display the Ruler, select **View/R**uler or press Alt+Shift+F3 (Ruler). To remove the display, again select **View/R**uler or press Alt+Shift+F3 (Ruler).

This section explains how to use the Ruler to change margins, tabs, justification, and line spacing. In later chapters, you will learn how to use the Ruler to change fonts and type size, select styles, and create tables and columns. Figure 2.9 shows the default Ruler, and points out many of its most important features.

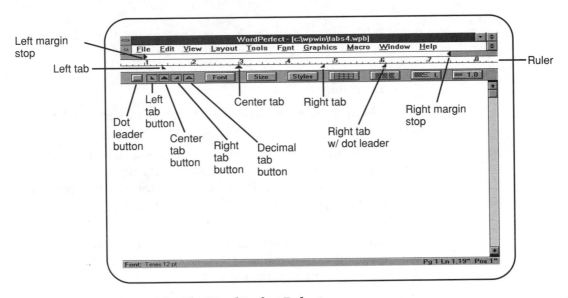

Figure 2.9   The WordPerfect Ruler.

Using the Ruler to Change Margins

1. Place the cursor in the paragraph where you want the new margin settings to begin.

2. Place the mouse pointer on the margin marker for the margin you want to change.

3. Drag the marker to the new margin setting. While you are dragging the marker, you can return the marker to its original position by dragging the mouse pointer to the top of the document window.

A vertical guideline appears when you drag the marker. You can use the guideline to help you align the marker with the Ruler markings and text. WordPerfect also displays the margin measurement on the status line as you drag the marker.

When you change margins, WordPerfect inserts a [L/R Mar:] code at the beginning of the paragraph containing the cursor. This code replaces any other [L/R Mar:] code at the beginning of the paragraph (see "Automatic Code Placement" later in this chapter).

The Ruler measures in increments of 1/16"; for example, you can set margins at 1 or 1.06 but not at a number in between. If you need margins that are in between, place the mouse pointer on either margin marker or on either gray margin area and double-click the mouse button. This displays the Margins dialog box, which you can use to set precise margins (see "Setting Left and Right Margins," earlier in this chapter).

If you change the left margin and you have relative tab settings (that is, settings measured from the left margin), the tab markers on the Ruler will shift because they'll be measured relative to the new left margin.

Using the Ruler to Change Justification

1. Place the cursor in the paragraph where you want the new justification to begin.

2. Place the mouse pointer on the Justification button (see Figure 2.9).

3. Press and hold the mouse button to display the pop-up list of justification properties (Left, Right, Center, and Full), drag the mouse pointer to the option you want to select, and release the mouse button.

When you release the mouse button, WordPerfect inserts a [Just:] code at the beginning of the paragraph containing the cursor. This code replaces any other [Just:] code at the beginning of the paragraph (see "Automatic Code Placement" later in this chapter).

Using the Ruler to Change Line Spacing

1. Place the cursor in the paragraph where you want the new line spacing to begin.

2. Point to the Line Spacing button (see Figure 2.9) with the mouse pointer.

3. Press and hold the mouse button to display the pop-up list of Line Spacing options (1.0, 1.5, and 2.0), drag the mouse pointer to the option you want to select, and release the mouse button.

When you release the mouse button, WordPerfect inserts a [Ln Spacing:] code at the beginning of the paragraph containing the cursor. This code replaces any other [Ln Spacing:] code at the beginning of the paragraph (see "Automatic Code Placement" later in this chapter).

To select line spacing other than 1.0, 1.5, or 2.0, double-click on the Line Spacing button. This displays the Line Spacing dialog box, which you can use to set any line spacing. See "Changing Line Spacing" earlier in this chapter.

Selecting a Group of Tabs

1. Place the mouse pointer in the tab ruler, below and to the left of the group of tabs you want to select. Make sure the pointer does not touch a tab marker.

2. Hold down the left mouse button and drag the mouse pointer to the right until the gray bar extends just past the last tab you want to select.

When you select a group of tabs, the mouse pointer is available only within the gray bar and the tab button area. If you move the mouse pointer outside these areas, it changes to a no-entry sign.

Next let's change the tabs. Before proceeding, note the following:

• When you drag a tab marker, WordPerfect displays a vertical guideline that can help you align the marker with text in a document.

• As you drag a marker, WordPerfect also displays the tab measurement on the status line.

• While dragging a tab marker, you can restore it to its original position if you drag the mouse pointer to the top of the document window before you release the mouse button.

- If you drag a tab to or near the location of another tab, the moved tab replaces the old one.

Using the Ruler to Change Tabs

1. Place the cursor in the paragraph where you want the new tab settings to begin.

2. Complete one or more of the actions in Table 2.2 to modify your tab settings.

Table 2.2   Changing tab settings using the ruler

Desired Result	Steps
Move a tab	Drag the tab marker to the new location.
Move a group of tabs and add them to other tabs in the area	Select the group and drag them to the new area.
Move a group of tabs and replace other tabs in the area	Select the group and hold the Shift key while dragging the group to the new area.
Copy a tab	Hold the Ctrl key while dragging the tab to a new location.
Copy a group of tabs and add them to other tabs in the area	Select the group and hold the Ctrl key while dragging them to the new area.
Copy a group of tabs and replace other tabs in the area	Select the group and hold Ctrl+Shift while dragging the group to the new area.
Delete a tab or group of tabs	Drag the tab marker or group of tabs off the Ruler.
Delete all tabs	Double-click on any tab marker or tab button, select Clear Tabs, and select OK.

continues

Table 2.2   Continued.

Desired Result	Steps
Add a tab	Move the mouse pointer to the tab button for the type of tab you want. Press and hold the mouse button to display a tab marker at the mouse pointer tip. Drag the new tab marker to the desired tab location on the tab ruler.
Add a tab with a dot leader	Select the Dot Leader button before adding the tab.
Change the tab type (left tab, right tab, etc.) for a tab or group of tabs	Select the tab (or group) and select the tab button for the new tab type.

When you change the tab settings, WordPerfect inserts a [Tab Set:] code at the beginning of the paragraph containing the cursor. This code replaces any other [Tab Set:] code at the beginning of the paragraph (see "Automatic Code Placement" later in this chapter).

Shortcut

The Ruler measures in increments of about 1/16"; for example, you can set tabs at 1" or 1.06" but not at a number in between. If you need tabs that are in between, hold down Shift while dragging the marker. This allows you to set tabs in finer increments. You can also double-click on any tab marker or tab button to display the Tab Set dialog box, which you can use to set precise tabs (see "Setting Tabs" earlier in this chapter).

Changing the Date

Beginner's Tip

Your computer keeps track of the date and the time. You may have entered the date and time when you turned on your computer, or your computer may have an internal clock. In either case, WordPerfect can insert the date and time directly from your system into any WordPerfect document.

When we created the memo application, we used the Date Text function to insert the date directly from the computer into the document. To use this function, select **Tools/Date/Text** or press Ctrl+F5 (Date Text). This inserts today's date at the cursor position.

If you intend to use MEMO.APP for a template, however, you might prefer it to display the *current* date. To have WordPerfect automatically enter the current date whenever you open or print the document, delete the date and insert a Date Code as follows.

Inserting a Date Code

1. Move the cursor to the line where you want the date to appear.

2. Select **Tools/Date/Code** or press Ctrl+Shift+F5 (Date Code).

WordPerfect inserts the current date at the cursor location, just as if you had used the Date Text function. However, if you display the Reveal Codes area, you'll see the [Date:] code. This code tells WordPerfect to insert the current date from your computer.

Whether you enter the date by using Date Text or Date Code, WordPerfect inserts the date in a fixed format. The default format is: Month (*word*), Day (*number*), Year (*number*)—for example, *April 3, 1992*. You can change the format at any time to a predefined format or to a format you define.

Changing the Date Format to a Predefined Format

1. Select **File/Preferences/Date Format** or press Ctrl+Shift+F1 and type **f**. WordPerfect displays a dialog box that lets you change how the date is displayed. The dialog box, shown in Figure 2.10, displays the current date format in the **E**dit Date Format box.

2. Select the **P**redefined Dates pop-up list button and then select a format from the pop-up list.

3. Select OK to close the dialog box and save the format setting.

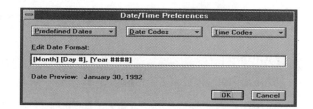

Figure 2.10   The Date/Time Preferences dialog box.

Defining Your Own Date Format

1. Select **File/Preferences/Date** Format or press Ctrl+Shift+F1 and type **f**. WordPerfect displays a dialog box that lets you change how the date is displayed. The dialog box, shown in Figure 2.10, displays the current date format in the **Edit Date Format** box.

2. Delete unwanted date codes from the **Edit Date Format** box by pressing Delete or Backspace. Notice that a code is treated as a single character—you cannot delete a portion of a code, only the entire code.

3. To insert new date codes in the **Edit Date Format** box, select the **Date Codes** pop-up list button and then select a date code from the pop-up list. Refer to Table 2.3 for examples of the date codes. When you select a code, it appears in the **Edit Date Format** box at the location of the cursor.

4. Repeat Step 3 to select additional format codes.

5. To display the time with the date, select time codes from the **Time Codes** pop-up list.

6. Type punctuation such as commas and spaces from the keyboard.

7. Select OK to close the dialog box and save the format setting.

You cannot enter codes by typing them from the keyboard; this simply enters the typed text into the date. For example, if you type **[Month]**, your date will contain [Month] rather than the name of the current month. You also cannot type numbers, the dollar sign ($), or the percent sign (%).

Table 2.3   Date Codes and examples of what they represent

Date Code	Examples (Bold Text)
[Day #]	May **9**, May **10**
[Day 0#]	May **09**, May **10**
[Day _#]	May **9**, May **10** (an extra space precedes the 9)
[Month #]	**12**/92, **1**/93
[Month 0#]	**12**/92, **01**/93
[Month _#]	**12**/92, **1**/93 (an extra space precedes the 1 in 1/93)

Date Code	Examples (Bold Text)
[Month]	**January**
[Abbr. Month]	**Jan**
[Year ##]	January **92**
[Year ####]	January **1992**
[Weekday]	**Monday**, **Tuesday**
[Abbr. Weekday]	**Mon**, **Tue**

Automatic Code Placement

WordPerfect has a feature called *Auto Code Placement*, which determines the placement of some format codes when you insert them in a document. It affects codes that you typically want to affect an entire paragraph or page.

When you change left or right margins, for example, you usually want the margin change to affect an entire paragraph or more, not just a few lines in a paragraph. If Auto Code Placement is turned on and you select new margins, WordPerfect automatically inserts the [L/R Mar:] code at the beginning of the paragraph, regardless of the cursor's location in the paragraph. (If you select text and then change the margins, the code appears at the beginning of the first paragraph containing the selected text.)

If Auto Code Placement is turned off, the code is inserted at the cursor location. If that new setting conflicts with the current line or page setting (for instance, if you change the left margin in the middle of a line or change the top margin in the middle of a page), WordPerfect inserts a hard return or a page break just before the new code.

The following codes are placed automatically when Auto Code Placement is turned on.

- Codes inserted at the beginning of the paragraph: Codes indicating left and right margins, line spacing, justification, justification limits, tab settings, line height, columns, letter and word spacing, paragraph and line numbering, hyphenation zone.

- Codes inserted at the beginning of the page: Codes indicating top and bottom margins, page numbering, centered page, page size, suppressed (headers, footers, etc.).

The default setting for Auto Code Placement is to have it turned on.

Changing Auto Code Placement

1. Select **File/Preferences/Environment**, or press Ctrl+Shift+F1 (Preferences) and type **e**.

2. Select Auto Code **P**lacement. If Auto Code Placement is already on (denoted by an X in the check box), selecting it turns it off.

3. Press Enter or select OK.

Saving Time with Button Bars

WordPerfect's Button Bar feature allows you to place the functions you most commonly use at your fingertips. Button Bars, such as the one shown in Figure 2.11, contain buttons that represent functions. You can select the function simply by selecting the button. If the button represents a function, such as Print, then selecting the button typically displays the dialog box for that function. If the button represents a command, such as Bold, then selecting the button executes the command.

You must use the mouse to select buttons.

WordPerfect comes with the following ready-made Button Bars:

- Main Button Bar (wp{wp}.wwb): The defualt Button Bar, containing general-purpose buttons such as Save, Print, and Speller, and other functions used in most documents. This Button Bar is illustrated in Figure 2.11.

- Tables Button Bar (tables.wwb): Contains buttons for working with tables.

When you install WordPerfect, the Main and Tables Button Bars are installed and stored in the default WordPerfect macros directory (for example, `c:\wpwin\macros`). Also during installation, WordPerfect automatically selects the Main Button Bar. To view it, select **View/Button Bar**. To remove the Button Bar display, select **View/Button Bar** again. If you create a Button Bar for the memo, it appears at the tip of the window. You can switch back to the Main Button Bar or another Button Bar at any time.

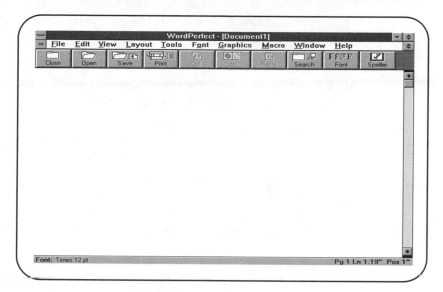

Figure 2.11   A Button Bar.

Creating a Button Bar

You can easily create a Button Bar tailored to any application. For the memo application, for example, you might want to create a Button Bar that has buttons for the following functions: Save As, Save, Cut, Copy, Paste, Ruler, Date Text, Center Page, Speller, and Print. Then you can center a short memo by selecting just the Center button (rather than **Layout/Page/Center Page**) and have easy access to the Ruler, from which you can view and change margins, tabs, justification, and line spacing.

Creating a Button Bar

1. Select **View/Button Bar Setup/New**. The Edit Button Bar dialog box appears.

2. Select a menu item that you want placed on a button. To create a button that will toggle the Ruler display on and off, for example, select **View/Ruler**. Notice that the mouse pointer changes to a hand holding a button when it is in the menu or Button Bar. When you select a menu item, a new button appears in the Button Bar.

3. Repeat Step 2 until you have added all the buttons you want. There is no limit to the number of buttons you can create. If they extend beyond the window area, scroll arrows appear; use them to scroll to the buttons you can't see.

73

4. To move a button, drag it over the two buttons between which you want it inserted.

5. To delete buttons, drag them from the Button Bar.

6. When you are satisfied with the Button Bar, select OK in the dialog box. The Save Button Bar dialog box appears.

7. Type a Button Bar name in the Save **As** field. If you don't want the Button Bar saved in the current directory named in the dialog box, type the full path and file name in the Save **As** field.

You don't need to add an extension to the file name. WordPerfect automatically assigns the extension .wwb. You can type a different extension, but this is not recommended because the Select Button Bar dialog box lists only Button Bar names having the extension .WWB.

8. Select **Save**. The Button Bar you saved under the name you entered in Step 7, is automatically selected as the current Button Bar, and is displayed in the document window.

   You can also assign macros to buttons. This is discussed in Chapter 12.

Selecting a Different Button Bar

Selecting a Button Bar

1. Select **View/Button Bar Setup/Select**. The Select Button Bar dialog box appears.

2. Select the Button Bar name from the **Files** list or type it in the **Filename** text box. If the file is not in the current directory named in the dialog box, enter the full path name in the **Filename** text box.

3. Choose **Select**. WordPerfect returns to the main window and displays the Button Bar.

Special window Button Bars, such as the Print Preview Button Bar that automatically appears in the Print Preview window, are available only in their respective windows and cannot be selected in the main document window.

To remove the Button Bar display, select **View/Button** Bar. You can redisplay the currently selected Button Bar at any time by selecting **View/Button** Bar again.

Editing a Button Bar

You can edit any of the WordPerfect Button Bars to suit your needs by adding, deleting, and rearranging the buttons. You also can change the position and display of a Button Bar—to conserve window space, for example, you might want to display only button function names.

Note in the following directions that the first step for editing document window Button Bars (that is, the Main and Tables Button Bars and Button Bars you create) differs slightly from editing the Button Bars in special windows, such as the Print Preview window.

Editing a Button Bar

1. *For document window Button Bars:*

   Select the Button Bar you want to edit. (See "Selecting a Button Bar" earlier in this section.)

   For Button Bars in the Print Preview, Equation Editor, and Figure Editor windows:

   Display the window containing the Button Bar. To edit the Print Preview Button Bar, for example, select **File/Print Preview** or press Shift+F5 to display the Print Preview window.

2. Select **View/Button Bar Setup/Edit**. The Edit Button Bar dialog box appears. Notice that the mouse pointer changes to a hand holding a button when it is in the menu or Button Bar.

3. To add a button, select the menu item you want placed on a button. When you select the menu item, a new button appears in the Button Bar. If the buttons extend beyond the window area, scroll arrows appear; use them to scroll to the buttons you can't see.

4. To move a button, drag it over the two buttons between which you want it inserted.

5. To delete buttons, drag them from the Button Bar.

6. When you are satisfied with the Button Bar, select OK in the dialog box. The Button Bar is saved under the original name.

Changing the Button Bar Position and Display

1. *Document window Button Bars:*

   Select the Button Bar you want to edit. (See "Selecting a Button Bar" earlier in this section.)

   Button Bars in the Print Preview, Equation Editor, and Figure Editor windows:

   Display the window containing the Button Bar. To edit the Print Preview Button Bar, for example, select **File/Print Preview** or press **Shift+F5** to display the Print Preview window.

2. Select **View/Button Bar Setup/Options.** The Button Bar Options dialog box appears.

3. To change the Button Bar position, select **Left, Right, Top,** or **Bottom.**

4. To change the display of the buttons, select Text Only, **Picture** Only, or Picture **and** Text.

5. Select OK.

Summary

While memos might seem like minor documents, their preparation and use accounts for a great deal of interoffice communication. Once you have fine-tuned the memo application for your own use, using the formatting features described here, you'll be able to create and send memos quickly and easily, without having to think about formatting them.

The Memo Application

Memo

September 2, 1992

To:

From:

Memo

September 2, 1992

To: All department heads

From: Neil S., Department Chair

We have a good deal of work to accomplish during our next meeting. Please come prepared to discuss the following issues, which were raised during our last meeting:

1. Partnership considerations

2. Building committee plans for the facility

3. Scheduling for the upcoming convention

4. Time estimates for the convention planning activities

I have assigned the following persons to the committees created at the last meeting:

Promotion	Building	Convention
Jake	Deb	Ruth
Beverly	Al	Barbara
Bill	Stephen	Kirk
Marie	Jean	Walt

Import graphics file into existing figure box

1. Select **Graphics/Figure/E**dit or press Shift+F11.

2. Type the Figure box number and select OK.

3. Select **F**ile/**R**etrieve or the Retrieve button.

4. Enter *<drive>:\<directory>\<filename.ext>*, and select **R**etrieve.

5. Select **F**ile/**C**lose or the Close button.

Change column widths

1. Select **L**ayout/**C**olumns/**D**efine, or press Alt+Shift+F9 and type **d**.

2. Type the left/right margin settings or select **E**venly Spaced and type the distance between columns.

3. Select OK.

Edit horizontal line

1. Place the cursor after the [HLine] code but before any other [HLine] code.

2. Select **G**raphics/**L**ine/Edit **H**orizontal.

3. Enter the changes and select OK.

Change graphics box size, position, and type

1. Select **G**raphics.

2. Select the box type and then select **P**osition.

3. Type the graphics box number and select OK.

4. Select the new options and then select OK.

Change graphics box and caption options

1. Move the cursor before the code for the first graphics box of the type whose options you want to change.

2. Select **G**raphics.

3. Select the box type and then select **O**ptions.

4. Type the graphics box number and select OK.

5. Select the new options and then select OK.

Edit figure

1. Select **G**raphics/**F**igure/**E**dit or press Alt+F11.

2. Type the Figure box number and select OK.

3. Edit the figure.

4. Select **F**ile/**C**lose or the Close button.

Create graphics box

1. Select **G**raphics.

2. Select the box type and select **C**reate.

3. Enter the box contents and select any options.

4. Select **F**ile/**C**lose or the Close button.

Create caption

1. Select **G**raphics.

2. Select the box type and select **C**aption.

3. Type the box number and select OK.

4. Type the caption.

5. Select **F**ile/**C**lose or the Close button.

BUSINESS
SHORTCUTS

Newsletter Cover

There's no better way to communicate with employees, clients, and colleagues than through a regularly published newsletter. Good ones are full of current, accurate, and interesting information, and are visually pleasing as well. The newsletter application described in this chapter provides you with a newsletter cover that you can customize for your own use. As you manipulate the application, you'll learn how to work with graphics boxes, one of WordPerfect's most powerful desktop publishing tools.

About the Application

The newsletter application, illustrated in Figure 3.1, consists of three Text boxes, two graphic lines, and one Figure box:

- Text Box 1 is for the newsletter title. It is 1" wide, runs along the left margin, and has no border. The title text can be rotated, as illustrated in Figure 3.1.

- Text Box 2 is where text for articles is entered. It is about 6" × 8.8". In Figure 3.1, Text Box 2 contains the articles "Thank You" and "Where We Stand." A single line borders Text Box 2 on the top, right, and bottom. A thicker line borders it on the left, where it touches Text Box 1.

- Figure Box 1 contains a handshake figure emphasizing the "Thank You" message in the first article in Text Box 2. (You can retrieve a different graphic into this Figure box.) The Figure box, superimposed on Text Box 2, is anchored on the page so it won't interfere with the text in Text Box 2. The Figure box has no borders.

- Thick horizontal graphic lines form the top and bottom borders of the top article (the "Thank You" message in the example). The lines have 50% gray shading.

- Text Box 3 can contain highlights of the contents. In Figure 3.1, these highlights are titled "What's Inside." Text Box 3 is superimposed on Text Box 2. A single-line border around Text Box 3 visually separates it from the underlying Text box.

To better understand how the newsletter application was created, press Alt+F3 (Reveal Codes) when the application is displayed. This will show you the Text box, Figure box, and Horizontal Line codes and their sequence.

Opening the Application

To customize the newsletter application for your own use, open the file called *NEWS.APP*. The application appears as shown in Figure 3.2.

To view the full page, select File/Print Preview or press Shift+F5 (Print Preview), and select the Full Page button.

Graphics and the Print Preview window both require a significant amount of memory. If you have the minimum amount of memory required to run WordPerfect for Windows (2 megabytes), you might receive an error message when you try to display several graphics in the Print Preview window. See the reference manual that accompanied your WordPerfect for Windows package for suggestions on freeing up memory.

If you plan do a significant amount of desktop publishing with WordPerfect for Windows (or any other program that supports it), you will want at least 4 megabytes of memory (RAM) in your computer. If you have only 2 megabytes, consider purchasing more memory. It is relatively inexpensive ($40-$60 per megabyte) and it will enhance the performance of nearly all your Windows applications.

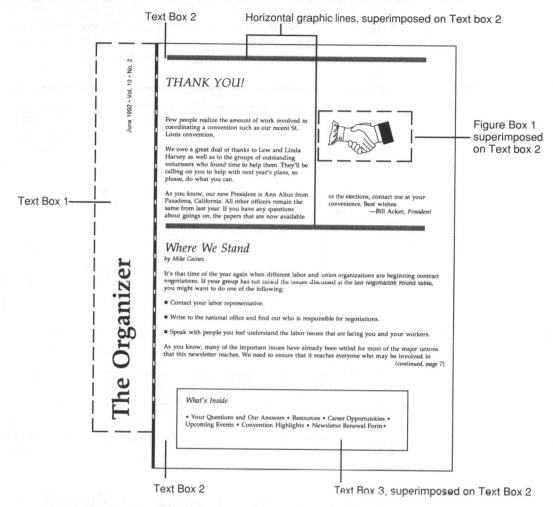

Text Box 2

Horizontal graphic lines, superimposed on Text box 2

June 1992 · Vol. 10 · No. 2

The Organizer

THANK YOU!

Few people realize the amount of work involved in coordinating a convention such as our recent St. Louis convention.

We owe a great deal of thanks to Lew and Linda Harvey as well as to the groups of outstanding volunteers who found time to help them. They'll be calling on you to help with next year's plans, so please, do what you can.

As you know, our new President is Ann Altus from Pasadena, California. All other officers remain the same from last year. If you have any questions about goings on, the papers that are now available

or the elections, contact me at your convenience. Best wishes.
—Bill Acker, *President*

Figure Box 1 superimposed on Text box 2

Text Box 1

Where We Stand
by Mike Gaines

It's that time of the year again when different labor and union organizations are beginning contract negotiations. If your group has not raised the issues discussed at the last negotiation round table, you might want to do one of the following:

■ Contact your labor representative.

■ Write to the national office and find out who is responsible for negotiations.

■ Speak with people you feel understand the labor issues that are facing you and your workers.

As you know, many of the important issues have already been settled for most of the major unions that this newsletter reaches. We need to ensure that it reaches everyone who may be involved in

(continued, page 7)

What's Inside

• Your Questions and Our Answers • Resources • Career Opportunities • Upcoming Events • Convention Highlights • Newsletter Renewal Form •

Text Box 2

Text Box 3, superimposed on Text Box 2

Figure 3.1   The newsletter cover consists of three Text boxes, one Figure box, and two horizontal graphic lines.

Customizing the Application

Beginner's Tip

The newsletter application is formatted for a PostScript printer. When you open the file, WordPerfect for Windows automatically formats it for the printer you installed. The appearance of your newsletter cover will depend on your printer's capabilities. If your printer does not support anything larger than 12-point type, for example, you cannot use a large font for the title of your publication. Whenever you change the newsletter, select File/Print Preview or press Shift+F5 (Print Preview) to see the effects of the change before printing.

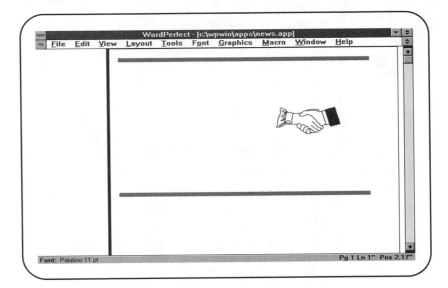

Figure 3.2   The newsletter cover displayed in the document window.

After you retrieve the newsletter application, you can type the text you want on the cover, including the title of your publication. You can also manipulate the appearance of the cover by changing the options for the various boxes—altering box size, borders, shading, and other variables.

Entering a Title for Your Publication

Shortcut

Map your design on graph paper before you begin working with WordPerfect for Windows graphics. This allows you to see where different elements of the design will fall and how they will look. More importantly, the graph paper provides you with exact values for sizes (such as a 1" × 8" Text box).

Follow the upcoming steps to place the title of the publication in Text Box 1. Notice that if you rotate the text, you need to increase the box size before you enter the title. This gives WordPerfect enough room to rotate the text. You can reset the box size after you rotate the text.

It's important that you stay in the Text Box Editor window while the box size is in flux; otherwise, WordPerfect might move the Text box code in the document window, adjusting for the new box size. If the codes move, the Text box numbers might change, causing you some confusion the next time you try to edit that text box.

Entering the Text Box Editor Window

1. Select **G**raphics/Text **B**ox/**E**dit or press Alt+Shift+F11 (Text Box Edit). The Edit Text Box dialog box appears. If you receive a message that the system hasn't enough memory for this operation, see the Beginner's Tip that follows Step 2 for an alternate procedure.

2. Type **1** and select OK. The Text Box Editor window for Text Box 1 appears, as shown in Figure 3.3. The window looks like a regular document window and has the regular WordPerfect for Windows menu bar. In addition, it has the buttons Close, Cancel, Box **P**osition, and **R**otate.

If you have a mouse, you can replace the first two steps with the following: Place the mouse pointer within Text Box 1. The status line displays the prompt:

```
Text Box 1 - Use right mouse button to display Graphics menu.
```

Click the *right* mouse button and then place the mouse pointer on Edit Text Box and click the *left* mouse button. This procedure works for any Graphics box that isn't superimposed on another graphics box (in that case, you can use this method to select only the underlying box).

Resizing Text Box 1 to Allow for Text Rotation

If you'll be rotating the text, you should maximize the box size before you type the text. (You want to allow WordPerfect for Windows enough room to rotate the text.)

3. In the Text Box Editor window, select Box **P**osition. The Box Position and Size dialog box appears.

4. Select the **S**ize pop-up list button and then select Auto **H**eight in the pop-up list.

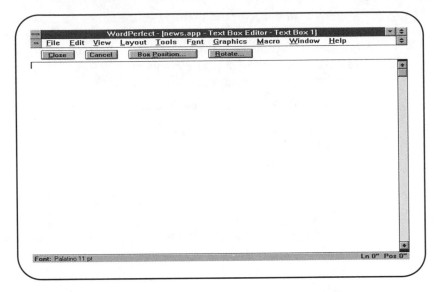

Figure 3.3   The Text Box Editor window.

5. Type **6** in the Width text box, to make the box height 6". (If you are using a unit of measurement other than inches, enter the equivalent of 6" in your default unit of measure.)

6. Select OK. WordPerfect for Windows returns to the Text Box Editor window.

Typing a Title in Text Box 1

7. In the Text Box Editor window, select Font/Font or press F9 (Font). The Font dialog box appears.

8. Select the font you want to use for the title; if you select a scalable font, also select the point size. In the application, the title is in 36-point Palatino Bold.

9. Select OK. WordPerfect for Windows inserts a hidden [Font] code.

10. Type the text for the title of your publication.

Shortcut

If your printer cannot rotate type, you cannot print your title sideways as in the example. Instead, you could stack the letters by pressing Enter after typing each letter. If you stack the letters, use center justification so that the letters are centered over each other (place the cursor at the beginning of the title and press Ctrl+J to insert the Center Justification code).

11. Select **Layout/Line/Flush Right** or press **Alt+F7** (Flush Right) to move the cursor flush right.

12. Repeat Steps 7 through 9 to change the font for the date and volume number. In the example, the font is 9-point Helvetica.

13. Type the date and volume number. To insert date text from your computer, select **Tools/Date/Text** or press **Ctrl+F5** (Date Text). To insert a date code, select **Tools/Date/Code** or press **Ctrl+Shift+F5** (Date Code).

If your printer cannot rotate type, stack the date over the volume number by pressing Enter after typing the date. You'll need to enter another flush right code before the volume number.

Rotating Text in the Text Box

14. With your title in the Text Box Editor window, select **Rotate**. The Rotate dialog box appears.

15. Select Rotate 90° and then select OK. Although it doesn't appear so in the Text box, the text is rotated 90° counterclockwise. If your printer cannot rotate type, leave Rotate None selected.

Sizing the Text Box after Rotating Text

If you changed the text box size to allow WordPerfect for Windows room to rotate text, you can now reset the box width and height.

16. With your title in the Text Box Editor window, select the Box Position button. The Box Position and Size dialog box appears.

17. Select the **Size** pop-up list button and then select **Set Both** from the pop-up list.

18. Type **1** in the **Width** text box to set the width at 1". (If you are using a unit of measurement other than inches, enter the equivalent of 1" in your default unit of measure.)

19. Type **8** in the **Height** text box. (If you are using a unit of measurement other than inches, enter the equivalent of 8" in your default unit of measure.)

Note: Steps 18 and 19 assume the title has a type size of 36 points. If the type size of your title is different, enter it instead of what is indicated in steps 18 and 19.

20. Select OK. WordPerfect for Windows returns to the Text Box Editor window.

21. Select **File/Close** or the Close button. WordPerfect for Windows returns you to the main document window. To see the rotated text, display the document in the Print Preview window (press Shift+F5).

Using a Different Graphic in the Figure Box

WordPerfect for Windows can do some amazing things, but it cannot create a graphic within a graphic. In other words, you cannot place a Figure box inside a Text box. You can achieve the same effect, however, by creating a Text box and a Figure box separately and then specifying the box positions so that the Figure box is superimposed over the Text box.

Using the handshake figure on your newsletter cover adds a nice touch, but you may want to use some other image for your publication, and you may want to change the appearance of the Figure box that contains the image.

The WordPerfect for Windows program disks contain compressed WordPerfect Graphics (.WPG) files. If you performed a basic installation (or a custom installation in which you chose to copy those files), then the files were uncompressed into the default graphics directory (for example, C:\WPWIN\GRAPHICS). If you have those files, you can replace the handshake figure with one of them. If you have your own graphics files, and if they're in a format that WordPerfect supports, you can import one of those figures instead. The reference manual that accompanied your WordPerfect for Windows package lists the formats supported by WordPerfect.

You can change the name of the default graphics directory by selecting **File/Preferences/Location of Files**. The graphics directory is specified in the **Graphics Files** text box.

Importing a Different Graphic into an Existing Figure Box

1. Select **Graphics/Figure/Edit** or press Shift+F11 (Figure Edit). WordPerfect for Windows prompts you to enter the number of the Figure box you want to edit.

2. Type the figure box number and select OK. (To edit the handshake figure, type **1** and select OK.) The Figure Editor window appears, displaying the current graphic image.

3. Select **File/Retrieve** or the Retrieve button. WordPerfect for Windows displays the Retrieve Figure dialog box, which lists graphics files in your default graphics directory.

4. Enter a file name, including the full directory path if the file is not in the default graphics directory. (For information about listing files in other directories, see Appendix D.)

5. Select **Retrieve**. WordPerfect for Windows returns to the Figure Editor window, which displays the new figure.

6. Select **File/Close** or the Close button. WordPerfect for Windows saves the change and returns to the document window.

While in the Figure Editor window, you can change the size and position of the Figure box and manipulate the graphic image. For more on the Figure Editor window, see "Editing Figures" later in this chapter.

Entering Text for Articles

Now that you have your figure in place, you can enter the text in the newsletter articles. Keep in mind that you now have to work around the Figure box to keep the text from overlapping it.

Entering Text in Text Box 2

1. Select **Graphics/Text Box/Edit** or press Alt+Shift+F11 (Text Box Edit). The Edit Text Box dialog box appears.

2. Type **2** and select OK. The Text Box Editor window for Text Box 2 appears. Although the window is blank, the file has several important formatting codes.

3. Select **View/Reveal Codes** or press Alt+F3 (Reveal Codes). The Reveal Codes area appears, as shown in Figure 3.4.

4. Move the cursor past the [Font:Palatino 18pt] code, and type the text you want to appear as the heading for this section. **Thank You!** was entered in the example shown at the end of the chapter. Whatever you type is in 18-point Palatino, and in italics (because of the [Italc On] code before the [Font] code). You can change the font by deleting the existing [Font] code and entering a new [Font] code as explained earlier for Text Box 1.

Beginner's Tip

When WordPerfect for Windows opened the file, it formatted it for your default printer. If your printer does not support the Palatino font, or 18-point size, these settings were changed to something supportable. The font code you actually see on-screen in Step 4 may vary, depending on your printer. For example, it may be [Font:Times Roman 18 pt] instead.

5. Move the cursor past the [Italc Off] code and press Enter twice. This places space between the heading and the main text. By moving the cursor past [Italc Off], you make sure that the rest of the text will appear without italics.

6. Enter a [Font] code specifying the font you want to use for the main text. For example, you may want to stay with Palatino but make the point size smaller, as in [Font:Palatino 12 pt].

7. Type the text that you want to appear in the left column. Keep an eye on the Ln number on the status line to determine how much text you can add before it runs into the horizontal graphic line. The horizontal line is at approximately 3.5", so stop just short of this number.

8. Press Ctrl+Enter to insert a hard page break. This ends the left column and starts the right column.

9. Press Enter several times, until the Ln number on the status line is greater than 2.5". This ensures that the text you type won't interfere with the bottom of the figure.

10. Type the remaining text for this section, making sure you stop short of the line at 3.5".

11. Select **File/Close** or the Close button to save the text and return to the document window.

12. Select **File/Print Preview** or press Shift+F5 (Print Preview) to see if the text interferes with any of the graphic elements.

If the text you entered overlaps the figure or the horizontal lines, reopen the Text Box Editor window and add or delete hard returns to move the text up or down. You can also move the Figure box (see "Changing the Position, Size, and Type of Graphics Box" and "Using the Mouse to Move and Size Graphics Boxes," later in this chapter). In addition, you can change the widths of the columns, as explained in the steps that follow.

Be careful if you narrow a column: The column might lengthen to accommodate the same amount of text and might run into the horizontal line.

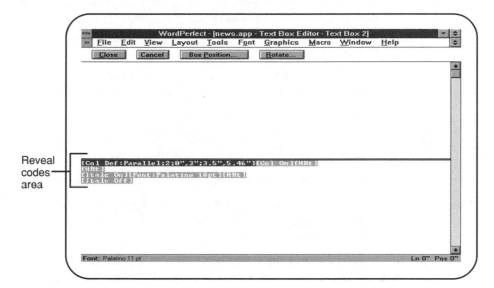

Reveal codes area

Figure 3.4   The Reveal Codes screen for Text Box 2.

Changing Parallel Column Widths

1. Display Text Box 2 in the Text Box Editor window.

2. Move the cursor just past the [Col Def] code.

3. Select **L**ayout/**C**olumns/**D**efine, or press Alt+Shift+F9 (Columns) and type **d**. The Define Columns dialog box appears.

4. *To create columns of equal width*, select the Evenly Spaced check box and type the distance you want to separate the columns in the **D**istance Between Columns text box. WordPerfect for Windows automatically enters the margins in the **M**argins text boxes.

   To create columns of unequal width, go to the **M**argins text boxes and type the left and right margin settings for each column. WordPerfect for Windows automatically deselects the Evenly Spaced check box. The next time you open the dialog box, the **D**istance Between Columns box also is updated.

5. Deselect the Column **On** check box. (The Column feature is turned on already; leaving this selected would insert unnecessary additional codes).

6. Select OK to return to the Text Box Editor window. If you are using WordPerfect's default setting for Auto Code Placement, WordPerfect for Windows replaces the original [Col Def] code with the new one. (See Chapter 2 for information on the Auto Code Placement feature.)

After you've entered text for the top part of Text Box 2, you must turn the Column feature off to prevent the text in the lower half of the box from appearing in columns.

Turning Columns Off

1. Display Text Box 2 in the Text Box Editor window.

2. Move the cursor just past the last character you typed.

3. Select **Layout/Columns/Columns Off**, or press Alt+Shift+F9 (Columns) and type **f**. WordPerfect for Windows inserts a [Col Off] code at the cursor location.

Type the text in the lower half of the box, being careful to begin after the line at about 3.9" (to avoid the horizontal graphic line) and to stop short of the line at 6.8" (where the "What's Inside" box starts). Remember, you can change fonts, add appearance attributes, and change the margins to customize the look of your text.

The bullets in the example were added by pressing Ctrl+W, entering 4,2 in the Number box, and selecting Insert. However, the characters that you can print depend upon your printer. Print the file called *CHARMAP.TST* using each of your available fonts to see what characters your printer can produce.

When you're done typing the text in Text Box 2, display the Text Box Editor window for Text Box 3, the "What's Inside" box, and type the text you want to appear in that box.

When you're finished, display the newsletter cover in the Print Preview window to check for overlapping text and graphics. Remember that the document window displays only an approximation of the real thing. The Print Preview window is a much more accurate representation. Text that appears to overlap in the document window might not actually overlap.

Make no changes until you display the document in the Print Preview window and verify that they are necessary. However, even the Print Preview window isn't 100% accurate; so, when in doubt, print it out.

Using Lines

The final touch on the newsletter consists of the two horizontal lines that separate the President's thank-you message from the rest of the text. Since these are graphics, they could not be entered in the Text box itself, but had to be created outside the Text box and positioned in their current location. You can edit either or both of these lines as follows.

Editing Horizontal Lines

1. In the Reveal Codes area, place the cursor so that it follows the [HLine] code for the line you want to edit, but precedes the code for any subsequent lines.

2. Select **G**raphics/**L**ine/Edit **H**orizontal. WordPerfect for Windows searches backward for the first horizontal line, and presents the Edit Horizontal Line dialog box for it.

3. Enter your changes in the dialog box. You can change the horizontal and vertical positions of the line and the line thickness, length, and gray shading. For more information about your options, see Chapter 8.

4. Select OK to save the change and close the dialog box. WordPerfect for Windows updates the [HLine] code to reflect the new line settings.

Changing the Position, Size, and Type of Graphics Box

To change the size of Text Box 1, you used the Box Position and Size dialog box. This is a generic dialog box used for all types of graphics boxes. You can use this dialog box, shown in Figure 3.5, to change the following:

Box Type: WordPerfect for Windows allows the following graphics box types: Figure, Table, Text, User, and Equation. Each box type is numbered separately from the other types. You also can set different options for each box type. To have two boxes of different types that you want to share attributes and numbering, change the box type of one of them to match the other. (Select the **B**ox Type pop-up list button and then select a new box type.) For example, to have a Text box be numbered with Figure boxes, change its **B**ox Type to **F**igure. The box will have the characteristics set by the last [Fig Opt] code.

Beginner's Tip

Changing the box type doesn't affect the box contents or the editor window for the box. If you later edit the box in the example just given, you will still use the Text Box Editor window, not the Figure Editor window.

Anchor To: If you choose this pop-up list button, WordPerfect for Windows presents the following options: **P**aragraph, which anchors the box to the paragraph the cursor was in when you created the box; Pa**g**e, which anchors the box to the page; and **C**haracter, which treats the box as a single character inserted at the cursor position (text leads into the left side of the box and out the right side on the same line).

Size: If you select this pop-up list button, WordPerfect for Windows presents a list of sizing methods. To have WordPerfect for Windows automatically size the graphics box, select **A**uto Both. To enter your own dimensions, select **S**et Both and enter dimensions for the box in the **W**idth and **H**eight text boxes. To set one dimension and have WordPerfect for Windows set the other, select Auto **W**idth (you set the height) or Auto **H**eight (you set the width). Enter the dimension you want to set in the appropriate text box below the **S**ize button. (It will be the only available text box; the other will be dimmed.)

Vertical Position: Select this pop-up list button to display options for positioning the box vertically on the page. Your options depend on the anchor type.

If you anchored the box to the page, select **F**ull Page to extend the box from the top to bottom margin; select **T**op to place it at the top of the page; select **C**enter to center it between the top and bottom margins; select **B**ottom to place it at the bottom of the page; or select **S**et Position to specify an exact location. If you select **S**et Position, enter the distance between the top of the page and the top of the box in the **P**osition text box.

If you anchored the box to a paragraph, **S**et Position is automatically selected. You can use the **P**osition text box to specify a distance between the top edge of the paragraph and the top of the box (including outside border space).

If you anchored the box to a character, select **T**op to align the top of the box with the surrounding text; select **C**enter to align the center of the box with the surrounding text; or select **B**ottom to align the bottom of the box with the surrounding text. Select **B**aseline to align the baseline of the graphics box contents with the baseline of the surrounding text.

Horizontal Position: Select this pop-up list button to display options for positioning the box horizontally on the page. As with **V**ertical Position, your options depend on the anchor type.

If you anchored the box to the page, you can align it with the left or right margins (Margin, **L**eft, or Margin, **R**ight), center it between the left and right margins (Margin, **C**enter), extend it from the left to the right margin (Margin, **F**ull), or set an exact position (**S**et Position). You specify the exact position in the **P**osition text box. If you have columns, you also can align the box with or between one or more columns; you specify the column or range of columns in the text box below the pop-up list button.

If you anchored the box to a paragraph, you can align it with the left or right edge of the paragraph (Margin, **L**eft; or Margin, **R**ight), center it between the left and right edges (Margin, **C**enter), extend it from the left to the right edge (Margin, **F**ull), or set an exact position from the left edge of the paragraph (**S**et Position). You specify an exact position in the **P**osition text box.

If you indented the paragraph, the edge depends on where the [Indent] code is. If the [Indent] code precedes the [Box] code, the left edge is the indent position.

If you anchored the box to a character, you cannot set a horizontal position.

Wrap Text Around Box: If you deselect this check box to prevent the text from wrapping around the box, text may be printed over the box. Deselect this check box only if you want to superimpose text over the box.

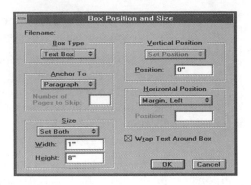

Figure 3.5   The Box Position and Size dialog box. These are the settings for Text Box 1.

Changing the Box Position, Size, and Type

1. With the cursor anywhere in the document, select **Graphics**, select the appropriate box type (for example, Text **B**ox or **F**igure), and then select **P**osition. WordPerfect for Windows prompts you to enter the box number. If you receive a message that the system doesn't have enough memory for this operation, see the Beginner's Tip at the end of Step 4 for an alternate procedure.

2. Type the box number and select OK. The Box Position and Size dialog box appears. In the document window, markers appear at the corners and sides of the Graphics box.

3. Select the box options you want.

If you change the position of Figure Box 1 in the newsletter, remember to reposition the text in Text Box 2 so that the figure and the text won't overlap.

4. Select OK. WordPerfect for Windows returns to the document window. You can see the effects of the change by displaying the Print Preview window (press Shift+F5).

If you have a mouse, you can replace Steps 1 and 2 with the following: Place the mouse pointer within the graphics box (the status line should indicate you are in the Graphics box) and click the *right* mouse button. A pop-up menu appears. Type P or place the mouse pointer on Box **P**osition and click the *left* mouse button. This procedure works for any Graphics box that is not superimposed on another box (in that case, the procedure displays the dialog box for the underlying box).

Changing the Graphics Box Appearance

Whenever you create a graphics box, WordPerfect for Windows formats the box according to default settings for that box type. The default for Figure boxes, for example, is a thin black line bordering all four sides and no gray shading inside the box. The default for a Text box is a thick black line at the top and bottom and 10% gray shading. In the application, we modified the appearance as follows:

- Text Box 1: Removed the border and gray shading.

- Text Box 2: Changed the border to be a single-black-line border at the top, right, and bottom, and a thick-black-line border at the left. Removed the gray shading.

- Text Box 3: Changed the border to be a single-black-line border on all sides and removed the gray shading.

- Figure Box 1: Removed the border.

The options are denoted by a [Txt Opt] code before each Text box and a [Fig Opt] code before the Figure box; other graphics boxes have similar codes. You can change these settings by entering a different [*box type* Opt] or [Fig Opt] code before the graphics box whose format you want to change. To do this, you use the Options dialog box for the box type. The name of the dialog box depends on the box type (for example, Text Box Options dialog box or Figure Options dialog box), but the options are the same, as shown in Figure 3.6.

Border Styles: Select a border style for each side of the box. To select a single line border for the left side, for example, select the Left pop-up list button and then select Single from the pop-up list.

Border Spacing: Type the amount of white space you want between the borders and the text (or graphic) inside and outside each border.

Gray Shading: Enter a percentage of gray in the Gray Shading text box. You can type the percentage or use the increment buttons to enter the percentage. Enter 0 to have no gray shading.

Minimum Offset from Paragraph: If you anchored the box a specific distance from the top of a paragraph and the paragraph falls at the bottom of the page, WordPerfect for Windows might have to move the box up to fit it on the page. To control how WordPerfect for Windows moves a box in such cases, you can specify the minimum distance between the top of the paragraph and the top of the box. Type the distance in the Minimum Offset from Paragraph text box.

Caption Numbering and Caption Position: If your box has a caption, you can select different caption options. (You'll learn about captions later in this chapter.)

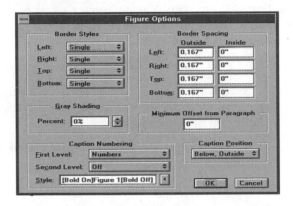

Figure 3.6 The Figure Options dialog box. The Text Box Options dialog box has the same options.

Changing Graphics Box Options

1. Select View/Reveal Codes or press Alt+F3. The Reveal Codes area appears.

2. Highlight the [*box type* Box] code for the graphics box, so that the [*box type* Opt] code will be inserted just before that box.

3. Select Graphics, select the appropriate box type (for example, Text Box), and then select Options. The Options dialog box for that box type appears.

4. Select the box options you want.

5. Select OK. WordPerfect for Windows returns you to the document window and inserts a [*box type* Opt] code (for example, [Txt Opt]) specifying the new options.

A [*box type* Opt] code (for example, [Fig Opt], [Txt Opt]) affects all subsequent boxes of that box type up to the next [*box type* Opt] code. If you want to return to the previous options, be sure to enter another [*box type* Opt] code after the box.

An easy wat to recreate the options used for a graphics box is to copy the [opt] code for that graphics box and paste it before the graphics box you want the options to affect. See Chapter 1 for information on copying and pasting.

Editing Figures

In addition to letting you import a wide variety of graphics into your documents, WordPerfect for Windows lets you manipulate those graphics and save the new version. The Figure Editor window, introduced earlier in this chapter, has a menu bar that offers the following options (see Figure 3.7).

File: Save and retrieve figures. Change the box position and size. Cancel changes. Close the window.

Edit: Manipulate the image.

View: Display or suppress the Figure Editor window Button Bar. Edit the Button Bar.

Help: Get help with WordPerfect for Windows.

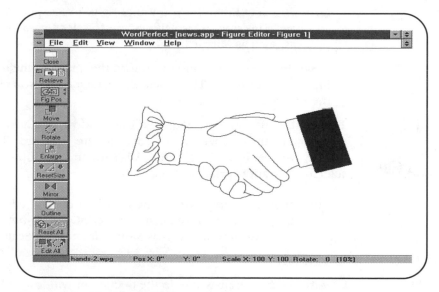

Figure 3.7   The Figure Editor window.

Using the Figure Editor Edit Menu

You can use the Edit menu to modify images by moving them, rotating them, resizing them, converting color images to black-and-white, and more. The following is a list of the Edit menu options:

Move: Lets you move the image horizontally and vertically in the window.

Rotate: Lets you rotate the image around its center point.

Scale: Lets you zoom in on, enlarge, reduce the image and reset it back to its original scale and position (but not its original rotation).

Mirror: Select this to change the image to be its mirror image.

Invert: Select this option to invert the colors for bit-mapped graphics. Colors are changed to their complementary colors. Black-and-white images are not affected.

Outline: Select this to display a color image as a line drawing. Colors are changed to white with a black outline. Black-and-white images are not affected.

Black and White: Select this option to change any colors in a color image to black.

Edit All: Select Edit All if you want to give exact specifications for an image. This option also allows you to select many of the other options, such as Mirror Image.

Reset All: Select this option to return the image to the original image you retrieved. This resets all characteristics you changed in the Figure Editor window.

Shortcut

The Button Bar in the Figure Editor window contains the most common of these operations: Move, Rotate, Enlarge, Reset Size, Mirror, Outline, Reset All, and Edit All. You can select these by simply selecting the appropriate button.

The following steps give the basic procedure for editing a figure. Following those steps are more detailed descriptions of some of the more complex Edit menu options, such as Move, Rotate, and Scale.

Editing a Figure

1. With the cursor anywhere in the document window, select **Graph-ics/Figure/Edit** or press Shift+F11 (Figure Edit). WordPerfect for

Windows prompts you to enter the number of the Figure box you want to edit.

2. Type the box number and select OK. The Figure Editor window appears.

3. Using the Figure Editor window options, edit the graphic image.

4. Select **File/Close** or the Close button to save the changes and return to the document window.

Moving an Image

The Move option lets you move the image horizontally and vertically in the window. Select Move, then use the mouse or the arrow keys to move the image.

To use the mouse, hold down the mouse button while moving the mouse pointer the distance you want the image to move. Release the mouse button to fix the new position.

To use the arrow keys, first press Insert to specify the percentage (1%, 5%, 10%, or 25%) you want the image to move each time you press an arrow key; the percentage is displayed in the status bar. When you press an arrow key, the image moves in the direction of the arrow by that percentage.

Rotating an Image

The **R**otate option lets you rotate the image about its center. When you select **R**otate, x and y axes appear as a guide.

To use the mouse to rotate the image, drag the right end of the x axis to a new orientation and then release the mouse button; the degree of rotation appears on the status line. You can also just click on the spot where you want the right end of the x axis to point. The image rotates so that the right end of the x axis points to the spot where you clicked.

To use the keyboard to rotate the image, first press Insert to specify the percentage (1%, 5%, 10%, or 25%) you want the image to rotate; the percentage is displayed in the status bar. Press Ctrl+Right Arrow to move the image clockwise by that percentage and Ctrl+Left Arrow to move it counterclockwise.

Scaling an Image

The **S**cale option lets you enlarge and reduce the image and reset it back to its original scale and position (but not its original rotation). When you select **S**cale, a cascading menu appears, displaying the following options: **E**nlarge Area, **E**nlarge %, Re**d**uce %, or **R**eset Size.

The Enlarge Area option lets you zoom in on an area. If you select this option, WordPerfect for Windows attaches a crosshair to the mouse pointer. Move the mouse pointer to one corner of the area you want to zoom in on, hold down the mouse button, and drag the mouse pointer to the diagonally opposite corner. The area you defined enlarges to fill the window.

Select Enlarge % and Reduce % to enlarge and reduce the image by the percentage shown in the status bar. Press the Insert key to specify the percentage before you select the option. You can also use the keyboard: Press Ctrl+Up Arrow to enlarge the area and Ctrl+Down Arrow to reduce the area by the percentage shown in the status bar.

Select Reset Size to reset the image to its original size and location. This does not affect its rotation. To reset everything in an image back to the original specifications, select Edit/Reset All or select the Reset All button.

Specifying Exact Measurements

Select Edit All if you want to give exact specifications for an image. WordPerfect for Windows displays a dialog box in which you can enter exact measurements for the horizontal and vertical position (negative numbers move it down and left; positive numbers move it up and right), x- and y-axis scales (entered in percentages), and the angle of rotation (measured in degrees counterclockwise). These measurements are relative to the original image data. You can also select Mirror Image, Outline, Invert, and Black and White.

To see the changes without leaving the dialog box, select Apply. Select OK to apply the changes and close the dialog box.

Beginner's Tip

If you enter a different percentage for horizontal (x axis) and vertical (y axis) scaling, you will distort the image. For example, if you enter 50 for the x value and leave the y value at 100, the image will be half as wide but will retain its original height.

Using the Figure Editor File Menu

The File menu gives you the following options:

Retrieve: Retrieve a figure into the Figure Editor window. For additional information, see "Using a Different Graphic in the Figure Box," earlier in this chapter.

Save As: Save a figure under a different name. Edits to the figure are not saved.

Graphic on Disk: Save a figure in a separate file from the document file. When you open the document file, it retrieves the figure file into the document. (Edits to the figure are not saved.) Use **Graphic on Disk** when you want to conserve file space. Becuase the graphic isn't saved as part of the document file, the document file size is smaller than if you used Save **As** and saved the graphic with the document. **Graphic on Disk** is the only way you can save a graphic in a style.

Box Position: Change box size, position, and type. For additional information, see "Changing the Position, Size, and Type of Graphics box," earlier in this chapter.

Cancel: Close the Figure Editor window without saving changes.

Close: Close the Figure Editor window and save the changes.

The Button Bar in the Figure Editor window has buttons for the **Retrieve, Box Position** (Fig Pos button), and **Close** options. You can quickly select these options by selecting the button.

The handshake figure included in the newsletter application does not come with WordPerfect for Windows. If you think you might want to use this graphic again, you can save it using either Save **As** or **Graphic on Disk.** =

Using the Mouse to Move and Size Graphics Boxes

A nice feature of WordPerfect for Windows is that you can drag graphics to new positions and resize them in the document window. This lets you see changes as you are making them. When you change the box size or position this way, WordPerfect for Windows automatically updates the settings in the Box Position and Size dialog box. In the following directions, note that the procedure for selecting a graphics box depends on whether you selected **W**rap Text Around Box (see "Changing the Position, Size and Type of Graphics Boxes" earlier in this chapter).

Using the Mouse to Move a Graphics Box

1. Place the mouse pointer inside the graphics box and click the left mouse button. Markers appear at the sides and corners of the selected box, as shown in Figure 3.8. If you deselected **W**rap Text

Around Box, click the right button instead, and then choose **Select** Box in the pop-up menu.

2. Place the mouse pointer inside the box. The pointer should change to a *four-directional arrow,* as shown in Figure 3.8.

3. Press and hold the left mouse button while dragging the box to its new location.

4. Release the mouse button to fix the box in its new location.

You can deselect a graphics box by moving the mouse pointer outside the box and clicking the mouse button.

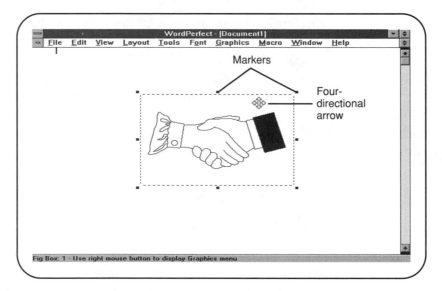

Figure 3.8 Markers appear at the sides and corners of a selected graphics box. When inside the box, the cursor is a four-directional arrow, indicating that you can drag the box to a new location.

Using the Mouse to Move a Graphics Box

1. Place the mouse pointer within the graphics box and click the left mouse button. Markers appear at the sides and corners of the selected box, as shown in Figure 3.8. If you deselected Wrap Text Around Box, click the right button instead, and then select **Select** Box in the pop-up menu.

2. Place the mouse pointer on the marker at the corner or side you want to move to resize the box. The pointer should change to a *two-directional arrow,* as shown in Figure 3.9.

3. Press and hold the left mouse button while dragging the box to its new size.

4. Release the mouse button to fix the new size.

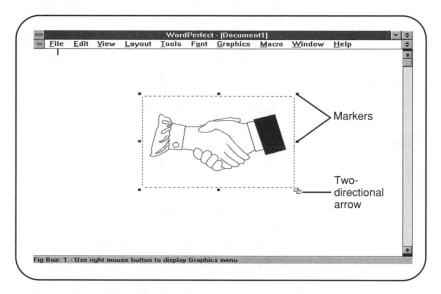

Figure 3.9 *A two-directional arrow over a marker indicates you can drag the marker to resize the box.*

Creating Additional Graphics Boxes

You can customize the newsletter application even further by adding your own graphics boxes. The process is similar for any type of graphics box you want to create: Figure, Text, Equation, and so on; you simply create the graphics box. You can then edit the box contents, position and size, and appearance options, as explained earlier in this chapter.

Creating a Graphics Box

1. Move the cursor anywhere on the page on which you want the graphic to appear. Normally, you need to be more careful about cursor placement, but since we're "pasting" the figures in exact locations, you needn't worry about the cursor location.

2. Select **Graphics**. The **Graphics** menu appears, listing the various graphics boxes.

3. Select the type of graphics box you want to create, and select **Create**. The editor window for the selected graphics box appears.

4. Enter the box contents and select any options. If you're creating a Figure box, for example, you can open a graphics file, edit it, and position and size the box. You needn't enter changes at this point; you can edit this box any time.

5. Select **File/Close** or press the Close button. WordPerfect for Windows returns to the document window, inserts the graphic, and inserts a [*box type* Box] code at the cursor location. If you have other Graphics boxes of the same type in the document, WordPerfect for Windows automatically renumbers the boxes.

You can delete a graphics box at any time by highlighting its code in the Reveal Codes area and pressing Delete. You can use **Edit/Undelete** (Alt+Shift+Backspace) or **Edit/Undo** (Alt+Backspace) to restore the code.

WordPerfect for Windows offers some shortcuts for creating Figure and Text boxes. To create a Text box, for example, you can use the following steps instead of the full procedure just given.

Creating a Text Box

1. Place the cursor as noted in step 1 of "Creating a Graphics Box."

2. Press Alt+F11 (Text Box Create). This displays the Text Box Editor window.

3. Continue with steps 4 and 5 of "Creating a Graphics Box."

Creating a Figure Box

1. Place the cursor as noted in step 1 of "Creating a Graphics Box."

2. Select F11 (Figure Retrieve). WordPerfect for Windows displays the Retrieve Figure dialog box, which lists graphic files in your default graphics directory.

3. Enter a file name, including the full directory path if the file is not in the default graphics directory. (For information about listing files in other directories, see Appendix D.)

4. Select **Retrieve**. WordPerfect for Windows returns to the document window, which displays the new figure. You can edit the figure as described earlier in this chapter.

Adding a Caption

You can enter captions for any graphics box. If you use a Text box to set off a quotation, for example, you may want to add a caption that cites the reference. The following outlines the steps necessary to create and edit a caption.

Creating or Editing a Caption

1. Select **Graphics**. The **Graphics** menu appears, listing the various graphics boxes.

2. Select the type of graphics box for which you are adding or editing the caption, and then select **Caption**. WordPerfect for Windows prompts you to enter the box number.

3. Type the box number and select OK. The Caption Editor window appears, as shown in Figure 3.10.

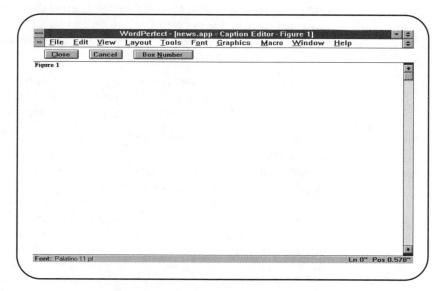

Figure 3.10   The Caption Editor window.

4. Enter the caption or edit the existing caption. To edit the caption, use the menu bar as you would in a normal document window. Select the Box Number button to automatically enter the box number (indicated by a [Box Num] code at the cursor location).

5. Select File/Close or the Close button to save the caption and return to the document window.

You can also display the Caption Editor window by clicking the right mouse button inside the graphics box in the document window. A pop-up menu appears. Select Edit Caption by typing **a** or by clicking on it.

Changing Caption Options

Each box type has a default style for the caption number. To change this style, select different options in the Options dialog box for that box type (for example, the Figure Options dialog box). To display the dialog box, place the cursor before the first graphics box whose options you want to change, select **Graphics** to display the **Graphics** menu, select the box type, and then select **Options**. This dialog box gives you the following caption-related options:

Caption Position: Select this pop-up list button to display a list of available caption positions (for example, **B**elow, Outside; **A**bove, Inside) and select a position from the list. Your selection appears on the face of the button.

Caption Numbering - First Level: Select this pop-up list button to display available number styles (for example, **N**umbers, **L**etters) and select a style. Your selection appears on the face of the button.

Caption Numbering - Second Level: If your caption has two numbering levels (for example, 1.1, 1.2; 1-1, 1-2), select this pop-up list button to display available second-level number styles (for example, **N**umbers, **L**etters) and select a style. The default is **O**ff, meaning there is no second level. If you select a numbering style for the second level, you can insert a character to separate the two levels in the **S**tyle text box. To specify captions having the style 1.1, 1.2, 1.3, for example, the text in the **S**tyle text box should be 1.2. Always use **1** to denote the first-level number and **2** to denote the second-level number, even if you selected Letters as the numbering style.

Caption Numbering - Style: Use this text box to enter any text you want to accompany the caption number. For figures, for example, you might want to insert the word *Figure* and a space ahead of the caption number. Select the arrow button to display available appearance attributes (for example, **B**old, Small **C**aps). Also see the preceding discussion on "Caption Numbering - Second Level."

Select OK when you have entered your changes. WordPerfect for Windows returns to the document window and at the cursor position inserts an [*box type* Opt] code (for example, [Fig Opt]).

Summary

WordPerfect for Windows' graphics boxes and editors provide you with all the tools you need to create an appealing layout. With these tools in hand, with the techniques you learned in this chapter, and with the basic template included with this book, you're only a few short practice sessions away from creating your own newsletters.

The Newsletter Application

June 1992 • Vol. 10 • No. 2

The Organizer

THANK YOU!

Few people realize the amount of work involved in coordinating a convention such as our recent St. Louis convention.

We owe a great deal of thanks to Lew and Linda Harvey as well as to the groups of outstanding volunteers who found time to help them. They'll be calling on you to help with next year's plans, so please, do what you can.

As you know, our new President is Ann Altus from Pasadena, California. All other officers remain the same from last year. If you have any questions about goings on, the papers that are now available or the elections, contact me at your convenience. Best wishes.

—Bill Acker, *President*

Where We Stand
by Mike Gaines

It's that time of the year again when different labor and union organizations are beginning contract negotiations. If your group has not raised the issues discussed at the last negotiation round table, you might want to do one of the following:

■ Contact your labor representative.

■ Write to the national office and find out who is responsible for negotiations.

■ Speak with people you feel understand the labor issues that are facing you and your workers.

As you know, many of the important issues have already been settled for most of the major unions that this newsletter reaches. We need to ensure that it reaches everyone who may be involved in

(continued, page 7)

What's Inside

• Your Questions and Our Answers • Resources • Career Opportunities •
Upcoming Events • Convention Highlights • Newsletter Renewal Form •

Create master document

1. Display blank document window.

2. Select **T**ools/**M**aster Document/ **S**ubdocument.

3. Type the *drive:\directory\filename.ext* for the subdocument you want to include and select Include.

4. Repeat steps 2 and 3 for each subdocument.

Check spelling

1. Select **T**ools/**S**peller or press Ctrl+F1.

2. Select Speller options.

3. Select **S**tart.

Expand master document

1. Retrieve the master document.

2. Select **T**ools/**M**aster Document/ **E**xpand Master.

Condense master document

1. Select **T**ools/**M**aster Document/ **C**ondense Master.

2. Confirm whether to save changes to subdocuments.

BUSINESS SHORTCUTS

Office Rental Lease

Many businesses are either tenants or landlords. In either case, an Office Rental Lease plays an important role. The rental lease in this chapter consists of two parts: a Premises section and a Rules and Regulations section. In this chapter, you'll learn how to combine the two sections into one master document, and edit the master document using the Search function to quickly find where to insert information that varies from lease to lease. You'll also learn how to change fonts to customize the appearance of the text, and how to use the WordPerfect for Windows Speller to check for typos and misspellings.

About the Application

The Office Rental Lease application contains standard language with asterisks inserted where you must supply information that differs from lease to lease (the lessee's name, for example).

The lease application consists of two sections, "Premises" and "Rules and Regulations." You can use either section separately or, if you need to generate an index or table of contents for the entire lease, you can generate a master document comprising both sections. A completed Office Rental Lease is shown at the end of this chapter. The italicized text marks the places where information was substituted for asterisks.

Opening the Application

The two sections of the application are each in a separate file. The section "Premises" is in the PREMISES.APP file, and the section "Rules and Regulations" is in the RULES.APP file. To edit either section individually, open it in the WordPerfect document window (refer to Chapter 1).

You can also combine the two sections into one *master document*. A master document is a special WordPerfect for Windows document that contains codes naming other WordPerfect for Windows documents you want included in the master. When included in a master document, WordPerfect for Windows documents are called *subdocuments*. Any WordPerfect for Windows document can be a subdocument; you don't need to save it as a special file.

To combine the documents named in a master document, you *expand* the master document. WordPerfect then retrieves each document into the master document. When you're finished with the master document, you can *condense* it back to only the subdocument codes, saving changes with the subdocuments if desired.

Creating a Master Document

1. Display a blank WordPerfect document window.

2. Select **T**ools/**Ma**ster Document/**S**ubdocument. The Include Subdocument dialog box appears.

3. Type or select *drive:\directory***premises.app** and then select Include. For example, if PREMISES.APP is in the C:\WPWIN\APPS directory, type **c:\wpwin\apps\premises.app**. WordPerfect inserts in the document window a comment box showing the path and file name you just entered, as shown in the example in Figure 4.1.

4. Repeat steps 2 and 3 for the RULES.APP file.

5. Select **F**ile/**S**ave **A**s or press F3 (Save As). WordPerfect displays the Save As dialog box.

6. Specify *drive:\directory\filename.ext* for the master document file, and select **S**ave. For example, you could type **c:\wpwin\master1.app** to save the master document master1.app to the WPWIN directory on the C drive. WordPerfect saves the file to the specified drive and directory under the specified file name.

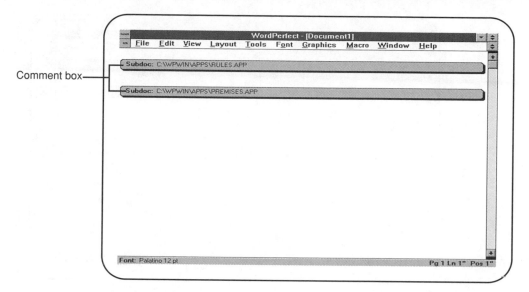

Comment box

Figure 4.1   WordPerfect inserts the name of the file in a comment box.

Beginner's
Tip

To move around the master document, use the right and left arrow keys. Notice that WordPerfect skips over each subdocument name. This is because they are just comments indicating that a subdocument code is entered at that location. If you display the Reveal Codes screen, as shown in Figure 4.2, you'll see the subdocument codes. You can move and delete these codes as you would any WordPerfect codes. To delete a subdocument link, just delete the subdocument code. Deleting the code has no effect on the subdocument itself; only on its link with the master document.

Customizing the Application

You now have three documents: two subdocuments and a master document that links the subdocuments. Before you start entering the information specific to a particular rental agreement, you should edit and customize each of these three documents. By carefully editing these individual documents early, you will avoid having to edit each rental agreement later.

Customizing this application is fairly simple because there's not much to customize. In the master document, you can:

• Specify a page numbering format so that the pages of the combined subdocuments will be numbered consecutively.

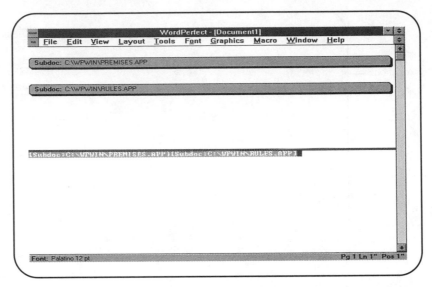

Figure 4.2   Subdocument comment boxes and codes in the master document.

- Change the initial document font.

- Replace the asterisks with the necessary information.

It's best to change the font in the master document *before* expanding the master document. Then, whenever you expand the master document, the font will be in effect.

In the subdocuments, you can:

- Change the appearance attributes of heading text (for example, make the headings bold or italic).

- Change the size of heading text.

- Edit the text so that the boilerplate text is suitable for your company. (Do not make edits that are specific to a particular lease.)

You should replace the asterisks with specific information only *after* you expand the master document. That way, the subdocuments remain unchanged for future use, while the document you created by linking the subdocuments contains the information specific to a particular rental agreement.

Specifying the Page Numbering

When the master document is expanded, it will be about six pages long. For easier reference, you can number those pages. The simplest way is to specify a page number format in the master document. Then you needn't worry about page numbering in the individual subdocuments. (If you specified page numbering in each subdocument, you would always have to check the last page number in the previous subdocument and then start the next subdocument's numbering where the previous subdocuments ended.)

Specifying the Page Numbering

1. With the master document displayed in the window, press Ctrl+Home to go to the top of the document, before the [Subdoc] codes.

2. Select **L**ayout/**P**age/**N**umbering, or press Alt+F9 and type **n**. The Page Numbering dialog box appears.

3. Select the **P**osition pop-up list button and then an option (for example, Top **R**ight) from the pop-up list (see Appendix B for information about selecting pop-up list buttons).

4. For this example, accept the default numbering type which is Arabic numerals (for example, 1, 2, 3). Select OK to close the dialog box. WordPerfect inserts a [Pg Numbering] code at the top of the document.

When creating master documents, it's important to decide which codes belong in the master document and which are better placed in the subdocuments. Codes for features involving all subdocuments generally belong in the master document. Examples of such codes are the [Def Mark:ToC] code, which defines the placement and format of the table of contents; the [Pg Numbering] code; and the [Def Mark:Index] code, which defines the placement and format of the index. The following section on fonts further illustrates this. But basically, just construct your master document as you would any other document. However, instead of typing text for the body of the document, insert the appropriate [Subdoc] codes.

Changing Fonts

To select a font for text in the expanded master document, you can specify a *document initial font* in the master document. A document initial font is a base font you select for the current document—in this case, the master document. When you expand a master document, the document initial font in the master document overrides any document initial fonts selected for the subdocuments, ensuring that the expanded document has a consistent font throughout (the original subdocument files are not affected).

Selecting an Initial Document Font

1. With the master document displayed in the window, select **L**ayout/**D**ocument/Initial **F**ont, or press Ctrl+Shift+F9 and type **f**. The Document Initial Font dialog box appears.

2. In the **F**onts list box, which displays the names of the installed fonts, select a font. (Highlight the font name and press Tab, or click on the name.)

3. If your printer can scale fonts (for example, if you have a PostScript printer), enter a point size in the Point Size text box.

4. Select OK.

The seleted font is the document initial font for the master document. Within the master document or subdocuments, you can override the document initial font by entering a [Font] code that specifies a different font, or modify it by using an appearance or size attribute code (for example, [Bold On] or [Large On]). In the subdocuments, for example, the heading "OFFICE LEASE" has the size attribute Very Large and the appearance attributes Bold and Italic. You could change these attributes by using the Font dialog box. (See Chapter 17 for other methods of changing size and appearance attributes.)

Changing Size and Appearance Attributes within a Document

1. Open PREMISES.APP in the document window.

2. Press Alt+F3 to display the Reveal Codes screen.

3. Delete the unwanted attribute codes before OFFICE LEASE.

4. Select OFFICE LEASE (see Chapter 1 for selection methods).

5. Select Font/**F**ont or press F9 (Font). The Font dialog box appears.

6. To select a size attribute, select one of the following Size check boxes: **F**ine, **S**mall, **L**arge, **V**ery Large, or **E**xtra Large.

7. To select an appearance attribute, select one of the following Appearance check boxes: **B**old, Underline, **D**ouble Underline, Italic, Outline, Shadow, or Small **C**ap.

8. Select OK. The highlighted text is now formatted with the size and appearance attribute. To see the new format, particularly if you selected a smaller size, you might need to display the text in the Print Preview window (press Shift+F5).

9. Repeat steps 3 through 8 to set the attributes for the "Premises" heading.

10. Select File/Save or press Shift+F3 (Save), and save the document. The changed document overwrites the original PREMISES.APP. If you don't want to overwrite this file, select File/Save As or press F3 (Save As) and save the document under a descriptive file name, such as OFF.APP.

You can use the same prodecure to change heading attributes in RULES.APP.

Beginner's Tip

To delete the hidden size attribute codes, press Alt+F3 to display the Reveal Codes screen, and then use Delete or Backspace to delete the code.

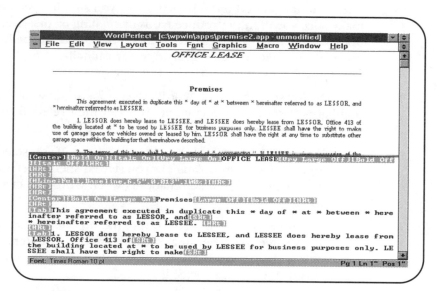

Figure 4.3   Changing fonts within a document.

117

Editing Subdocuments

Before you combine the subdocuments PREMISES.APP and RULES.APP into a master document, read each subdocument thoroughly. If necessary, edit the standard language to reflect your company's policies. To edit a subdocument retrieve it, and then use the editing techniques discussed in Chapter 1 to modify the document. When you are satisfied with it, save it again.

Submit a copy of the edited lease to your lawyer, and consult with your lawyer before using it. State and local rules may vary. You'll save yourself time and trouble in the future by consulting with your lawyer before signing the lease.

Spell Checking the Subdocuments

After you have edited the subdocuments, you should spell check them to make sure you didn't introduce typos or spelling errors. Even though the documents are short, it's easy to overlook typos and misspellings. You also can have WordPerfect check for irregular capitalization, duplicate words (such as *the the*), and words with numbers.

During spell checking, WordPerfect stops at questionable words and highlights them in the document. You can then select from among the following command buttons:

Suggest: List suggested alternative spellings. If you selected the Suggestions check box before you started spell checking, alternative spellings appear automatically when WordPerfect stops at the word.

Add: Adds the questioned word to the supplementary dictionary and resume spell checking. If WordPerfect encounters the word again, it finds the spelling in the supplementary dictionary and considers the word correctly spelled.

Skip Once: Resume spell checking but have WordPerfect stop again the next time it encounters the word.

Skip Always: Resumes spell checking and have WordPerfect will ignore the word during the rest of the spell check.

Replace: Replaces the word with the text in the Word text box and resumes spell checking. WordPerfect remembers the correction and corrects any other occurrences of the word. (WordPerfect will not remember the correction the next time you open the Speller window.)

Close: Closes the Speller window without changing the word.

 Spell Checking a Document

1. With the cursor anywhere in the document, select **T**ools/**S**peller or press Ctrl+F1. WordPerfect displays the Speller window, as shown in Figure 4.4. Note that the Speller window has its own Menu bar, which you use to tailor the spell checking process.

2. In the Speller menu, display the **O**ptions menu and deselect any options you don't want WordPerfect to look for (for example, **I**rregular Capitalization). Select **M**ove to Bottom if you want the Speller window to appear at the bottom of the screen (this allows you to see the questioned words as they are highlighted in the document).

3. If the **C**heck pop-up list button doesn't say "Document," select the button to display a pop-up list of options and then select **D**ocument from the list (for information about selecting from pop-up lists, see "Selecting Pop-up list Buttons" in Chapter 1).

4. To have WordPerfect display suggested alternative spellings whenever it encounters a questionable spelling, select the **S**uggestions check box. (The Speller is faster if this is not selected.)

5. Select St**a**rt. The **C**heck button changes to "To End of Document." The Speller stops on the first questioned word. If you selected **S**uggestions in step 4, the Speller lists alternative spellings in the display area below the **S**uggestions check box and places the first suggested alternative in the **W**ord text box, as illustrated in Figure 4.5. If you didn't select **S**uggestions in step 4, the questioned word appears in the **W**ord text box.

6. If the word is correct, select one of the command buttons to specify the action you want to take.

7. If the word is not correct, select the correct spelling from the list of suggestions, or type the correct spelling in the **W**ord text box and then select **R**eplace. Edit the text box as you would any text. You can use the Edit menu (select **E**dit in the Speller window) to cut, copy, and paste text, and to undo edits.

If you didn't select **S**uggestions in step 4, you can select the **S**uggest button now to have WordPerfect list suggestions.

8. Repeat steps 6 and 7 until you reach the end of the document. When WordPerfect displays a dialog box indicating the spell check is complete, press Enter to remove the dialog box message.

9. Select **C**lose to exit the Speller.

You can check the spelling of a selected block of text by highlighting the block before selecting the Speller.

You can move between the document window and the Speller window by clicking the mouse button while the mouse pointer is in the window you want to be active. If you move to the document window, you can resume spell checking by selecting **R**esume in the Speller window.

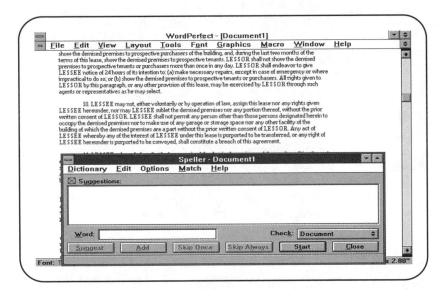

Figure 4.4   The Speller window.

Word in question ―

Suggestions ―

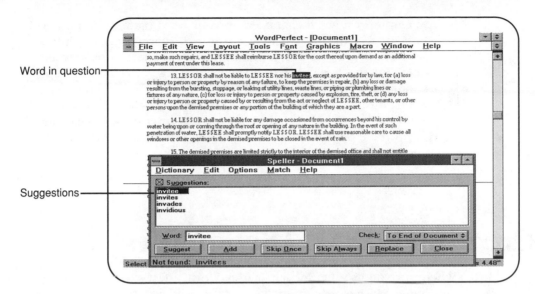

Figure 4.5   You can have the Speller display suggested alternatives.

Although the Speller is a time saver, be careful how much you depend upon it. This utility does not check your spelling as much as it checks your typing skills. For example, if you type **on** when you meant to type **in**, the Speller won't catch the error. Nor does the Speller check grammar or the legality of the text. Be sure to read the document word-for-word before using it in its final form.

Looking Up a Word's Spelling

You can use the Speller's **S**uggest feature at any time to check the spelling of a word. Select **T**ools/**S**peller or press Ctrl+F1 to display the Speller window. In the **W**ord text box, type the word or word pattern you want to check. Type the word as you think it is spelled; you don't have to type the entire word. Then select **S**uggest. WordPerfect displays a list of suggested spellings for the series of characters you typed. If you type **occurance**, for example, WordPerfect suggests the following: occupance, occurrence.

You can use wild-card characters in your word patterns. Type **?** to represent any single character, or type ***** to represent any string of characters. If you type **a?t**, for example, WordPerfect displays three-letter words that begin with *a* and end with *t:* act, aft, alt, amt, ant, apt, art, aut. If you type **can*a**, WordPerfect displays words of any length that begin with *can* and end with *a:* candel, candelabra, candida. If you forget the wild-card characters, you can enter them by selecting **Match** on the Speller Menu bar and then selecting **1** Character (to enter a ?) or **Multiple Characters** (to enter a *).

Creating Special Dictionaries

Whenever you use the Speller, it uses WordPerfect's main dictionary to determine which words are spelled correctly and which ones are not. This dictionary is contained in a file called WP{WP}*NN*.LEX, where *NN* denotes the language of the dictionary. (If you set up WordPerfect so that the base language is U.S. English, for example, the dictionary is WP{WP}US.LEX.)

You can create a supplementary dictionary by adding words during a spell check. When you choose to add a word (that is, when you select **Add** in the Speller window), WordPerfect stores the word in a file called WP{WP}*NN*.SUP (for example, WP{WP}US.SUP for U.S. English). WordPerfect then considers that word correct on all future spell checks. You can edit this file as you would edit any other file.

You needn't add only specialized words to the supplementary dictionary. Your name, for example, is probably not recognized by WordPerfect's main word lists so every time you use your name in a letter, the Speller will stop on it. Use the **Add** option for words such as your name, address, business title, and so forth.

You can create additional supplementary dictionaries just as you create regular text files, and edit them as you would any document. To make the dictionary easily accessible, save it in the default speller directory (that is, C:\WPC) and use the file extension .SUP. For example, you can create a dictionary called LEGAL.SUP to include all the legal terms you use. To use the supplementary dictionary, select **Dictionary/Supplementary** in the Speller window menu. Enter the dictionary name or select it from the list of files, and then choose Select.

Expanding and Condensing the Master Document

Now that you have edited the subdocuments and checked your spelling to ensure perfection, you can expand the master document to combine the two subdocuments into one. You can then view the document and determine if it needs any final adjustments.

Expanding a Master Document

1. Open the master document.

2. Select **T**ools/**M**aster Document/**E**xpand Master. WordPerfect expands the master document.

When the master document is expanded, WordPerfect displays a comment box at the beginning and end of each subdocument, showing where each subdocument begins and ends. In Figure 4.6, you can see the end of the first subdocument and the beginning of the second.

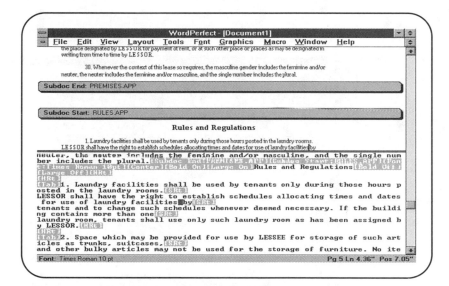

Figure 4.6   The expanded master document.

Now that the master document is displayed in the window, you can preview how it will appear in print. Go to the top of the document and select **F**ile/Print Preview or press Shift+F5 (Print Preview). The first page of the master document appears on-screen. Select the 100% or 200% buttons to view text in the document (selecting Full Page displays layout only).

Scroll through the document using the Next Page and Previous Page buttons, or any of the cursor movement keys. (Refer to Table 1.1 for a list of these keys.) Look at the overall layout first. This may reveal some problems. In Figure 4.7, for example, you can see that the "Rules and Regulations" heading overlaps the text in the previous paragraph. In such a case, you must go into the master document and insert two or three hard returns between the Subdoc 1 and Subdoc 2 comment boxes in the master document.

To place the cursor between the comment boxes, move the cursor to immediately following the period at the end of the first subdocument, and then press the right arrow key. You can also use the Reveal Codes screen for guidance. When the [Subdoc Start:*drive:\directory* RULES.APP] code is highlighted, the cursor is between the comment boxes. This is where you insert the hard returns.

Once you've reviewed the document, and made notes concerning any necessary formatting changes, you can condense the master document to return it to its original form.

Heading overlapping text—

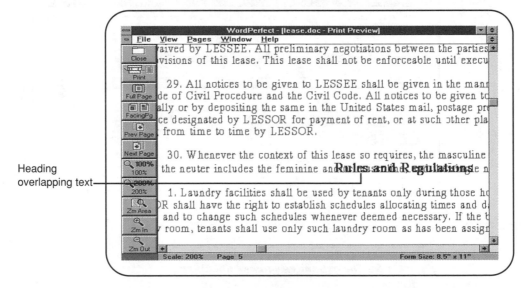

Figure 4.7   Use the Print Preview window to look for any formatting problems in the master document.

As you review the master document, you'll inevitably note other corrections you should make to the text and the format. If the corrections are minor, it might be easiest to enter them in the master document. When you condense the master documents, as explained in the following directions, you can have WordPerfect for Windows automatically make the changes to the subdocuments as well. If the corrections are extensive, you probably will find it easier to enter them in the subdocuments, which are smaller and therefore easier to work with. Before you edit the subdocuments, condense the master document to its original form.

Condensing a Master Document

1. Select **Tools/Master** Document/Condense Master. WordPerfect displays a dialog box asking whether you want to save all subdocuments.

2. Select **No**, if you did not make changes to the subdocuments. WordPerfect condenses the master document into its original form. If you inserted hard returns between the [Subdoc] codes, they remain in the master document. The next time you expand the master document, the subdocuments will be separated by those same hard returns.

3. If you edited the subdocuments within the master document and you want to save the changes in the subdocument files, select **Yes**. You receive the following prompt in a dialog box:

   ```
   Replace Existing File?
   ```

   ```
   PREMISES.APP
   ```

   Select **Yes** to direct WordPerfect to replace the old subdocument with the version you edited in the master document. Select **No** to enter a new file name for the subdocument. To replace, without any further prompts, all of the subdocuments with the new, edited versions, clear the **Prompt** Before Replacing Subdocuments check box.

   If you decided to enter the corrections in the subdocuments (rather than the master document), make the changes to the individual documents and save those changes to disk. By doing this, you save the changes to those files you will use in the future. That is, whenever you expand the master document again, you won't have to reenter those changes.

Editing the Office Lease

Once you've customized the master document and two subdocuments for your own use, you're ready to customize the application for this particular rental agreement. That is, you're ready to replace the asterisks with the information that pertains to this specific rental agreement.

Editing the Master Document

1. Open the master document.

2. Expand the master document as described earlier.

3. Select **Edit/Search** or press F2. The Search dialog box appears.

4. In the Search For text box, type ***** and then press Enter to select Search. WordPerfect searches for an asterisk and stops just past the first asterisk it finds.

5. Press Backspace and then type the required information.

6. Press Shift+F2 to search for the next asterisk.

7. Repeat steps 5 and 6 until you've replaced all the asterisks with the required information.

Saving the Master Document

Now that you have a customized office lease for this particular rental agreement, you should save the file under a file name that's unique for this agreement. See Chapter 1 for information about saving files.

Saving the Specific Office Lease

1. Select **File/Save As** or press F3. WordPerfect displays a dialog box with the following prompt:

   ```
   Document is expanded, condense it?
   ```

2. Select **No**. WordPerfect displays the Save As dialog box.

3. Type a file name that will help you remember this particular rental agreement, and select **Save**. For example, type the last name of the other person who will sign the agreement. WordPerfect saves the file under the name you typed.

When you save the file in its expanded form, it is still a master document. To remove its links to the subdocument, just delete the [Subdoc] codes. Deleting the codes does not affect the text in the document.

Summary

The Master Document feature gives you the power to edit subdocuments quickly and easily, while at the same time letting you treat a master document as a single unit. With this feature, you can create as many individual documents as you need, perfect those documents, and assemble them at any time and in any combination to create documents that suit your needs. You can then print the subdocuments as a single document, create a table of contents or index for the master document, and paginate the document as a single unit.

The Office Rental Lease Application

(Page 1 of 6)

1

OFFICE LEASE

Premises

This agreement executed in duplicate this *5* day of *March* at *315 Main Street, Carmel, IN,* between *Jack Jordan* hereinafter referred to as LESSOR, and *Doug Springer* hereinafter referred to as LESSEE.

1. LESSOR does hereby lease to LESSEE, and LESSEE does hereby lease from LESSOR, Office 413 of the building located at *1000 Corporate Square, Carmel, IN,* to be used by LESSEE for business purposes only. LESSEE shall have the right to make use of garage space for vehicles owned or leased by him. LESSOR shall have the right at any time to substitute other garage space within the building for that hereinabove described.

2. The terms of this lease shall be for a period of *one year* commencing *January 1, 1992.* If LESSEE is given possession of the demised premises prior to the date specified for the commencement of this lease, the occupancy of LESSEE during such period shall be subject to the provisions of this lease. This lease shall not be extended except by an instrument in writing executed by both parties. The holding over by LESSEE after the expiration of the terms set forth above shall not be deemed a month to month tenancy or any other lawful tenancy in the absence of an agreement in writing executed by both parties establishing such tenancy.

3. LESSEE shall pay to LESSOR a monthly rental of *$850,* the said sum payable in advance, without demand, on the *first* day of each month during the term of this lease. Rent shall be paid to LESSOR at *the office* or at such other place as LESSOR may hereafter designate by notice in writing.

4. LESSEE shall deposit with LESSOR upon the execution of this agreement the sum of *$850* as security for payment of the rent reserved under this lease and for the performance by LESSEE of the terms of this lease. If LESSEE should fail to perform any obligation imposed upon him under this agreement, LESSOR shall have the right to apply such security deposit against the damage suffered by LESSOR by reason of LESSEE breach in defaulting on the payment of rent, causing damage to the premises, and the expense of cleaning the premises upon termination. The security deposit, or such portion of it as may remain after allowable offsets, shall be returned to LESSEE after expiration of the terms of this agreement. LESSOR shall not be obligated to hold the security deposit in a special account nor shall LESSOR be accountable to LESSEE for interest, if any, earned upon the said sum, nor shall LESSOR be under restriction with respect to the use of the said deposit. If LESSOR should sell the property containing the demised premises, LESSOR shall have the right to transfer the security deposit to the vendee for the benefit of LESSEE, and LESSOR shall thereupon be released by LESSEE from all liability for the return of such security.

5. Occupation of the demised premises during the term of this lease or any extension thereof shall be limited to the following parties: *Members of the lessee's business.*

6. LESSEE shall pay for all utilities used or consumed upon the demised premises subject to the following exceptions: *no charges for water.*

7. LESSEE shall execute a receipt for all keys furnished by LESSOR. LESSEE shall pay to LESSOR a deposit not to exceed $1.00 for each key furnished. The said deposit shall not be returned to LESSEE upon return of the keys in good condition upon termination of this lease.

8. If LESSEE has executed an application for lease form prior to the execution of this lease, the representations made by LESSEE to LESSOR in such form are hereby incorporated and made a part of this

The Office Rental Lease Application

(Page 2 of 6)

2

agreement as though set forth in full. The execution of this lease by LESSOR is acknowledged by LESSEE to have been induced by the representations set forth in such application form by LESSEE. If it should be determined at any time that the representations made in such application form, or any of them, are not true, LESSOR shall have the right to consider such misrepresentation by LESSEE as a breach of this agreement, and LESSOR shall have the right to terminate this agreement or exercise any other right given herein to LESSOR upon breach by LESSEE.

9. LESSOR shall have the right to retain a passkey to the demised premises. LESSOR shall have the right to enter upon the demised premises at reasonable hours during the day for the purpose of making necessary repairs upon the demised premises or upon any other portion of the building which may require access through the demised premises. LESSOR may, between the hours of 1.30 P.M. and 4.00 P.M. of any day except Sunday, show the demised premises to prospective purchasers of the building, and, during the last two months of the terms of this lease, show the demised premises to prospective tenants. LESSOR shall not show the demised premises to prospective tenants or purchasers more than once in any day. LESSOR shall endeavor to give LESSEE notice of 24 hours of its intention to: (a) make necessary repairs, except in case of emergency or where impractical to do so; or (b) show the demised premises to prospective tenants or purchasers. All rights given to LESSOR by this paragraph, or any other provision of this lease, may be exercised by LESSOR through such agents or representatives as he may select.

10. LESSEE may not, either voluntarily or by operation of law, assign this lease nor any rights given LESSEE hereunder, nor may LESSEE sublet the demised premises nor any portion thereof, without the prior written consent of LESSOR. LESSEE shall not permit any person other than those persons designated herein to occupy the demised premises nor to make use of any garage or storage space nor any other facility of the building of which the demised premises are a part without the prior written consent of LESSOR. Any act of LESSEE whereby any of the interest of LESSEE under this lease is purported to be transferred, or any right of LESSEE hereunder is purported to be conveyed, shall constitute a breach of this agreement.

11. LESSEE acknowledges that he has examined the demised premises and the good condition thereof except as herein otherwise specified. Upon expiration of this lease from any cause whatever, LESSEE shall surrender the premises in their original good condition, reasonable wear and tear excepted. LESSEE shall remove all trash and debris from the premises and shall leave the premises in broom clean condition. All appliances shall be cleaned by LESSEE and turned back to LESSOR in good operating condition.

12. LESSEE shall forthwith repair at his expense all damage resulting from the act or neglect of LESSEE and those persons who came into any portion of the building of which the demised premises are a part as the invitee of LESSEE. If LESSEE fails to make such repairs, LESSOR may, but shall not be obligated to do so, make such repairs, and LESSEE shall reimburse LESSOR for the cost thereof upon demand as an additional payment of rent under this lease.

13. LESSOR shall not be liable to LESSEE nor his invitees, except as provided for by law, for (a) loss or injury to person or property by reason of any failure, to keep the premises in repair, (b) any loss or damage resulting from the bursting, stoppage, or leaking of utility lines, waste lines, or piping or plumbing lines or fixtures of any nature, (c) for loss or injury to person or property caused by explosion, fire, theft, or (d) any loss or injury to person or property caused by or resulting from the act or neglect of LESSEE, other tenants, or other persons upon the demised premises or any portion of the building of which they are a part.

14. LESSOR shall not be liable for any damage occasioned from occurrences beyond his control by water being upon or coming through the roof or opening of any nature in the building. In the event of such penetration of water, LESSEE shall promptly notify LESSOR. LESSEE shall use reasonable care to cause all windows or other openings in the demised premises to be closed in the event of rain.

15. The demised premises are limited strictly to the interior of the demised office and shall not entitle LESSEE to any use of the ground space surrounding the building of which the demised premises form a part, other than for the purpose of ingress and egress. The furnishing by LESSOR to LESSEE of any storeroom, use of laundry,

The Office Rental Lease Application

(Page 3 of 6)

3

or any other facility outside of the demised premises, shall be deemed to be furnished gratuitously. The use of any such laundry room, storeroom, or other facilities shall be at the risk of the person using the same, and neither LESSOR nor his agents or employees shall be liable for any injury to person, loss by theft or otherwise, or damage to property resulting from use of such facilities, except as provided by law.

16. LESSEE shall make no alterations, additions or improvements in or to the demised premises without the prior written consent of LESSOR. All additions, fixtures, or improvements that may be made or installed upon the demised premises shall be surrendered to LESSOR upon termination of this lease. All shades, curtain or drapery fixtures, and any items specially designed to be used upon the demised premises, which are installed upon the premises by means of a fastening device of any nature, shall remain upon the premises and be surrendered to LESSOR upon termination of this lease. LESSEE shall not change any lock nor shall LESSEE alter any lock so that the keys originally furnished by LESSOR will not operate the same.

17. The Rules and Regulations set forth at the end of this lease are a part of this lease. LESSEE agrees to abide by such Rules and Regulations for himself and for all persons upon the demised premises with his consent. Whenever, in the sole discretion of LESSOR, it is deemed necessary or desirable to promote the safety, care or cleanliness of the building, or the preservation of the good order, or the comfort, quiet, or convenience of other occupants of the building of which the demised premises are a part, LESSOR may modify, delete, or add to, the said Rules and Regulations, and such altered Rules and Regulations shall be, from the time of their adoption by LESSOR, a part of this lease. LESSOR may serve notice of such changes of the Rules and Regulations upon LESSEE by leaving a copy thereof in the mail box of LESSEE. Nothing contained herein shall be deemed to impose any liability upon LESSOR for any violation of said Rules and Regulations, or the breach of any covenant or condition in any lease, by any tenant or occupant in the building. Continued violation of the Rules and Regulations by LESSEE shall constitute a breach of this lease by LESSEE, and LESSOR shall have all those rights given to him under this lease by reason thereof as in the case of any other breach of this lease.

18. If LESSOR, his agents or employees, should render any service to LESSEE, such as acceptance of packages, or any other service of any kind or character, or in the event LESSOR permits any person or firm not in the employment of LESSOR access to the building of which the demised premises are a portion for the purpose of performing services such as, but not limited to, car washing and polishing, the rendition of such accommodation services or the granting of access to such persons for the purpose of performing any service function is a courtesy to LESSEE for which no charge has been included in the sum charged as rent. LESSOR shall not be obligated to perform, or permit the performance of, such services, nor the continuation thereof. Neither LESSOR, his agents or employees, shall be responsible for any loss, damage or injury of any nature which may result from the rendition of such accommodation services or by reason of the activities of any person or firm given access to the premises as hereinabove set forth.

19. LESSOR shall maintain all appliances and equipment furnished to LESSEE or the use of which is made available to LESSEE. LESSEE shall be obligated to acquaint himself with the proper use of all such appliances and equipment. If repair or servicing of any appliances or equipment is, in the opinion of the person or firm servicing or repairing the same, required by reason of the improper use or neglect of the same by LESSEE, LESSOR shall have the right to charge all costs incurred by reason of such improper use or neglect to LESSEE, and such costs shall be reimbursed by LESSEE as an additional payment of rent under this lease upon demand by LESSOR. If any facility, equipment, appliance, or item of any nature furnished for use of the LESSEE should require repair or servicing, LESSOR shall have a reasonable time after notification to have such repair or servicing work performed, but in no event shall LESSOR be liable to LESSEE for damage or inconvenience suffered by LESSEE by reason of the failure of any such facility, equipment, appliance or item of any nature, except as provided by law.

20. The word "premises" as used in this lease shall include all carpeting, carpets, furniture, appliances or other personal property, if any, furnished by LESSOR. LESSEE shall execute a receipt for all items received, provided, however, that as to such items which are permanently affixed to the demised premises, such as, but not limited to, carpeting and built-in appliances, no receipt shall be executed. All items of personal property furnished

The Office Rental Lease Application

(Page 4 of 6)

4

by LESSOR shall be subject to the provisions of this lease insofar as they are applicable. LESSEE shall turn over possession of all such personal property to LESSOR at the termination of this lease in it original good condition, reasonable wear and tear excepted.

21. The demised premises shall not be used for any illegal purpose nor contrary to any provision of law affecting the same.

22. Should LESSOR, for any reason, be unable to deliver possession of the demised premises at the time specified for the commencement of the term of this lease, LESSOR shall not be liable for any damage caused thereby, except as provided for by law, and LESSEE shall be entitled to appropriate credit on the rent reserved hereunder for such period as delivery of possession cannot be made. If LESSOR is unable to deliver possession within 7 days after the time specified for commencement of this lease, LESSEE shall have the right to cancel this lease and to a refund of all sums paid to LESSOR.

23. Neither the delivery of keys by LESSEE to LESSOR, his agents or employees, nor any act on the part of LESSEE shall serve to constitute a termination of this lease prior to the expiration of the term hereof unless such delivery or other act is acknowledged in writing by LESSOR as constituting a termination of this lease.

24. If LESSEE shall fail to pay the rent reserved herein when the same becomes due and payable, or if LESSEE shall fail to keep, observe or perform any other covenant, condition or obligation of this lease on his part to be kept or performed, or if LESSEE shall abandon the premises (a period of 14 days absence while the tenant shall be in default in rent shall be deemed an abandonment for the purpose of this lease), LESSOR may serve notice upon tenant that said failure to pay rent, failure to perform, failure of condition, or abandonment of the premises must be remedied within three (3) days, and if no such remedy is effected, within the legally prescribed time period, LESSOR, in addition to all other rights and remedies he may have at law, shall have the option to do any of the following:

(a) Upon court order, immediately re-enter and remove all persons and property from the premises, storing said personal property in a public warehouse or elsewhere at the cost of, and for the account of, the LESSEE. No such re-entry or taking possession of the premises by LESSOR shall be construed as an election on the part of LESSOR to terminate this lease unless a written notice of such intention is given by LESSOR to LESSEE.

(b) To collect any suit or otherwise each installment of rent or other sum as it becomes due hereunder, or to enforce by suit or otherwise, any other term or provision hereof on the part of LESSEE required to be kept or performed.

(c) Terminate this lease, in which event LESSEE agrees to surrender immediately possession of the premises, and to pay LESSOR, in addition to all other sums to which LESSOR may be entitled, all damages suffered by LESSOR by reason of LESSEE's default, including the cost of recovering the premises.

In the event that any personal property remains upon the demised premises upon termination of this lease or upon re-entry by LESSOR under rights given to LESSOR by this lease, LESSOR shall, upon court order, have the right to remove the same and he shall have a lien upon all such property. Notice of sale, and the sale to enforce said lien, shall be governed by *the Indiana* Civil Code. The proceeds realized upon any such sale shall be applied first to the payment of expenses of the sale, reimbursement of costs to remove the property from the demised premises, costs of storage pending sale, and reasonable attorney's fees incurred in connection therewith; any balance remaining shall be applied to the payment of other sums which may then or thereafter be legally due to LESSOR from LESSEE; after satisfying all of the obligations previously enumerated, the balance, if any, shall be paid over to LESSEE.

25. The prevailing party shall be entitled to recover all expenses which may be incurred, including

The Office Rental Lease Application

(Page 5 of 6)

reasonable attorney's fees, by reason of any breach of this agreement.

26. Neither the acceptance by LESSOR of any installment of rent after its due date nor the waiver by LESSOR of any other breach by LESSEE of this agreement shall constitute a waiver by LESSOR of any future default on the part of LESSEE.

27. Upon vacation of the demised premises LESSEE shall furnish written notice to LESSOR of the address to which LESSEE is moving. All refunds to which LESSEE is entitled under this lease shall be mailed to such address.

28. This lease contains the entire agreement between LESSEE and LESSOR relating to the leasing of the demised premises. No representation which is not incorporated herein shall be binding upon LESSOR, and all representations which have been made are incorporated herein, or if not so incorporated, shall be deemed to have been waived by LESSEE. All preliminary negotiations between the parties are merged into, and superseded by, the provisions of this lease. This lease shall not be enforceable until executed by both LESSEE and LESSOR.

29. All notices to be given to LESSEE shall be given in the manner provided by applicable sections of the Code of Civil Procedure and the Civil Code. All notices to be given to LESSOR shall be given in writing personally or by depositing the same in the United States mail, postage prepaid, and addressed to the LESSOR at the place designated by LESSOR for payment of rent, or at such other place or places as may be designated in writing from time to time by LESSOR.

30. Whenever the context of this lease so requires, the masculine gender includes the feminine and/or neuter, the neuter includes the feminine and/or masculine, and the single number includes the plural.

Rules and Regulations

1. Laundry facilities shall be used by tenants only during those hours posted in the laundry rooms. LESSOR shall have the right to establish schedules allocating times and dates for use of laundry facilities by tenants and to change such schedules whenever deemed necessary. If the building contains more than one laundry room, tenants shall use only such laundry room as has been assigned by LESSOR.

2. Space which may be provided for use by LESSEE for storage of such articles as trunks, suitcases, and other bulky articles may not be used for the storage of furniture. No item may be stored which would increase the risk of fire nor which would result in increasing the rate of fire insurance upon the building.

3. LESSEE shall not himself make, nor permit to be made by other members of his family, servants, agents, or visitors or invitees of any nature, any disturbing noises upon the demised property or in the building of which they are a part that will interfere with the rights, comforts or convenience of other tenants. If the playing of any musical instrument, or the operation of any phonograph, radio or television set upon the demised premises between the hours of eleven o'clock P.M. and the following eight o' clock A.M. shall disturb or annoy other occupants of the building, LESSEE shall not play or permit to be played, such musical instrument, nor operate, nor permit to be operated, any phonograph, radio or television set upon the demised premises during such hours. Operation of phonographs, radios and television sets, and the playing of musical instruments, must at all times be conducted with regard to the rights of other tenants of the building to the peaceful enjoyment of their offices. LESSEE shall avoid any unnecessary running of water between the hours of eleven o' clock P.M. and the following eight o' clock A.M., and the operation of garbage disposal units and washing machines during such hours is prohibited.

4. Baby carriages, velocipedes, bicycles or other like articles shall not be allowed to remain in the passageways, garage areas or patio areas of the building. Garbage cans, trash receptacles, kitchen supplies and other similar articles shall not be placed or left in the hallways, public areas of the building, or any area under the control

The Office Rental Lease Application

(Page 6 of 6)

6

of tenant which is exposed to public view. Public entrances, sidewalks, and parking areas shall not be obstructed nor used for any purpose other than for ingress to and egress from the offices.

5. LESSEE shall not shake or hang from the windows, doors, patio or porch areas, any linens, cloth, clothing, bedding, curtains, rugs, mops, or items of any nature, nor shall LESSEE sweep any dirt, dust or debris of any nature from the interior of the demised premises onto any patio, porch or hall areas.

6. The water closets, basins, and other plumbing fixtures shall not be used for any purpose other than for which they were designed. No sweepings, rubbish, rags, or any other improper articles shall be thrown into the same. Deposit of trash, and those of items of garbage which cannot be handled by garbage disposal units into the trash chute shall be made in accordance with instructions. LESSEE shall familiarize himself with the proper operation of all items of equipment furnished for his use, and LESSEE shall use such items in accordance with recommended procedures. LESSEE shall clean all filtering devices upon equipment furnished for his use at regular intervals so as to insure proper operation of the equipment and to avoid damage to the same. Elevators shall not be used for the moving of furniture or any articles which cannot be carried by hand without the prior consent of LESSOR, and any damage to the elevators or the premises caused by the movement of furniture or other items shall be repaired at the expense of LESSEE.

7. No aerial or antenna may be erected on the roof or exterior walls without the written consent of LESSOR. No shades, awnings, venetian blinds, window guards or similar items may be installed without the prior written consent of LESSOR. No dogs, cats, or pets of any nature shall be kept upon the demised premises without the prior written consent of LESSOR. Running of exposed wires for electrical appliances or fixtures in violation of applicable building codes is prohibited.
LESSOR:

By

Lessor

Lessee

Mark heading for table of contents

1. Select the heading.

2. Select **Tools**/**Mar**k Text/Table of Contents, or press F12 and type **c**.

3. Enter the heading level.

4. Select OK.

Define table of contents

1. Move the cursor to where you want the table of contents to begin.

2. Select **Tools**/De**f**ine/Table of Contents, or press Shift+F12 and type **c**.

3. Select the number of levels and the numbering format.

4. Select OK.

Change page numbering

1. Select **Layout**/**P**age/**N**umbering, or press Alt+F9 and type **n**.

2. Select the new page number and number type.

3. Select OK.

Generate table of contents

1. Select **Tools**/**G**enerate or press Alt+F12.

2. Select **Yes**.

**BUSINESS
SHORTCUTS**

Business Plan

*Before you start a business or commit your company to a new venture,
you must have the resources—the financial backing. In order to get that
backing, you must convince prospective investors that your product or
service is useful and will provide a respectable return on the investment. A well-designed and thorough business plan is often the first step
in securing funds from investors. This chapter and the accompanying
application provide a table of contents for a standard business plan.
You'll learn to customize the plan by entering text under each heading,
changing the fonts of the headings to emphasize them, and generating
your own table of contents to help prospective investors find their way
through the plan.*

About the Application

The business plan application is an outline consisting of three sections:
Business, Projected Financial Statements, and Appendices. These sections
are further divided into subsections that let you expand upon the main
topic. The section and subsection headings are marked to be included in a
table of contents, so once you finish typing your text, you can tell WordPerfect
to generate an updated table of contents for the plan. The example at the
end of this chapter shows the application after the table of contents was
generated. Note that WordPerfect automatically inserted a page number for
each heading.

Retrieving the Application

To customize the business plan application for your own use, open the file BP.APP. Once the application is displayed, you can begin creating your business plan.

By saving the application under another name, you can change it without affecting BP.APP. That way, if you delete a heading by mistake, you can open BP.APP and recover the heading.

Customizing the Application

Since this application consists of a general outline, you customize the application by adding, deleting, and rearranging headings as necessary, and by entering information under each heading. You can also change the font for the entire document and for the headings.

Before you begin, press Alt+F3 (Reveal Codes) or select **View/Reveal Codes** to display the Reveal Codes screen for the application, as shown in Figure 5.1. Notice that each heading is bracketed by a [Mark:ToC] code on the left and an [End Mark:ToC] code on the right. These codes mark each heading for the table of contents. Whenever you edit this application, you work with these codes, so it's a good idea to keep the Reveal Codes screen displayed.

Adding, Deleting, and Moving Headings

Before you begin entering text under the various headings, you should review the outline to determine if you need additional headings, or if you need to delete headings that don't apply to your plan. You can then add or delete headings as necessary. Since each heading is a separate paragraph, it's easy to delete a heading.

If you delete a heading by mistake, press Alt+Shift+Backspace (Undelete), or select **Edit/Undelete**. With **U**ndelete, you can restore up to three of your previous deletions. Select **N**ext or **P**revious to display these deletions on-screen. When the deletion you want to restore is displayed, select **R**estore.

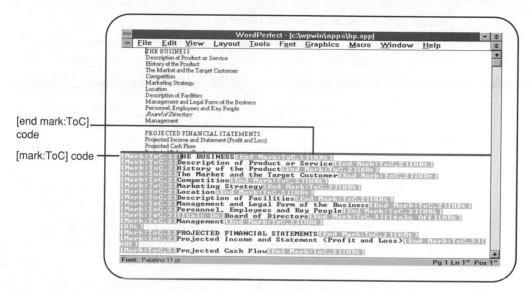

[end mark:ToC] code

[mark:ToC] code

Figure 5.1 The Reveal Codes screen for the business plan application.

Deleting a Heading

1. Move the cursor anywhere in the heading you want to delete.

2. Select **Edit/Select/Paragraph**. WordPerfect highlights the heading.

3. Press the Delete key. WordPerfect deletes the heading.

Once you've trimmed away the unnecessary headings, you can add headings of your own. This process is a little more complex because not only must you enter text for the headings, but you must also mark the headings to be included in the table of contents.

Adding a Heading

1. Position the cursor in front of the hard return code [HRt] that follows the heading under which you want to insert the new heading. (Use the Reveal Codes screen for guidance; the highlight should be on the [HRt] code.)

2. Press Enter to create a new line.

3. Type the text you want to use for the heading, adding any attributes, such as bold or italic.

4. Repeat steps 1 through 3 for all the headings you want to add.

After you've typed all the new headings, you can mark them so they will appear in the table of contents.

Marking the Heading for the Table of Contents

1. Select the heading you want to mark. (See Chapter 1 for methods of selecting text.) If you include type style codes such as [Italc On] in the selection, the heading will have that type style in the table of contents. Do not select the [HRt] code that follows the heading. (Note that you should not use **E**dit/**S**elect/**P**aragraph in this case, because that method selects the hard return following the heading.)

2. Select **T**ools/**M**ark Text or press F12.

3. Select Table of Contents. The Mark Table of Contents dialog box appears, asking you to specify the level of this heading in the table of contents.

4. In the Level text box, type the heading level (a number between 1 and 5) or use the increment buttons to enter a level.

5. Select OK. WordPerfect places a [Mark:ToC,n] code in front of the entry and an [End Mark:ToC,n] code after the entry. The number n in the [Mark:ToC,n] code indicates the level of the heading. In Figure 5.2, for example, the code [Mark:ToC,1] marks THE BUSINESS as a level one head.

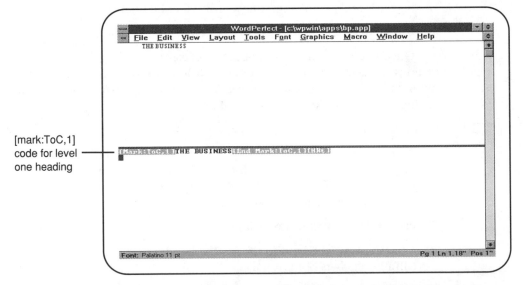

[mark:ToC,1] code for level one heading

Figure 5.2   Headings are marked with a code that indicates the heading level in the table of contents.

After you review your headings, you might decide to reorganize them. To move a heading within the outline, use the **Cut** command to move the heading to the Clipboard, and then the **Paste** command to insert it at the desired location.

Moving a Heading

1. Position the cursor anywhere in the heading you want to move.

2. Select **Edit/Select/Paragraph**. WordPerfect highlights the heading.

3. Select **Edit/Cut** or press Shift+Delete.

4. Position the cursor just before the [Mark:ToC] code below the line where you want the heading inserted. (Use the Reveal Codes screen for guidance; the highlight should be on the [Mark:ToC] code.)

5. Select **Edit/Paste** or press Shift+Insert. The heading is inserted on the line above the [Mark:ToC] code you highlighted.

If you decide you'd rather move the heading elsewhere, select **Edit/Undo** or press Alt+Backspace. WordPerfect then reverses your last edit, which was to paste the heading in the document. The cut heading remains on the clipboard, so just repeat steps 4 and 5 to paste the heading in a different location.

Marking Level Two Headings with a Macro

If you have many entries that must be marked as level two headings, place the cursor anywhere in the heading you want to mark, and then use the macro TOC2.WCM. To use the macro, select **Macro/Play** or press Alt+F10. When the Play Macro dialog box appears, type **toc2** in the Filename text box and then select **Play**. This macro automatically marks the line in which the cursor is located as a level two entry in the table of contents. The macro saves you the following steps:

Keystroke	*Function*
Home, Home	Returns to the beginning of the line, before any formatting codes
F8 (Select)	Turns Select on

continues

Keystroke	*Function*
End	Stretches highlight to end of line
F12	Selects the Mark Text function
C	Selects the Table of Contents option
2 Enter	Marks the text as a level two heading

Before you can run TOC2.WCM, you must copy it from the book disk to your default macros directory. (For example, c:\wpwin\macros.) If you don't know the name of the directory, select File/Preferences/Location of Files. The default macro directory is listed in the Files text box (under Macros/Keyboards/Button Bars).

Entering Text

Once you're satisfied with your outline, you can begin entering running text—the text under each heading. Although this process is simple, it is complicated by the existence of the [Mark:ToC] and [End Mark:ToC] codes. If you enter any text between those codes, that text will appear in the table of contents heading.

Entering Running Text

1. Move the cursor to the hard return code [HRt] after the heading under which you want to type text.

2. Press Enter two or three times to insert space between the heading and the text you are about to type.

3. Type the text you want to include under the heading.

4. Press Enter once or twice to insert space between the end of the text and the following heading.

Changing Fonts

The applications on the disk that accompanies this book are formatted for a QMS PS-810 PostScript printer. When you open an application in the document window, WordPerfect automatically reformats the application for the printer that's installed on your system, selecting the closest available fonts. You can change to a different font at any time, assuming your printer supports other fonts.

You might want to change the fonts for the entire document or for the headings. To change the font for the running text, change the font for the entire document, rather than for each block of text; you can then change the font for the headings, if desired. To change the font for headings of a particular level, change the font individually for each heading at that level.

Changing Fonts for the Document

1. With the business plan displayed in the document window, select **Layout/Document/Initial Font**, or press Ctrl+Shift+F9 and then type **f**. The Document Initial Font dialog box appears, as shown in Figure 5.3.

2. In the Fonts list box, which displays the names of the installed fonts, select a font. (Highlight the font name and press Tab, or click on the name.)

3. If your printer can scale fonts (for example, PostScript printers), enter a point size in the Point Size text box.

4. Select OK.

The selected font applies to all text in the document, including headers, footers, footnotes and endnotes. Because this is a document setting, WordPerfect does not insert a format code. The Status line, however, displays the new default font for this document.

This font will not override any fonts that you change for individual headings. For example, if you change the font for the heading THE BUSINESS, you insert a [Font] code that overrides the document initial font you just set.

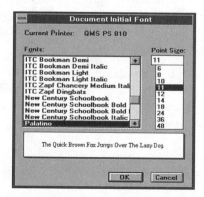

Figure 5.3   The Document Initial Font dialog box.

Changing Fonts for the Headings

1. Select the heading text.

2. Select Font/Font or press F9. The Font dialog box appears, as shown in Figure 5.4.

3. In the Font list box, which displays the names of the installed fonts, select a font. (Highlight the font name and press Tab, or click on the name.)

4. If your printer can scale fonts (for example, PostScript printers), enter a point size in the Point Size text box.

5. Select OK.

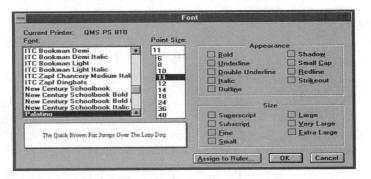

Figure 5.4   The Font dialog box.

If you look in the Reveal Codes screen, you'll find that WordPerfect has inserted a [Font:*heading font name*] code at the beginning of the heading, and a [Font:*document initial font name*] code after the heading, as illustrated in Figure 5.5. As this indicates, the font has changed only for the heading text you selected.

You can also distinguish different heading levels by capitalization, appearance attributes, and size attributes. For example, you can use all uppercase bold characters for level one heads, bold text for level two heads, and italics for level three heads.

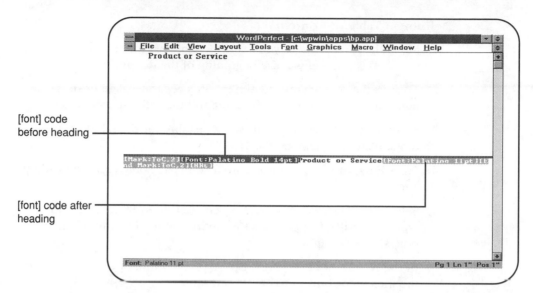

[font] code before heading

[font] code after heading

Figure 5.5 The new font affects only the heading, as indicated by the [Font] codes before and after the heading.

Creating a Table of Contents

Now that your business application is in its final form, you can create a table of contents for the document. This table will list the headings you marked, including the number of the page on which each heading appears. The process requires two basic steps: defining the table of contents and generating it.

Defining the Table of Contents

Before you can generate a table of contents, you must define some of its basic characteristics: its location, the number of heading levels to include, and the page number format for each level. After you finish defining the table of contents, WordPerfect inserts a [Def Mark:ToC] code at the cursor location. When you generate the table, it is inserted at this position in the format you specified.

A *dot leader* is a series of dots inserted between the heading and the page number. This series of dots leads the reader's eyes to the page number.

Defining a Table of Contents

1. Move the cursor where you want the table of contents to be located. This is usually at the beginning of the document.

2. To start the rest of your document on a separate page from the table of contents, press Ctrl+Enter and then the up arrow key.

3. Press Shift+F7 (Center) and type a heading for the table of contents. For example, type **CONTENTS**.

4. Press Enter one or more times to insert space between the heading and the table.

5. Select Tools/Define/Table of Contents, or press Shift+F12 and type **c**. WordPerfect displays the Define Table of Contents dialog box, shown in Figure 5.6.

6. In the Number of Levels text box, type the number of levels or use the increment button to enter a number.

7. In the Numbering Format group, select the number format for each level. Note that the Level buttons are pop-up list buttons. The format shown on the button is the current format. To display your other options, select the Level button for that heading level. The display screen to the right of the Level buttons illustrates the format you have selected. Note that each level is indented to the right of the previous level.

8. If you want to display the last level of your table in wrapped format, select the Last Level in Wrapped Format check box.

9. Select OK. WordPerfect returns to the document window and inserts a [Def Mark:ToC] code at the cursor location, as shown in Figure 5.7. When you generate the table, it starts at the position of this code.

To see an example of wrapped format, select the Last level in wrapped format check box and then look at the last level shown in the display screen. If you don't want that format, clear the check box and then select the level format you want (see step 7).

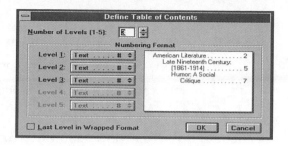

Figure 5.6   The Define Table of Contents dialog box.

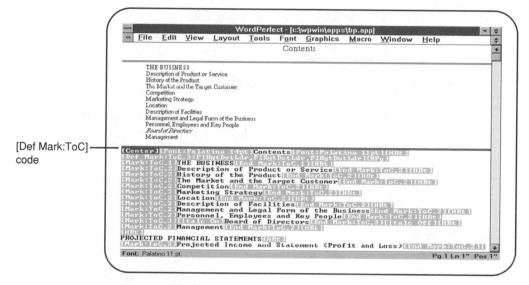

Figure 5.7   When you generate the table of contents, it appears at the location of the [Def Mark:ToC] code.

The Define Table of Contents Macro

On the disk that accompanies this book is a macro that can help you define a table of contents. This macro, called DEFTC.WCM, automatically generates a table of contents including up to three levels of headings. Dot leaders are inserted between the heading and the page numbers. To use the macro, move the cursor where you want the table of contents to appear, and press Ctrl+Enter and up arrow if you want the table to appear on a separate page. Next, select **Macro/Play** or press Alt+F10, type **deftc**, and press Enter. The macro saves you the following keystrokes:

Keystroke	Function
Shift+F12	Selects the Define function
C	Selects the Table of Contents option
3	Enters 3 as the number of heading levels
Enter	Saves the definition and exits the dialog box

Before you can run DEFTC.WCM, you must copy it from the book disk to your default macros directory (for example, c:\wpwin\macros). If you don't know the name of the directory, select **File/Preferences Location** of Files. The default macro directory is listed in the Files text box (under Macros/Keyboards/Button Bars).

Generating the Table of Contents

After you define your table of contents, generating it is easy. You enter the command and WordPerfect does the rest. Before you generate the table, though, consider your page numbering scheme. If the [Def Mark:ToC] code is at the beginning of the document, the generated table will take up one or more pages ahead of the other text, altering the page numbering for the rest of your document. If you want page numbering to begin with the first page of the document, use the New Page Number option before you generate the table.

Changing Page Numbers

1. Press Ctrl+Home twice to move the cursor to the top of the first page of the document, before the formatting codes. (Be sure the cursor precedes the [Def Mark:ToC] code.)

2. Select **Layout/Page/Numbering**, or press Alt+F9 and type **n**. WordPerfect displays the Page Numbering dialog box, shown in Figure 5.8.

3. Select an option for Numbering Type (this is a pop-up list button; for information on displaying the list and selecting from it, see Chapter 1). To have the pages of the table of contents numbered with lowercase Roman numerals, for example, select **i**, ii, iii, iv.

4. In the New Page Number text box, type the page number for the first page of the table of contents (that is, **1** if you want the first page of the table of contents to be numbered 1 or i). Enter the desired page number using an Arabic numeral (1, 2, and so on), regardless of the numbering type you have selected.

5. Press Enter or select OK. WordPerfect enters a [Pg Num:] code in the document, as shown in Figure 5.9. The code indicates the page number and number type, for example, [Pg Num:i] or [Pg Num:1].

6. Move the cursor to the top of the page that follows the table of contents.

7. Repeat steps 2 through 5. If you used roman numerals for the table of contents, select **1**, 2, 3, 4 in step 3. This tells WordPerfect to start numbering the body of the business plan with Arabic numerals.

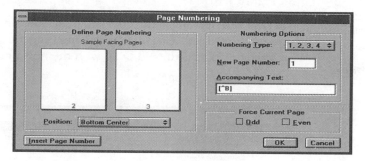

Figure 5.8   The Page Numbering dialog box.

Page number for table of contents

New page number for body of document

Figure 5.9   You can number your table of contents separately from the body of the business plan.

Generating a Table of Contents

1. Select **T**ools/**G**enerate or press Alt+F12. The Generate dialog box appears, warning you that you are about to replace any existing tables, indexes, or cross references, and asking you to confirm.

2. Select **Y**es to continue, or select **N**o to cancel the operation. If you continue, the generation begins. A counter in the Status line shows the progress of the generation. When WordPerfect has finished, the table of contents appears followed by an [End Def] code, as shown in Figure 5.10.

If you change a heading in the business plan, you can update the table of contents to reflect the change by regenerating the table of contents. WordPerfect replaces the old table with the new one.

[End Def] code ——————

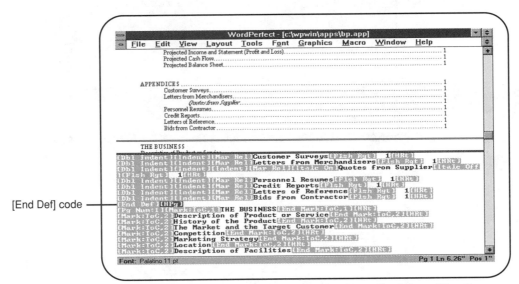

Figure 5.10   The [End Def] code marks the end of the table of contents.

Summary

A good business plan presents your ideas and products, and proves their value to prospective investors and board members. With the outline provided here and with a few simple tools, you can create a well-organized business plan in a visually appealing format.

The Business Plan Application

Contents

Add rows or columns

1. Move the cursor to the row or column where you want to insert the new rows or columns.

2. Select **Layout/Tables/Insert**, or press **Ctrl+F9** and type **i**.

3. Select **Rows** or **Columns**.

4. Type the number of rows or columns to add.

5. Select **OK**.

Delete rows or columns

1. Move the cursor to the first row or column you want to delete.

2. Select **Layout/Tables/Delete**, or press **Ctrl+F9** and type **d**.

3. Select **Rows** or **Columns**.

4. Type the number of rows or columns to delete.

5. Select **OK**.

Join cells

1. Select cells you want to join.

2. Select **Layout/Tables/Join**, or press **Ctrl+F9** and type **j**.

Split cell

1. Place the cursor in the cell.

2. Select **Layout/Tables/Split**, or press **Ctrl+F9** and type **s**.

3. Select **Column** or **Row**.

4. Type the number of columns or rows in which you want the cell split.

5. Select **OK**.

Create a table

1. Place the cursor where you want the table to begin.

2. Select **Layout/Tables/Create**, or press **Ctrl+F9** and type **c**.

3. Specify the number of rows and columns.

4. Select **OK**.

Change cell format and shading

1. Move the cursor to the cell or select a group of cells.

2. Select **Layout/Tables/Cell**, or press **Ctrl+F9** and type **e**.

3. Select the options you want.

4. Select **OK**.

Lock a cell

1. Move the cursor to the cell or select a group of cells.

2. Select **Layout/Tables/Cell**, or press **Ctrl+F9** and type **e**.

3. Select **Lock**.

4. Select **OK**.

Create a table header

1. Move the cursor inside the table.

2. Select **Layout/Tables/Options**, or **press Ctrl+F9** and type **o**.

3. Go to the **Attributes** text box.

4. Type the number of rows you want in the header.

5. Select **OK**.

BUSINESS
SHORTCUTS

Net Worth

When a business or individual applies for a loan, the lending institution generates a net worth statement that shows the financial condition of the business or individual. The net worth application covered here lets you create a net worth statement of your own, using WordPerfect's Tables feature. While customizing the net worth application, you'll learn how to enter your own information in the table, perform basic mathematical calculations on the values you enter, add and delete rows and columns from the table, and change the format and appearance of individual cells within the table.

About the Application

The *net worth application*, which appears at the end of this chapter, consists of two categories: "Assets," which lists the income sources, and "Liabilities," which lists expenditures. By subtracting total liabilities from total assets, you determine net worth.

The application is a table, so it is easy to keep track of columns and rows and to add and subtract values. The type size and style used for various entries and labels are varied; this creates a more interesting appearance, and emphasizes certain values (such as total liabilities). You can change any aspect of the table easily after you open the application.

Opening the Application

To customize the net worth application for your own use, open the file NETWORTH.APP. The net worth table appears on-screen, without the numerical entries shown in the example at the end of the chapter.

 Save the application under another name, such as MYWORTH.APP, so you can change the file without affecting the original NETWORTH.APP file. Then, if you make a mistake, you can open the NETWORTH.APP file and begin again.

Customizing the Application

WordPerfect for Windows' tables are a lot like spreadsheets you may have used in other applications such as Lotus 1-2-3 or Microsoft Excel.

 In case you're not familiar with spreadsheets, here is a brief guide. A *spreadsheet* (or *table*) consists of a series of *rows* and *columns*. Rows are identified by number (row 1, row 2, and so on) and columns by letter (column A, column B, and so on). Where a row and column intersect, a *cell* is formed. Each cell has a *letter/number* coordinate that specifies its position in the table. For example, the cell in the upper-left corner is A1. The cell to its right is B1. The cell below A1 is A2.

The following sections will familiarize you with WordPerfect's tables as you customize the sample to create your own net worth statement.

Entering the Values

You can customize the application simply by entering your own values next to each asset and liability heading. To move the cursor from cell to cell, use the keystrokes listed in Table 6.1. If you are using a mouse, just click on the desired cell and the cursor will move to it. The Status bar displays the coordinates of the cell containing the cursor.

To enter the values, type them into the cells. You don't have to enter values in every cell. If you leave a cell blank, WordPerfect assumes the value is 0.00. If you include decimal points in the values, WordPerfect aligns the values around the decimal points.

Beginner's Tip

If a value is wider than the cell in which you're typing, you may not see the entire number (or the number might wrap to the next line in the cell). As explained later in this chapter, you can widen the cell, or use a smaller font to fit the number onto one line within the cell.

Table 6.1 *Moving the cursor in a table*

Press	*To move*
Up or down arrow	Up or down one cell in single-line cells; up or down one line in multiline cells
Ctrl+Right Arrow or Ctrl+Left Arrow	Right or left one word
Alt+Up Arrow or Alt+Down Arrow	Up or down one cell
Tab or Alt+Right Arrow	Right one cell
Shift+Tab or Alt+Left Arrow	Left one cell
Home Home	First cell in row
End End	Last cell in row
Alt+Home	First line of a multiline cell
Alt+End	Last line of a multiline cell

You can also use the Go To feature to move the cursor in a table. Place the cursor in the table, and press **Ctrl+G** to display the Go To dialog box (shown in Figure 6.1). Select the **P**osition pop-up list button, and then select an option from the pop-up list (see Figure 6.1). If you select Go to **C**ell or **G**o to Page Number, type the cell coordinate or page number in the text box. Select **OK** to go to the new position.

Performing the Calculations

Now that you have some values, you can calculate net worth. Hidden in the table are the formulas that WordPerfect calculates. A + in the Total Assets cell (B19) and the Total Liabilities cell (D11) tells WordPerfect to add all the numbers in the cells above them, and to insert the respective totals in B19 and D11. The Net Worth cell (D20) contains a formula, B19 - D11 (B19 minus D11), which tells WordPerfect to subtract the total liabilities in cell D11 from the total assets in cell B19.

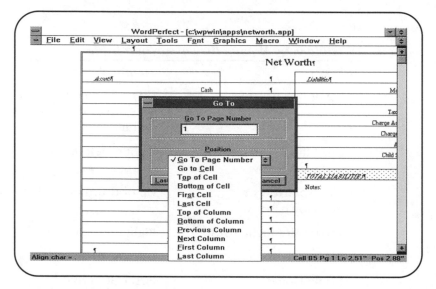

Figure 6.1   The Go To dialog box.

Beginner's Tip

To check a formula, place the cursor in the cell containing the formula and look at the left end of the Status bar. The formula is displayed there. If the cell contents are aligned about a character and the cursor is to the left of the alignment character, then the Status bar also shows the alignment character.

Calculating Net Worth

1. Position the cursor anywhere in the net worth table.

2. Select **L**ayout/**T**ables/**C**alculate, or press **Ctrl+F9** (Tables) and type **a**.

Shortcut

You can recalculate your net worth any time you change a value in the table. This makes the table useful for planning a course of action. You can set a goal for your net worth, and experiment with the different values in the table to determine how you can achieve your goal most efficiently.

WordPerfect has several table calculation options. You can have WordPerfect ignore a specific cell in calculations; you can change the number of digits to the right of the decimal point; and you can display negative numbers in parentheses, rather than using the minus sign. For further information, see "Changing Cell Characteristics," "Changing Column Characteristics," and "Setting Table Options" later in this chapter.

Adding and Deleting Rows and Columns

If you don't use some of the rows in the table, or if you need more rows listing your particular assets and liabilities, you can add or delete rows.

When you *delete* a row, you delete the entire row, all the way across the table. For example, in the NETWORTH application, if you delete the row that contains the Cash cell, the Mortgage cell is deleted, too. Before you delete a row, therefore, you should move any words or numbers that you want to save to a different row. To delete Cash, for example, highlight the word Cash and delete it as you normally would. You can then move one of the remaining words up into the Cash cell, or type a new entry in the cell.

When you delete row or columns: they are deleted from *below* or *to the right* of the cursor position forward. When you *add* rows or columns, the opposite is true: rows are added *above* the row containing the cursor, and columns are inserted immediately *to the left* of the column containing the cursor. To add rows to the bottom of the table or add columns to the right of the table, change the table size. See "Setting Table Options" later in this chapter.

After you have rearranged the text in the existing cells to suit your needs, you can add rows if you need more, or delete rows if excessive rows make the table look too airy. Keep in mind that when you add or delete a row, it is added or deleted across the entire table.

Adding Rows or Columns

1. Move the cursor to the row or column where you want to insert the new rows or columns.

2. Select **Layout/Tables/Insert**, or press **Ctrl+F9** (Tables) and type **i**. The Insert Columns/Rows dialog box appears.

3. Select the **R**ows or **C**olumns radio button. The text box to the right of the radio button becomes available.

4. In the text box, type the number of rows or columns you want to add.

5. Select **OK**. The additional rows or columns are inserted immediately before the row or column that contained the cursor in Step 1.

 The new rows or columns have the same format as the row or column that contained the cursor in Step 1.

 Deleting Rows or Columns

1. Move the cursor to the first row or column you want to delete.

2. Select **Layout/Tables/D**elete, or press Ctrl+F9 (Tables) and type **d**. The Delete Columns/Rows dialog box appears.

3. Select the **R**ows or **C**olumns radio button. The text box to the right of the radio button becomes available.

4. In the text box, type the number of rows or columns you want to delete.

5. Select **OK**. The specified rows or columns are deleted from the cursor position forward.

If you mistakenly add or delete rows or columns, you can reverse the mistake by pressing **Alt+Backspace** (Undo) or selecting **Edit/Undo**. You must use Undo before making any other edits.

WordPerfect provides several shortcuts for adding and deleting single rows. These are listed in Table 6.2.

Table 6.2   *Shortcuts for adding and deleting rows*

Press	*To*
Alt+Insert	Insert a single row above the row containing the cursor

Press	To
Alt+Shift+Insert	Insert a single row below the row containing the cursor
Alt+Delete	Delete the row containing the cursor

Joining and Splitting Cells

You can join two or more adjacent cells to form one large cell. The title in the application, for example, is in a cell formed by joining all the cells in the top row. You can also split larger cells into individual, smaller cells. Figure 6.2 shows a row of five cells before and after they were joined. In this case, the first three cells were joined to form one cell, and the last two were joined to form another.

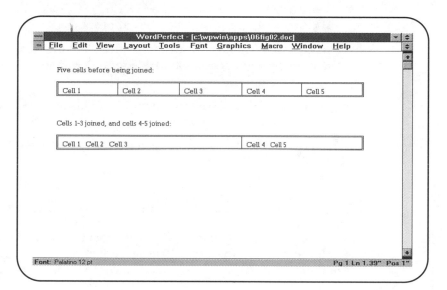

Figure 6.2   Cells before and after being joined.

Beginner's Tip

To reverse the effect of joining and splitting cells, press **Alt+Backspace** (Undo) or select **E**dit/Undo. You must use Undo before making any other edits.

Joining Cells

1. Select the cells you want to join. You can use normal selecting procedures (see Chapter 1) or the special all selection procedure described later in the chapter in "Selecting Table Text and Structure."

2. Select **Layout/Tables/Join**, or press **Ctrl+F9** (Tables) and type **j**. WordPerfect joins the cells.

You can also *split* cells, creating several cells that occupy the same space as the cell that was split. Figure 6.3 shows a cell before and after being split. A row was split to produce two rows, and then the lower cell in the row was split into two columns.

Splitting Cells

1. Move the cursor to the cell you want to split. To split several cells, select the cells.

2. Select **Layout/Tables/Split**, or press Ctrl+F9 (Tables) and type **s**. The Split Column/Row dialog box appears.

3. Select the **Column** or **Row** radio button. The text box next to the selected button becomes available for entering text. The other text box is dim, indicating it is not available.

4. In the text box, type the number of columns or rows into which you want the cell to be split.

5. Select **OK**. WordPerfect divides the highlighted cell(s) into the number specified.

Including and Editing Formulas

Formulas consist of two types of entries: cell coordinates that specify the location of the values you want to use in the formula, and math operators (+ – * /) that tell WordPerfect which calculations to perform on the values.

If you added or deleted rows in the table, you altered the cell coordinates used in the net worth equation (joining and splitting cells may also change coordinates). B19 minus D11 will no longer give you a correct result for net worth. The other two formulas (the plus signs) will still work unless you deleted the cells that contain those formulas (the Total Assets and Total Liabilities cells).

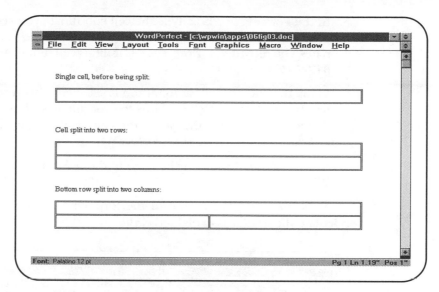

```
                    WordPerfect - [c:\wpwin\apps\06fig03.doc]
  File   Edit   View   Layout   Tools   Font   Graphics   Macro   Window   Help


     Single cell, before being split:



     Cell split into two rows:




     Bottom row split into two columns:





  Font: Palatino 12 pt                                          Pg 1 Ln 1.19"  Pos 1"
```

Figure 6.3   Cells before and after being split.

The following steps are directions for editing the net worth formula. To edit the formula, you need to change the current cell coordinates, B19 and D11, to the new coordinates of the cells containing the total assets and total liabilities values. Note that there are cells immediately to the right of the Total Liabilities cell, the Total Assets cell, and the Net Worth cell. These rightmost cells appear to be part of the cells to their left (since they have no line borders on the left side), but they are actually separate cells. You can see the cells by displaying the Reveal Codes screen. Each cell is enclosed by [Cell] codes.

Editing the Net Worth Formula

1. Move the cursor to the cell immediately to the right of the Total Assets cell, and note the cell's coordinates (for example, B17). The cell's coordinates are displayed on the Status bar, as illustrated in Figure 6.4.

2. Move the cursor to the cell immediately to the right of the Total Liabilities cell, and record the cell's coordinates (for example, D12).

3. Move the cursor to the cell immediately to the right of the Net Worth cell.

4. Select **Layout/Tables/Formula**, or press Ctrl+F9 (Tables) and type **f**. The Tables Formula dialog box appears, as shown in Figure 6.5.

5. In the Formula text box, type the cell coordinate you recorded for the Total Assets cell, type a minus sign (-), and type the coordinates you recorded for the Total Liabilities cell. For example, type **B17-D12**.

6. Verify that the **To** Cell radio button is selected. Also verify that the text box next to **To** Cell contains the coordinates of the cell immediately to the right of the Net Worth cell. (Unless you changed the coordinates, they should be correct.)

7. Select **OK**. The formula is inserted in the cell to the right of the Net Worth cell.

Now that you have corrected the formula for net worth, you can recalculate the results as explained earlier.

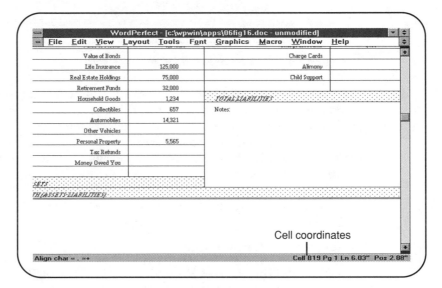

Figure 6.4   Check the Status bar to determine a cell's coordinates.

Figure 6.5   The Tables Formula dialog box.

The single plus sign (+) in the Total Assets and Total Liabilities cells is the Subtotal function. It tells WordPerfect to add the numbers in the column above the cell containing the function, and to insert the result in the cell. Other special math functions are the following:

- Total (=): Adds all Subtotals in the column above the cell containing the Total function, and inserts the result in the cell.

- Grand Total (*): Adds all totals in the column above the cell containing the Grand Total function, and inserts the result in the cell.

These functions can be entered in a cell the same way as you enter a formula: in the Tables Formula dialog box, enter + (for Subtotal), = (for Total), or * (for Grand Total).

Fitting Text in a Cell

You may find that when you enter text in a cell, the text wraps to the next line and the row gets taller, as shown in Figure 6.6. If you want to keep the text on one line, either change the type size of the text, or increase the width of the column. It's easiest to change the width of the column, but if the column is already as wide as the margin settings allow, you may have to change the type size.

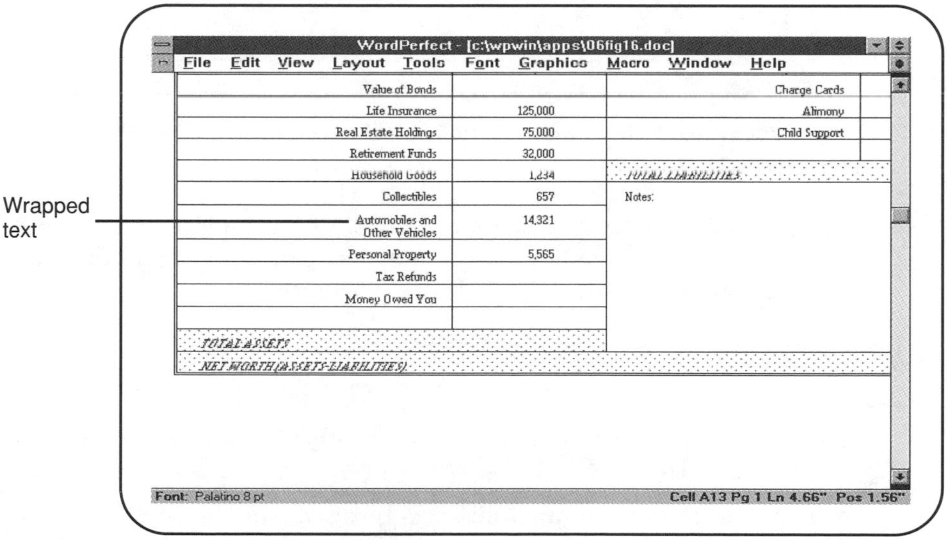

Figure 6.6   Text wrapping in a cell.

Changing Column Widths

1. Place the cursor anywhere in the table.

2. Select **View/Ruler** or press **Alt+Shift+F3** (Ruler). In the ruler, inverted triangles mark the column margins, as shown in Figure 6.7.

3. Place the mouse pointer on the marker for the column margin you want to change and drag the marker to a new position.

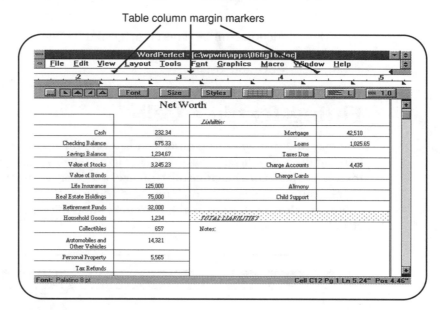

Figure 6.7 ***Inverted triangles on the Ruler mark the table column margins.***

Another way to change the width of a column is to enter a precise measurement in the Format Column dialog box. To display the dialog box and enter the column width, follow these steps.

 Setting Precise Column Widths

1. Place the cursor in the column whose width you want to set.

2. Select **Layout/Tables/Column**, or press **Ctrl+F9** and type **u**. The Format Column dialog box appears.

3. Go to the Column Width text box and type the width.

4. Select **OK**.

If the column is already as wide as the margin settings allow, you can reduce the type size so that all text fits on one line. To change the type size, change the font.

Changing Fonts for the Entire Table

1. Display the Reveal Codes area by selecting **V**iew/Reveal **C**odes or pressing **Alt+F3** (Reveal Codes).

2. Highlight the [Tbl Def] code for this table.

3. Select **F**ont/F**o**nt or press **F9**. The Font dialog box appears, displaying a list of available fonts.

4. Select the smaller font you want to use. If your printer can scale fonts, also select a point size.

5. Select **OK**. WordPerfect inserts a [Font] code at the cursor location.

6. To change the font back to the initial document font, move the highlight just past the [Tbl Off] code, and repeat steps 3 through 5. WordPerfect inserts another [Font] code; any text that follows the table appears in the font selected for the document.

You can also change the font, size, and appearance attributes (for example, **bold**) within individual cells. Simply select the text and then select the font, size, or appearance attribute from the Font dialog box. This inserts on and off codes for the size or attribute. If you change the font, it inserts a [Font] code before the selected text, and after the selected text it inserts a [Font] code that reselects the initial document font. For another way to change cell characteristics, see "Changing Cell Characteristics," later in this chapter.

Creating Tables

If many of the entries in the net worth application do not apply to you, you may find it easier to create a net worth table from scratch, rather than try to edit the application. You can create your own tables by using the Layout menu or the Ruler. The methods are equally easy.

Using the Layout Menu to Create a Table

1. Place the cursor where you want the table to begin.

2. Select **L**ayout/**T**ables/**C**reate, or press **Ctrl+F9** (Tables) and type **c**. The Create Table dialog box appears, with the cursor in the Columns text box.

3. In the **Columns** text box, type the number of columns you want in the table.

4. In the **R**ows text box, type the number of rows you want in the table.

5. Select **OK**. WordPerfect inserts the table structure for a table having the number of columns and rows you entered. Enter and format information in the table, and modify the table structure, as you learned earlier in this chapter.

Using the Ruler to Create a Table

1. Place the cursor where you want the table to begin.

2. Select View/**R**uler or press **Alt+Shift+F3** to display the Ruler.

3. Click on the Table button (shown in Figure 6.8) and hold the mouse button down. WordPerfect displays a grid representing table rows and columns, as shown in Figure 6.9.

4. Drag the mouse pointer to highlight the number of rows and columns you want in the table. In Figure 6.9, for example, the mouse pointer has selected 4 columns and 3 rows.

5. Release the mouse button. WordPerfect inserts the table structure for a table having the number of columns and rows you selected. Use the techniques described in this chapter to enter and format text in the table and to modify the table structure.

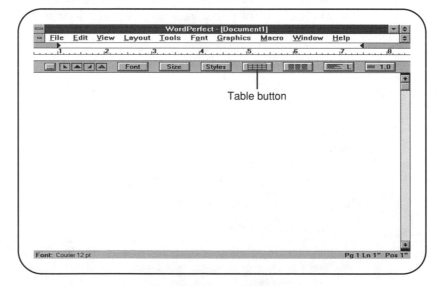

Figure 6.8   The Table button on the Ruler.

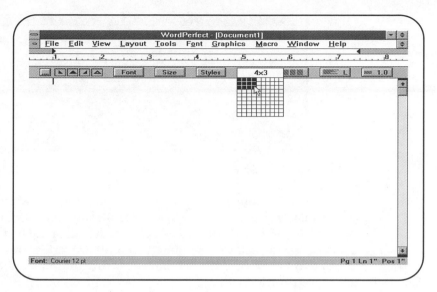

Figure 6.9   When you select the Table button, WordPerfect displays a grid representing table rows and columns.

Formatting Tables

In tables it's important to distinguish between the table structure and the text within the table, because you can format them independently. To format text alone, you use the normal formatting options. Earlier in this chapter, for example, you learned how to use the Font menu to change the type size of table text. To include formatting in the table *structure*, you can use the normal formatting options or the special cell and column formatting options that appear when you select Layout/Tables/Cell or Layout/Tables/Column.

The normal formatting options and special table options are often the same. If you select Layout/Tables/Cell, for example, WordPerfect displays the Format Cell dialog box (shown in Figure 6.10); notice that it has many of the options found in the Font dialog box. In fact, most of the normal Font menu options are also available as special table cell and column options: you can make text bold, italic, large, fine, justified, and so forth by using either set of options.

165

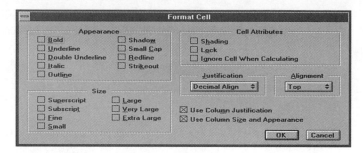

Figure 6.10   The Format Cell dialog box.

When deciding how to proceed, consider the following. If you select and format only text, WordPerfect inserts the format codes in the text; you can see the codes in the Reveal Codes area. If you format text by specifying a format for the cell or column structure, WordPerfect stores the format information with the cell or column structure information, and does not insert any format codes.

Although formatting a column of cells is faster if you simply specify a format for the entire column structure, codes can be useful:

- They indicate immediately the type of formatting in a cell.

- They allow you to remove formatting simply by deleting the codes.

- You can search for and replace them.

The formatting options that are available to you depend on whether you select text alone or text and table structure together. Before we discuss formatting, therefore, we need to explain the different selection methods.

Selecting Table Text and Structure

The normal methods of selecting text—with a mouse, the Shift key, or F8 (Select)—also work for selecting text within a cell. If you select two or more cells, you automatically select the cell structures, too.

WordPerfect also provides some special cell selection methods. If you have a mouse, you can use the *selection arrow* to select cells, including text and structure. The selection arrow is a mouse pointer that appears when you place the normal mouse pointer (the I-beam-shaped pointer) on the top or left edge of a cell. When at the top of the cell, the selection arrow points up, as shown in Figure 6.11. When at the left of the cell, the arrow points left, as shown in Figure 6.12. You can use the selection arrow to select a cell, row, column, or the entire table. Table 6.3 lists the methods for selecting each.

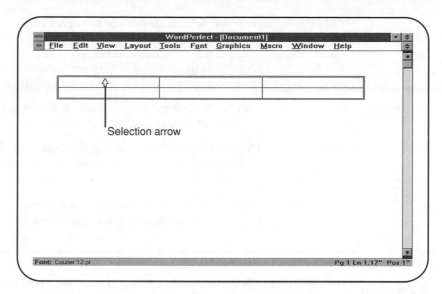

Figure 6.11   The selection arrow points up when at the top border of a cell.

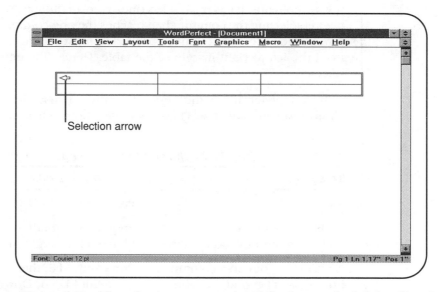

Figure 6.12   The selection arrow points left when at the left border of a cell.

Table 6.3   Using the selection arrow to select cells

To select	Follow these steps
A cell	Display in the cell the left- or upward-pointing selection arrow, and click the mouse button.
A row	Display the left-pointing selection arrow in any cell in the row, and double-click the mouse button.
A column	Display the upward-pointing selection arrow in any cell in the column, and double-click the mouse button.
The table	Display the left- or upward-pointing selection arrow in any cell, and rapidly click the mouse button three times.

Beginner's
Tip

If a table contains a row that has only one column, then selecting any column may select the entire table. The table title, for example, might be in a one-column row—that is, a cell that extends across the entire table. The rest of the table, however, might consist of rows containing several columns. If you try to select one of those columns, WordPerfect begins selecting the column, then reaches the one-column row at the top. And to select that column, WordPerfect must expand the selection from the left to right margin of the table. Hence, the entire table is selected.

If you prefer using the keyboard, you can use the cell selection methods given in Table 6.4. These also select both cell structure and text.

Table 6.4   Using the keyboard to select cells

To select	Follow these steps
A cell	Press Shift+8
Cells one by one in a row, including text beyond the table	Press Shift+F8; then Shift+Left or Right Arrow.
Cells one by one in a column, but not text beyond the table	Press Shift+F8; then Shift+Alt+Up or Down Arrow.
Cells one by one in a column, including text beyond the table	Press Shift+F8; then Shift+Up or Down Arrow.

To select	Follow these steps
The beginning of the current row	Press Shift+F8; then Shift+Home.
The end of the current row	Press Shift+F8; then Shift+End.
The current row	Press Shift+F8; then Ctrl+Left or Right Arrow.
The current column	Press Shift+F8; then Ctrl+Up or Down Arrow.
From the cursor to the beginning of the document (outside the table)	Press Shift+F8; then Shift+Ctrl+Home.
From the cursor to the end of the document (outside the table)	Press Shift+F8; then Shift+Ctrl+End.

When both text and structure are selected, you can format the cells—using either the standard formatting options (for example, those on the Font menu), or the special table options that appear when you select Layout/Tables (or press **Ctrl+F9**). When text alone is selected, you can use only the standard formatting options.

Changing Cell Characteristics

Beginner's Tip

WordPerfect uses *inches* as its default unit of measure. When you enter a number to set the height or width of a cell, the number you entered is in inches. You can change the unit of measure to use centimeters, 1200ths of an inch, or points (approximately 72 points in an inch). To change the unit of measure, select File/Preferences/Display. Select the Display and Entry of Numbers pop-up list button, and then select the unit of measure from the pop-up list.

As noted earlier, you can use the Tables feature to format the text within a cell—changing text appearance, size, and justification. You can also use the Tables feature to change other cell characteristics. The new characteristics are stored as part of the cell structure, and no format codes are inserted in the text.

The application uses standard formatting codes to make the table title extra large and the column and totals headings italic. You may want to assign these characteristics to the cells themselves. Then, when you enter text, you won't need to worry about inserting the text between the formatting codes—the text will automatically have the correct format. If you set the formats for the cell, be sure to delete the format codes entered in the application. To change cell characteristics, use the Format Cell dialog box (which was shown in Figure 6.10). Display the dialog box by selecting **L**ayout/**T**ables/**C**ell, or by pressing **Ctrl+F9** and typing **e**. The dialog box has the following options:

Appearance: Use these check boxes to change the appearance of text and numbers within a cell. The options are the same as those in the Font dialog box: **B**old, **U**nderline, **D**ouble Underline, **I**talic, **O**utline, **S**hadow, Small **C**ap, **R**edline, and Strikeout. If you also use the Font dialog box to change the appearance, the Font dialog box settings are combined with the Format Cell dialog box settings. For example, if you use the Format Cell dialog box to format a cell for bold type, and then use the Font dialog box to italicize the text in that cell, the text is bold *and* italic.

Size: These check boxes let you change the size attributes of a cell: S**u**perscript, Su**b**script, **F**ine, **S**mall, **L**arge, **V**ery Large, and **E**xtra Large. The Font dialog box also contains these options. If you select size attributes in both the Format Cell dialog box and the Font dialog box, the larger size overrides the smaller size. For example, if you select Fine in the Format Cell dialog box, and then use the Font dialog box to select Large for one word in the cell, the word will have the Large size attribute and other cell text will retain the Fine size attribute. If, however, you select Large in the Format Cell dialog box and then use the Font dialog box to select Fine for a word, the word will still have the Large size attribute.

Justification: Select this pop-up list button to list justification options you can select. By default, text in cells is left-justified. You can change this justification setting to right-justify, center, or fully justify the entry. You can also choose to align numbers around a decimal point, as in the net worth table.

Alignment: By default, when you enter a single line in a table, it is automatically aligned with the top edge of the cell. If you enter more than one line in a cell, you may want to align the contents of the cell with the top, bottom, or the center of the cell. (Figure 6.13 illustrates each of these alignment options.) Use this option only when at least one of the cells in a row has more than one line. To view the different alignment, you may have to display the document in the Print Preview window.

If you select several cells and the cells have different formats, the check boxes in the Format Cell dialog box will be shaded if the box is selected in some cells but not in others. If the justification or vertical alignment differs among the cells, **Mixed** will be selected on the Justification and Alignment pop-up lists.

Use Column Justification and Use Column Size and Appearance: When you format a column, WordPerfect applies that format to all cells in the column unless these check boxes are cleared. If you select a cell size, appearance, or justification option other than the column default, these check boxes are automatically deselected. If you later decide to use the column defaults, you can easily reapply them by selecting the Use Column Justification and Use Column Size and Appearance check boxes.

Cell Attributes: These check boxes let you specify whether to shade or lock the cell and whether to ignore the cell in calculations. If you select **Sh**ading, the cell has the percentage of gray shading specified in the Table Options dialog box (see "Setting Table Options," later in this chapter). To protect the contents of a cell, you can lock the cell by selecting **Lock**. You cannot move the cursor into a locked cell; the cursor skips over it. To unlock the cell, select the cell and then deselect **Lock**. (To unlock all cells temporarily, see "Setting Table Options" later in this chapter.)

If you have a mouse, you can select a locked cell with the selection arrow. To use the keyboard, you must place the cursor in the cell before the locked cell, and then extend the selection past the locked cell.

Locked cells are still included in calculations. To exclude a number from a calculation, select **I**gnore Cell When Calculating.

Now that you're familiar with the formatting options, follow these steps to change the format of one or more cells.

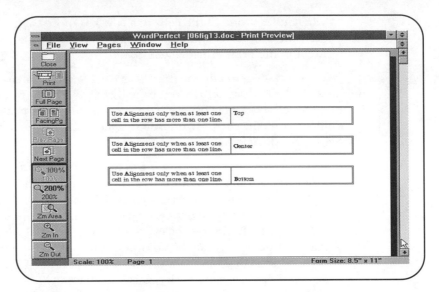

Figure 6.13   Vertically aligned text in cells.

Changing Cell Format

1. Move the cursor to the cell you want to change. To change several cells, select them. (Select the entire cell, not just the text.)

2. Select Layout/Tables/Cell, or press **Ctrl+F9** (Tables) and type **e**. The Format Cell dialog box appears.

3. Select the options you want.

4. Select **OK**.

The Lock Cell Macro

On the disk that accompanies this book is a macro that provides an easy way to lock a cell. To use the macro, move the cursor to the cell you want to lock, select Macro/Play or press **Alt+F10** (Macro Play), type **lock**, and select Play. The macro saves you the following keystrokes:

Keystroke	*Function*
Ctrl+F9	Displays the Tables cascading menu.
e	Selects Cell to display the Format Cell dialog box.
Alt+O	Selects Lock.
Enter	Selects OK to save the change and close the dialog box.

Changing Column Characteristics

You can format all the cells in a column without highlighting the cells by selecting **Layout/Tables/Column** or by pressing **Ctrl+F9** (Tables) and typing **u**. When you choose Col**u**mn, WordPerfect displays the Format Column dialog box, which is similar to the Format Cell dialog box. It has the same Appearance, Size, and Justification options discussed earlier in "Changing Cell Characteristics." In addition, it has these options:

> *Column Width:* You can enter a specific measurement for the width of the column.

> *Digits:* You can enter the number of digits you want to the right of the decimal point.

Changing the attributes of a column is often handy when you need to place an entire column of values in a different font or style (such as bold or italics). In the net worth application, where text in the Assets and Liabilities columns is right-justified, you may want to change the column attributes to select left justification. Change the options the same way you changed the options in the Format Cell dialog box.

Cell format settings have precedence over column format settings. For example, if you select center justification for the first cell in a column, and decimal-align justification for the column, all cells in the column except the first cell are aligned about the decimal points. The first cell retains the center justification.

Changing Table Lines

The lines that surround the table and define the cells can be a variety of styles: single, double, dashed, dotted, thick, and extra thick; they can also be removed. You can define the line style for each side of each cell individually, or you can select a group of cells and define the line styles for the entire group at once.

If your printer doesn't support graphics, these lines won't show up when you print.

Modifying Lines in a Table

1. Select the cell or cells whose lines you want to alter.

2. Select **Layout/Tables/Lines**, or press **Ctrl+F9** (Tables) and type **L**. The Table Lines dialog box appears.

3. Choose the pop-up list button for the border you want to change (**Left**, **Right**, **Top**, **Bottom**, **Inside**, or **Outside**) and then select the new line style or **None** from the pop-up list. Note that the **Inside** pop-up list button is available only when you select multiple cells. It applies the line style to all cell borders inside the selected group; it does not affect the style of the group's outside border.

4. Repeat Step 3 for each border you want to change. Figure 6.14 shows the effects of various borders.

5. Select **OK**. WordPerfect makes the changes, and returns to the document window.

If you select a group of cells, the border refers to the *group* border, not to the borders of the cells within the group. For example, if you select a group of cells and then select **Left** as the border you want to change, the left border of the group is changed, not the left border of each cell within the group.

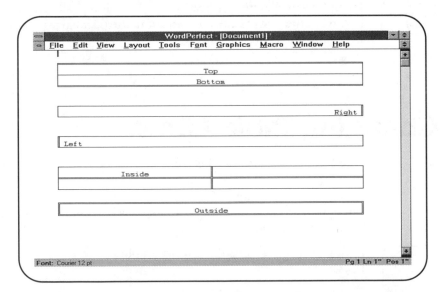

Figure 6.14   Changing the line border for different parts of a cell.

Setting Table Options

Shortcut

If you are having trouble determining where on your page you want to place a table, use a ruler. Measure from the left edge of the page to where you want the leftmost line in the table to appear. Then use the Table Options dialog box to enter your measurement.

The Table Options dialog box offers the following options that let you control the overall appearance and position of the table. To display the dialog box (shown in Figure 6.15), select **L**ayout/**T**ables/**O**ptions, or press **Ctrl+F9** (Tables) and then type **o**. The following are the options you will encounter there.

Table Size: You can change the number of columns and rows in a table by typing different numbers in the **C**olumns and **R**ows text boxes. WordPerfect adds and deletes columns at the right side of the table, and adds and deletes rows at the bottom of the table.

Position: You can select justification from one of the Position radio buttons: **L**eft, **R**ight, Ce**n**ter, **F**ull, or Fr**o**m Left Edge. From Left Edge allows you to set the position of the table from the left edge of the page. If you select the **F**ull radio button (to fully justify the table), WordPerfect expands the table so it is flush with the left and right margins. To set the position, select Fr**o**m Left Edge, and then type into the text box the position of the table from the left edge of the page (not from the left margin). The net worth application is left-justified, you may want to center it to give it a more balanced appearance especially if you reduce the table width.

Cell Margins: With this group of text boxes, you can set the spacing between the text within a cell and the lines that make up the four borders of the cell: **L**eft, **R**ight, **T**op, and **B**ottom.

Negative Result Display: The default selection is **M**inus Sign. When WordPerfect performs the calculations in a table, by default it displays any negative results with a minus sign before the value. You can select **P**arentheses to have WordPerfect display the results within parentheses instead.

Shading: This lets you specify the percentage of gray that WordPerfect uses in shaded cells. You can set only one percentage in any one table. Type a percentage from 0 to 100, or select the increment buttons to enter a percentage. The net worth application

10% gray shading appears in the cells that show the totals. (We used the cell Format dialog box to shade those cells; see "Changing Cell Characteristics" earlier in this chapter.)

Attributes Header Rows: If a table is more than one page, you might want to repeat the first few rows as a header on the next page of the table. To specify a header, type in the **Attributes** text box the number of rows you want in the header. To have the first row repeat as a header, for example, type **1**. To have the first two rows repeat as a header, type **2**.

Disable Cell Locks: If you have locked several cells in a table (see "Changing Cell Characteristics," earlier in this chapter), you can disable them temporarily by selecting the **D**isable Cell Locks check box. This allows you to enter text and numbers in locked cells. When you want to enable the locks again, clear this check box.

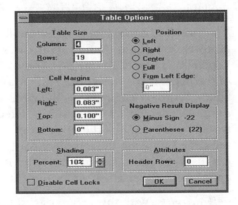

Figure 6.15   The Table Options dialog box.

Summary

The net worth application is useful for determining the financial condition of a business or an individual. With this application and WordPerfect's Tables feature, you can create a net worth statement of your own that is accurate, thorough, and professional. You can use the application to determine whether a loan applicant represents an acceptable risk, or whether you or your business can afford to repay a loan. You can also use the application to set goals for your financial future.

The Net Worth Application

Net Worth

Assets		Liabilities	
Cash	232.34	Mortgage	42,510
Checking Balance	675.33	Loans	1,025.65
Savings Balance	1,234.67	Taxes Due	
Value of Stocks	3,245.23	Charge Accounts	4,435
Value of Bonds		Charge Cards	
Life Insurance	125,000	Alimony	
Real Estate Holdings	75,000	Child Support	
Retirement Funds	32,000		
Household Goods	1,234	TOTAL LIABILITIES	47,970.65
Collectibles	657	Notes:	
Automobiles	14,321		
Other Vehicles			
Personal Property	5,565		
Tax Refunds			
Money Owed You			
TOTAL ASSETS	259,164.57		
NET WORTH (ASSETS-LIABILITIES)			211,193.92

Sort by line

1. Select **Tools/Sort** or press Ctrl+Shift+F12.

2. Select **Line**.

3. Select sort order and key definitions.

4. Select OK.

Sort by paragraph

1. Select **Tools/Sort** or press Ctrl+Shift+F12.

2. Select **Paragraph**.

3. Select sort order and key definitions.

4. Select OK.

Sort by table

1. Place cursor in table.

2. Select **Tools/Sort** or press Ctrl+Shift+F12.

3. Select sort order and key definitions.

4. Select OK.

Define sort keys

1. Select **Tools/Sort** or press Ctrl+Shift+F12.

2. Select key type.

3. Type Field number, Line number, Word number, and Cell number, as necessary.

Extract and sort records

1. Select **Tools/Sort** or press Ctrl+Shift+F12.

2. Select record type, sort order, and key definitions.

3. Type extraction criteria in **Record Selection** text box.

4. Select OK.

Extract records without sorting

1. Select **Tools/Sort** or press Ctrl+Shift+F12.

2. Select record type and key definitions.

3. Select **No Sort**.

4. Type extraction criteria in **Record Selection** text box.

5. Select OK.

BUSINESS SHORTCUTS

Client Records

No business can do without clients and customers, but managing their records can be difficult and time-consuming. While many different programs are designed specifically to manage data, WordPerfect for Windows, with its Sort feature, can perform many of those same tasks while offering you the flexibility of a powerful word processing program. In this chapter, you will create a collection of records and organize them by sorting and extracting them in a variety of ways.

If you plan on retrieving information from your client records to create customized documents, such as mailing labels, letters, and phone lists, you should use the Merge feature to set up your list, instead of using the templates in this chapter. Refer to Chapter 9 for more information.

About the Application

Two templates were prepared for this chapter: *CLIENT1.APP* and *CLIENT2.APP*, which appear at the end of this chapter. Both templates contain the same information, but the information is organized differently in each. In both cases, the information for each client makes up a *record*. Each piece of client information is entered in a *field*, and within each field are one or more *words*. These terms are important, because later you'll be telling WordPerfect for Windows to sort the records according to a particular field, and perhaps by a particular word as well.

Planning Your Database

Before you begin customizing either application, you should make a list of the types of information you want to include for each client. For the templates in this chapter, the list includes Last Name, First Name, Account #, Rep Name, Region #, and Last Order date. You may want to include a street address, city, state, ZIP code, telephone number, and person's title.

The list should be thorough, because when WordPerfect for Windows sorts the records, it expects each record to be organized in the same way. For example, if you sort the records in CLIENT2.APP according to the entries on Line 5 (Region #), WordPerfect for Windows counts the lines from the top of the record down, to find Line 5. If a record is missing a First Name line (Line 2), then Line 6 becomes Line 5, and the records are sorted improperly. You don't have to enter information on each line or in each field, but all the records must have the same number of lines or fields listed in exactly the same order, or the sort won't work. When your list is complete, select a format for your records: lines (as in CLIENT1.APP) or paragraphs (as in CLIENT2.APP).

Which Application Should I Use?

In CLIENT1.APP, the information for each client is entered in a line across the page; in CLIENT2.APP, the information is entered in a paragraph. Use whichever application is better for your situation (CLIENT1.APP or CLIENT2.APP). If you already have client records organized in a certain fashion, or if you're importing the records from a database program, their current form may dictate which template is better.

If you're entering records for the first time and your records are brief, it would be better to organize the records by line. Then, you can enter column heads once and simply type the field entries for each record. If the records are long, however, you might not be able to fit each record on one line. In that case, you must use the paragraph method instead, because lines can be no wider than the page.

Now that you know what your database needs are, and have decided on a type, open the appropriate application (CLIENT1 or CLIENT2) and then follow the text in the appropriate section(s) in this chapter based on your choice.

Opening the Application

When you open either CLIENT1 or CLIENT2, a list of records appears on-screen. You can either use the existing records to experiment with the various ways to sort and select records, as explained later in the chapter, or you can customize the application by entering your own records, as explained next.

Save the application under another name, so that you can change it without affecting the original application file. For example, you could save the file under MYCLIENT.WPF and then use that file for storing your own records.

Customizing the Application

You can customize either application by entering information about your clients. The following two sections explain how to customize CLIENT1 and CLIENT2. Follow the instructions appropriate to your choice—or, gain valuable experience by trying both ways.

Entering Records in Lines (CLIENT1)

To enter records in lines, use CLIENT1.APP. In line records, each field must be separated by a single tab, as shown in Figure 7.1. WordPerfect for Windows uses the tabs to determine field numbers. If you press the Tab key twice between fields, you throw off the field numbering sequence. The field numbering sequence is also disrupted if the information in a field runs into the next tab stop. If the field numbering sequence is off, the records will be sorted improperly.

Change the tab stops (if needed) in CLIENT1.APP so that the information you're going to enter in each field in the line fits between the tab stops. For information about changing tab stops, refer to Chapter 2.

A good way to determine field length is to type the longest entry you can imagine having in each field, and then use the Ruler to set the tab stop so that the text in each field does not overlap the next tab stop.

181

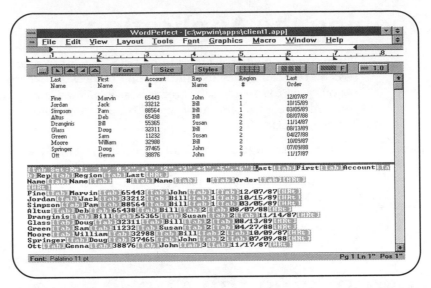

Figure 7.1   Each field is separated by a [Tab] code, which appears in the Reveal Codes screen.

Next, type the headings for your columns, using the list you developed earlier. You can delete all the headings in the template and type in your own, or you can modify the existing ones for your own use. Since the headings will not be included in the sorting operation, you can insert extra spaces and tabs to align the headings if needed.

Beginner's Tip

Although headings are not essential, they help you enter all the information for your records in the correct sequence.

Now it's time to enter your own records. You'll probably want to delete the example records after you have set the tab stops; they'll only get in the way. To do this, select all the records in the template, and press Delete or Backspace to delete them. Then, type your own records, being sure to press the Tab key once—and *only* once—between each field in a line. If you don't have the necessary information for a field, press Tab to leave the field blank; this keeps the field numbering sequence in order.

After you have typed the records, check them and enter any necessary corrections. Save a copy of the file to disk under another name in case anything happens to it as you work through this chapter. Save another copy of the file onto a floppy disk and take the disk home with you, so if anything happens to your hard disk or computer, you have a back-up copy of your client records.

As you're typing the information for your records, save the file every five to ten minutes, so you never lose more than ten minutes of work if the power fails. You can also have WordPerfect save your work automatically; by default, WordPerfect for Windows saves the file in a backup copy every 20 minutes. You can change the default to have a backup copy saved more frequently, as explained in Appendix C.

Entering Records in Paragraphs (CLIENT2)

To enter records in paragraph form, you'll use the CLIENT2.APP file as a template. Before you begin entering the paragraph records, type the headings you want to use for your entries, using the list you developed earlier. After each heading, press Enter. At the end of the last heading, press Enter twice to indicate the end of the record. Type only one of these templates, and then copy it for each record you need to enter, as shown in the following steps.

WordPerfect for Windows recognizes a paragraph record by the presence of at least two hard returns. Each line is separated by a single hard return, and each record is separated by two hard returns.

Copying a Block

1. Select the template you just created, including the two [HRt] codes at the end of the template. (Reveal Codes will help you find the [HRt] codes.)

2. Select **Edit/Copy** or press Ctrl+Insert.

3. Move the cursor just below the two [HRt] codes in the block you copied. (If you did not move the cursor after step 2, the cursor should already be in the correct place.)

4. Select **Edit/Paste** or press Shift+Insert. A copy of the block is inserted at the cursor location.

5. Repeat Step 4 for as many records as you need to enter. Another copy of the block is inserted at the cursor location each time you repeat the step.

When you're done, type the information required for each record. If you don't have the necessary information for an entry, leave the space blank (the line should contain only the [HRt] code). After you have typed the records, check them and enter any necessary corrections. Save a copy of the file to your hard disk under another name, and save a copy of the file to a floppy disk.

Shortcut

When copying the template, make one more copy than you will need, and leave the blank one at the end of the file. That way, the next time you need to add records, you will still have the blank template to copy.

Sorting Records

Now that you have a collection of records (either in line or paragraph form), you can sort the records in many ways. You can sort them alphabetically by last name, numerically by ZIP code (to take advantage of bulk mailing rates), numerically in descending order by outstanding bills (to determine billing priorities), or other ways depending on your needs.

When you choose the Sort option, WordPerfect for Windows displays the Sort dialog box, shown in Figure 7.2. The dialog box contains options that let you control the way WordPerfect for Windows sorts your records:

Record Type: Lets you choose the type of record: **L**ine, **P**aragraph, **M**erge Record, or **T**able Row. **T**able Row is dimmed unless the cursor is in a table when you select Sort. Once you select a particular type, that type stays in effect for your entire WordPerfect for Windows work session. If you sort by paragraph and then want to sort by line, go back and select **L**ine for Record Type. For more information about the merge sort, refer to Chapter 9.

Key Definitions: Lets you enter sort criteria that WordPerfect for Windows will use to sort the records. For example, you can tell WordPerfect for Windows to sort the records by account numbers in numerical ascending order or by last name in alphabetical descending order. More about keys later.

Sort Order: Determines the order of the sort: **A**scending (from A to Z or from 0 to 9) or **D**escending (from Z to A or from 9 to 0). If you want to extract records without sorting them, select **N**o Sort.

Record Selection: Lets you extract a group of records based on a *selection statement* regarding the contents of lines or fields. For example, you can enter a selection statement that extracts records for only those clients whose last name begins with the letter *S*, or all clients who are in a certain region, such as Region 1. To extract the records without sorting them, go to the Sort Order radio buttons and select No Sort. Otherwise, the extracted records are sorted.

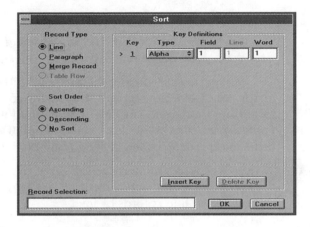

Figure 7.2   The Sort dialog box.

You can use the Sort feature to sort all the records in a file, or you can select a group of records and sort only the records in that selection. If you sort a selection, the selected records are replaced by the sorted records.

Using Keys to Enter Sort Criteria

Each key in the Sort dialog box represents a sort criterion. To define the criterion, you specify the type of sort (alphanumeric or numeric) and the entry that will be sorted to determine the new order.

To specify the key type, select the pop-up list button across from the key number and then select Alpha (for alphanumeric) or Numeric. (You can select the pop-up list button with the mouse or by typing the key number; for example, type **1** to select the button for key 1.) An alphanumeric key can be used to sort any type of information: letters or numbers or both. A numeric key can sort only numbers (without regard to letters) whether the entry has the same or a different number of digits. For example, you could sort the following set of account numbers using an alphanumeric key, since each number has the same number of digits:

```
12-506-665343
43-675-798989
544-58-687887
```

But, if the number of digits were unequal, such as

```
1-506-665
43375-798989
54-58-6878
```

you would have to identify that key as being numeric for the sort to be successful. Most of the time, you'll be using alphanumeric keys.

To specify the word on which sorting will be based, identify its location in the Key Definitions group. If you are sorting paragraph records, its location is determined by line number, field number (if the lines contain fields separated by tabs), and word number. If you are sorting line records, its location is determined by field number and word number.

Beginner's Tip

If you choose Line for Record Type, the Line text box under Key Definitions is dim, signifying that it is not available. This is because you cannot sort line records by line.

If you are sorting paragraph records, type a number in the Line box to indicate which line the sort will focus on. For example, you could enter **1** to sort the records according to the last names, which are on Line 1. If you are sorting line records, type a number in the Field box to indicate which Tab field is the focus of the sort.

Type a number in the Word text box to specify which word in the specified line or field is the basis for the sort. Words consist of text or numbers separated by spaces, dashes, or forward slashes (/). For example, to sort the line records in CLIENT1.APP by the year of the client's last order, Key 1 would look like this:

```
Key     Type     Field     Line     Word
1       Alpha    6                   3
```

WordPerfect for Windows would then base the sort on the third word (which is the year: 87, 88, 89) in the sixth field (Date of Last Order).

To base the sort on more than one word, use more than one key. Order the keys by the priority of each sort criterion, with the Key 1 criterion having highest priority. For example, if you want to sort first by region number, specify the Region # field in the Field text box for Key 1. To sort those in the same region by last name, specify the Last Name field in the Field text box for Key 2.

Shortcut

WordPerfect for Windows normally counts the fields and words from left to right, and the lines from top to bottom. To have WordPerfect count from right to left or from bottom to top, enter a negative number. This is useful, for example, if the field is the last one in the line, but you can't remember how many fields preceded it. If this is the case, just enter **-1**. You can also use this method to prevent problems when fields have different numbers of words. If sorting by last name, for example, enter **-1** in the Word text box to sort fields that might contain "John Smith" or "Jill A. Jones."

To add another key, select **I**nsert Key. The new key appears below Key 1. If you have more than one key, the new key is inserted above the currently active key (denoted by a >). To delete a key, use the mouse or press Tab and Shift+Tab to select the key (the > marker should precede the key number), and then select **D**elete Key. The Sort dialog box in Figure 7.3 illustrates several keys.

You can use up to nine keys for sorting. WordPerfect for Windows first sorts the records according to the sort criterion defined for Key 1, then according to the sort criterion defined for Key 2, and so on.

Beginner's Tip

Remember, whatever options you select remain in force the next time you sort. Always check the Sort dialog box options before selecting OK to begin the sort, because you cannot undo a sort once it is done.

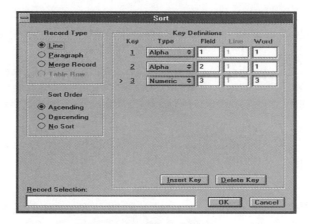

Figure 7.3   Enter sort criteria by defining keys.

Sorting by Lines

If you entered the information for your records in lines, you must either select the records before sorting them (in order to exclude the headings from the sort) or delete the headings before sorting the records.

If you delete the headings as a block, after the sort you can use Alt+Shift+Backspace (Undelete) to restore the headings.

Golden rule of sorting! *Always* save whatever you are working on before you sort. Then, if you make an error, you can open the saved file and begin again.

Sorting a File by Line

1. Open the file you want to sort. To sort only a group of records, select (highlight) the group.

2. Select **Tools/Sort** or press Ctrl+Shift+F12 (Sort). The Sort dialog box appears.

3. Select the **Line** radio button.

4. Select the sort order (**A**scending or **D**escending).

5. Select the pop-up list button across from the desired key number. From the pop-up list, select **A**lpha (to sort alphanumerically) or **N**umeric (to sort numerically).

6. In the Field text box, type the number of the field containing the word you want to sort. For example, if you want to sort records by last name, and the last name is in Field 2, type **2**.

7. In the Word text box, type a number to specify which word in the specified field is the basis for the sort. For example, if you're sorting by year and the entry in the date field is in the form *month/ day/year*, you would type **3** to base the sort on the third "word" (remember that words can be separated by spaces, forward slashes, or dashes).

8. If you want to use another key, select **Insert Key** and repeat steps 5 through 7.

9. Select OK. WordPerfect for Windows sorts the files and displays the sorted list in the window.

Sorting by Paragraphs

You can sort paragraphs by highlighting the paragraphs you want to sort or by sorting an entire file. The procedure is nearly the same as the procedure for sorting by lines.

Sorting a File by Paragraph

1. Open the file you want to sort. To sort only a group of records, select (highlight) the group.

2. Select **T**ools/**So**rt or press Ctrl+Shift+F12 (Sort). The Sort dialog box appears.

3. Select the **P**aragraph radio button.

4. Select the sort order (**A**scending or **D**escending).

5. Select the pop-up list button across from the desired key number. From the pop-up list, select **A**lpha (to sort alphanumerically) or **N**umeric (to sort numerically).

6. In the Line text box, type the number of the line containing the word you want to sort. For example, if you want to sort records by last name, and the last name is on Line 2, type **2**.

7. If the line contains tab fields, go to the Field text box and type the number of the field containing the word you want to sort.

8. In the Word text box, type a number to specify which word in the specified field is the basis for the sort. For cxamplc, if you're sorting by year and the entry in the date field is in the form *month/ day/year*, you would type **3** to base the sort on the third "word" (remember that words can be separated by spaces, forward slashes, or dashes).

9. If you want to use another key, select **I**nsert Key and repeat steps **5** through **8**.

10. Select OK. WordPerfect for Windows sorts the files and displays the sorted list in the window.

Sorting Tables

Shortcut

A simple way to organize records is to use WordPerfect's Tables feature. You can create a table that includes a cell for each required entry. You can then sort the records according to the entries in any given cell. For more information about the Tables feature, refer to Chapter 6.

WordPerfect for Windows sorts tables by row. To specify in what order those rows are sorted, you indicate the cell containing the "word" that is the basis for the sort. If the cell has more than one line, you also specify the line number. Other than that, the sorting procedure is similar to that for line records and paragraph records. Note that the definition of *cell* is somewhat different from that normally used. Here, a cell is really a column and the cell number is the column number, numbered from left to right.

Sorting Records in a Table

1. Place the cursor anywhere in the table.

2. Select Tools/Sort or press Ctrl+Shift+F12 (Sort). The Sort dialog box appears. The Table Row radio button is automatically selected.

3. Select the sort order (Ascending or Descending).

4. Select the pop-up list button across from the desired key number. From the pop-up list, select Alpha (to sort alphanumerically) or Numeric (to sort numerically).

5. In the Cell text box, type the number of the cell (column) containing the word you want to sort. For example, if you want to sort records by last name, and the last name is in Cell 2 (the second column), type **2**.

6. If the cell contains lines, go to the Line text box and type the number of the line containing the word you want to sort.

7. In the Word text box, type a number to specify which word in the specified field is the basis for the sort.

8. If you want to use another key, select Insert Key and repeat Steps 4 through 7.

9. Select OK. WordPerfect for Windows sorts the table rows and displays the sorted rows in the window.

Extracting Records

If your customer file consists of hundreds of records, you probably want to work with only a select group of records at any one time. To do that, you can enter *record selection* criteria, telling WordPerfect for Windows which records you want to extract. For example, you can direct WordPerfect for Windows to extract records for only those clients who have ordered in 1989, or only those whose last name begins with the letter *S*. You can also specify more complex criteria; for example, you can select records of all those clients with an account number greater than 60000 in Region #2. And you can select and sort the records in a single operation.

You enter the selection criteria in the **R**ecord Selection text box, which is in the Sort dialog box (see Figure 7.4). To enter the selection criteria, you can use the operators described in Table 7.1. WordPerfect for Windows reads the criteria from left to right, step-by-step, unless you group steps within parentheses. The following entries, for example, specify different criteria:

```
key1=Florida * key4>1990 + key5=N
key1=Florida * (key4>1990 + key5=N)
```

Given the first statement, two types of records are extracted: those in which Key 1 is "Florida" *and* Key 4 is greater than 1990; and those in which Key 5 is "N." Given the second statement, only one type of record is extracted: those in which Key 1 is "Florida" *and* in which either Key 4 is greater than 1990 or Key 5 is "N."

Table 7.1 *Operators used in selection criteria*

Operator	*Selects*	*Example*
+	Records meeting either condition.	key1=Sam+key2=2. Select all records with key 1 equal to Sam *or* key 2 equal to 2.
*	Records meeting both conditions.	key1=Sam*key2=2. Select all records with key 1 equal to Sam *and* key 2 equal to 2.
=	Records containing exactly the same information.	key1=Sam. Selects only records with key 1 equal to Sam.
<>	Records that don't match the criteria.	key1<>Sam. Select all records with key 1 not equal to Sam.
>	Records that have information greater than criteria.	key1>Sam. Select all records with key 1 past Sam in alphabetical order.

continues

Table 7.1   Continued.

Operator	Selects	Example
<	Records that have information less than criteria.	key2<6000. Select all records with key 2 less than 6000.
>=	Records that have information greater than or equal to criteria.	key1>=Sam. Select all records with key 1 equal to Sam or after Sam in alphabetical order.
<=	Records that have information less than or equal to criteria.	key2<=6000. Select all records with key 2 less than or equal to 6000.

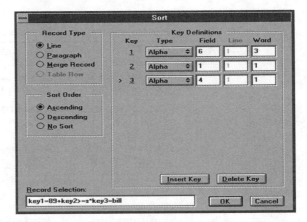

Figure 7.4   Enter a Record Selection statement to extract a group of records.

Beginner's Tip

If you forget to define the keys in your selection statement, WordPerfect for Windows displays a reminder when you select OK. Remember to define all the keys you name in the **R**ecord Selection text box.

WordPerfect for Windows also has a global key, *keyg*, which you can use to define any word in the file. To extract only those records containing the word *rabbit*, for example, you would enter the criterion **keyg=rabbit**. Records having *rabbit* in any field would be extracted.

You can extract files and sort them at the same time, or you can extract them without sorting them. To extract them without sorting, select **No** Sort for Sort Order in the Sort dialog box.

Entering a Selection Statement

1. Open the file from which you want to extract records.

2. Select **Tools**/Sort or press Ctrl+Shift+F12 (Sort). The Sort dialog box appears.

3. Enter your key definitions as described earlier in this chapter.

4. Go to the **Record** Selection text box and type your criteria. For example, if you're using Key 1 to sort the records by the Last Order date in Field 6, you can type **key1=89** to select the records for only those customers who placed an order in 1989. Remember, this is Key 1 using Field 6, not Key 6 (which is a very common mistake).

5. Enter any other sort criteria you want to use to sort the selected group of records. Or select **No** Sort to extract the records without sorting them.

6. Select OK.

Summary

Sorting and selecting records is one of WordPerfect for Windows' most useful features for organizing information. You can use it to manage everything from a simple list of names to a complex file of financial information. All it takes is an understanding of key definitions and the use of conditional statements to define records you want extracted.

Customer Records Entered by Lines

Last Name	First Name	Account #	Rep Name	Region #	Last Order
Fine	Marvin	65443	John	1	12/07/87
Jordan	Jack	33212	Bill	1	10/15/89
Simpson	Pam	88564	Bill	1	03/05/89
Altus	Deb	65438	Bill	2	08/07/88
Dranginis	Bill	55365	Susan	2	11/14/87
Glass	Doug	32311	Bill	2	08/13/89
Green	Sam	11232	Susan	2	04/27/88
Moore	William	32988	Bill	2	10/09/87
Springer	Doug	37465	John	2	07/09/88
Ott	Genna	38876	John	3	11/17/87

Customer Records Entered by Paragraphs

Last Name: Jordan
First Name: Jack
Account #: 33212
Rep Name: Bill
Region #: 1
Last Order: 10/15/89

Last Name: Green
First Name: Sam
Account #: 11232
Rep Name: Susan
Region #: 2
Last Order: 04/27/88

Last Name: Simpson
First Name: Pam
Account #: 88564
Rep Name: Bill
Region #: 1
Last Order: 03/05/89

Last Name: Altus
First Name: Deb
Account #: 65438
Rep Name: Bill
Region #: 2
Last Order: 08/07/88

Last Name: Glass
First Name: Doug
Account #: 32311
Rep Name: Bill
Region #: 2
Last Order: 08/13/89

Last Name: Moore
First Name: William
Account #: 32988
Rep Name: Bill
Region #: 2
Last Order: 10/9/87

Last Name: Springer
First Name: Doug
Account #:34765
Rep Name: John
Region #: 2
Last Order: 07/09/88

Last Name: Fine

First Name: Marvin
Account #: 65443
Rep Name: John
Region #: 1
Last Order: 12/07/87

Last Name: Ott
First Name: Genna
Account #: 38876
Rep Name: John
Region #: 3
Last Order: 11/17/87

Last Name: Dranginis
First Name: Bill
Account #: 55365
Rep Name: Susan
Region #: 2
Last Order: 11/14/87

Advance text

1. Select Layout/Advance.

2. Select an option in the Advance options group.

3. Type the distance you want to advance.

4. Select OK.

Edit line (using the menu bar)

1. Position the cursor after the Line code but before any later Line codes.

2. Select Graphics/Line.

3. Select Edit Horizontal or Edit Vertical.

4. Enter changes.

5. Select OK.

Edit line (using the mouse)

1. Double-click on the line to be edited.

2. Enter changes in the dialog box.

3. Select OK.

Create horizontal line

1. Select Graphics/Line/Horizontal or press Ctrl+F11.

2. Select line options.

3. Select OK.

Create vertical line

1. Select Graphics/Line/Vertical or press Ctrl+Shift+F11.

2. Select line options.

3. Select OK.

Turn kerning on/off

1. Select Layout/Typesetting.

2. Select the Automatic Kerning check box.

3. Select OK.

BUSINESS SHORTCUTS

Report Cover

The first thing that greets the reader of an important paper or report is the cover. An effective cover must tell the reader clearly and succinctly what's inside, while enticing the reader to continue reading. The cover must also present an air of professionalism without appearing overly stylized. The report cover described in this chapter provides you with a businesslike design that you can quickly customize for your own use. As you create your cover, you'll learn how to move text around the page and to create and edit horizontal and vertical lines.

About the Application

The report cover application, illustrated at the end of this chapter, consists of several horizontal lines at specific locations on the page. Text in various fonts appears between the horizontal lines. This text has been removed from the version you have on disk, so you can enter your own text. The Advance feature is used to adjust the position of the text in relation to the lines. In the example at the end of the chapter, WordPerfect's Kerning feature is used to tighten loose character pairs such as *Yo*, *We*, and *Ta*.

Open the Application

To customize the report cover application for your own use, you must first open the file called *RC.APP*. The file consists of several horizontal lines that form a design at the top and bottom of the page.

Hidden codes define the horizontal lines. To see the codes, select **Edit/ Reveal Codes** or press **Alt+F3** (Reveal Codes). To see the horizontal lines as they will appear in print, select **File/Print Preview** or press **Shift+F5** (Print Preview) and then select the Full Page button. Throughout this chapter, you can use the Print Preview window to view your page layout.

Customizing the Application

In this application, the horizontal lines have already been fixed in place. You customize the application by entering the text you want to appear on the cover and then adjusting the position of that text.

Entering a Title

The horizontal lines are placed in absolute locations on the page. As you can see in Figure 8.1, the locations are set relative to the top edge of the page. Were you to type the title of your report at the top of the page, whatever you typed would be printed over the horizontal lines already there. To prevent this, the application contains an [AdvToLn:4.5"] code that advances the text to a line that's 4.5" from the top of the page. Just for reference, the bottom of the fifth graphic line is 3.3" from the top of the page.

If you are creating complex sets of lines that have to be placed precisely, draw a rough sketch of the design on .125-inch graph paper, using the upper left corner of the page as your zero point. This will give you the precise measurements that you need to position lines and advance text.

Typing a Title

1. If the Reveal Codes area is not displayed, display it by selecting Edit/Reveal Codes or pressing Alt+F3.

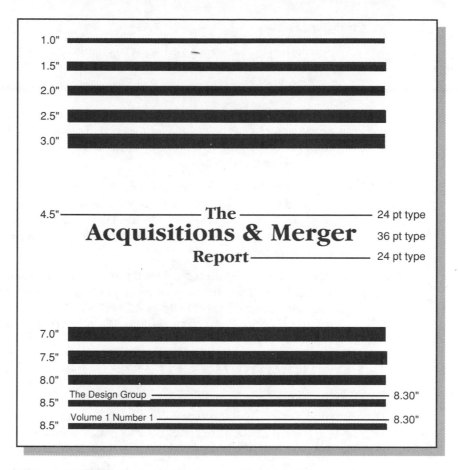

1.0"
1.5"
2.0"
2.5"
3.0"

4.5" — The — 24 pt type
Acquisitions & Merger 36 pt type
Report — 24 pt type

7.0"
7.5"
8.0"
The Design Group — 8.30"
8.5"
Volume 1 Number 1 — 8.30"
8.5"

Figure 8.1 The horizontal lines are placed in absolute locations on the page.

2. Move the cursor just to the right of the [AdvToLn:4.5"] code.

3. To center the title as in the example, press Ctrl+J or select **Layout/ Justification/Center**. A [Just:Center] code appears at the beginning of the paragraph (before the [AdvToLn:4.5"] code).

4. Type the text for your title, pressing Enter whenever you want to start a new line. The text is automatically centered on the page.

You now have the text for your title, but it is set in the default font you selected for your printer or document. To change the font for some or all of the title text, perform the following steps. For more about fonts, refer to Chapter 17.

Changing Fonts

1. Select the text for which you want to change the font. (See Chapter 1 for information about selecting text.)

2. Select Font/Font or press F9 (Font). The Font dialog box appears.

3. Select the font you want to use. If your printer supports several type sizes, check the Point Size text box. To enter a point size other than the one in the text box, select from the list below the text box or type it in the text box.

4. Select OK. WordPerfect inserts [Font] codes before and after the selected text. The [Font] code preceding the selected text changes the font to the one you chose in the Font dialog box. The [Font] code following the selected text returns the font to the default document font.

5. Repeat steps 1 through 4 for each block of text you want to appear in a different font. In the printed example at the end of the chapter, The and Report are set in 24-point ITC Bookman Demi, and Acquisitions & Mergers is set in 36-point ITC Bookman Demi.

Positioning the Title

In the template, the position of the title is 4.5" from the top of the page. If you typed a title of a different length, or if you used different fonts, the 4.5" position may not be appropriate. Your title may even run into the bottom lines. Use the Print Preview window to check the appearance of the title.

You can reset the title position by using WordPerfect's Advance feature. This feature lets you offset printed text up, down, left, or right from the cursor position, or to a specific position on the page. Because all the horizontal lines are set to absolute positions from the top of the page, it's best in this case to advance the title to a specific line on the page rather than disturb the horizontal lines.

Advancing Text to a Line

1. Delete the [AdvToLn] code just before the title you typed.

2. Select Layout/Advance. The Advance dialog box appears.

3. Select the To Line radio button.

4. In the **A**dvance text box, type a number specifying the line position to which you want the text advanced. For example, to place the bottom of the first line of text 4.0" from the top of the page, type **4**. Unless you changed the unit of measure in the document (see Appendix C), the line position is displayed in inches.

5. Select OK. WordPerfect inserts an [AdvToLn] code that specifies the new line position.

You can use the other Advance options to shift the text to an absolute position measured from the left edge of the page, or to shift the text in increments left, right, up, or down from the current position. If you shift the text in increments, WordPerfect inserts at the cursor location an [Adv] code, which affects all subsequent text. To cancel the Advance setting for subsequent text, you must enter another [Adv] code where you want to cancel the Advance. This second code must advance the text the same distance in the *opposite* direction, to put things back to normal. If you advance text 1" to the right of the left margin, for example, you return subsequent text to the left margin by advancing that text 1" to the left.

Typing Additional Text

In the example shown in Figure 8.1, you can see other text, including the report authors (the Design Group) and the volume number (Volume 1 Number 1). You can enter any text and position it anywhere on the page using the Justification and Advance features. In the example, The Design Group is left-justified, set in 14-point Helvetica, and advanced to line 8.3" so it sits just above the top of the ninth graphic line. Since the top of the ninth line is 8.50" from the top of the page, the bottom of The Design Group is .2" (8.5"-8.3") from the top of the line. Volume 1 Number 1 is also left-justified and set in 14-point Helvetica. Since the top of the tenth line is 9" from the top of the page, the volume number is advanced to 8.8".

The [AdvToLn] codes for these two entries are in the application on disk. You can type text after either code to set text above lines 9 and 10 as in the example, or you can delete the codes and enter your own codes to position text anywhere on the page. You can also center text between the lines or right-justify a date or any other information you want to include on your cover.

Be sure to view the layout in the Print Preview window after you make a change. The document window is only an approximate representation of the layout.

Deleting Lines

If you typed a long title, or if you selected a large font for your title, it may not fit in the space between the two sets of lines. In that case, you can delete either or both of the thickest lines to open up the center. To delete a line, highlight the code for the line in the Reveal Codes area and press Delete.

Editing Lines

You can edit any horizontal line in the template to change its thickness, length, position, or shading. To edit a line, you can use the menu bar or a mouse (both methods are described later in this section). In both cases, WordPerfect displays the Edit Horizontal Line dialog box for that line, as shown in Figure 8.2. This dialog box offers the following options:

Vertical Position: For a horizontal line, this option lets you set the line on the current baseline or at a specific position measured from the top edge of the page. For a vertical line, this option lets you position the line against the top or bottom margin, extend the line from the top to the bottom margin, center the line between the top and bottom margins, or set the position of the line to an absolute location measured from the top edge of the page. If you extend the line from the top to the bottom margin, you cannot set the line length (see "Length" in this section).

Horizontal Position: For a horizontal line, this option lets you left-justify, right-justify, center, or fully justify the line. You can also set the position of the line to an absolute location. If you use full justification, the line is extended to both margins; you cannot set its length. For a vertical line, this option lets you set the line at the left or right margin, between columns, or at a specific position measured from the left edge of the page.

Length: Lets you set the length of the line. If you chose to extend a line from margin to margin, this option is not available.

Thickness: Lets you specify the line thickness. Figure 8.3 shows how various line thicknesses appear in print. In the figure, the thinnest line is .1", and the lines increase in thickness by .05", up to the thickest line, which is .30". You can create line as thick as 27".

Gray Shading: Lets you control the shading of a line. Shading of 100% is black (the default), 50% is medium gray, and 10% is light gray. Figure 8.4 shows a variety of shadings.

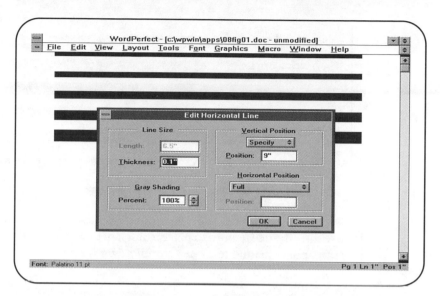

Figure 8.2   The Edit Horizontal Line dialog box. The Edit Vertical Line dialog box is similar.

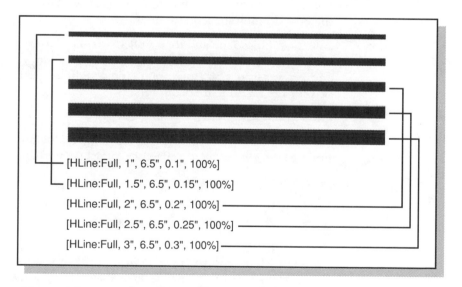

Figure 8.3   Horizontal lines in a variety of thicknesses.

Figure 8.4   Horizontal lines illustrating gray shading percentages.

For an interesting effect, create a thick line with 10% gray shading, and use the Advance feature to place a block of text in the line. The line will appear as a shaded text box, complete with text.

Using the Menu Bar to Edit a Line

1. In the Reveal Codes area, place the cursor so that it follows the [HLine] or [VLine] code for the line you want to edit, but precedes the code for any subsequent lines.

2. Select Graphics/Line and then Edit Horizontal or Edit Vertical. WordPerfect searches backward for the type of line you specified, and presents the Edit Horizontal Line or Edit Vertical Line dialog box for the first one it encounters.

3. Enter your changes in the dialog box.

4. Select OK to save the change and close the dialog box. WordPerfect updates the Line code to reflect the new line settings.

Using the Mouse to Edit a Line

1. Place the tip of the mouse pointer on the line you want to edit. The mouse pointer should look like an arrow when it's on the graphic line.

2. Double-click the mouse button. WordPerfect presents the Edit Horizontal Line or Edit Vertical Line dialog box for the selected line.

3. Enter your changes in the dialog box.

4. Select OK to save the change and close the dialog box. WordPerfect updates the Line code to reflect the new line settings.

You can also use the mouse to move and resize graphic lines. Place the mouse pointer on the line and click the mouse button once. Markers appear at the corners and sides of the line. The mouse pointer is a four-directional arrow when it is on the line, and a two-directional arrow when it is on a marker. To move the line, place the mouse pointer on the line (make sure the pointer appears as a four-directional arrow) and drag the line to a new location. To resize the line, place the mouse pointer on the marker at the side or corner you want to *pull* (make sure the mouse pointer appears as a two-directional arrow), and drag the marker to resize the line.

Creating Lines

You can customize the report cover even further by adding your own horizontal or vertical lines (or both). If you edited the horizontal lines earlier, the process will seem familiar. Don't worry about getting the line just right; at any time you can change the dimensions, shading, or position of the line, as explained earlier in this chapter.

Creating a Line

1. If you're creating a horizontal line positioned along the baseline, place the cursor in the line where you want the horizontal graphic line to appear. For any other type of graphic line, place the cursor anywhere on the page on which you want the line to appear. The cursor can be anywhere, because you set the line position as an absolute location.

2. To create a horizontal line, select Graphics/Line/Horizontal or press Ctrl+F11 (Horizontal Line). To create a vertical line, select Graphics/Line/Vertical or press Ctrl+Shift+F11 (Vertical Line).

   WordPerfect displays a dialog box that has the same options as the Edit Horizontal Line dialog box, shown in Figure 8.2. In completing the remaining steps, refer to the descriptions of those options in the previous section titled "Editing Lines."

3. Select an option from the **V**ertical Position pop-up list. To specify a position, select **S**pecify from the pop-up list and then type the position in the **P**osition text box.

4. Select an option from the **H**orizontal Position pop-up list. To specify a position, select **S**pecify from the pop-up list, and then type the position in the **P**osition text box.

5. If you did not choose full justification (that is, you did not choose to extend the line from margin to margin), enter a measurement for the line length in the **L**ength text box.
6. Enter a line thickness in the **T**hickness text box.
7. To make the line gray instead of black, enter a percentage less than 100 in the **G**ray Shading text box. You can use the increment buttons to enter a percentage, or you can type the percentage. The lower the percentage, the lighter the shade of gray.
8. Select OK. This inserts the line code into your document at the cursor position.

To repeat the same line in several positions, highlight the code for that line, and select **E**dit/**C**opy or press Ctrl+Insert. Select **E**dit/**P**aste or press Shift+Insert to insert as many copies of the line as you need. Note that this works best if the original line is placed on the baseline rather than at a set position. If you copy a line whose position is set, you must then go back and edit the copied lines to set their positions.

Kerning

Some letter pairs, because of the shape of the individual letters, give an illusion of greater-than-normal letter spacing. Examples are *WA*, *Vo*, and *To*. The effect, which is more pronounced in larger type sizes, is illustrated in Figure 8.5.

Closing up the space between the letter pairs is called *kerning* the letters. WordPerfect offers a feature that automatically kerns certain letter pairs; you simply turn the feature on to use it.

Yo We To Tr Ta Wo Tu Tw Ya Te — Unkerned

Yo We To Tr Ta Wo Tu Tw Ya Te —— Kerned

Figure 8.5 The effects of kerning.

Turning Kerning On or Off

1. Move the cursor where you want to turn kerning on or off.

2. Select Layout/Typesetting. The Typesetting dialog box appears.

3. Select the Automatic Kerning check box.

4. Select OK. WordPerfect inserts a [Kern:On] or [Kern:Off] code at the cursor location.

 If WordPerfect does not kern a character pair to your liking, you can manually kern the pair by inserting an [Adv] code between the two characters to shift the second character. You also can use the Manual Kerning feature: Place the cursor between the characters you want to kern, select Layout/Typesetting, and then select Manual Kerning. Enter a negative number to decrease the space between the characters, or a positive number to increase the space. Use the Preview screen in the dialog box to guide you. WordPerfect enters an [Adv] code at the cursor location.

 The Kerning feature is printer and font dependent. That is, your printer or the font you use may not support the Kerning feature. The KERN.TST file included with WordPerfect includes the most frequently kerned pairs of letters. A printout of this file is shown in Figure 8.6. You can open this file and print it to see how character pairs will be kerned for your printer. By changing the document initial font for the file before printing, you can test kerning for different fonts.

KERN.TST
Format this document for the printer you are working with by choosing that printer as your current Printer Selection. Insert a font change to the appropriate ps font before printing the kern pairs. Adjust the values in the kern table until the kern pairs look right.

Common ASCII Kern Pairs:
"A 'A 'd 'o 'r 's 't 'v 'w 'y °A ,1 -A .1 01 1, 1. 10 11 12 13 14 15 16 17 18 19 21 31 41 51 61 71 74 77 81 91 A- A" A' A' A* AA Aa Ab AC Ac Ad Ae Ag AG AO Ao Aq AQ AT At Au Av AV AW Aw AY Ay BA BT BV BW BY CA CO CT CV CW CY DA DT DV DW DY F, F- F. FA Fa Fc Fd Fe Fi Fo Fr Fu fy GA GT GV GY K- Ka KC Ke KG Ko KO Ku Ky L- L" L' L' L* LA LC Le LG LO Lo LS LT Lu LV LW LY Ly NA Na NC Ne NG No NO Nu OA OT OV OW OX OY P- P, P. PA Pa Pe PJ Po Pu R- R" R' R' R* RA Ra RC Rc Re RG Ro RO RT Ru RV RW Ry RY T, -T T- T. T: T; TA Ta TC Tc Td Te Tg TG Ti To TO Tr Ts TS Tu TV Tw Ty TY U, U. Um Un Up V, V- -V V. V: V; Va VA Vc VC Ve VG Vg Vi VO Vo Vr VS Vu Vy -W W, W- W. WA Wa WC Wc Wd We WG Wg Wi WO Wo Wr Ws WS Wu Wy X- Xa Xe Xo XO Xu Xy Y, -Y Y- Y. Y: Y; YA Ya YC Yc Ye YG Yi YO Yo YS Yu Zy aj av aw ay a' by ch ck ev ew ey e' fa fe ff fi fl fo fs ft f' hy ij k- ka ke kg ko ks my ny n' ov ow ox oy py qy r- r. r, ra rc rd re rf rg rm rn ro rr rs rt ru rv rw rx ry rz r' st s' t' u' v- v. v, va vc ve vg vo w- w. w, wa wc we wg wo ws x- xa xc xe xo y- y. y, ya yc ye yo

Sample kerning in 300ths:
-00: MN MN MN MN MN
-05: MN MN MN MN MN
-10: MN MN MN MN MN
-15: MN MN MN MN MN
-20: MN MN MN MN MN
-30: MN

Unkerned:
WordPerfect AVAILABLE Available Kerning available wonderful you Wonderful You

Kerned:
WordPerfect AVAILABLE Available Kerning available wonderful you Wonderful You

Figure 8.6   The KERN.TST file shows some common pairs that need to be kerned when printed in larger sizes.

Summary

WordPerfect's Line feature is a versatile tool that lets you place vertical and graphic horizontal lines at an absolute location on the page or on a baseline. The Advance feature lets you position text at absolute locations on the page or advance the text in specified increments from the current position. Used together, these two features let you electronically paste lines and text on a page to create a simple, businesslike cover design.

The Report Cover
Application

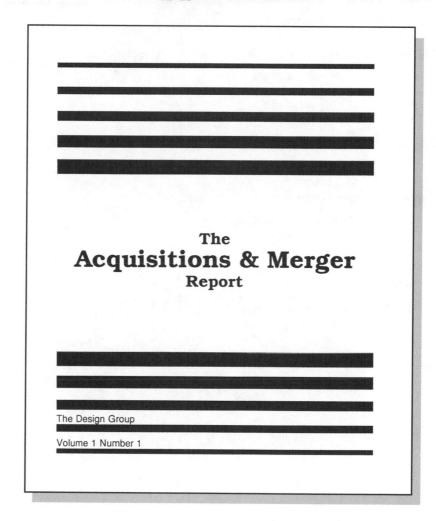

End Field

1. Press Alt+Enter.

End Record

1. Press Alt+Shift+Enter.

Enter {FIELD} code

1. Select Tools/Merge or press Ctrl+F12.
2. Select Field.
3. Type the field number or name.
4. Select OK.

Enter merge code

1. Select Tools/Merge/Merge Codes, or press Ctrl+F12 and type c.
2. Select the code.
3. Select Insert.
4. If a dialog box appears, enter the requested information and select OK.
5. Select Close.

Merge files

1. Select Tools/Merge/Merge, or press Ctrl+F12 and type m.
2. Type the name of the primary file.
3. Type the name of the secondary file.
4. Select OK.

**BUSINESS
SHORTCUTS**

Personalized Letters
& Merge

*Everyday business activities often require you to create several copies
of the same letter to send to different people. While you could write
an individual letter and edit the letter to change the inside address,
greeting, and content, the WordPerfect for Windows Merge feature offers
an easier way. With the Merge feature, you can create a single form
letter, leaving codes where you want letter-specific information inserted. You can then merge the letter with a file containing the specific
information, and print an entire stack of personalized letters.*

About the Application

Before you can use the Merge feature to generate a series of letters, you must
have two files: a *primary file* and a *secondary file*. The secondary file
contains a list of all names, addresses, phone numbers, and other information that commonly changes from letter to letter. If you created a client
record file in Chapter 7, you can adapt that file for use as your secondary file.
The primary file contains a template for the document you are creating, such
as a form letter, memo, mailing label, or phone list. This template can
include text and must include codes that tell WordPerfect for Windows
where to insert information from the secondary file.

Two applications are used in this chapter: PRI.APP (for the primary file) and SEC.APP (for the secondary file). Printouts of both files appear at the end of the chapter. SEC.APP contains a list of customers and information about each customer, including the customer's name, address, and telephone number, and the name and phone number of his or her sales representative. PRI.APP contains a form letter announcing a new product line. Figure 9.1 shows the personalized letters you can create by merging the two files.

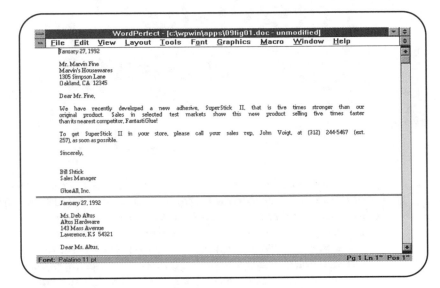

Figure 9.1 *The results of merging the primary and secondary files.*

Opening the Application

Since you are working with two applications, open each file in a separate document window. First, open the file called PRI.APP (by selecting **File/Open** or pressing F4). Then open SEC.APP the same way without closing PRI.APP. It appears in a second document window. Select **Window/Tile** to display both document windows in the WordPerfect for Windows window.

Beginner's Tip

You can move between the document windows by clicking anywhere inside the window that you want to be active. You can also switch to the other window by selecting **Window** to display the **Window** menu, and then selecting the document name from the **Window** menu.

You can use the example files provided to experiment with the Merge feature, as explained later in this chapter. Or, you can customize the application right away by entering your own records and editing the letter, as explained next.

Customizing the Application

In this chapter, you must customize two applications: the list of records and the form letter. It doesn't matter which file you customize first.

Customizing the Secondary File

A secondary file consists of a list of *records*. Each record consists of one or more *fields* containing text, with an {*END FIELD*} code at the end of each field. A field can be more than one line or paragraph long. The first field is Field 1, the second is Field 2, and so on. At the end of each record, there is an {*END RECORD*} code and a hard page break. Note that some merge terms, such as record and field, are similar to terms used in describing the Sort feature (see Chapter 7). Although the terms have similar meanings in merge and sort, merging and sorting are very different processes. Also, the method of entering fields and records differs between merge and sort.

Shortcut

You can adapt Sort paragraph records to be secondary Merge records. In adapting the paragraph records, remember to make the following changes:

- Delete any column definition codes and any unwanted formatting codes.

- Add field names, if desired (see "Naming Fields" later in this section).

- Delete the current hard return code ([HRT]) at the end of each paragraph line, replacing each [HRT] code with an {END FIELD} code. Inserting an {END FIELD} code automatically inserts a [HRT] code also, which you should leave in.

  Note that paragraph records are separated by two hard returns. Replace only the first of these hard returns with an {END FIELD} code.

- Replace the second hard return code [HRT] following each paragraph record with an {END RECORD} code. Inserting an {END RECORD} code automatically inserts a hard page break also, signalling the end of that merge record.

Beginner's Tip

At the top of the SEC.APP window is a {*FIELD NAMES*} code and a list of names assigned to the fields; the names are separated by tildes (~). Move the cursor to the first field entry, Mr. In the lower left corner of the status bar, you'll see the name assigned to this field, title. Move the cursor down another line to see the name of the next field, first name. Field names let you work more intuitively with fields; instead of referring to fields by number, you can refer to them by name. If you're going to use this template as is, without adding or deleting fields, you can keep these names. If you add or delete fields, however, the names will no longer correspond to the right fields. You'll learn how to enter your own field names later.

A primary file contains the text and graphics that will be common to all the final documents. It also contains {*FIELD*} codes, which tell WordPerfect for Windows where to insert the information from the secondary file. Where you want to insert the text from Field 2, for example, you enter **{FIELD}2~**. If you name the fields, you can specify the field by name (for example, **{FIELD}first name~**) rather than by number.

Before you begin, make a list of the fields you want to use for each record. For example, the list might include last name, first name, address, phone number, the person's title, and spouse's name. The list should be thorough, because you may want to use the information contained in this file to generate other customized files, including phone lists, mailing lists, lists of overdue payments, and so on.

Once you've completed the list, count the number of fields you need for each record. You can now create a template that you can use to enter information for each record. Select the contents of SEC.APP and delete them, so you can start from scratch.

Creating Merge Fields

1. Move the cursor to the top of the document.

2. Press Alt+Enter once for each field you want to create. Each time you press Alt+Enter, an {END FIELD} code and a [HRt] code are inserted at the cursor location, and the cursor moves to the next line.

3. Press Alt+Shift+Enter. WordPerfect for Windows inserts an {END RECORD} code and a hard page break at the end of the record.

A secondary file can contain more than text. For example, you can include a figure as a field entry. Just insert the entry as you would an entry in any other document, and end it with the {END FIELD} code. If you save the figure as a graphic on disk (see Chapter 3), your secondary file will be smaller and the merge will run faster.

Your file should look similar to the one in Figure 9.2. This gives you a template that you can use to enter information for each record. Type only one of these templates, and then copy it for as many records as you need to enter.

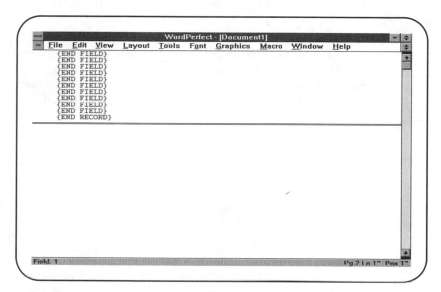

Figure 9.2   A template for creating records.

Copying a Block

1. If the Reveal Codes screen isn't displayed, press Alt+F3 (Reveal Codes) or select **View/Reveal Codes** to display it.

2. Select the template you just created, including the [HPg] code following the {END RECORD} code. (Use the Reveal Codes screen for guidance in selecting the codes.)

3. Select **Edit/Copy** or press Ctrl+Insert.

4. Leave the cursor in its current position (at the end of the selected text).

5. Press F8 to deselect the highlighted text.

6. Select **Edit/Paste** or press Shift+Insert. A copy of the block is inserted at the cursor location.

7. Repeat step 6 for as many records as you need to enter. Another copy of the block is inserted at the cursor location each time you repeat the step.

When copying the template, make one more copy than you will need, and leave the blank one at the end of the file. That way, the next time you need to add records, you will still have the blank template to copy.

When you're done, you can type the information required for each record, entering the information to the left of the {END FIELD} codes. But first, you may want to name the fields to help you remember the type of information that belongs in each field. This is optional.

Naming Fields

1. Move the cursor to the top of the document.

2. Select **Tools/Merge/Merge Codes**, or press Ctrl+F12 and type **c**. The Insert Merge Codes dialog box appears. It displays a list of merge codes, as shown in Figure 9.3. You can use the scroll bar or press Page Up, Page Down, and the arrow keys to scroll through the list. If you know the name of a merge code, you can highlight it quickly by typing the first few letters of the code name.

3. Type **f** to move the cursor to the first code name starting with *F,* and then press the down arrow key to highlight the following merge code:

   ```
   {FIELD NAMES}name1~...nameN~~
   ```

4. Select **Insert**. The Merge Field Name(s) dialog box appears, as shown in Figure 9.4. The dialog box shows the syntax for the merge code and indicates the number of the field you are naming: 1. The cursor is in the Field Name text box.

5. Type a name for Field 1 and select **Add**. The name appears in the list below the Field Name text box.

6. Move the cursor back to the Field Name text box and type the name for the next field. As soon as you begin typing, the Field Number indicator increases by 1. Select **Add** to add the name to the list of field names.

7. Repeat step 6 until you've named all the fields.

8. Select OK. WordPerfect for Windows returns to the Insert Merge Codes dialog box.

9. Select Close. WordPerfect for Windows places a {FIELD NAMES} code at the top of the document, followed by the names you entered, listed in sequence and separated by a tilde. Whenever you move the cursor into a field in this file, a prompt will appear in the lower left corner of the status bar, displaying the name of the field.

If you have more fields than field names, the additional fields are numbered.

Figure 9.3   The Insert Merge Codes dialog box.

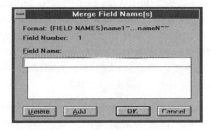

Figure 9.4   The Merge Field Name(s) dialog box.

Beginner's Tip

To make the field names easier to read, you can place them on separate lines. For example, you can format the names in this way:

```
{FIELD NAMES}
title~
first name~
last name~
company name~
~{END RECORD}
```

The hard returns won't affect the merge.

Now that you have your fields set up, type the information for each field in each record, entering the information to the left of the {END FIELD} codes. Make sure you enter the correct information in each field. WordPerfect for Windows uses field numbers or names to identify the location of the information, and expects the field entries to be listed in the same order for each record. For example, if the primary file is a letter containing a code to insert addresses from Field 3, the merged file will include the information from Field 3 (regardless of what information is in that field). If Field 3 for one of your records contains a phone number instead of an address, the phone number is inserted into the letter.

If you don't have the necessary information for a particular field, leave the field blank. But, leave the {END FIELD} code in the record so you don't throw off the field numbering for subsequent entries. When you have typed the records, check them and enter any necessary corrections. Save a copy of the SEC.APP file to your hard disk under another name, and also save a copy of the file to a floppy disk. This protects the file in case anything happens to it during the course of this chapter.

Customizing the Primary File

Select the document window for the PRI.APP file. The file contains a {*DATE*} code and several {FIELD} codes that tell the Merge feature where to insert information from the secondary file. To customize this file, change the {FIELD} codes, if necessary, so they correspond to the field numbers or names in your secondary file. To delete any of the existing {FIELD} codes, select the code, the field number, and the tilde (~), and press Delete. (The tilde signals the end of a field.)

If you're not sure which field has the information you want to reference, go back to your secondary file. Move the cursor to the information in question. The field name or number appears in the lower left corner of the status bar.

Inserting {FIELD} Codes

1. Move the cursor where you want to insert a {FIELD} code.

2. Enter any formatting code you want to affect this field entry. For example, if you want to center the entry, press Shift+F7.

3. Select **Tools/Merge/Merge Codes**, or press Ctrl+F12 and type **c**. The Insert Merge Codes dialog box appears. It displays a list of merge codes (see Figure 9.3). You can use the scroll bar or press

Page Up, Page Down, and the arrow keys to scroll through the list. To move quickly to a code, type the first few letters of its name.

4. Type **f** to move the cursor to the first code name starting with *F*:

   `{FIELD}field~`

5. Select **Insert**. The Insert Merge Code dialog box appears.

6. Type the name or number of the field you want to use, and select OK.

7. Select **Close**. WordPerfect for Windows inserts a {FIELD} code in the form {FIELD}*field~* (where *field* is the name or the number of the field).

You can also insert a {FIELD} code by selecting **T**ools/**M**erge/**F**ield, or by pressing Ctrl+F12 and typing **f**. When the Insert Merge Code dialog box appears, type the field name or number and select OK.

You can insert additional merge codes, such as the {DATE} code at the top of the PRI.APP file. Some of these codes are explained later in the chapter. To insert a code from the list, highlight the code name and select **Insert**, or double-click on the code name. If a dialog box appears, provide the requested information and select OK. When you're finished entering merge codes, select Close.

To finish customizing the primary file, delete the text in the letter and enter your own text. You can also change formatting options, such as margins and fonts, to affect the letters created by the merge. For example, the primary file we created contains a [Center Pg] code at the top of the document that centers the letter on the page; this is especially useful for short letters. If your letter is long, however, you may want to delete the code. You can also use text boxes and figure boxes at the top of your letter to create custom letterhead. For more information about creating custom letterhead, refer to Chapter 14.

Enter most of your formatting codes as initial document settings for the primary file. That way, when you merge the primary and secondary files, each letter you create will have the correct format, but the codes won't be inserted in each document. To enter initial document settings, place the cursor anywhere in the primary file, and select **L**ayout/**D**ocument/**I**nitial Codes, or press /Ctrl+Shift+F9 (Document) and type **c**. The Document Initial Codes window appears. Enter the format codes you want to apply to the document, and then select **F**ile/**C**lose or the Close button to return to the main document.

If you are using graphics, enter the graphics as graphics on disk; it makes the merge much faster. See Chapter 3 for information about saving graphics on disk.

Merging the Primary and Secondary Files

Once you've customized the primary and secondary files and saved the files to disk, you can merge the two files to create several individualized letters.

Merging Files

1. Close both document windows. Make sure you start with a blank window.

2. Select **Tools/Merge/Merge**, or press Ctrl+F12 and type **m**. The Merge dialog box appears.

3. Type the name of the primary file in the **P**rimary File text box. Include a path name if needed. You can select the list button to the right of the text box to display the Select File dialog box, which allows you to select a file from a directory.

4. Type the name of the secondary file in the **S**econdary File text box. Include a path name if needed. You can select the list button to the right of the text box to display the Select File dialog box, which allows you to select a file from a directory.

5. Select OK. A status bar prompt indicates that the merge is in progress.

When the merge is complete, the letters created by the merge appear. Each letter is separated by a page break, so that if you print the document, each letter is printed on a separate page. You can now save the file to disk or print the document.

Sorting and Selecting Records

You can use the WordPerfect for Windows Sort feature to create letters for selected records in your list, or to create letters that are sorted by region, city, ZIP code, or another criterion. To do this, you must first sort and, if desired, select the records in your secondary file. For basic information concerning sorting and selecting records, refer to Chapter 7.

Sorting a Secondary File

1. Open the file you want to sort. To sort only a group of records, highlight the group.

2. Select **Tools/Sort** or press Ctrl+Shift+F12. The Sort dialog box appears, as shown in Figure 9.5.

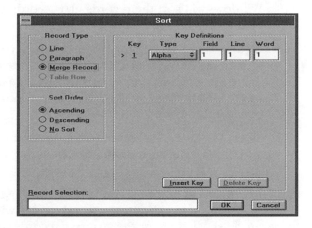

Figure 9.5   The Sort dialog box.

3. Select the **Merge Record** radio button.

4. Select the sort order (Ascending or Descending). Or, select **No Sort** to extract records without sorting them.

5. Select the pop-up list button, across from the key number. From the pop-up list, select **Alpha** (to sort alphanumerically) or **Numeric** (to sort numerically).

6. In the Field text box, type the number of the merge field containing the word on which the sort or selection is based. For example, if you want to sort records by ZIP code and the ZIP code is in Field 8, type **8**.

7. If the field is more than one line, go to the Line text box and type the number of the line containing the word you want to sort. For example, you may have an address field that contains a street address on the first line, the city and state on the second line, and the ZIP code on the third line. To sort by state, you would type **2** to specify the second line.

8. In the Word text box, type a number to specify which word in the specified field is the basis for the sort. For example, if you're sorting by year and the entry in the date field is in the form *month/day/year,* you would type **3** to base the sort on the third "word" (remember that words can be separated by spaces, forward slashes, or dashes).

9. If you want to use another key, select **I**nsert Key and repeat steps 5 through 8.

10. Repeat step 9 for each key you want to add. WordPerfect for Windows will sort the records first according to the sort criteria next to Key 1, then by the sort criteria next to Key 2, and so on.

11. If you want to select only certain records, type the selection criteria in the **R**ecord Selection text box. For example, if you're using Key 1 to sort the records by ZIP code in Field 8, you can type **key1>=12345*key1<=54321** to select records for all ZIP codes between 12345 and 54321.

12. Select OK. WordPerfect for Windows sorts and/or selects the files and displays the sorted/selected list in the window.

The sorted/selected list of records appears in the document window. Save this document as your secondary file and close the document window. Then you can merge the new secondary file with your primary file to generate a list of letters for the group of records you selected, in the order in which you sorted the records.

Creating Mailing Labels

You can also use the information in your secondary file to generate various other documents, including mailing labels. If you sorted or selected records as previously explained, you can use the resulting list to create the mailing labels for that same group of records, in the same order in which the letters were generated.

Begin by creating a separate primary file that includes all the information you want printed on the mailing label. The easiest way to create this file is to highlight the {FIELD} codes that make up the inside address in PRI.APP, and use Ctrl+Ins to copy the highlighted block. Next, select **F**ile/**N**ew or press Shift+F4 to open a new file in a second document window. Press Shift+Ins to paste the copied codes into the new document. The resulting file should look similar to this:

```
{FIELD}1~ {FIELD}2~ {FIELD}3~
{FIELD}4~
{FIELD}5~
{FIELD}6~, {FIELD}7~  {FIELD}8~
```

Save the file under a name such as MAIL.PRI. Merge this primary document with your list of records to create a list of mailing labels. The primary file will use the information from the previously created secondary file to create labels such as:

```
Mr. Marvin Fine
Marvin's Housewares
1305 Simpson Lane
Oakland, CA   12345

Ms. Deb Altus
Altus Hardware
143 Mass Avenue
Lawrence, KS   54321
```

After you create a list of addresses, you must tell WordPerfect for Windows how to format the list for the sheet of labels you're using. WordPerfect for Windows needs the dimensions of both the page of labels (the *physical page*) and the label itself (the *logical page*). You can enter this information in either of two ways. The easiest way is to run the WordPerfect for Windows Labels macro. This macro presents a list of several common label formats from which you can select. If the dimensions of your labels do not appear on this list, however, you must enter the dimensions manually. The following steps lead you through both alternatives.

Formatting Labels Using the WordPerfect for Windows Labels Macro

1. Move the cursor to the beginning of your file.

2. Select **Macro/Play** or press Alt+F10. The Play Macro dialog box appears.

3. Type **labels** and select **Play**. WordPerfect for Windows runs the Labels macro. It displays a dialog box asking whether you want to check to see if a WordPerfect for Windows printer driver is selected (the macro won't run properly if you don't select a WordPerfect for Windows printer driver).

Beginner's Tip

The first time you play the macro, you will have to wait a few seconds while WordPerfect for Windows compiles it. Thereafter, the macro will run almost instantaneously.

4. Select **Yes** if you're not sure whether a WordPerfect for Windows printer driver is selected. Select **No** otherwise.

5. If you selected **Yes** in step 4, WordPerfect for Windows displays the Select Printer dialog box, and prompts you to select a WordPerfect for Windows printer. Make sure WordPerfect for Windows is selected under Printer Drivers. Then select a printer and choose **Select**.

6. The Main Options menu appears. Select the label type: **Page** (laser/inkjet) labels or **Tractor**-feed (dot matrix) labels. Then select OK.

   WordPerfect for Windows presents a list of label dimensions, as shown in Figure 9.6. You can press Page Down and the arrow keys to see the rest of the list.

   If the dimensions for your labels are not on the list, select Cancel to exit the macro and format the labels manually (as explained in the *"Formatting Labels Manually"* steps later in this chapter).

7. Highlight the dimensions that represent the labels you're using and press the space bar to select it. You can select more than one label definition. To deselect a definition, move the selection box to it and press the space bar again. When you've selected all the definitions you want, select Install. If you need to return to the Main Options menu and change the label type, select **Menu**.

8. In the dialog box that appears, select **Continuous**-feed labels, **Manual**-feed labels, or **Bin**-feed labels and then select OK.

   WordPerfect for Windows notifies you that the labels you specified are now installed for the currently selected printer, and asks whether you want the label definition inserted in the document.

9. Select **Yes** or **No**. If you select **Yes**, WordPerfect for Windows inserts the [Paper Sz/Typ] code for the label in the Document Initial Codes window. A dialog box notifies you that the macro is finished.

10. Select OK.

Beginner's Tip

WordPerfect for Windows saves the [Paper Sz/Typ] codes as a document initial code. Had it entered the code directly in the document, WordPerfect for Windows would have applied the [Paper Sz/Typ] code to each label. This doesn't hurt anything; it's just not very efficient. To see the [Paper Sz/Typ] code, select Layout/Document/Initial Codes, or press Ctrl+Shift+F9 (Document) and type **c**. The Document Initial Codes window appears, displaying the [Paper Sz/Typ] code. Select File/Close or the Close button to return to the main document.

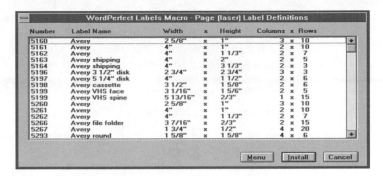

Figure 9.6   A list of preformatted label dimensions.

If the Labels macro does not list your label size, you must format the labels manually, defining a paper size and label characteristics. The information is inserted in a [Paper Sz/Typ] code in your document. We recommend that you insert the code as a document initial code, rather than insert the code directly in the document. Otherwise, the [Paper Sz/Typ] code is applied to each label, which, as noted earlier, is not very efficient.

Formatting Labels Manually

1. Move the cursor to the beginning of your document and delete any [Paper Sz/Typ] code that appears.

2. Select Layout/Document/Initial Codes, or press Ctrl+Shift+F9 (Document) and type **c**. The Document Initial Codes window appears. If this window contains a [Paper Sz/Typ] code, delete the code.

3. Select **L**ayout/**P**age/Paper **S**ize, or press Alt+F9 and type **s**. The Paper Size dialog box appears. A list of paper formats appears.

4. Select **A**dd. The Add Paper Size dialog box appears.

If the Edit Labels dialog box appears instead (after a message), then the current printer driver is a Windows printer driver. If you want to use the Windows printer driver, enter the label information in the Edit Labels dialog box and select OK; and then continue with step 12. Otherwise, choose Cancel and then Close to exit the dialog boxes, select a WordPerfect for Windows printer driver (**F**ile/Se**l**ect Printer), and begin with step 1 again.

5. Select the Paper **T**ype pop-up list button, and then select **L**abels from the pop-up list.

6. Select the Paper Size pop-up list button, and then select the paper size that represents the dimensions of the *physical* page (that is, the full sheet containing the labels). To enter your own dimensions, select **Other** and type the dimensions in the text boxes.

7. Select the paper orientation, paper location, and print options.

8. Select **Labels**. The Edit Labels dialog box appears.

9. Enter the required information for each option. You need to specify the width and height of the label, the number of columns and rows of labels, the distance of the first label from the upper left corner of the page, the distance between labels, and the label margins.

10. Select OK. You return to the Add Paper Size dialog box.

11. Select OK. You return to the Paper Size dialog box.

12. Highlight the paper size and type that represents the labels you're using and choose **Select**. WordPerfect for Windows returns to the Document Initial Codes window and inserts a [Paper Sz/Typ] code at the top of the page. (If you have turned off the Auto Code Placement feature, the code appears at the cursor location; see Chapter 1 for more information on Auto Code Placement).

13. Select **File/Close**, the **Close** button, or press Ctrl+F4 (Close), to save the change and return to the document window.

After formatting your list for the printer, print the list on regular paper to make sure the addresses will print correctly on the labels. If you don't like where the addresses are printing, you can make the necessary adjustments before printing on expensive labels.

Adjusting Your Labels

1. Select **Layout/Document/Initial Codes** or press Ctrl+Shift+F9 and type **c**. The Document Initial Codes window appears.

2. Delete the old [Paper Sz/Typ] code.

3. Select **Layout/Page/Paper Size**, or press Alt+F9 and type **s**. The Paper Size dialog box appears.

4. Highlight the Labels paper type and select **Edit**. The Edit Paper Size dialog box appears.

5. Under Text Adjustments, select the direction of the adjustment (**Up** or **Down**) for **Top**, and then enter the adjustment in the text box. For **Side**, select **Left** or **Right** and then enter the adjustment in the text box.

6. Select OK. WordPerfect for Windows inserts a new [Paper Sz/Typ] code.

7. Select **File/Close** or the Close button, or press Ctrl+F4. You return to the document window.

Advanced Merge Codes

Throughout this chapter, you worked with the three most common merge codes: {END FIELD}, {END RECORD}, and {FIELD}*n*~. In addition to these common codes, WordPerfect for Windows offers some advanced codes that you may find useful. To view a list of these codes, select **Tools/Merge/Merge Codes**, or press Ctrl+F12 and type **c**. The Insert Merge Codes dialog box appears, displaying a list of merge codes (see Figure 9.3). You can use the scroll bar or press Page Up, Page Down, and the arrow keys to scroll through the list. You can select a code from the menu in any of the following ways:

- Use the cursor keys to highlight the code name, and then select **Insert**.

- Double-click on the code name.

- Type the first few letters of the code name. As you type, the highlight moves to the first code name that begins with those letters. Continue typing letters until the highlight is on the name of the code you want to select, and then select **Insert**.

You can also select the more commonly used codes from the cascading menu that appears when you select **Tools/Merge** or press Ctrl+F12. The most commonly used merge codes, {END FIELD} and {END RECORD}, can be inserted even more easily—by pressing Alt+Enter and Alt+Shift+Enter, respectively.

The following sections describe some of the more commonly used merge codes and their functions.

{DATE}

The {DATE} code tells WordPerfect for Windows to insert the current system date at the location of the code. If you're inserting the date in a letter of correspondence, you may want to right justify the code by pressing Alt+F7 before entering the code. That way, the date will be inserted flush against the right margin.

{KEYBOARD}

When WordPerfect for Windows encounters the *{KEYBOARD}* code, it pauses and waits for you to type information. When you're done typing, press Alt+Enter to continue the merge operation. This code is useful if you're creating a series of letters, and in each letter you need to enter information that's not included in the secondary merge file. For example, in Figure 9.7, the {KEYBOARD} code was used to pause the merge operation so that the user could type an appointment date and time for each individual.

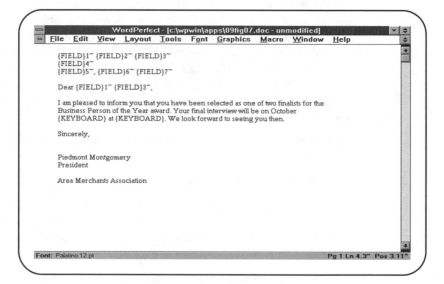

Figure 9.7   Using the {KEYBOARD} code.

{BELL}

If you have a very long document (such as a contract) and you have only two or three places where WordPerfect for Windows stops and needs your attention to type information, you can use the *{BELL}* code just before the {KEYBOARD} code. This tells WordPerfect for Windows to beep when you need to enter information.

{INPUT}message~

Imagine that you run an employment agency and you would like everyone who comes through the door to complete some type of form. Rather than have them write out information on paper, which you may then have to retype, you can have them enter it directly into a WordPerfect for Windows document using the *{INPUT}* code.

The {INPUT} code makes WordPerfect for Windows pause, as does the {KEYBOARD} code, but it also displays a message on the screen and waits for input from the keyboard. Pressing Alt+Enter continues the merge operation. Figure 9.8 shows an example of a file that uses the {INPUT} code to lead an applicant through filling out a form.

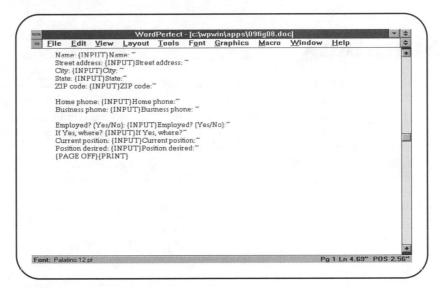

Figure 9.8   Using the {INPUT} code to request information.

{PRINT}

The file shown in Figure 9.8 includes a *{PRINT}* code on the last line. This code tells WordPerfect for Windows to print the file after the applicant types the last entry and presses Alt+Enter.

{PAGE OFF} and {PAGE ON}

You can use the *{PAGE OFF}* code to eliminate the hard page breaks between the merged records. This is particularly useful when you are merging to the printer. If no {PAGE OFF} code precedes the {PRINT} code, a blank page follows each printed record. The file shown in Figure 9.8 includes a {PAGE OFF} code before the {PRINT} code on the last line. You can also use {PAGE OFF} when you want a document to contain more than one merged record.

The {PAGE OFF} code can be inserted in either the primary or secondary merge files and remains in effect until the merge encounters a *{PAGE ON}* code. The {PAGE ON} code reinstates the hard page breaks.

Summary

The WordPerfect for Windows Merge feature is a powerful tool that lets you combine the standard information in one file with the specifics from another file, to mass-produce letters, mailing labels, phone lists, mailing lists, and other documents. Combined with the Sort feature, Merge lets you create sorted lists for selected groups of records.

The Secondary File

{FIELD NAMES}title~first name~last name~company name~street address~city~state~zip code~
phone number~sales rep~reps phone~~{END RECORD}

Mr.{END FIELD}
Marvin{END FIELD}
Fine{END FIELD}
Marvin's Housewares{END FIELD}
1305 Simpson Lane{END FIELD}
Oakland{END FIELD}
CA{END FIELD}
12345{END FIELD}
(000) 445-7689{END FIELD}
John Voigt{END FIELD}
(000) 244-5467 (ext. 257){END FIELD}
{END RECORD}

Ms.{END FIELD}
Deb{END FIELD}
Altus{END FIELD}
Altus Hardware{END FIELD}
143 Mass Avenue{END FIELD}
Lawrence{END FIELD}
KS{END FIELD}
54321{END FIELD}
(000) 324-3456{END FIELD}
Bill Shaver{END FIELD}
(000) 244-5467 (ext. 259){END FIELD}
{END RECORD}

The Primary File

{DATE}

{FIELD}1~ {FIELD}2~ {FIELD}3~
{FIELD}4~
{FIELD}5~
{FIELD}6~ , {FIELD}7~ {FIELD}8~

Dear {FIELD}1~ {FIELD}3~,

We have recently developed a new adhesive, SuperStick II, that is five times stronger than our original product. Sales in selected test markets show this new product selling five times faster than its nearest competitor, FantastiGlue!

To get SuperStick II in your store, please call your sales rep, {FIELD}10~, at {FIELD}11~, as soon as possible.

Sincerely,

Bill Shtick
Sales Manager

GlueAll, Inc.

Define outline style

1. Select **Tools/Outline/Define** or press Alt+Shift+F5.

2. Select the options you want to change.

3. Select OK.

Turn outline on

1. Place the cursor after the [Par Num Def] code.

2. Select **Tools/Outline/Outline On**.

Turn outline off

1. Place the cursor after the last Outline entry.

2. Select **Tools/Outline/Outline Off**.

Change to next lower level

1. Place the cursor immediately before or after the paragraph number.

2. Press Tab.

Change to next higher level

1. Place the cursor immediately before or after the paragraph number.

2. Press Shift+Tab.

Delete outline family

1. Move the cursor to the first line in the family.

2. Select **Tools/Outline/Delete Family**.

3. Select **Yes**.

Move outline family

1. Move the cursor to the first line in the family.

2. Select **Tools/Outline/Move Family**.

3. Press the Up or Down Arrow key.

4. Press Enter.

5. To cancel the operation at any time, press Esc.

Copy outline family

1. Move the cursor to the first line in the family.

2. Select **Tools/Outline/Copy Family**.

3. Press the Up or Down Arrow key.

4. Press Enter.

5. To cancel the operation at any time, press Esc.

BUSINESS SHORTCUTS

Capital Investment Analysis

If you plan on starting a new business, producing a new product, or acquiring a company, you need to examine your prospects and gather enough information to make a well-educated decision. To collect the right information, you must ask the right questions. This chapter and the application that accompanies it provide a capital investment analysis outline of questions designed to help you gather the necessary information. You'll learn to customize the application by adding your own questions to the outline, adding brief answers to the questions, and changing the outline structure. You'll also learn how to display the outline with another document window open so that you can refer to the outline when writing a capital investment report.

About the Application

The capital investment analysis application, which appears at the end of this chapter, is an outline consisting of nine main headings. Under each main heading are subheadings that let you expand upon the main heading. The outline is defined so that the first level is numbered with Arabic numerals (1, 2, 3); the second level uses lowercase letters (a, b, c); and the third level uses lowercase Roman numerals (i, ii, iii). The Outline function is turned on at the beginning of the outline. You'll learn more about defining outlines and turning the Outline function on and off later.

Retrieving the Application

To customize the capital investment analysis application for your own use, you must first open the file called *CAPITAL.APP* from disk to the WordPerfect window. Although the file is formatted for a QMS PS-810 PostScript printer, WordPerfect automatically reformats the file for your installed printer.

Customizing the Application

You can use this application as a general outline and type responses to the various questions following each entry. You can change questions by deleting the question to the right of the outline number or letter and typing a question that's more relevant to your investment activities.

To revise the outline further, you can add or delete headings, add or delete entire sections of the outline, change the numbering style for the outline, and rearrange sections to provide a more logical flow for your needs. The following sections explain in detail the various ways you can customize the outline.

Changing the Outline Numbering Style

Before you create an outline, you must define it. When you define the outline, WordPerfect inserts a [Par Num Def] code at the cursor location. The code tells WordPerfect how to number the various outline levels. To use a different numbering style for the capital investment analysis form, delete the existing [Par Num Def] code and insert a new one.

Beginner's Tip

To use WordPerfect's default style, Outline, you don't have to insert a [Par Num Def] code. The first level paragraphs are numbered with uppercase Roman numerals (I, II, III), the second level with uppercase letters (A, B, C), the third level with Arabic numerals (1, 2, 3), the fourth level with lowercase letters (a, b, c), and so on, as shown in Figure 10.1. To number outline headings in some other way, however, you must insert a [Par Num Def] code.

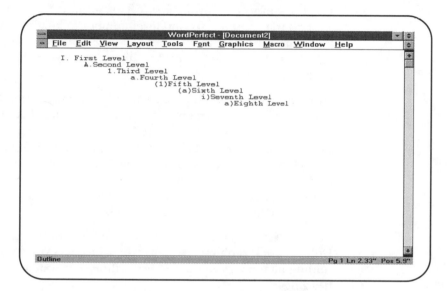

Figure 10.1   The default paragraph numbering style, Outline.

To insert a new [Par Num Def] code, you use the Define Paragraph Numbering dialog box, shown in Figure 10.2. It has the following options:

Predefined Formats: A pop-up list button that lets you display a pop-up list of standard numbering schemes and select a scheme from the list. The current numbering scheme is named on the pop-up list button and illustrated in the Level Style list box.

Style: Lets you create your own paragraph number style. Use this text box in conjunction with the Level Style list box. In the Level Style list box, select the level for which you want to enter a style. Then enter the style for that level in the Style text box. You can enter the number style by typing it or by selecting the Styles pop-up list button (denoted by the left-pointing arrowhead) and then selecting a style from the list. To display the new style in the **Level Style** list box, go to the list box and select the level again. If you enter your own format, WordPerfect automatically selects **User-Defined for Predefined Formats.**

Attach Previous Level: Lets you attach the paragraph number to the paragraph number used for the previous level. Select the lower level in the **Level Style** list box, and then select Attach **Previous** Level. For example, if your first level is A. and your second level is 1., and you want the second level number to attach to the first level number (A.1.), then select 1. in the **Level Style** list box and select Attach **Previous** Level. An asterisk appears in the **Level Style** list box next to the 1..

Starting Outline Number: Lets you select a starting number for your outline. You must enter Arabic numerals for this setting or leave it blank. Leaving it blank tells WordPerfect to continue with the previous numbers in use before Outline was turned off. Although you enter an Arabic numeral, WordPerfect resumes numbering with the original style you selected. This is useful if you want to interrupt an outline with a block of text, and you want the numbering to pick up where it left off.

Change: Lets you create and use a style for your outline headings. Unlike a paragraph numbering style, which lets you format only the outline numbers, you can use an outline style to format outline headings.

Enter Inserts Paragraph Number: When Outline is on and you press Enter, WordPerfect automatically enters a paragraph number, such as I or A. To discontinue this, deselect the **Enter Inserts Paragraph Number** check box. If you deselect this option, you must use the Paragraph Numbering function each time you want to insert a paragraph number (see Chapter 13).

Auto Adjust to Current Level: When Outline is on and you press Enter to insert an automatic paragraph number, WordPerfect assumes you want that number to be at the same level as the previous one. If the previous number is at level two, for example, the next number will also be at level two. To change it to the first level, press Shift+Tab. If you deselect this check box, WordPerfect treats each entry as though it's a first-level entry and you can change levels only by pressing Tab.

Outline On: Lets you turn Outline on and off. Select this check box to turn Outline on. Deselect it to turn it off.

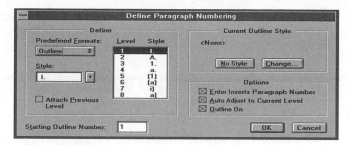

Figure 10.2   The Define Paragraph Numbering dialog box.

Redefining an Outline

1. Select View/Reveal Codes or press Alt+F3 (Reveal Codes) so you can see the [Par Num Def] code.

2. Delete the [Par Num Def] code. If you want to use WordPerfect's default numbering style, you can skip the rest of the steps.

3. Select Tools/Outline/Define or press Alt+Shift+F5 (Paragraph Def). The Define Paragraph Numbering dialog box appears.

4. Select the options you want to change.

5. Select OK. WordPerfect returns to the document window and inserts the [Par Num Def] code at the cursor position.

Turning Outline On and Off

In addition to the [Par Num Def] code, the Outline feature needs an [Outline On] code that turns the feature on. This code already exists in CAPITAL.APP, but if you delete the code by mistake, perform the following steps to insert the code that turns on Outline.

Turning Outline On

1. Place the cursor after the [Par Num Def] code.

2. Select Tools/Outline/Outline On. WordPerfect inserts the [Outline On] code at the cursor position and Outline appears on the status line. Pressing Enter now inserts a first-level paragraph number.

Turning Outline Off

1. Place the cursor after the last outline entry.

2. Select **Tools/Outline/Outline Off**. WordPerfect inserts the [Outline Off] code at the cursor position and `Outline` disappears from the status line. Pressing Enter now inserts a hard return instead of a paragraph number.

   To turn Outline on again later, select **Tools/Outline/Outline On**.

Adding Headings

Once your outline is defined and the Outline feature is on, you can type the entries in the capital investment analysis outline, and WordPerfect takes care of the formatting. As you are typing and editing your entries, you can use special cursor movement keys to move the cursor from one level to the next in the outline; these keys are listed in Table 10.1.

Table 10.1   Moving the cursor in an outline.

Press	*To Move*
Alt+left arrow	To the previous paragraph number
Alt+right arrow	To the next paragraph number
Alt+up arrow	To the previous paragraph number of the same level or higher
Alt+down arrow	To the next paragraph number of the same level or lower

Typing Entries

1. Make sure the cursor is between the [Outline On] and [Outline Off] codes. `Outline` should be displayed on the status line.

2. Place the cursor at the end of the entry immediately above where you want the new entry. The cursor should immediately precede the hard return code [HRT] at the end of that entry.

3. Press Enter to create a paragraph number. WordPerfect inserts a paragraph number for the level (and also inserts a [Par Num:Auto] code in the Reveal Codes area).

4. Press Tab as many times as needed to change the paragraph number to the desired level. Each time you press Tab, the cursor moves one tab to the right, and the paragraph number changes to the next lower level. To move back a level, press Shift+Tab.

5. Press F7 (Indent) or the space bar to insert space after the paragraph number. You can't use the Tab key to insert space. Pressing Tab when Outline is on changes the level of the paragraph number.

6. Type text for the current outline entry.

7. Press Enter to create another paragraph number. The cursor moves to the next line and inserts the next paragraph number for this level.

8. Repeat steps 2 through 7 until the outline is complete.

To change the level of a paragraph number after you've entered it, place the cursor immediately before or after the paragraph number and press Tab or Shift+Tab.

Restructuring the Outline

The Outline feature offers three options to help you edit the capital investment analysis outline. These options let you move, copy, and delete groups of outline entries called *families*. A family consists of a paragraph number and its text plus all subsequent paragraph numbers and text below that level. If you move the cursor to 4. Pricing and select one of the Family options, for example, WordPerfect highlights 4. Pricing and the a, b, c, d, and e lines beneath 4. Pricing, as shown in Figure 10.3.

Deleting a Family

1. Place the cursor anywhere in the first line of the family.

2. Select **T**ools/**O**utline/**D**elete Family. WordPerfect highlights the family and displays a dialog box asking you to confirm that you want to delete the family.

3. Select **Y**es to delete the family or **N**o to cancel the operation.

4. If you select **Y**es, the family is erased.

If the deleted family is one of the last three deletions you made, you can restore the family anywhere by selecting Edit/**U**ndelete or pressing Alt+Shift+Backspace, and then selecting **R**estore.

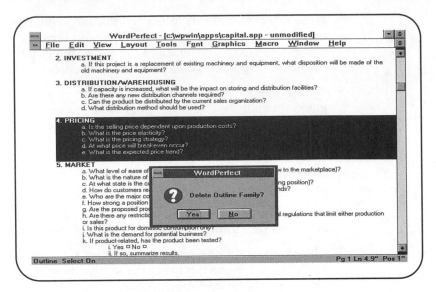

Figure 10.3   A family about to be deleted.

Moving or Copying a Family

1. Place the cursor anywhere in the first line of the family.

2. Select **Tools/Outline/M**ove Family or **Tools/Outline/C**opy Family. WordPerfect highlights the family. In the typing area, the mouse pointer changes to a no-entry sign, indicating you cannot use the mouse.

3. Use the arrow keys to move the highlighted family, and press Enter. As you move the family, the number of the first level changes, indicating the new position in the outline.

4. To cancel the operation at any time, press Esc.

Working with the Outline

After you customize the capital investment analysis outline, you can use it several ways. The easiest way is to treat the outline as a form. You can enter brief answers after each question as a type of brainstorming session. However, you might not want to add a great deal of text within the outline itself, because that would clutter the outline and defeat its purpose.

To use the outline more effectively, you can open a second document window and display it with the first window, as shown in Figure 10.4. Keep the outline displayed in one window, and use the other window to answer the questions and formulate a comprehensive capital investment analysis report. For more information about displaying windows, see Appendix B.

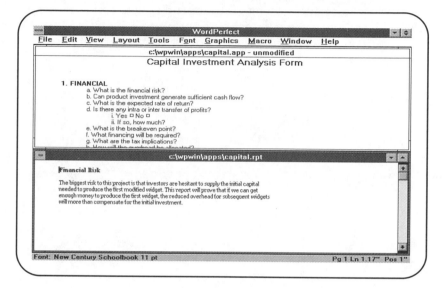

Figure 10.4   Two open document windows displayed in the WordPerfect window.

Displaying A New Window

1. Select **File/New** or press Shift+F4. A new document window fills the WordPerfect window.

2. Select **Window/Tile**. The two document windows appear with one beneath the other, as shown in Figure 10.4. The highlighted (or colored) title bar indicates the active window. You can move and resize the windows as described in Appendix B.

3. Switch between documents by placing the mouse pointer in the window and clicking the mouse button or by pressing Ctrl+F6 (Next Doc).

If your outline is not already displayed, open it into one of the windows. Use the outline as a reference tool. Use the other window to create your capital investment analysis report. Since the Outline feature is not on in this new document, you can format the document as you normally would.

Summary

The outline for the capital investment analysis is a useful tool for collecting the information you need to develop an intelligent investment strategy. With WordPerfect's Outline feature, you can customize the outline to fit the investment challenge you face and to help you analyze the prospects. You can then use this analysis to prove to yourself, to board members, or to potential investors whether or not the investment poses an acceptable risk.

The Capital Investment Analysis Application

Capital Investment Analysis Form

1. FINANCIAL
   a. What is the financial risk?
   b. Can product investment generate sufficient cash flow?
   c. What is the expected rate of return?
   d. Is there any intra or inter transfer of profits?
      i. Yes ▢ No ▢
      ii. If so, how much?
   e. What is the breakeven point?
   f. What financing will be required?
   g. What are the tax implications?
   h. How will the overhead be allocated?

2. INVESTMENT
   a. If this project is a replacement of existing machinery and equipment, what disposition will be made of the old machinery and equipment?

3. DISTRIBUTION/WAREHOUSING
   a. If capacity is increased, what will be the impact on storing and distribution facilities?
   b. Are there any new distribution channels required?
   c. Can the product be distributed by the current sales organization?
   d. What distribution method should be used?

4. PRICING
   a. Is the selling price dependent upon production costs?
   b. What is the price elasticity?
   c. What is the pricing strategy?
   d. At what price will breakeven occur?
   e. What is the expected price trend?

5. MARKET
   a. What level of ease of entry by competitors exists (if the product is new to the marketplace)?
   b. What is the nature of the market, i.e. size, industry, etc.?
   c. At what state is the current market (expanding, contracting, maintaining position)?
   d. How do customers react to changes in the economy, needs, and trends?
   e. Who are the major competitors?
   f. How strong a position do the competitors have in the marketplace?
   g. Are the proposed products competitive?
   h. Are there any restrictions set forth by the marketplace or governmental regulations that limit either production or sales?
   i. Is this product for domestic consumption only?
   j. What is the demand for potential business?
   k. If product-related, has the product been tested?
      i. Yes ▢ No ▢
      ii. If so, summarize results.
   l. Are there any additional costs involved in promoting the product?

6. TECHNICAL
   a. What are the risks in completing the project?
   b. How likely are the chances of changes in technology or the risk of obsolescence?
   c. If this is a new process, what are the potential problems?
   d. Are there any additional requirements for maintenance?
      i. Yes ▢ No ▢
      ii. If so, explain.
   e. What is the technical know-how needed for the proposed project?
   f. Will machinery and equipment require new design?

245

       i. Yes ☐ No ☐
       ii. If so, explain.
  g. Does the project require new plant layout?
       i. Yes ☐ No ☐
       ii. If so, explain.
  h. Will the start-up situation require additional resources?
       i. Yes ☐ No ☐
       ii. If so, explain.
  i. Can technical service be provided to new customers for new products?
       i. Yes ☐ No ☐
       ii. If so, explain.
  j. Are any patent problems involved?
       i. Yes ☐ No ☐
       ii. If so, explain.
  k. Are there any sellable by-products as a result of this project?
       i. Yes ☐ No ☐
       ii. If so, explain.

7. PRODUCTION
  a. How will this project affect production rates?
  b. Does the projected volume of production seem reasonable compared to the current rate?
  c. How flexible are the planned facilities for future expansion?
  d. What changes to current production facilities are necessary?
  e. What is the history of repair and maintenance costs, if equipment and machinery are being replaced?
  f. Can new facilities produce other related products?
  g. Is the product seasonal, and if so, what is impact on production levels?

8. LABOR
  a. Will project require any additional labor?
       i. Yes ☐ No ☐
       ii. If so, estimate requirements.
  b. Will project reduce labor costs?
       i. Yes ☐ No ☐
       ii. By how much?

9. INVENTORY
  a. Are new sources of raw materials needed?
       i. Yes ☐ No ☐
       ii. If so, explain.
  b. What are the required inventory levels?
  c. How accessible are producers of raw material to production facilities?
  d. Is there more than one supplier of raw materials?
       i. Yes ☐ No ☐
       ii. List prospective suppliers.

Define parallel columns

1. Select-Layout/Columns/**D**efine, or press Alt+Shift+F9 and type **d**.

2. Type the number of columns.

3. Select **P**arallel or Parallel **B**lock Protect.

4. Enter margin settings, or select **E**venly Spaced and type the distance between columns.

5. Select OK.

Turn Columns on

Select-Layout/Columns/**C**olumns **O**n, or press Alt+Shift+F9 and type **o**.

Turn Columns off

Select-Layout/Columns/**C**olumns **O**ff, or press Alt+Shift+F9 and type **f**.

Set column margins

1. Select-Layout/Columns/**D**efine, or press Alt+Shift+F9 and type **d**.

2. Enter margin settings, or select **E**venly Spaced and type the distance between columns.

3. Select OK.

Set number of columns

1. Select-Layout/Columns/**D**efine, or press Alt+Shift+F9 and type **d**.

2. Type the number of columns.

3. Select OK.

Set distance between columns

1. Select-Layout/Columns/**D**efine, or press Alt+Shift+F9 and type **d**.

2. Enter margin settings, or select **E**venly Spaced and type the distance between columns.

3. Select OK.

Protect block in column

1. Select-Layout/Columns/**D**efine, or press Alt+Shift+F9 and type **d**.

2. Select Parallel **B**lock Protect.

3. Select OK.

**BUSINESS
SHORTCUTS**

Telephone
Reference Form

*Almost every job application requires that the applicant supply a list of
references. Before you hire the applicant, you need to verify the references and obtain additional information about the applicant's past job
performance. The telephone reference form, described in this chapter
and included on disk, provides a form containing 17 important questions about a prospective employee. You can fill in the answers while
you're on the telephone with the applicant's reference.*

About the Application

The *telephone reference form*, shown at the end of this chapter, consists of
a list of questions and possible answers. The columns are set up as *parallel*
columns, so that each entry on the left has a corresponding entry on the
right. Hanging indents, used for the entries are indented from the left
column margins, making the question numbers stand out from the text.

Beginner's
Tip

An *indent* moves all lines in paragraph one tab stop to the right. You
can format an existing paragraph with an indent, or format as you type.
In either case, insert the indent by pressing F7. This inserts an Indent
code.

You can change the distance the text is indented by changing the tab stop positions. In parallel columns, relative tabs are "relative" to the left margin of every column (see Chapter 2 for information about relative and absolute tabs), this allows you to specify relative tabs for all columns simply by choosing one set of relative tabs; WordPerfect for Windows will automatically apply those tabs relative to each left column margin. If you set a relative tabs of 0.3", for example, pressing F7 (Indent) or Tab in any column will move the cursor 0.3" from the left margin of that column.

If you prefer using tables to using parallel columns, you can use the Table feature to create a table containing your text (see Chapter 6). After you have entered text, you can remove the lines from the table to make the table columns appear as parallel columns. To convert existing columns into a table, select the columns; then select **L**ayout/**T**ables/**C**reate, or press Ctrl+F9 (Tables) and type **c**. If the columns are parallel columns, select **P**arallel Column. If you set up the columns using tabs, select **T**abular Column. Select OK to make the conversion. To remove the lines, highlight the entire table; then select **L**ayout/**T**ables/**L**ines, or press Ctrl+F9 (Tables) and type **l**. Select **N**one for **I**nside and **O**utside and select OK.

Opening the Application

To customize the telephone reference form, open the file TELREF.APP. This template is a duplicate of the one shown at the end of this chapter, but it may appear different in print, depending on the printer you installed. To see how the form will look in print, press Shift+F5 (Print Preview) or select **F**ile/Print Preview.

Customizing the Application

The most basic way to customize this application is to replace the asterisks with the information that applies to the particular applicant and reference. Use the Search (F2) and Search Next (Shift+F2) features to search for the asterisks. When WordPerfect for Windows finds an asterisk, it stops to the right of the asterisk. Press Backspace to delete the asterisk, and then type your entry. When you're done, you can print the file and write your answers on the printed form. To customize the application further (as explained in this chapter), you can delete or add questions, and redefine the parallel columns. You can also use different fonts, as explained in Chapter 17.

Moving Between Columns

The easiest way to move the cursor in parallel columns is to use the mouse. Place the mouse pointer where you want the cursor, and then click the mouse button.

If you use the keyboard, keep in mind that the cursor moves differently in parallel columns than it does in normal text. When you use the Left and Right Arrow keys or Ctrl+Left Arrow and Ctrl+Right Arrow to move the cursor one character or word left or right, the cursor moves through the entry in one parallel column before going to the corresponding entry in the next parallel column. Similarly, pressing Home and End move the cursor to the beginning and end of a line (respectively) within a column.

You can use Go To to move the cursor to a page, to the top or bottom of a column, to the next or previous column, or to the first or last column. Press **Ctrl+G** or select **E**dit/**G**o To to display the Go To dialog box. Select the **P**osition pop-up list button, and then select the position to which you want to move the cursor. Select **OK** to move the cursor.

Caution: Before you edit parallel columns, display the Reveal Codes area. Compare the position of the highlight in the Reveal Codes screen with the position of the cursor in the normal document window. With some machines, these positions differ. The highlight shows the true position of the cursor. If you have this problem, call WordPerfect's customer support at 1-800-228-1029. A representative will make sure you receive the release that corrects this for your machine. In the meantime, always work with the Reveal Codes screen displayed.

By default, WordPerfect for Windows displays your columns side by side so you can see how they'll appear when printed. Although this view of your columns can help you when you're creating them, it can slow you down when you're entering and editing text. To speed up the process, you can change the default so the columns appear staggered on screen. In this mode, WordPerfect for Windows reformats edited text more quickly.

Turning Side-by-Side Display Off

1. Select **F**ile/**P**references/**D**isplay, or press Ctrl+Shift+F1 (Preferences) and type **d**. The Display Settings dialog box appears.

2. Deselect the Display **C**olumns Side-by-Side check box.

3. Select OK. The columns appear staggered on screen and separated by page breaks, as shown in Figure 11.1. This has no effect on the printed document. If you print it (or use the Print Preview feature), WordPerfect for Windows displays the columns side by side.

Columns are staggered and on separate pages.

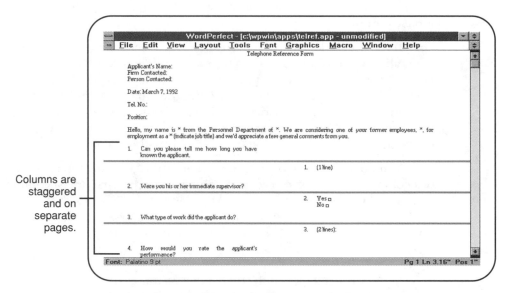

Figure 11.1   Side-by-side display turned off.

Deleting and Adding Questions

Once you have moved into a particular column, you can edit the text as you would in any WordPerfect for Windows document, deleting or adding questions as needed. If your changes affect the numbering of the questions, be sure to go back and renumber them.

Beginner's Tip

When editing parallel columns, turn on Reveal Codes. That way you can see the formatting codes (such as [Col On] and [Col Off]). This is especially important if you want to move items from one location to another. For the text you move to be formatted correctly, you must select the formatting codes along with the text.

Deleting a Question

1. Using the Reveal Codes screen as a guide, move the cursor so that the Reveal Codes highlight is on the [Col On] code before the question you want to delete. Begin your selection here.

2. Select the text, including the [Col On] code in step 1. Stretch the highlight over the entire question and the corresponding choices in the right column, to just past the [Col Off] code.

3. Press Delete. The question is deleted.

4. If extra space appears between the previous question and the next one, highlight the [HRt] code in the Reveal Codes screen, and press Delete.

Adding a Question

1. Move the cursor just past an entry in the right column but before the [Col Off] code for that entry.

2. Press Ctrl+Enter. WordPerfect for Windows inserts a [HRt] code and [Block Pro:On][Col On] and [Col Off] codes at the cursor location, as shown in Figure 11.2. The [HRt] code adds space between the previous entry and this one. The [Col On] and [Col Off] codes turn the Columns feature on and off for this question. And the [Block Pro:On] code turns on the Block Protect feature.

3. Type the question number, type a period (.), press F7 (Indent), and then type the text of the question.

4. Press Ctrl+Enter to move the cursor to the right column. WordPerfect for Windows inserts a [HPg] code, and the cursor moves to the right column. If you have side-by-side display turned on, the cursor is on the same line as the first line of the question.

5. Type the save question number you typed in step 3, type a period (.), press F7 (Indent), and then type the choices or directive for the question you entered in step 3.

6. Repeat steps 2 through 5 to enter another question.

Beginner's Tip

If your printer supports WordPerfect's character sets, you can use WordPerfect's Compose feature to insert the small check boxes shown in the example. Move the cursor where you want the box to appear. Press Ctrl+W. The WordPerfect Characters dialog box appears, and the **Number** text box is highlighted. Type 6,93 and select **Insert** or **Insert and Close**. (The 6 stands for the WordPerfect character set. The 93 stands for the number of the character in that set.) Use the Print Preview feature to see how the box will appear in print.

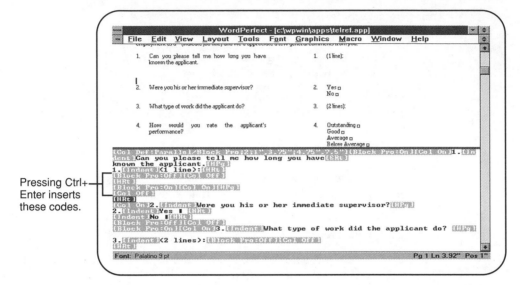

Pressing Ctrl+
Enter inserts
these codes.

*Figure 11.2   Press Ctrl+Enter at the end of the entry in the right
column to start a new series of columns.*

Formatting Columns

If you revised the content of the form extensively, you might want to change
the column widths, the number of columns, or the distance between
columns for the new version. To do so, you must replace the existing [Col
Def] code with a new one, as explained in the following steps.

Redefining the Parallel Columns

1. Move the cursor just past the [Col Def] code.

2. Select **L**ayout/**C**olumns/**D**efine, or press Alt+Shift+F9 (Columns)
   and then type **d**. The Define Columns dialog box appears, as shown
   in Figure 11.3.

3. Select the type of parallel columns you want: **P**arallel or Parallel
   Block Protect. Choose Parallel **B**lock Protect to keep list items from
   splitting across a page break.

4. In the Number of **C**olumns text box, type the number of columns
   you want. WordPerfect for Windows automatically assumes you
   want evenly spaced columns separated by 0.5", calculates the
   column margins, and enters the results in the **M**argins text boxes.

5. To change the distance between columns, type a new measurement in the **Distance Between Columns** text box. WordPerfect for Windows automatically recalculates the margins and enters them in the **Margins** text boxes.

6. To create columns of unequal width, go to the **Margins** text boxes and type the left and right margin settings for each column. WordPerfect for Windows automatically deselects the **Evenly Spaced** check box. The next time you open the dialog box, the **Distance Between Columns** box also is updated.

7. Deselect the **Column On** check box. (The Columns feature is turned on already, so leaving this selected would insert unnecessary additional codes).

8. Select OK to return to the Text Box Editor window. If you are using WordPerfect's default setting for Auto Code Placement, WordPerfect for Windows replaces the original [Col Def] code with the new one. (See Chapter 1 for information on the Auto Code Placement feature.)

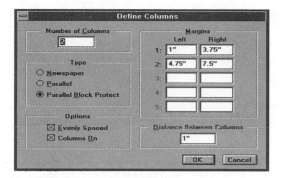

Figure 11.3 The Define Columns dialog box.

You can also use the Ruler to change parallel column margins. Refer to Chapter 13 for further information.

> ▶ You can have several different column definitions in one document. To enter a new definition, turn Columns off, enter a [Col Def] code as explained above, and then turn Columns on. See Chapter 13 for information about turning Columns on and off.

Summary

The telephone reference form will help you collect the information required for assessing job candidates. With the application in this chapter, and WordPerfect's Parallel Columns feature, you are well on your way to creating a custom form that can fulfill your needs. If you can type while talking on the phone, you may even be able to type answers directly onto the form while talking to the applicant's reference!

Telephone Reference Form

(Page 1 of 2)

Telephone Reference Form

Applicant's Name:
Firm Contacted:
Person Contacted:

Date: March 7, 1992

Tel. No.:

Position:

Hello, my name is * from the Personnel Department of *. We are considering one of your former employees, *, for employment as a * (indicate job title) and we'd appreciate a few general comments from you.

1.	Can you please tell me how long you have known the applicant.	1.	(1 line)
2.	Were you his or her immediate supervisor?	2.	Yes ☐ No ☐
3.	What type of work did the applicant do?	3.	(2 lines):
4.	How would you rate the applicant's performance?	4.	Outstanding ☐ Good ☐ Average ☐ Below Average ☐
5.	Can you tell me why?	5.	(2 lines):
6.	Was the applicant a hard worker?	6.	Yes ☐ No ☐
7.	How would you rate the applicant's attendance and punctuality?	7.	(2 lines):
8.	What would you say the applicant's strong points were?	8.	(2 lines):
9.	In what areas might the applicant need some improvement?	9.	(2 lines):
10.	How would you rate the applicant's personality, tact, and ability to get along with others?	10.	Favorable ☐ Questionable ☐ Unfavorable ☐
11.	Why did the applicant leave your employ?	11.	(2 lines):
12.	Approximately, what dates was the applicant employed by you?	12.	From: To :

Telephone Reference Form

(Page 2 of 2)

13. Would you rehire the applicant?

13. Yes ☐
    No ☐
    (If "No") Can you tell me why?

14. Interviewer, when you are through with this interview, you should have a feeling about how the person you spoke to felt about the applicant, by such things as tone of voice, candidness of answers, etc. Write your evaluation as completely as possible. Do not exceed six lines.

Signature _____

Date: March 7, 1992

Run a macro

1. Select **Macro/Play**, or press Alt+F10.

2. Type the macro name and select **Play**.

Edit a macro

1. Open the macro file.

2. Edit it as you would any document.

3. Save the changes.

Enter comment in macro

1. Open the macro file.

2. Move cursor where you want to insert comment.

3. Type / /, followed by the comment.

4. Press Enter.

Record a macro

1. Select **Macro/Record**, or press Ctrl+F10.

2. Type a macro name.

3. If desired, enter a description and abstract.

4. Select **Record**.

5. Complete the tasks you want recorded.

6. Select **Macro/Stop**, or press Ctrl+Shift+F10.

Add a macro to the Macro menu

1. Select **Macro/Assign** to Menu.

2. Select **Insert**.

3. Enter the macro name.

4. Type the text you want to appear on the Macro menu.

5. Select OK to close the Insert Macro Menu Item dialog box.

6. Select OK to close the Assign Macro to Menu dialog box.

Add a macro to the Button Bar

1. Select **View/Button Bar Setup/Edit**.

2. Select **Assign Macro to Button**.

3. Enter the macro name.

4. Select **Assign**.

5. Select OK.

BUSINESS
SHORTCUTS

Telephone Message Form

The telephone plays an important role in any business. To use the phone effectively, you must make sure that important phone calls are documented and that messages are relayed to the right people. The telephone message application explained in this chapter is a macro that you can use while talking on the phone. The macro prompts you to enter various pieces of information about the caller, including the caller's name, affiliation, and phone number. Then, the macro prints the message and asks if you want to save the message to disk.

About the Application

The telephone message application, TEL.WCM, differs from the other applications in this book. This application is not a WordPerfect for Windows document like the others. Instead, it's a macro: a set of commands that you can play back to perform a task. The telephone message macro leads the user through the process of recording information on a telephone message form. The resulting form looks like the example shown at the end of this chapter.

The macro opens a new document window and then begins creating the telephone message form. It first creates a Text box for the message. This allows the message to be enclosed by the border shown in the example at the end of the chapter. The macro includes several PauseKey commands that make the macro pause while you type information. After you type the information and press Enter, the macro continues. Once you type the last entry on the form, the macro prints the message and displays the Save As dialog box. You can enter a file name and choose Save to save the message, or choose Cancel to close the dialog box without saving the message. After you choose Save or Cancel, the macro closes the document window, and returns you to your original document window.

Taking a Message

The telephone message macro begins with a command that automatically opens a new document window. This command was included so that you won't accidentally insert the telephone message in an existing document. The macro ends with a command that closes the new window, returning you to the window in which you were working.

To stop a macro during its execution, press Esc (Cancel). The macro will stop, and WordPerfect for Windows will display a message that the macro was canceled at your request. Select OK to clear the message from the window.

The best way to understand what the macro does is simply to run it. Go ahead and run it now (making up a phony telephone message), using the steps that follow.

Running the Macro

1. Select **Macro/Play**, or press Alt+F10 (Macro Play). The Play Macro dialog box appears.

2. Type **tel** and select **Play**. WordPerfect for Windows starts running the macro. A new document window opens, "While You Were Out" appears at the top of the window, and the prompt To: appears on screen.

3. Type the name of the person being called, and press Enter. The macro proceeds to the next line and automatically inserts the date and time next to `Date/Time:`. The prompt `Mr./Ms?` appears on screen.

4. Type **Mr.** or **Ms.**, and press Enter.

5. Continue entering information as prompted. Whenever you press Enter, the macro proceeds to the next prompt. (When the `Left message:` prompt appears, remember to type the message in one paragraph. You cannot use Enter to begin a new paragraph.) After you enter your last response, the macro prints the message and then displays the Save As dialog box.

6. To save the message, type a file name and select **S**ave. If you don't want to save the message, select Cancel. After you select **S**ave or Cancel, the macro closes the message window, returning you to the window you were in when you began playing the macro.

The first time you play a macro, you will notice a slight delay before the macro begins. The delay occurs because WordPerfect for Windows is *compiling* the macro, placing it in a form more easily read by the computer. A macro is compiled the first time it is played and remains compiled thereafter. The next time you play the macro, it begins without delay.

As you saw from running the macro, a command is included that automatically inserts the date from your computer system after `Date/Time:` on the message form. By default, WordPerfect for Windows inserts only the date in the form `Month(word), day(number), year(number)`. For example: February 24, 1992. You can include the time of day by changing the date format.

Note that when the macro is running, it takes the date format from WordPerfect for Windows' current settings rather than from any fixed setting included in the macro. That means that if several people use the macro, the date formats on telephone messages may vary throughout the office.

Changing the Date/Time Format to Include Time

1. Select **File/Preferences/Date Format**. The Date/Time Preferences dialog box appears.

2. Go to the **Edit Date Format** text box and place the cursor where you want to insert the time—for example, after the [Year] code.

3. Type any punctuation or spaces that should precede the time.

4. Select the **Time Codes** pop-up list button, and then select an [Hour] time code. To display time on a 24-hour clock, for example, select [Hour(24)#]. The code appears in the **Edit Date Format** text box; an example of the date and time format is displayed in the Date Preview field.

5. Type a colon to separate the hours from the minutes.

6. Select the **Time Codes** pop-up list button, and then select a [Minute] time code. To display minutes with a zero pad, for example, select [**Minute** 0#]. (A zero pad means single-digit numbers are preceded by a zero. For example: 08, 09, 10.) The code appears in the **Edit Date Format** text box.

7. If you selected a 12-hour clock format in Step 4, you might want to add *am* or *pm* after the time. To do so, select the **Time Codes** pop-up list button again, and then select [AM/PM]. WordPerfect for Windows will automatically include the correct setting, am or pm, for the time of day.

8. Review the example in the Date Preview field to make sure you are satisfied with it. If you are not, modify the codes or punctuation in the Edit Date Format text box.

9. Select OK. WordPerfect for Windows returns to the document window.

From now on, whenever you use WordPerfect for Windows' Date feature to insert the date from your computer system into your document, the program will insert the date and time in this new format. (For more information about using the Date/Time Preferences dialog box, see Chapter 2.)

If you don't want to change the date/time format, you can edit the macro (as explained later) to have it pause so you can type the date and time.

Customizing the Application

You can edit the telephone message macro to modify the prompts that appear in the form. You can also add or delete macro commands to make the macro perform other functions. Keep in mind that there are two types of macro commands: WordPerfect for Windows product commands and programming commands.

- A *product command* implements a WordPerfect for Windows feature, such as Print Preview, or an activity you normally perform while using the program, such as inserting text or moving the cursor. The product command FileNew(), for example, opens a new document window; it is equivalent to selecting **File/New**. The product command HardReturn() inserts a hard return. Most product commands have easily recognizable names, so you can tell at a glance what function or activity a command performs.

- A *programming command* allows you to pause a macro, set up conditions under which the macro will run, and change the flow of the macro. The PAUSE command, for example, stops the macro until the user resumes the macro by selecting **Macro/Pause**.

The macro TEL.WCM, shown in Figure 12.1, contains product commands and programming commands.

```
Application (WP;WPWP;Default;"WPWPUS.WCD")
//This macro opens a new document window and creates a telephone message
form,  pausing to let you type information in the form. When you are
finished, the macro prints the telephone message and then displays the
Save As dialog box. You can save the file or cancel saving. After you
choose whether to save, the macro closes the window.

//Open a new document window:
FileNew()

//Specify a double-line border and no gray shading for the text box:
BoxOptions

        (Type:Text!;LeftBorder:Double!;RightBorder:Double!;TopBorder:Double!;
        BottomBorder:Double!;GrayShade:0)

//Create the text box, set its width and height, and center it between
the left and right margins:
TextBoxCreate()

BoxPosition
        (AutoMode:SetBoth!;Width:5.0";Height:6.5";HorizontalType:Center!)

//Center the form title, make it bold and in large type, and type the
title: "While You Were Out."
LineCenter()
FontBold(State:On!)
FontLarge(State:On!)
Type(Text:"While You Were Out")

//Move the cursor past the [Bold Off] and [Large Off] codes:
PosCharNext()
PosCharNext()

//Insert space between the form title and the first line of text:
HardReturn()
HardReturn()
HardReturn()
//
//In each of the following groups of commands, the macro enters some
boilerplate form text, turns on italics so that your response is in
italics, pauses to let you type your response, (except for the date,
which is automatically entered), and then moves the cursor past the
[Italc Off] code.

        //Enter name of message recipient:
Type(Text:"To:   ")
FontItalic(State:On!)
PauseKey (Key:Enter!)
PosCharNext()
```

Figure 12.1   A complete listing of the commands in TEL.WCM. (1 of 3)

```
        //Enter date from system:
HardReturn()
HardReturn()
Type(Text:"Date/Time: ")
FontItalic(State:On!)
DateText()
PosCharNext()

        //Enter Mr. or Ms.:
HardReturn()
HardReturn()
HardReturn()
Type(Text:"Mr./Ms.? ")
FontItalic(State:On!)
PauseKey (Key:Enter!)
PosCharNext()

        //Enter caller's name:
HardReturn()
HardReturn()
Type(Text:"Name: ")
FontItalic(State:On!)
PauseKey (Key:Enter!)
PosCharNext()

        //Enter caller's affiliation:
HardReturn()

HardReturn()
Type(Text:"Of: ")
FontItalic(State:On!)
PauseKey (Key:Enter!)
PosCharNext()

        //Enter message:
HardReturn()
HardReturn()
Type(Text:"Left message: ")
FontItalic(State:On!)
PauseKey (Key:Enter!)
PosCharNext()

        //Enter caller's phone number:
HardReturn()
HardReturn()
LineFlushRight()
Type(Text:"Please call at: ")
FontItalic(State:On!)
PauseKey (Key:Enter!)
PosCharNext()
```

Figure 12.1   A complete listing of the commands in TEL.WCM. (2 of 3)

267

```
        //Enter whether message is urgent:
HardReturn()

LineFlushRight()
Type(Text:"Urgent?")
FontItalic(State:On!)
PauseKey (Key:Enter!)
PosCharNext()

        //Enter  whether the caller will call again:
HardReturn()
LineFlushRight()
Type(Text:"Will call you again? ")
FontItalic(State:On!)
PauseKey (Key:Enter!)
PosCharNext()

        //Enter whether caller was returning a call:
HardReturn()
LineFlushRight()
Type(Text:"Returned your call? ")
FontItalic(State:On!)
PauseKey (Key:Enter!)
PosCharNext()

//Close the Text Box Editor window:
Close()

//Print the telephone message:
PrintFull()

//Set up macro so that user can select Cancel in the Save As dialog box
without canceling the macro:
ONCANCEL (nosave@)

//Display the Save As dialog box. The macro continues after you select
Save or Cancel.
FileSaveAsDlg()

LABEL (nosave@)//If user selects Cancel, in the Save As dialog box, the
macro skips to this line.

//Close the document window:
CloseNoSave(Verify:0)
Close(Save:0)
```

Figure 12.1   A complete listing of the commands in TEL.WCM. (3 of 3)

The following list describes these commands and their functions. In both the following list and the figure, programming commands, such as LABEL, are distinguished by uppercase letters. Notice that the product commands have the general form:

CommandName( )

or

CommandName(parameter:value;parameter:value;)

In both forms, the command is followed by open and closed parentheses. In the second form, the parentheses enclose information about *parameters* and *values*. Commands having that form require additional information before they can run; you supply the information by specifying values for certain parameters. To specify boldface in a macro, for example, you use the command FontBold(State:On!). *FontBold* is the command name, *State* is the parameter, and *On* is the value for that parameter. Programming commands may also have parameters enclosed in parentheses, or they may just be a command name, such as PAUSE, with no following parentheses.

//: This is the comment command, a programming command that lets you insert comments in the macro explaining a step or series of steps. The comments do not affect the operation of the macro, but they can help you edit the macro later. A comment can contain about 500 characters.

FileNew(): Opens a new document window so you don't accidentally insert the message in an existing document.

BoxOptions(Type:Text!; etc.): Inserts a [Txt Opt] code that specifies double-line borders for the Text box and no gray shading. To specify this, values were entered for the following parameters: Type:Text! indicates the options are for a Text box; LeftBorder:Double!, RightBorder:Double!, TopBorder:Double!, and BottomBorder:Double! select double-line borders for the Text box; and GrayShade:0 specifies 0 as the percentage of gray shading in the Text box.

TextBoxCreate(): Creates the Text box and opens the Text Box Editor window.

BoxPosition(AutoMode:SetBoth!; etc.): Sets the Text box size and the horizontal position of the box on the page. Automode:SetBoth! specifies that both box dimensions are being set, rather than having WordPerfect for Windows set them. Width:5.0" and Height:6.5" set the Text box width at 5" and height at 6.5". You can edit these numbers (5.0 and 6.5) just as you would edit text in a normal document window. HorizontalType:Center! centers the text box between the left and right margins.

LineCenter(): Inserts a [Center] code so that the title "While You Were Out" will be centered inside the Text box.

FontBold(State:On!)FontLarge(State:On!): Inserts [Bold On][Large On][Large Off][Bold Off] codes, positioning the cursor after the On codes. These codes set the title text, which is entered next, in boldface, large type.

Type(Text:"While You Were Out"): Enters the title text. Notice that text entered as the value for the Text parameter must be enclosed by quotation marks.

PosCharNext(): Moves the cursor right one character, that is, to the *next* character. This command appears throughout the macro. It is used to move the cursor past attribute codes such as [Bold Off], [Large Off], and [Italc Off], so that subsequent text will not have those attributes.

HardReturn(): Inserts a [HRt] code in the text and moves the cursor down to the next line.

FontItalic(State:On!): Inserts [Italc On] and [Italc Off] codes after the prompts on the form. When you type your response to the prompts, the text is inserted between the codes, making it italic.

PauseKey(Key:Enter!): Tells the macro to pause for user input and to continue after the user presses the Enter key. Although this looks like a programming command, it really is a product command.

DateText(): Enters the date from your system.

LineFlushRight(): Enters a [Flsh Rgt] code. This command was used to make the last four entries flush with the right margin.

Close(): Closes the Text Box Editor window.

PrintFull(): Prints the full document.

ONCANCEL(nosave@): Directs the macro to skip to the label *nosave@* if you select Cancel in a dialog box. Without this command, selecting Cancel would cancel (that is, stop) the macro. (See LABEL later in this list.)

FileSaveAsDlg(): Opens the Save As dialog box. This was included to give you the option to save the telephone message. After you save the message or cancel saving, the macro continues.

LABEL(nosave@): If you select Cancel in the Save As dialog box, the macro goes to this label. A label is a place marker. In this case, it was necessary to direct the macro to continue if you selected Cancel in the Save As dialog box (see ONCANCEL, above). To instruct it where to continue, a place (label) was specified and named *nosave*. The macro was told to continue there.

CloseNoSave(Verify:0)Close(Save:0): Closes the window containing the message. Because you already chose to save or not save the message, the macro closes the window without prompting you to save the document. To specify that no prompt be given, both Verify and Save have the value 0. Note that you must use both CloseNoSave and Close if you want to close a window without being prompted to save.

Editing the Telephone Message Macro

You might want to modify TEL.WCM to include different prompts or to modify the Text box characteristics. A macro file is a normal document file. To edit TEL.WCM, therefore, open the file and edit it as you would any other document. Just remember to strictly observe the syntax for the commands. If you type the command incorrectly, the macro will not run. The following sections give the syntax for the commands you are most likely to edit in TEL.WCM, and explain how to modify those commands.

Beginner's Tip

If you edit a macro, WordPerfect for Windows recompiles the macro the first time you run the edited version.

After you enter your changes, save the file as you would any document file, using **File/Save** or **File/Save As**. The next time you run the macro, the updated version will be compiled and then executed.

Editing the Telephone Message Prompts

As the macro TEL.WCM creates the telephone message, it inserts text such as `To:` and `Left Message:`. To insert this text, the macro uses the Type command:

```
Type(Text:"character expression")
```

where *character expression* is the text you want entered in the document. Notice that *character expression* is enclosed by double quotation marks. In the Type command, double quotation marks must enclose the text you want entered in the document. If you want to include quotation marks in that text, you must use two quotation marks to indicate each one. To insert *She said, "My what a big nose you have,"* for example, you would enter this Type command:

```
Type(Text:"She said, ""My what a big nose you have""")
```

In this example, the first quotation mark indicates that this is the beginning of the text you want to enter. The two quotation marks preceding My and the first two quotation marks following have tell WordPerfect for Windows to type one quotation mark at each location. The third quotation mark following have tells the program that this is the end of the text you want entered.

To help you visualize the macro as you edit it, print the macro document. Because a macro is a normal WordPerfect for Windows document, you can print it as you would any other document.

To edit a prompt in the telephone message macro, edit the text within the quotation marks in the Type command. You can use the Cut, Copy, and Paste features, the Delete and Backspace keys, and the Insert key, just as you do when typing text in a normal document. You may enter as many as 512 characters, including spaces and punctuation. Use characters only. Do not enter tabs, hard returns, or formatting; you enter these by inserting individual product commands. For example, the two lines:

```
Will call you again?
Returned your call?
```

are entered by the following commands:

```
Type(Text:"Will call you again?")
HardReturn()
Type(Text:"Returned your call?")
```

To delete a prompt, delete the entire Type command, including the command name, the text within the parentheses, and the parentheses. Do not leave any stray characters from the command; if you do, WordPerfect for Windows will detect a syntax error and *the macro will not run.*

To add a prompt in the same format as the other prompts, follow these steps.

Adding a Prompt

1. Place the cursor where you want to enter the prompt. To have the prompt appear on a separate line, make sure you place the cursor after a HardReturn( ) command.

2. Type the following:

   Type(Text:"character expression")

   where character expression is the prompt you want entered in the message form.

3. Press Enter to start the next command on a new line. This has no effect on the macro and does not insert a hard return in the telephone message. It just places the next macro command on a separate line so that the commands are easier to distinguish.

4. To set the response to the prompt in italics, type:

   FontItalic(State:On!)

   This inserts [Italc On] and [Italc Off] codes in the message form and places the cursor after the [Italc On] code.

5. Press Enter to start the next command on a new line.

6. To have the macro pause to let the user enter a response to the prompt, type:

   PauseKey(Key:Enter!)

   This specifies that the macro will pause until the user presses the Enter key. When the user presses Enter, the macro will continue.

7. Press Enter to start the next command on a new line, and then type:

   PosCharNext()

   This command tells WordPerfect for Windows to move the cursor one character to the right, moving the cursor past the [Italc Off] code following the user's response.

8. Press Enter to start the next command on a new line, and then type:

```
HardReturn()
HardReturn()
```

This inserts a blank line after the line containing the prompt and the user's response. You might want to type a third HardReturn() command to enter an additional blank line.

Changing the Text Box Size

You might find that the Text box is too small or large for your messages. To change the Text box size, you can edit the BoxPosition() command in the macro.

The BoxPosition() command has the following form in the macro:

```
BoxPosition(AutoMode:SetBoth!;Width:5.0";Height:6.5";
HorizontalType:Center!)
```

In this command, *BoxPosition* is the command name. Within the parentheses, we have specified values for several parameters:

- The parameter *AutoMode* has the value *SetBoth*. This specifies that we are setting both box dimensions (rather than having WordPerfect for Windows set them).

- The parameter *Width* has the value *5.0"*. This sets the box width at 5 inches.

- The parameter *Height* has the value *6.5"*. This sets the box height at 6.5 inches.

- The parameter *HorizontalType* has the value *Center*. This centers the box between the left and right margins.

The BoxPosition() command illustrates several characteristics of product commands:

- The command names are often similar to the names of menu items or dialog boxes. The names of command parameters and values are often similar to the names of buttons and options you would select in a dialog box. The BoxPosition() command, for example, corresponds to the Box Position and Size dialog box. The HorizontalType parameter is similar to the Horizontal Position button in that dialog box. Although the Box Position() command used in this macro specifies only four parameters, you could specify other parameters that correspond to those in the Box Position and Size dialog box.

- A colon separates a parameter and its value. For example: AutoMode:SetBoth! and Width:5.0".

- A semicolon separates parameter:value couples. For example: AutoMode:SetBoth!;Width:5.0";Height:6.5".

- Some parameters may have only certain values. The AutoMode parameter, for instance, may have one of the following values: AutoBoth, AutoWidth, AutoHeight, or SetBoth. No other value is permitted. The set of permissible values is called a *value set*. In a product command, values that are members of a value set are always followed by an exclamation point, for example, AutoMode:SetBoth! and HorizontalWidth:Center!.

Changing the PauseKey Command

The macro contains several PauseKey(Key:Enter!) commands, which pause the macro until the user presses the Enter key. The pause allows you to type information about the phone call and then continue the macro by pressing Enter. If you take messages that are longer than one paragraph, you should change the PauseKey command so that pressing a different key continues the macro. Then you can press the Enter key to end a paragraph and begin a new one without automatically continuing the macro. You can specify the following values for Key in the PauseKey command: Enter, Cancel (to use the Esc key), Close (to use Ctrl+F4), or a character key.

To use Cancel (Esc key), or Close (Ctrl+F4), edit the PauseKey command by replacing the word `Enter` with `Cancel` or `Close`. The resulting command should be PauseKey(Key:Cancel!) or PauseKey(Key:Close!).

You can type commands, parameters, and values in any combination of upper- and lowercase letters.

To use a character key, edit the PauseKey command by replacing the word `Enter` with `Character`, moving the cursor past the exclamation point, and then typing:

```
;Character:key
```

where *key* is the key character, for example: **a** or **?**. To use the *a* key, for example, the command would be:

```
PauseKey(Key:Character!;Character:a)
```

If you enter more than one character, only the first is recognized.

Removing the Automatic Date

The macro automatically inserts the date from your system. If you prefer to type the date, you can delete the command for the automatic date and add a PauseKey() command that pauses the macro so you can type the date.

Removing the Automatic Date and Inserting a Pause

1. Delete the command DateText(), which is near line 50 of the macro (look for the comment // Enter date from system.).

2. Type **PauseKey(Key:***key***)**, where *key* is *Enter*, *Cancel*, *Close*, or *Character*, depending on which key you want to press to continue the macro. (See "Changing the PauseKey Command" earlier in this chapter.)

Creating a Macro

Given the power of macros, you may find that you want to create many of your own. You can create macros by typing the commands. But an easier way to create simple macros is to have WordPerfect for Windows record the actions you use to accomplish a task. The program will then convert those actions into the appropriate macro commands.

When recording a macro, you cannot use a mouse to position the cursor or select text, but you *can* use it to select commands and navigate dialog boxes.

Recording a Macro

1. Select **Macro/Record**, or press Ctrl+F10. The Record Macro dialog box appears, as shown in Figure 12.2.

2. Type a macro name in the **Filename** text box. If you do not type a file extension, WordPerfect for Windows adds the default extension .WCM.

3. If desired, type a description of the macro in the **Descriptive Name** text box. You can type up to 68 characters. You can also type a more lengthy description in the **Abstract** text box, which can contain about 760 characters.

4. Select **R**ecord. The dialog box closes. From now until you stop recording, all your WordPerfect for Windows activities are recorded in the macro.

5. Complete the tasks you want recorded. You can select menu items, display and select from dialog boxes, enter text, or perform any other WordPerfect for Windows activity except selecting text or exiting the program.

6. When you have finished the tasks you want to record, select **M**acro/**S**top, or press Ctrl+Shift+F10.

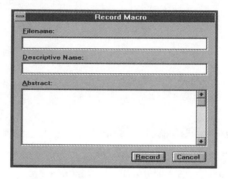

Figure 12.2   The Record Macro dialog box.

After creating the macro, you can view it by opening the macro file. Figure 12.3 shows a typical macro that has just been recorded. Notice that WordPerfect by default inserts an Application command at the top of the macro. This command specifies that the following commands are all performed in WordPerfect for Windows. Also notice that the commands are spread across several lines. The Box Options command in Figure 12.3 , for example, has this form:

```
BoxOptions
(
   Type:Text!;
   LeftBorder:Double!;
   RightBorder:Double!;
   TopBorder:Double!;
   BottomBorder:Double!;
   GrayShade:0
)
```

As this indicates, WordPerfect for Windows allows you to format a command in any way as long as the syntax is correct. This allows you to use tabs, indents, and hard returns to format a command so that it is easily readable. Remember, however, that a hard return following a Comment command always ends the comment. To continue the comment after a hard return, you must insert another Comment command (//) before typing the comment text.

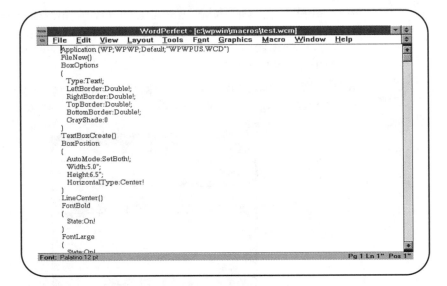

Figure 12.3   A newly created macro.

A macro is a normal WordPerfect document that can be opened, edited, saved, printed, and closed. You might want to edit a newly created macro to annotate it, to remove keystrokes you didn't mean to record, or to insert commands such as PauseKey (). You have already learned the basics of macro commands and some of the most common commands. If you would like to learn more about the more than 600 macro commands, we recommend that you obtain *WordPerfect for Windows Macros Manual*, which provides full descriptions of all macro commands. You can obtain this manual from WordPerfect Corporation.

Testing a Macro

Whenever you create or edit a macro, you should run the macro to have WordPerfect for Windows compile it. If the macro compiles and you receive no error messages, you're done. If the program encounters a syntax error during the compilation, it will display a message indicating the type of syntax error and the approximate location of the error.

Figure 12.4 illustrates such a message. You can choose to cancel compilation or to continue. If you continue, WordPerfect for Windows will compile the rest of the macro, displaying additional messages if it encounters syntax errors. You must fix all syntax errors before the macro will run. Use the information the program gave you in the syntax error messages to identify and correct the errors, then rerun the macro to compile it again.

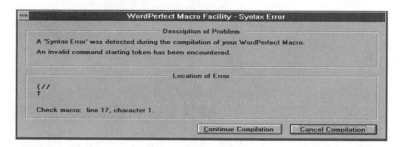

Figure 12.4   A syntax error message.

Adding Macros to the Macro Menu

If you frequently use certain macros, consider adding them to the Macro menu, where you can quickly select them. You can add up to nine macros to the Macro menu.

Adding a Macro to the Macro Menu

1. Select **Macro/Assign** to Menu. The Assign Macro to Menu dialog box appears, as shown in Figure 12.5. If you have assigned other macros to the Macro menu, they are listed in the dialog box.

2. Select Insert. The Insert Macro Menu Item dialog box appears, as shown in Figure 12.6.

3. Type the macro name in the Macro **N**ame text box. You can also enter a macro by selecting the List Button to display the Select File dialog box, and then selecting a file name from that dialog box.

4. In the Menu **T**ext text box, type the name you want to appear on the Macro menu. If you entered a descriptive name for the macro

when you created it, that name appears in the Menu **Text** text box. You can use this for the menu text, edit or delete it, and replace it with a different description.

5. Select OK. WordPerfect for Windows returns to the Assign Macro to Menu dialog box.

6. Select OK. You can now select the macro by selecting **M**acro to display the Macro menu and then selecting the macro item.

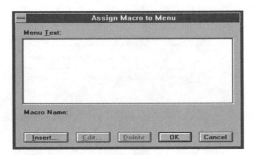

Figure 12.5   The Assign Macro to Menu dialog box.

To edit or delete a macro item on the Macro menu, display the Assign to Macro Menu dialog box, highlight the macro you want to edit or delete, and then select **E**dit or **D**elete. If you select Edit, the Edit Macro Menu Item dialog box appears. This is the same as the Insert Macro Menu Item dialog box, as shown in Figure 12.6. Edit the macro name and menu text, and then select OK to save it. The edited information appears in the Assign to Macro Menu dialog box. Select OK to close this dialog box.

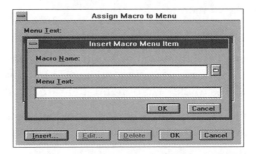

Figure 12.6   The Insert Macro Menu Item dialog box.

Adding Macros to the Button Bar

You can also assign macros to the Button Bar. To run the macro, just click on the button for that macro.

Adding a Macro to the Button Bar

1. Select **V**iew/Button Bar **S**etup/**E**dit. The current Button Bar and the Edit Button Bar dialog box appear.

2. Select **A**ssign Macro to Button. The Assign Macro to Button dialog box appears, listing the macros in your default macro directory.

3. Enter the macro name. If the macro is not in your default directory, also enter the directory path, for example, enter C:\WPWIN\TEL.WCM.

4. Select **A**ssign. WordPerfect for Windows adds a new button to the Button Bar. The button displays the macro name and an icon of a cassette (to symbolize a recording), as shown in Figure 12.7.

5. Select OK to close the Edit Button Bar dialog box.

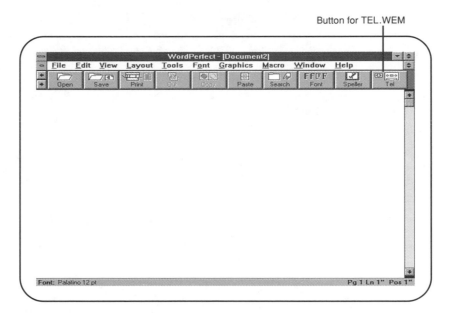

Figure 12.7   Button for the telephone message macro.

281

Summary

In this chapter, you learned how to run the telephone macro to document phone calls while working in WordPerfect for Windows. You also learned how to edit the macro for your own use. With this macro and the skills you learned, you can ensure that phone messages are documented in the proper format, and that the messages include all the necessary information. Since the messages are typed and printed using a computer, you'll no longer have to worry about receiving illegible messages.

The Telephone Message Application

While You Were Out

To: *Mary Kraynak*

Date/Time: *Feb 23, 1992*

Mr./Ms.? *Mr.*

Name: *Nicholas Alexander*

Of: *Alexander's Unlimited*

Left message: *Please call and confirm reservations for Friday's dinner.*

Please call at: *555-0000*

Urgent?: *N*

Will call again?: *Y*

Returned your call?: *N*

Turn side-by-side display off

1. Select **F**ile/**P**references/**D**isplay, or press Ctrl+Shift+F1 and type **d**.

2. Clear the Display **C**olumns Side by Side check box.

3. Select OK.

Define newspaper columns

1. Select **L**ayout/**C**olumns/**D**efine, or press Alt+Shift+F9 and type **d**.

2. Type the number of columns.

3. Select **N**ewspaper.

4. Enter margin settings or select **E**venly Spaced and then type the distance between columns.

5. Select OK.

Turn columns on

1. Select **L**ayout/**C**olumns/Columns **O**n, or press Alt+Shift+F9 and type **o**.

Turn columns off

1. Select **L**ayout/**C**olumns/Columns O**f**f, or press Alt+Shift+F9 and type **f**.

Set column margins

1. Select **L**ayout/**C**olumns/**D**efine, or press Alt+Shift+F9 and type **d**.

2. Enter margin settings or select **E**venly Spaced and type the distance between columns.

3. Select OK.

Set number of columns

1. Select **L**ayout/**C**olumns/**D**efine, or press Alt+Shift+F9 and type **d**.

2. Type the number of columns.

3. Select OK.

Set distance between columns

1. Select **L**ayout/**C**olumns/**D**efine, or press Alt+Shift+F9 and type **d**.

2. Enter margin settings or select **E**venly Spaced and type the distance between columns.

3. Select OK.

Protect block

1. Select the block of text you want to keep together.

2. Select **L**ayout/**P**age/**B**lock Protect, or press Alt+F9 and type **b**.

Insert paragraph number

1. Press Alt+F5 or select **T**ools/**O**utline/**P**aragraph Number.

2. Select **I**nsert.

BUSINESS
SHORTCUTS

Employee Questionnaire

In the past 10 years, a new emphasis has been placed on the relation-ship between hourly employees and management. Companies have found that listening to employees not only helps management make better decisions, but also makes the employees happier and more productive. The application in this chapter will help you gain insight into how your employees feel about their jobs, their supervisors, and the department in which they work. As you customize the application, you'll learn how to use the WordPerfect for Windows Newspaper Columns feature to modify the questionnaire and create similar forms.

About the Application

The employee questionnaire, included on disk and shown at the end of this chapter, consists of a series of questions, each with a set of corresponding choices. The application is formatted using the Newspaper Columns fea-ture, so the questions snake from the bottom of the left column to the top of the right column. Decimal tabs and indents are used to format the questions and choices. The decimal tabs align the question numbers at the period following each number, and the indents align the questions and choices to the right of the question numbers. To enter the question numbers, we used the Paragraph Numbering feature, which automatically enters the numbers in sequence. If you add or delete questions in the questionnaire, the question numbers automatically adjust so that they are sequential again.

Opening the Application

The employee questionnaire is in a file called EMPQUEST.APP on the disk that accompanies this book. When you open this file in the WordPerfect for Windows window, WordPerfect for Windows automatically reformats the file for the installed printer and displays the document on screen. You can then start to customize the document.

Customizing the Application

You can print the application as is and use it immediately, but you'll probably want to enter a few changes first. You may want to use a larger type size, add and delete questions and choices, or change the number of columns, the column widths, or the space between columns. The following sections explain how to make these adjustments.

Moving between Columns

The easiest way to move the cursor in newspaper columns is to use the mouse. Place the mouse pointer where you want the cursor and click the mouse button.

If you use the keyboard, remember that the cursor moves differently in columns than it does in normal text. Its movement in newspaper columns also differs slightly from that in parallel columns. Table 13.1 provides a list of the cursor movement keys and how they function in newspaper columns.

Table 13.1   Cursor keys for moving in newspaper columns

Press	To move
Left or Right Arrow	Left or right one character
Ctrl+Left arrow or Ctrl+Right Arrow	Left or right one word

Press	To move
Home	To the beginning of the line within the column
End	To the end of the line within the column
Up or Down arrow	Up or down one line
Alt+left arrow	One column to the left
Alt+Right Arrow	One column to the right

When you use the Left and Right Arrow keys, Ctrl+Left Arrow, and Ctrl+Right Arrow to move the cursor, the cursor snakes through the columns, moving through an entire column from top to bottom before moving to the top of the next column.

You can use the Go To command to move the cursor to a page, to the top or bottom of a column, to the next or previous column, or to the first or last column. Press Ctrl+G or select **E**dit/**G**o To to display the Go To dialog box. Next, select the **P**osition pop-up list button and then select the position where you want to move the cursor. Select OK to move the cursor to the selected position.

By default, WordPerfect for Windows displays columns side by side, so you can see how they'll appear when printed. Although this view of your columns is helpful when you're creating them, it can slow you down when you're entering and editing text. You can change the default so that the columns appear staggered on separate pages. In this mode, the cursor moves more quickly.

Turning Side-by-Side Display Off

1. Select **F**ile/**Pr**eferences/**D**isplay, or press Ctrl+Shift+F1 (Preferences) and type **d**. The Display Settings dialog box appears.

2. Deselect the Display **C**olumns Side by Side check box.

3. Select OK. The columns appear staggered on separate pages, as shown in Figure 13.1. This has no effect on the printed document. If you print it or use the Print Preview feature, WordPerfect for Windows displays the columns side by side.

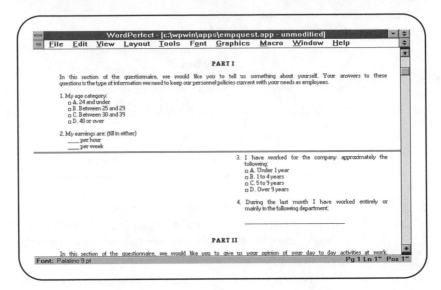

Figure 13.1   Side-by-side display turned off for newspaper columns.

Aligning Text

Before you begin customizing the document, view it in the Print Preview window to see how it will appear in print. To do this, press Shift+F5 or select **File/Print Preview**. The document may not look the same as the one at the end of this chapter. If your printer is set up to use a larger font, for example, the text may wrap differently, throwing off the alignment. A question that appears in the example as:

```
23. The cleanliness of the lunch room space is:
    ❑ A. Poor
    ❑ B. Fair
    ❑ C. Good
```

may appear in the Print Preview window as:

```
23. The cleanliness of the lunch room space is:
    ❑ A. Poor

    ❑ B. Fair

    ❑ C. Good
```

You can correct this problem in one of two ways. You can change the document initial font to use a 9-point type size (the size used in the example), or you can change the tab stops to realign the indents.

Changing a Document's Font

1. Select **L**ayout/**D**ocument/Initial **F**ont, or press Ctrl+Shift+F9 (Document) and type **f**. The Document Initial Font dialog box appears, listing available fonts.

2. Select a font that has a 9-point or 20-cpi (character per inch) type size. If you use a PostScript printer or scalable fonts, select any font on the list (size is not specified), and then type **9** in the Point Size text box.

3. Select OK. The selected font is now in effect for the document.

If you would rather use a larger type size, you can fix text alignment problems by changing the tab stop positions instead. The application contains a [Tab Set] code at the beginning of the document. The code sets the tab positions for the decimal tab and the indents in both columns of questions.

When you add a hanging indent to a paragraph, you move the entire paragraph (up to the next hard return to the right by one tab stop).

For example, in the following question

```
10. How well does your supervisor keep you
    informed on company policy plans and
    developments:
```

the period following the number 10 is aligned with the decimal tab stop which in the application is 0.25" from the left margin, and the question is indented to the next tab stop, five characters to the right of the first tab stop. The remaining two tab stops in the left column are also at intervals of 0.19". The right column has similar tab intervals. To change the tab stop position, follow these steps.

Adjusting Tab and Indents

1. Press Alt+F3 or select **V**iew/**R**eveal **C**odes to display the Reveal Codes screen.

2. Move the cursor immediately right of the [Tab Set] code at the top of the document.

3. Select **L**ayout/**L**ine/**T**ab Set, or press Shift+F9 (Line) and type **t**.

The Tab Set dialog box appears, as shown in Figure 13.2, listing the current tab stop positions in the **P**osition list box.

4. Highlight the tab stop position you want to change, and select Clear **T**ab. Notice that when you highlight a tab stop position, the position appears in the text box at the top of the **P**osition list box.

5. Select the **L**eft Align and Left **M**argin option buttons.

6. Place the cursor in the text box at the top of the **P**osition list box, delete any existing text, and type the position for the new tab.

7. Select **S**et Tab.

8. Select OK. WordPerfect for Windows returns you to the document window and inserts a [Tab Set] code, replacing any other [Tab Set] code there. (If you have turned Auto Code Placement off, the code does not replace any existing code.) The new tab stop settings take effect at this position.

Figure 13.2   The Tab Set dialog box.

You can also use the Ruler to change tab positions. Place the cursor where you want the new tab settings to begin. If the Ruler is not displayed, select Alt+Shift+F3 (Ruler) to display it. The current tab positions are shown by the triangles on the Ruler. Delete an existing tab by dragging it off the Ruler. Add a tab by dragging it from the tab button for that tab type to the Ruler. For additional information, see Chapter 2.

Replacing the Check Boxes

The small check boxes that appear next to the choices were created using WordPerfect for Windows Compose feature. This feature lets you insert characters from any of WordPerfect for Windows 13 character sets. You simply enter a code telling WordPerfect for Windows the number of the character set and the number of the character from that set. If your printer does not support the check box character, however, the check box might not appear in the printed version. In that case, replace the check box with a character that your printer does support, or with the underline character (_) from your keyboard.

If you have a laser or dot-matrix printer, WordPerfect for Windows will use its graphics capabilities to create the character if your printer does not specifically support the character.

Replacing the WordPerfect for Windows Character

1. Press Ctrl+Home to move the cursor to the top of the document.

2. Select **Edit/R**eplace or press Ctrl+F2 (Replace). The Search and Replace dialog box appears, as shown in Figure 13.3.

3. With the cursor in the Search For text box, press Ctrl+W to display the WordPerfect for Windows Characters dialog box (see Figure 13.3), type **6,93** in the **N**umber text box, and select Insert **a**nd Close. The specified WordPerfect for Windows character appears in the Search For text box.

4. Move the cursor to the Replace With text box.

5. To use the underline character from your keyboard, simply type that character. To use a WordPerfect for Windows character, press Ctrl+W to display with WordPerfect for Windows Characters dialog box; in the **N**umber text box, type the character set number, type a comma, and type the character number of the WordPerfect for Windows character you want to use; then select Insert **a**nd Close. The specified WordPerfect for Windows character appears in the Replace With text box.

6. Select Replace **A**ll to have WordPerfect for Windows replace all check boxes without asking you to confirm at each instance. Select Search **N**ext to have WordPerfect for Windows stop at each check box, allowing you each time to choose whether to replace it.

7. If you selected Search Next, WordPerfect for Windows stops on the first check box. Select **R**eplace to replace that check box and go to the next check box, or select Search Next to go to the next check box without replacing the current check box. You can also select Close to stop searching and replacing.

8. When WordPerfect for Windows finds no further check boxes, the Status bar displays the message `String not found`. Select Close in the Search and Replace dialog box to return to the document window.

You can move between the Search and Replace dialog box and the document window by just clicking on the window or the dialog box. This can be convenient if you want to search several noncontinous portions of a document. Search the first portion. Then, leaving the Search and Replace dialog box open, click on the document window and move the cursor to the beginning of the next part you want to search. Click on the Search and Replace dialog box to continue searching.

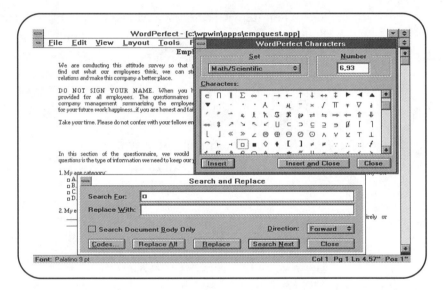

Figure 13.3   The Search and Replace dialog box and the WordPerfect for Windows Characters dialog box.

Deleting and Adding Questions

Once the text is aligned, you can delete or add questions to the questionnaire. Just remember to renumber the questions when you're finished.

Deleting a Question

1. Press Alt+F3 to display the Reveal Codes area. Each question is surrounded by several codes, as shown in Figure 13.4. When you

select a question, you should select the surrounding codes that affect it, to prevent wayward codes from affecting subsequent text.

2. Using the Reveal Codes area as a guide, move the cursor so that the Reveal Codes highlight in on the [Block Pro: On] code before the question you want to delete.

3. Select the entire question, including the [Block Pro: On] code preceding it, the lettered choices below it, and the [HRt][Block Pro: Off][HRt] codes following the choices.

4. Press Delete to delete the question and its corresponding choices. The question is deleted.

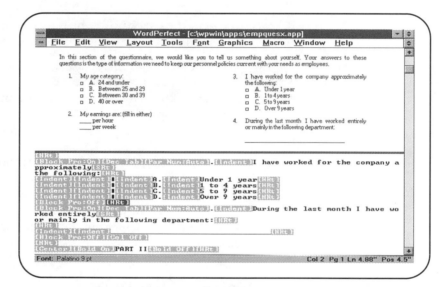

Figure 13.4 Reveal Codes shows codes that you might want to include in the selected block.

To add questions to the form, you must insert the decimal tab, automatic paragraph number, indent for each question, and insert the indents and check box for each choice listed under the question.

Adding Questions

1. Move the cursor just past the [Block Pro:Off] code that follows the preceding question, and press Enter to insert a one-line space between the questions.

2. Press Tab to insert the decimal tab.

3. Press Alt+F5 (Paragraph Number) or select Tools/Outline/Paragraph Number. In the Paragraph Numbering dialog box that appears, leave Auto selected and then select Insert. The question number appears in the document window and subsequent question numbers are automatically adjusted to follow in sequence. In the Reveal Codes screen, the number appears as a [Par Num: Auto] code.

4. Type a period following the question number.

5. Press F7 (Indent) to indent the question.

6. Type the question, and then press Enter to start the choices on the next line.

7. Press F7 twice to indent the check box (which you create in the next step) so that it is aligned flush left with the question.

8. Press Ctrl+W, then type **6,93** and select Insert and Close to create a check box before the choice. If your printer does not support this WordPerfect for Windows character, you can type an underline character (_) directly from your keyboard, instead.

9. Press F7.

10. Type the letter of the choice, type a period, and then press F7.

11. Type the text for the choice, and then press Enter.

12. Repeat steps 7 through 11 to list the remaining choices. The question and its choices should appear in the Reveal Codes area as shown in Figure 13.5.

Keeping a Block Together

In newspaper columns, any text that cannot fit in one column is automatically wrapped to the top of the next column. In a questionnaire, that could cause problems. You may end up with a question at the bottom of one column and the choices at the top of the next column or even on the next page. In the application, we used the Block Protect feature to keep each question with its set of choices. If you add new questions, you should use Block Protect to keep the new questions and choices form splitting across columns or pages.

Protecting a Block

1. Select the block you want to protect, including any codes that apply to the block. For example, if you want to protect a question and its

choices, highlight text and codes from the [Dec Tab] code before
the question to the [HRt] code at the end of the last choice. Don't
highlight the [HRt] code between questions. This [HRt] code can
float, giving WordPerfect for Windows some flexibility in breaking
the columns.

2. Select **L**ayout/**P**age/**B**lock Protect, or press Alt+F9 (Page) and
type **b**.

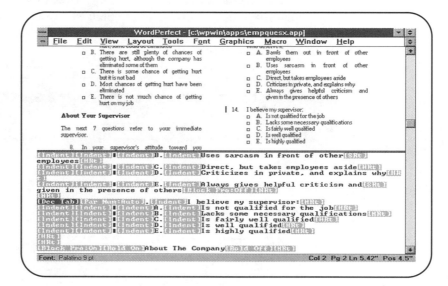

Figure 13.5 Question 14 as displayed in the Reveal Codes area.

Adding Text Outside Columns

In the application, you can see that several paragraphs do not appear in the
column format. To enter paragraphs such as these, you must turn Columns
off before entering the text, and then turn Columns back on afterward.

Turning Columns Off

1. Move the cursor where you want to turn Columns off.

2. Select **L**ayout/**C**olumns/Columns **Off**, or press Alt+Shift+F9
(Columns) and type **f**. WordPerfect for Windows inserts a [Col Off]
code at the cursor location.

Turning Columns On

1. Move the cursor to the line where you want to start typing text in columns.

2. Select **Layout/Columns/Columns On**, or press Alt+Shift+F9 (Columns) and type **o**. WordPerfect for Windows inserts a [Col On] code at the cursor location.

You can also use the Ruler, shown in Figure 13.6, to turn Columns on and off. Display the Ruler by pressing Alt+Shift+F3 or by selecting **View/Ruler**. Select the Columns pop-up list button and then select Columns On or Columns Off from the pop-up list.

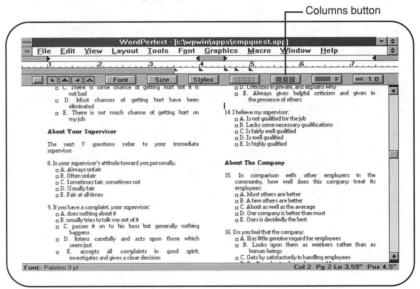

Figure 13.6   You can turn Columns on and off by selecting the Columns button and then selecting Columns On or Columns Off.

Modifying Columns

You can change column widths, the number of columns, and the distance between columns at any point in the document by redefining the columns. When you define columns, WordPerfect for Windows inserts a [Col Def] code at the cursor location. This code controls column formatting up to the next [Col Def] code or until the end of the document.

Redefining Columns

1. Move the cursor just past the [Col Def] code.

2. Select **Layout/Columns/Define**, or press Alt+Shift+F9 (Columns) and type **d**. The Define Columns dialog box appears, as shown in Figure 13.7.

3. In the **Number of Columns** text box, type the number of columns you want across the page.

4. Select **Newspaper** as the column type. WordPerfect for Windows assumes you want columns of equal width and calculates the column margins, assuming the distance between columns is 0.5". The **Margins** text boxes show the resulting margins for each column.

5. To change the distance between columns, type a new measurement in the **Distance Between Columns** text box. WordPerfect for Windows automatically recalculates the margins in the **Margins** text boxes.

6. To create columns of unequal width, go to the **Margins** text boxes and type the left and right margin settings for each column. WordPerfect for Windows automatically deselects the **Evenly Spaced** check box. The next time you open the dialog box, the **Distance Between Columns** box also is updated.

7. For this application, deselect the **Column On** check box. (The Column feature is turned on already, so leaving this selected would insert unnecessary additional codes).

8. Select **OK**. If you are using WordPerfect for Windows default setting for Auto Code Placement, WordPerfect for Windows replaces the original [Col Def] code with the new one. (See Chapter 2 for information on the Auto Code Placement feature.)

To change only the column margins, you can use the Ruler. The Ruler allows you to set margins in 1/16" increments (for more information on this, see the Ruler discussion in "Environment" of Appendix C). If you need more precise margins, use the Define Columns dialog box. You can use the Ruler to change the column widths for Newspaper or Parallel columns.

Beginner's Tip

You can display the Define Columns dialog box by double-clicking on the Columns button on the Ruler.

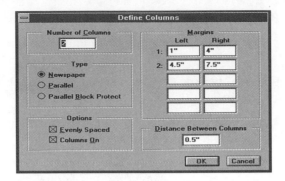

Figure 13.7   The Define Columns dialog box.

Using the Ruler to Change Column Widths

1. Place the cursor anywhere in the columns whose widths you want to change.

2. To display the Ruler, select **View/R**uler or press Alt+Shift+F3. Notice that the margin indicators on the Ruler show the column margins, as noted in Figure 13.8.

3. For each margin you want to change, drag the corresponding margin marker to the new position. WordPerfect for Windows revises the [Col Def] code to reflect the new column margins.

The Ruler also offers a way to create simple Newspaper columns. You can use it to define evenly spaced Newspaper columns having two to five columns. WordPerfect for Windows places 0.5" between each column. For more complicated columns, use the Define Columns dialog box.

Using the Ruler to Create Newspaper Columns

1. Move the cursor where you want the columns to begin. Make sure it is not within any current columns.

2. If the Ruler is not displayed, select **View/R**uler or press Alt+Shift+F3 (Ruler). The Ruler appears.

3. Place the mouse pointer on the Columns button and press and hold the mouse button to display a list of options.

4. Highlight the number of columns you want: 2, 3, 4, or 5 columns.

5. Release the mouse button. WordPerfect for Windows inserts a [Col Def] code and turns Columns on.

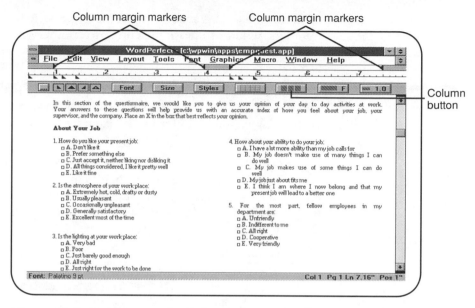

Figure 13.8 You can use the Ruler to create simple Newspaper columns and change column margins.

You can have several different column definitions in one document. To enter a new definition, turn Columns off, enter a [Col Def] code for the new columns as explained above, and then turn Columns on.

Changing the Paragraph Numbering

In Chapter 10, you learned how to use the Define Paragraph Numbering dialog box to select a style for automatic numbers. The numbering style EMPQUEST.APP is digits: 1, 2, 3, and so on. To define this style, you can follow these steps:

1. Place the cursor where you want the numbering style to take effect.

2. Select **T**ools/**O**utline/**D**efine or press Alt+Shift+F5 (Paragraph Def). The Define Paragraph Numbering dialog box appears, as shown in Figure 13.9.

3. In the **L**evel list box, Level 1 should be highlighted. If it isn't, highlight it.

4. Select the **S**tyle drop-down list button (denoted by a button with a left-pointing arrowhead), and then select **1** Digits from the

drop-down list. This action assigns the Digits style to first-level numbers. When you move the cursor to another option in the dialog box, the style appears across from Level 1 in the Level list box.

5. Clear the check boxes titled **Outline On** and **Enter Inserts Paragraph Number**. (Clearing the latter check box is optional: If you clear **Outline On**, the **Enter Inserts Paragraph Number** option cannot take effect even if selected.)

6. Select OK. The dialog box closes and a [Par Num Def] code appears in the Reveal Codes screen at the beginning of the paragraph containing the cursor (if Auto Code Placement is off, it appears at the cursor location). In EMPQUEST, the code is at the beginning of the columns in Part I.

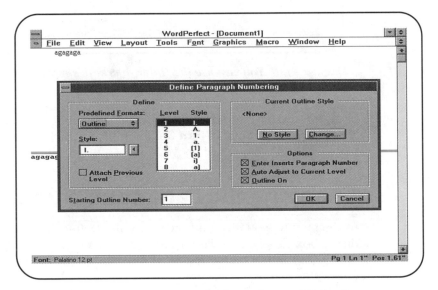

Figure 13.9   The Define Paragraph Numbering dialog box.

Since numbered lists typically only use one numbering level, you need not select a numbering style for other numbering levels in the Level list box. You can just leave the default entries.

If you want to use a different numbering style, open the Define Paragraph Numbering dialog box and select one of the predefined formats or define your own format. See Chapter 10 for details.

EMPQUEST.APP has a second [Par Def] code, at the beginning of Part II, which restarts the question numbers in Part II at 1. If you add a Part III, you might want to restart the question numbers again.

Restarting Paragraph Numbers

1. Place the cursor where you want the numbering to restart.

2. Select **T**ools/**O**utline/**D**efine or press Alt+Shift+F5 (Paragraph Def). The Define Paragraph Numbering dialog box appears, as shown in Figure 13.9.

3. If the value in the Starting Outline Number text box isn't 1, go to the text box and enter 1 (or whatever number you want as the starting number).

4. Clear the check boxes titled **O**utline On and **E**nter Inserts Paragraph Number.

5. Select OK. The dialog box closes and a [Par Num Def] code appears in the Reveal Codes screen at the beginning of the paragraph containing the cursor (if Auto Code Placement is off, it appears at the cursor location).

Summary

The employee questionnaire uses the Newspaper Columns feature to format columns of questions that wrap from one column to the next. Indents keep the entries from appearing cluttered and Block Protect keeps each question and its set of choices from splitting across columns and pages. Automatic paragraph numbering allows you to edit the numbered questions without having to manually renumber the questions. With these tools and the application included on disk, you can create and modify any form that requires wrapping columns and numbered lists—from newsletters and reports to phone lists and rosters.

The Employee Questionnaire

(Page 1 of 3)

Employee Questionnaire

We are conducting this attitude survey so that you can state clearly and openly how feel about your job. If we can find out what our employees think, we can strengthen and improve management policies and management-employee relations and make this company a better place.

DO NOT SIGN YOUR NAME. When you have finished filling out this questionnaire, place it in the locked box provided for all employees. The questionnaires will be tabulated and analyzed and a report will be made to the company management summarizing the employee viewpoints expressed in the surveys. This study can be important for your future work happiness...if you are honest and fair in your replies.

Take your time. Please do not confer with your fellow employees as to how you should answer any of the questions.

PART I

In this section of the questionnaire, we would like you to tell us something about yourself. Your answers to these questions is the type of information we need to keep our personnel policies current with your needs as employees.

1. My age category:
   - ☐ A. 24 and under
   - ☐ B. Between 25 and 29
   - ☐ C. Between 30 and 39
   - ☐ D. 40 or over

2. My earnings are: (fill in either)
   - ____ per hour
   - ____ per week

3. I have worked for the company approximately the following:
   - ☐ A. Under 1 year
   - ☐ B. 1 to 4 years
   - ☐ C. 5 to 9 years
   - ☐ D. Over 9 years

4. During the last month I have worked entirely or mainly in the following department:

   _____

PART II

In this section of the questionnaire, we would like you to give us your opinion of your day to day activities at work. Your answers to these questions will help provide us with an accurate index of how you feel about your job, your supervisor, and the company. Place an X in the box that best reflects your opinion.

About Your Job

1. How do you like your present job:
   - ☐ A. Don't like it
   - ☐ B. Prefer something else
   - ☐ C. Just accept it, neither liking nor disliking it
   - ☐ D. All things considered, I like it pretty well
   - ☐ E. Like it fine

2. Is the atmosphere of your work place:
   - ☐ A. Extremely hot, cold, drafty or dusty
   - ☐ B. Usually pleasant
   - ☐ C. Occasionally unpleasant
   - ☐ D. Generally satisfactory
   - ☐ E. Excellent most of the time

3. Is the lighting at your work place:
   - ☐ A. Very bad
   - ☐ B. Poor
   - ☐ C. Just barely good enough
   - ☐ D. All right
   - ☐ E. Just right for the work to be done

4. How about your ability to do your job:
   - ☐ A. I have a lot more ability than my job calls for
   - ☐ B. My job doesn't make use of many things I can do well
   - ☐ C. My job makes use of some things I can do well
   - ☐ D. My job just about fits me
   - ☐ E. I think I am where I now belong and that my present job will lead to a better one

5. For the most part, fellow employees in my department are:
   - ☐ A. Unfriendly
   - ☐ B. Indifferent to me
   - ☐ C. All right
   - ☐ D. Cooperative
   - ☐ E. Very friendly

The Employee Questionnaire

(Page 2 of 3)

6. Compared to other pay rates in the company, do you consider your rate:
   - ☐ A. Extremely low
   - ☐ B. On the low side
   - ☐ C. About right
   - ☐ D. Above average
   - ☐ E. Generous

7. How about the chances of getting hurt on your job:
   - ☐ A. There are lots of chances of getting hurt, some could be eliminated
   - ☐ B. There are still plenty of chances of getting hurt, although the company has eliminated some of them
   - ☐ C. There is some chance of getting hurt but it is not bad
   - ☐ D. Most chances of getting hurt have been eliminated
   - ☐ E. There is not much chance of getting hurt on my job

About Your Supervisor

The next 7 questions refer to your immediate supervisor

8. In your supervisor's attitude toward you personally,
   - ☐ A. Always unfair
   - ☐ B. Often unfair
   - ☐ C. Sometimes fair, sometimes not
   - ☐ D. Usually fair
   - ☐ E. Fair at all times

9. If you have a complaint, your supervisor:
   - ☐ A. does nothing about it
   - ☐ B. usually tries to talk me out of it
   - ☐ C. passes it on to his boss but generally nothing happens
   - ☐ D. listens carefully and acts upon those which seem just
   - ☐ E. accepts all complaints in good spirit, investigates and gives a clear decision

10. How well does your supervisor keep you informed on company policy, plans and developments:
    - ☐ A. None of the time
    - ☐ B. Seems not too well informed himself
    - ☐ C. Informs me some of the time
    - ☐ D. Informs me most of the time
    - ☐ E. Informs me all of the time

11. How well does he or she plan the work of your group:
    - ☐ A. There is no planning
    - ☐ B. Occasional planning, but not good
    - ☐ C. Tries to plan most of it
    - ☐ D. Plans regularly
    - ☐ E. Plans carefully and systematically

12. How well does he or she explain new things to employees:
    - ☐ A. Never bothers
    - ☐ B. Gives unclear explanations
    - ☐ C. Explains well sometimes
    - ☐ D. Gives clear instructions most of the time
    - ☐ E. Explains carefully and patiently all of the time

13. How well does he or she discipline employees who deserve it:
    - ☐ A. Bawls them out in front of other employees
    - ☐ B. Uses sarcasm in front of other employees
    - ☐ C. Direct, but takes employees aside
    - ☐ D. Criticizes in private, and explains why
    - ☐ E. Always gives helpful criticism and given in the presence of others

14. I believe my supervisor:
    - ☐ A. Is not qualified for the job
    - ☐ B. Lacks some necessary qualifications
    - ☐ C. Is fairly well qualified
    - ☐ D. Is well qualified
    - ☐ E. Is highly qualified

About The Company

15. In comparison with other employers in the community, how well does this company treat its employees:
    - ☐ A. Most others are better
    - ☐ B. A few others are better
    - ☐ C. About as well as the average
    - ☐ D. Our company is better than most
    - ☐ E. Ours is decidedly the best

16. Do you feel that the company:
    - ☐ A. Has little genuine regard for employees
    - ☐ B. Looks upon them as workers rather than as human beings
    - ☐ C. Gets by satisfactorily in handling employees
    - ☐ D. Really understands employee problems
    - ☐ E. Shows high regard for the employee's welfare

17. In its relationship with the community, I believe our company:
    - ☐ A. Has built ill will
    - ☐ B. Does not have the respect of the citizens
    - ☐ C. Should do more than it has
    - ☐ D. Has built some good will
    - ☐ E. Has built a lot of good will

18. When you tell your friends what company you work for, how do you feel:
    - ☐ A. Ashamed to admit it
    - ☐ B. Not happy about it
    - ☐ C. Neutral about it
    - ☐ D. Glad you don't work for certain other companies
    - ☐ E. Proud to tell it

The Employee Questionnaire

(Page 3 of 3)

19. In its relations between employees and management, I think the company:
    - ☐ A. Is doing a poor job
    - ☐ B. Has considerable room for improvement
    - ☐ C. Is about average
    - ☐ D. Is pretty good
    - ☐ E. Is decidedly outstanding

20. Which one of the following in your opinion shows greatest consideration to employees:
    - ☐ A. Your immediate supervisor
    - ☐ B. Manager of the department
    - ☐ C. Top management of the company

21. Which one of the following in your opinion shows the least consideration to employees:
    - ☐ A. Your immediate supervisor
    - ☐ B. Manager of the department
    - ☐ C. Top management of the company

22. The care and maintenance given to washrooms and toilets is:
    - ☐ A. Poor
    - ☐ B. Fair
    - ☐ C. Good

23. The cleanliness of the lunch room space is:
    - ☐ A. Poor
    - ☐ B. Fair
    - ☐ C. Good

24. The food and vending machines are:
    - ☐ A. Poor
    - ☐ B. O.K.
    - ☐ C. Good

25. Prices at the cafeteria are:
    - ☐ A. Entirely too high
    - ☐ B. O.K.
    - ☐ C. Reasonable

26. What percentage of profit on sales after paying taxes do you think the company makes:
    - ☐ A. 1%
    - ☐ B. 5%
    - ☐ C. 10%
    - ☐ D. 15%
    - ☐ E. 20% or more

27. What is your opinion of our method of inducting and training new employees:
    - ☐ A. Not enough attention is given to these new employees
    - ☐ B. I have no opinion on this matter
    - ☐ C. They are being treated well and are properly trained

28. How much do you think the company has to pay for hospitalization insurance for each employee annually:
    - ☐ A. $50-$99
    - ☐ B. $100-$149
    - ☐ C. $150-$199
    - ☐ D. $200-$249
    - ☐ E. $250 and over

29. Do you feel that prompt action is taken on safety recommendations:
    - ☐ A. No
    - ☐ B. Sometimes
    - ☐ C. Yes

30. Do you frequently receive orders from more than one person?
    - ☐ A. No
    - ☐ B. Yes

31. If you answered "yes" above, do orders sometimes conflict:
    - ☐ A. No
    - ☐ B. Yes

32. How do you feel about working overtime:
    - ☐ A. Do not like it at all
    - ☐ B. Do not mind it occasionally
    - ☐ C. Neutral about it
    - ☐ D. Like it all the time

Import a figure

1. Place the cursor where you want the figure.

2. Select **Graphics/Figure/Edit** or press Shift+F11.

3. Type the Figure box number and select OK.

4. Select **File/Retrieve** or select the Retrieve button.

5. Enter a file name.

6. Select **Retrieve**.

7. Select **File/Close** or the Close button.

Change figure box options

1. Highlight the [Fig Box] code for the figure box.

2. Select **Graphics/Figure/Options**.

3. Select the box options you want.

4. Select OK.

Designing Letterhead

The "business of business" is communication, and a large part of communication is handled through letters. From your initial contact with a customer through follow-up contacts, public relations messages, and announcements of new product lines, you use letters to communicate. You want those letters to look professional. Until now, you have probably had to hire a printer to design and print special letterhead, but with WordPerfect for Windows' Graphics feature and the application in this chapter, you can design your own letterhead and use it as a template when you send a letter. Your printer will print the letterhead at the same time it prints the letter.

About the Application

The letterhead application is simple. It consists of a 1" by 1" Graphics box in the Upper Left corner of the page. This box lets you import a figure, as shown in the example at the end of this chapter. The heading of the letter is set in a large font. A [Date] code following the heading inserts the current date from your computer into any letter you create using this template. The rest of the letter is a normal WordPerfect for Windows document.

Opening the Application

To customize the letterhead application, open the file named LETTER.APP, which is on the disk that accompanies this book. The file appears in the WordPerfect for Windows window as shown in Figure 14.1.

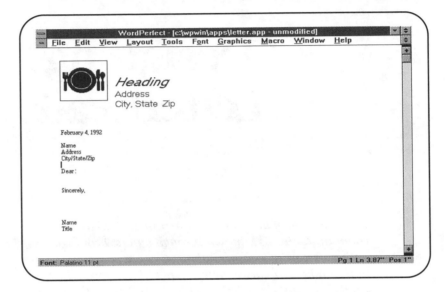

***Figure 14.1   LETTER.APP** displayed in the document window.*

Customizing the Letterhead

To customize the letterhead application, you import a graphics file into the Figure box and type your own text for the heading. You can also change the Figure box options to modify the border of the box and to add shading. To customize the letterhead even further, you can add vertical or horizontal lines and text boxes, as explained in Chapters 3 and 8.

Working with Graphics Files

The Figure box in the upper left corner of the application lets you import a graphics file into the document. You tell WordPerfect for Windows which directory contains the graphics file and the file name and WordPerfect for Windows imports the file into the box. You can then edit the figure, change its location and size, and change the Figure box borders and shading.

The WordPerfect for Windows program disks contain compressed WordPerfect for Windows graphics (.WPG) files. If you performed a basic installation (or a custom installation in which you chose to copy those files), then the files were placed in the default graphics directory (for example, C:\WPWIN\GRAPHICS). If you have other graphics files and they're in a format that WordPerfect for Windows supports, you can import one of those figures instead. The reference manual that accompanied your WordPerfect for Windows package lists the formats supported by WordPerfect for Windows.

Importing a Different Graphic

1. Select **Graphics/Figure/Edit** or press Shift+F11 (Figure Edit). WordPerfect for Windows prompts you to enter the number of the Figure box you want to edit.

2. Type **1** (the Figure box number) and select OK. The Figure Editor window appears, as shown in Figure 14.2, displaying the current graphic image.

3. Select **File/Retrieve** or select the Retrieve button. WordPerfect for Windows displays the Retrieve Figure dialog box, which lists graphics files in your default graphics directory.

4. Enter a file name, including the full directory path if the file is not in the default graphics directory. (For information about listing files in other directories, see Appendix D.)

5. Select **Retrieve**. WordPerfect for Windows returns to the Figure Editor window, which displays the new figure.

6. Select **File/Close** or the Close button. WordPerfect for Windows saves the change and returns to the document window.

Beginner's Tip

If you have a mouse, you can replace the first two steps with the following: Place the mouse pointer within Figure Box 1. The Status bar displays the prompt `Fig Box 1 - Use right mouse button to display Graphics menu`. Click the *right* mouse button; then click on Edit Figure with the *left* mouse button.

Figure 14.2   The Figure Editor window.

Editing the Figure

In addition to letting you import a wide variety of graphics into your documents, WordPerfect for Windows lets you manipulate those graphics. If you display the graphics in the Figure Editor window, shown in Figure 14.2, you can use the Figure Editor to rotate the figure, scale the figure height and width in different percentages to make the figure appear oblong, change color figures to black and white, and more. You can also move and resize the figure. Refer to Chapter 3 for more information.

Changing Figure Box Borders and Shading

When you create a Figure box, WordPerfect for Windows formats the box according to a list of default settings. By default, all Figure boxes have a thin black border on all four sides and no gray shading inside the box. You can change these settings by entering a [Fig Opt] code before the Figure box whose format you want to change. This code controls the appearance of all Figure boxes up to the next [Fig Opt] code or until the end of the document.

Enter Figure box settings in the Figure Options dialog box, shown in Figure 14.3. This dialog box offers the following options that you might find useful for this application:

Border Styles: You can select no lines or single, dashed, double, dotted, thick, or extra thick lines. You can vary line thickness to create a drop-shadow for your box. Set the border line to **Extra Thick** for the right and bottom borders and to **Single** for the left and top borders. Some examples are shown in Figure 14.4.

Border Spacing: Type the amount of white space you want between the borders and the graphic inside the box, and between the borders and the text outside the box. Use the Outside **Right** text box to enter the amount of space between the border and the letter heading.

WordPerfect for Windows increases the white space between the figure box border and the graphic inside the box by reducing the figure size. The box still displays the entire figure, just at a smaller size.

Gray Shading: Lets you shade your box. A value of 0% adds no shading. A value of 100% makes the box completely black. By default, Figure boxes have no shading.

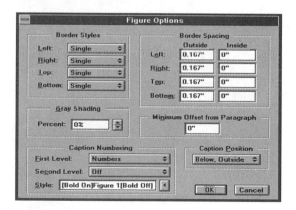

Figure 14.3   The Figure Options dialog box.

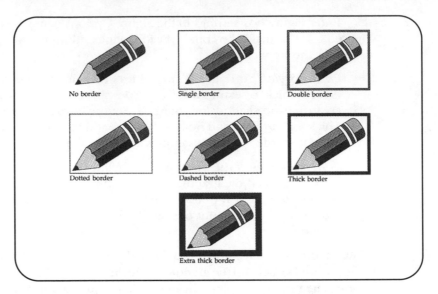

Figure 14.4   The effects of various border options.

Changing Figure Box Options

1. Select **V**iew/Reveal **C**odes or press Alt+F3. The Reveal Codes area appears.

2. Highlight the [Fig Box] code for the Figure box, so that the [Fig Opt] code will be inserted just before that box.

3. Select **G**raphics/**F**igure/**O**ptions. The Figure Options dialog box appears.

4. Select the box options you want.

5. Select OK. WordPerfect for Windows returns you to the document window and inserts a [Fig Opt] code specifying the new options.

6. If there is previous [Fig Opt] code for the Figure box whose options changed and the code does not set options for other figure boxes, you can delete that code.

Entering Text for the Heading

Once your graphics options are set, you can enter the heading, which is the name and address of your business or organization. Before you begin, press Alt+F3 to display the Reveal Codes area, so you can see the type style and font codes that affect the text. If you type the text outside these codes, it will not appear in the selected style.

Entering Text

1. Move the cursor after the [Italc On] code before the word Heading. The cursor must be between the [Italc On] and [Italc Off] codes for the company name to appear italic.

2. Type the name of your company or organization, and delete the word Heading.

3. Press the Right Arrow key three times to move the cursor past the [Italc Off] code and past the [Font] code for the address.

4. Type the street address of your business or organization, press Enter, and type the city, state, and ZIP code.

5. Delete the words Address, City, State, and Zip.

Adjusting Heading Size and Position

Your letterhead is nearing completion. Press Shift+F5 or select File/Print Preview to view it. Your printer may not support some of the fonts used to create the application, so you may need to change fonts or advance the text up, down, left, or right to fine-tune the template.

Changing Fonts

1. Move the cursor immediately before the first character you want the font change to affect. (In the Reveal Codes area, the highlight should be on the first character.)

2. Press F9 (Font) or select Font/Font. The Font dialog box appears, listing available fonts.

3. Select the font you want. If you have a PostScript printer or scalable fonts, enter a point size also.

4. Select OK. WordPerfect for Windows inserts a [Font] code for the selected font.

5. Press the Left Arrow key until the highlight in the Reveal Codes area is on the old [Font] code, and press Delete.

The best way to add more space between the Figure box and the text of the heading is to change the Figure box options as explained above, increasing the outside border space. If you want to move the text up or down in relation to the Graphics box, however, you can insert an [Adv] (Advance) code. This code shifts the text the specified distance and direction from its current location. For example, you can advance the text in the heading up near the top of the figure box, as shown in Figure 14.5.

Figure 14.5   Advancing text to adjust its position on the page.

Advancing Text

1. Move the cursor to the first character you want to advance.

2. Select **Layout/Advance**. The Advance dialog box appears.

3. Select the direction in which you want to advance the text: **Up**, **Down**, **Left**, or **Right**.

4. Go to the **Advance** text box and type the distance you want to advance the text.

5. Select OK. WordPerfect for Windows inserts an [Adv] code that specifies the distance and direction to advance the text.

Instead of advancing the text in increments from the current position, you can advance the text to an absolute position or line on the page, by selecting To **P**osition or To **L**ine from the list of options. To **P**osition lets you specify a position measured from the left edge of the page. To **L**ine lets you specify a position measured from the top edge of the page. Refer to Chapter 8 for more information.

Saving the Template

After you have customized your letterhead, save it to disk under another name. Whenever you need to create a letter, simply open the letterhead template, type the letter, print it, and save it under its own name.

 You can use this letterhead along with the Merge feature explained in Chapter 9. By typing {FIELD} codes in your letterhead template, you can have the template retrieve information, such as names and addresses, from another WordPerfect for Windows file. The information is inserted in the proper location in the template.

Summary

Now that you have a customized letterhead in an electronic file, creating and printing letters is a snap. You no longer have to worry about keeping enough letterhead paper in stock, positioning the letterhead correctly in your printer, or wasting expensive letterhead paper whenever you decide to revise a letter. You can change your letterhead without hiring a professional designer or waiting for letterhead to be printed. Just import a different graphic into the Figure box, change the fonts, and you have a completely new look.

The Letterhead Application

 Restaurant Association of America
1535 Sugar Way
Tempe, AZ 12345

February 4, 1992

Mr. Mike Ott
1812 Border Village Way
Boulder, CO 12345

Dear Restaurateur:

Once again, convention time is upon us. I am writing to see if you're interested in participating in some of the pre-session that will be offered at both the Williams-on-the-Court and the Evergreen Hotels on November 15 and 16. You should be receiving details about these sessions during the first week of August.

A matter of business that will be considered on the main convention floor is the election of new officers. Preliminary voting will be at 9 a.m. on the 15th. All the present officers hope that you can attend and listen to the candidates' statements on the issues that are before us.

If you have questions about convention business, including accommodations, please call me at your convenience. I look forward to seeing you in Seattle.

Sincerely,

Davis Michaels
Secretary
RAA

Compare documents

1. Open the revised document.

2. Select **Tools/Document Compare/Add Markings.**

3. Type the name of the disk file you want to compare.

4. Select **Compare.**

Remove redlining and strikeout

1. Select **Tools/Document Compare/Remove Markings.**

2. To keep redline text, select Leave **Redline** Marks check box.

3. Select OK.

Create a document summary

1. Select **Layout/Document/Summary,** or press Ctrl+Shift+F9 and type **s.**

2. Enter information.

3. Select OK.

Insert a nonprinting comment

1. Place the cursor where you want the comment inserted.

2. Select **Tools/Comment/Create.**

3. Type the comment.

4. Select OK.

Assign a password

1. Open the document to which you are assigning a password.

2. Select **File/Password.**

3. Type the password and select **Set.**

4. Type the same password again and select **Set.**

5. Save the file under its original name.

BUSINESS
SHORTCUTS

Real Estate Contract

Many businesses are involved with purchasing and selling property. Whether the property is land or a building, the parties involved in the exchange must sign a contract that sets forth the terms of the agreement. The real estate contract included on disk and explained in this chapter provides a starting point for such a contract. As you work through the chapter, you will revise the contract to suit your needs, and you will add nonprinting comments in the document to help a colleague understand your revisions. You'll also work with the Document Compare feature to determine how the contract has changed from revision to revision. Finally, you'll create a summary to help you find the document later.

About the Application

The real estate contract is one of the most basic WordPerfect for Windows documents included in this book. The heading of the contract is centered and set in a larger font than is the rest of the document, but the remaining text is straightforward. You can almost use the application "as is" by substituting specific information at each asterisk (*).

However, laws concerning real estate may vary from state to state or county to county, so you should have your lawyer check the contract before using it. And even after your lawyer enters changes, the contract may not be final. Most contracts vary from one transaction to another, depending on the property and parties involved. So, unlike previous chapters that focused on formatting the application, this chapter focuses on the features that help you manage a document from its inception to its final form: WordPerfect for Windows' Document Compare, Comment, and Document Summary features.

Opening the Application

To work with the contract, open the file named CONTRACT.APP. When you open the file, WordPerfect for Windows automatically reformats it for the selected printer, so the contract may differ in appearance from the example shown at the end of this chapter.

Customizing the Application

You can use this application as is by replacing each asterisk with information specific to this transaction. When you're done, the application should appear similar to the application at the end of the chapter.

Replacing Asterisks with Text

1. Select Edit/Search or press F2 (Search). The Search dialog box appears.

2. In the Search For text box, type * and then select Search. WordPerfect for Windows searches for an asterisk and stops to the right of the first asterisk it finds.

3. Press Backspace to delete the asterisk, and type the required information. Whatever you type appears in italics.

4. Press Shift+F2 to search for the next asterisk.

5. Repeat steps 3 and 4 until you've replaced all the asterisks with the required information.

The italics highlight the new text, making it easy for you to find and proofread it quickly. To remove the italics from the final contract, use the Replace feature to search for either the [Italc On] or the [Italc Off] code and replace it with nothing. When you delete one of these paired codes, WordPerfect for Windows automatically deletes the other.

Removing Italics

1. Place the cursor at the beginning of the document.

2. Select **Edit/R**eplace or press Ctrl+F2. The Search and Replace dialog box appears, with the cursor in the Search **F**or text box.

3. If the Search **F**or text box contains any text or codes, delete the text or codes.

4. Keeping the cursor in the Search **F**or text box, select the Codes button. The Codes dialog box appears.

5. Type **it** to highlight Italc Off. (You can highlight a code name by typing the first few letters of the code name.)

6. Select Insert and then select Close. An [Italc Off] code appears in the Search **F**or text box.

7. If the Replace **W**ith text box contains any text, delete it.

8. Select Replace **A**ll to have WordPerfect for Windows replace all [Italc Off] and [Italc On] codes without asking you to confirm at each instance. Select Search **N**ext to have WordPerfect for Windows stop at each [Italc Off] code, allowing you each time to choose whether to replace it.

9. If you selected Search **N**ext, WordPerfect for Windows stops on the first [Italc Off] code and displays the Search and Replace dialog box. Select **R**eplace to delete that set of paired [Italc] codes and go to the next [Italc Off] code, or select Search **N**ext to go to the next code without replacing the current code. You can also select Close to stop searching and replacing.

10. When WordPerfect for Windows finds no further [Italc Off] codes, the status bar displays the message String not found. Select Close in the Search and Replace dialog box to return to the document window.

Save the contract under a different file name, so that you still have the original application. You can then print the file and use it for your transaction.

Comparing Drafts

If you edit the contract application before using it, you may want to use WordPerfect for Windows' Document Compare feature to create an *edit trail*—a history of the various revisions. This feature compares the on-screen, revised document to the old version on disk and marks the on-screen version in the following ways, showing what has been added, erased, or moved:

- Redlined text—Redline codes ([Redln]) are inserted before and after text that has been added. On color monitors, the text between the codes is red. On monochrome monitors, redline text appears boldface.

- Strikeout text—Strikeout codes ([Stkout]) are inserted before and after text that has been deleted. Between the codes, the strikeout text is marked by a horizontal line through the text.

- Moved text—If text was moved, prompts appear before and after the section that has been moved.

Let's say that Joan Fisher (the seller) revises the contract. She sends the revised contract, on disk, to the purchaser, Michael Greenwald. He reviews the contract, enters his changes on disk, and returns the disk to Fisher.

Fisher opens the revised contract, but has no idea what changes Greenwald has made. To view the changes, she can compare Greenwald's version (on screen) to her original version (on disk). When she does, the changes appear on screen. Figure 15.1 shows how the changes appear in the document window.

Comparing Documents

1. Save the edited document under a different name from the disk version to which you are comparing it. This gives you the option of referring to the edited version after the comparison.

2. Select **Tools/Document Compare/Add Markings**. WordPerfect for Windows displays the Add Markings dialog box, which prompts you to enter the name of the file to compare.

3. Type the name of the disk file you want to compare. If you aren't sure of the file name or path, select the list button to the right of the text box to display the Select File dialog box and then select a file.

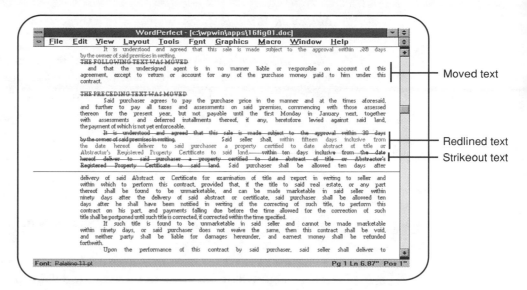

Figure 15.1 An edited contract as it appears in the document window, showing Moved, Redlined and Strikeout text.

4. Select **C**ompare. WordPerfect for Windows compares the documents and marks the open document with Redline and Strikeout codes. If text was moved, prompts appear before and after the moved section.

You can remove the redline text and the strikeout markings, restoring the open document to near its appearance before you used Document Compare. If there were many markings, however, the restored version might differ significantly from the original. This is another reason why it makes sense to save a backup copy of the open file before using Document Compare.

Removing Redlining and Strikeout

1. Select **T**ools/Doc**u**ment Compare/**R**emove Markings. The Remove Markings dialog box appears.

2. To keep the redline text, select the Leave **R**edline Marks check box.

3. Select OK.

By default, redlined (added) text is printed according to the method defined in your printer's definition file. For example, any text added during the revision may appear lightly shaded. If you prefer, you can select one of the following methods instead (to see how the redline text will appear in print, press Shift+F5 to display the text in the Print Preview window):

Mark Left Margin: Marks the text with a vertical line (|) in the left margin.

Mark Alternating Margins: Marks the text with a vertical line in the left margin on even-numbered pages and a vertical line in the right margin on odd-numbered pages.

If you select either option, you can select a different character to use in place of the vertical line.

Selecting a Redline Method

1. Select **L**ayout/**D**ocument/**R**edline Method, or press Ctrl+Shift+F9 (Document) and type **r**.

2. Select **P**rinter Dependent, Mark **L**eft Margin, or Mark Alternating Margins.

3. If you selected Mark **L**eft Margin or Mark Alternating Margins, you can enter a redline character other than the default character (|). Go to the **R**edline Character text box, delete the vertical line, and type a new character or use the Compose feature (Ctrl+W) to select a character.

4. Select OK.

This changes the redline method only for the document on which you are working. To change the method for all new documents, use the Print Settings dialog box. Select **F**ile/**P**references/**P**rint to display the dialog box, which includes the Redline Method options. Select the option you want and then select OK.

Creating and Using Nonprinting Comments

Another WordPerfect for Windows tool that's helpful in the revision process is the Comment feature. This feature lets you add nonprinting comments in the document. For example, if you send a revised contract on disk to your lawyer, you may want to add a comment that explains your revisions. Your lawyer will then see the comment after opening the file.

Adding a Comment

1. Move the cursor where you want the comment inserted.

2. Select **T**ools/Commen**t**/**C**reate. The Create Comment dialog box appears.

3. Type the comment. To enter a hard return, press Ctrl+Enter. (If you just press the Enter key, you select the active command button.)

4. To change the appearance of text, select the text and then select **B**old, **U**nderline, or **I**talic.

5. Select OK. WordPerfect for Windows inserts a [Comment] code at the cursor location, and the comment appears in a gray box, as shown in Figure 15.2.

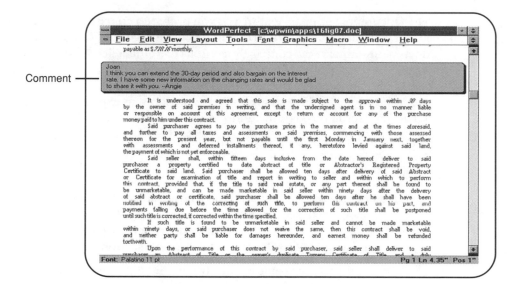

Figure 15.2   The comment as it appears on screen.

If the comment doesn't appear in the document window, select **V**iew/**C**omments to display it.

Although the comment is visible on screen, it will not appear when the document is printed. You can delete the comment by placing the cursor on the [Comment] code and pressing Delete.

To print a comment, first convert the comment into normal text. Move the cursor just past the [Comment] code for the comment you want to convert. Select **Tools/Comment/Convert to Text**. The gray comment box disappears, and the comment appears as normal text.

You can turn normal text into a comment as well. Select the text you want to turn into a comment, and then select **Tools/Comment/Create**. The text appears in a gray comment box. When you print the document, this text will not print.

Creating and Using a Document Summary

The Document Summary feature lets you prepare a concise summary of the important information about a document and have it readily available. Your document summary can contain the contract date, the seller's and purchaser's name, the property being sold, and other information specific to a particular transaction. If you add a document summary to a document, you can display the summary in the File Manager's Viewer window, as explained later in this section, to scroll through the entire document file to learn its contents.

When you create a document summary, you use the Document Summary dialog box, shown in Figure 15.3. This dialog box has the following options:

Descriptive Name: You can type a more descriptive name for the file, using up to 68 characters in the name. In the File Manager window, you can choose to display the descriptive name of files when listing files, as described later in this section.

Descriptive Type: You can specify a document type—such as contract, report, or letter—of up to 20 characters. In the File Manager window, you can choose to display the descriptive file type when listing files, as described later in this section. You can also have the File Manager sort files by type. (For information about the File Manager, see Appendix D.)

Creation Date: This is the date that the document summary (not the document itself) is created. Your creation date may be later than the revision date.

Revision Date: This date is automatically inserted, and you cannot change it in the dialog box. The revision date shows the last date and time the file was changed.

Author and Typist: You can type up to 60 characters for each entry.

Subject: You can enter up to 160 characters. If your document contains a subject statement preceded by RE:, you can select Extract to copy up to 160 characters of the RE: statement and insert it in the Subject text box.

Account: You can enter an account number up to 160 characters.

Keywords: You can enter up to 160 characters. If you enter keywords, you can use the Search menu in the File Manager to locate a document by searching for a specific keyword, such as the name of the seller or purchaser (see "Searching Through Document Summaries").

Abstract: This entry can have up to about 780 characters. One way to quickly enter an abstract is to select Extract, which enters in the text box the first 400 characters of the document.

When extracting text for the Subject text box, WordPerfect for Windows searches for RE: and then copies the text to the right of that statement. If your documents typically contain a subject statement other than RE:, such as Subject:, you can change the text for which WordPerfect for Windows searches. Select File/Preferences/Document Summary to display the Document Summary Preferences dialog box, enter a different search string, and select OK. This changes the search string for all documents. You can also use this dialog box to specify a default descriptive type.

Creating a Document Summary

1. Select Layout/Document/Summary, or press Ctrl+Shift+F9 (Document) and type **s**. The Document Summary dialog box appears, as shown in Figure 15.3.

2. Enter information for any item; no information is mandatory.

3. To copy a subject entry and an abstract from the document, select Extract. WordPerfect for Windows inserts the information in each text box.

4. Select OK.

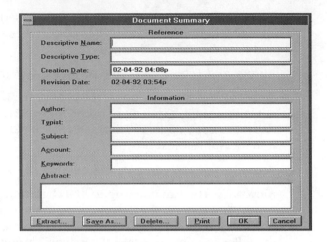

Figure 15.3   The Document Summary dialog box.

Beginner's Tip

You can delete a document summary by opening the document, displaying the Document Summary dialog box, selecting De1ete, and then selecting Yes.

Shortcut

You can have WordPerfect for Windows display the Document Summary dialog box whenever you save a document that doesn't already have a document summary. Select File/Preferences/Document Summary, select the Create Summary on Save/Exit check box, and select OK.

Viewing Descriptive Names and Types in the File Manager Window

The File List in the File Manager window lists for each file the file name, file size, and date and time of creation. The list can also display the descriptive names and types entered in the document summaries.

Displaying Descriptive File Names and Types in the File List

1. Select File/File Manager. The File Manager window opens.

2. Select View/Layouts/Wide FileList,Viewer to display the File List window, shown in Figure 15.4. You can display the File List in

other ways (see Appendix D), but this way ensures that the File List is wide enough for you to see the File List bar headings and the space to the right of those headings.

3. Place the mouse pointer in the File List bar to the right of the Time heading.

4. Press and hold the mouse button. A pull-down menu appears, as shown in Figure 15.4.

5. Drag the mouse pointer to highlight `Desc. Name` or `Desc. Type`.

6. Release the mouse button. A `Desc. Name` or `Desc. Type` heading appears in the File List bar. If a file has a document summary, the descriptive name or type is listed below the heading.

You can move a heading by dragging it to a new location on the File List bar. To remove a heading, drag it from the bar.

To close the File List, press Ctrl+F4. To exit the File Manager window, press Alt+F4. For additional information on the File Manager, see Appendix D.

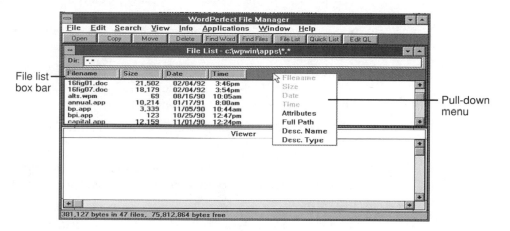

Figure 15.4   The File Manager window displays the wide view of the File List. If you click on an empty space in the File List bar, a pull-down menu appears.

Viewing and Editing the Document Summary

Now that your document has a summary, you can view the summary when the document is open by selecting **Layout/Document/Summary**. The File Manager window also allows you to view document summaries to help you quickly scan the contents of files.

Viewing a Document Summary in the File Manager

1. Select **File/File Manager**. The File Manager window opens.

2. Select **View/Options**. The View Options dialog box appears.

3. Select the Doc Summary in **Viewer** check box.

4. Select OK.

5. Highlight a file name in the File Manager window. The descriptive name and descriptive type from the document summary appear at the top of the Viewer window, as shown in Figure 15.5. The first few lines of the file contents, normally displayed in the Viewer window, appear below the document summary information. (To view the rest of the file contents, click on the scroll bar to move forward and backward through the document.)

6. Select the Summary button to display the rest of the document summary. The button name changes to Text. Select the Text button to display the document contents again.

7. Repeat steps 5 and 6 to view the document summaries for other files.

8. To stop viewing the document summaries, select **View/Options**, clear the Doc Summary in **Viewer** check box, and select OK.

9. Press Alt+F4 or select **File/Exit** to leave the File Manager window and return to the WordPerfect for Windows document window.

You cannot edit a document summary when it is displayed in the File Manager window. To change the contents of a document summary, open the document in the WordPerfect for Windows window, and use the Document Summary feature to display the summary.

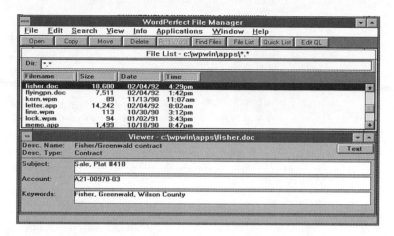

Figure 15.5 A document summary shown in the File Manager window.

Editing a Document Summary

1. Open the file whose summary you want to edit.

2. Select Layout/Document/Summary, or press Ctrl+Shift+F9 (Document) and type **s**. The Document Summary dialog box appears.

3. Enter your changes.

4. Select OK. WordPerfect for Windows returns to the document window.

5. Save the file to save the changes in the summary.

You can save the summary as a separate file, independent of the document. When the Document Summary dialog box is displayed, select Save As. Type a file name for the summary, and select Save. The file is now a document file, and you can treat it as any other document file.

Searching through Document Summaries

Although you can use the Search menu in the File Manager window to search for files that contain a specific word or phrase, a more efficient method is to search through the document summaries for a keyword. For example, you can search for a contract between a particular seller and buyer if you entered the seller's and buyer's names as keywords in the document summary **Keywords** text box. You just tell WordPerfect for Windows to find only those contracts that include *both* names as keywords in the document summary. WordPerfect for Windows finds the files, and then displays a Search Results window listing them. Table 15.1 shows the types of search phrases you can enter and the results you can expect.

Table 15.1   *Examples of search phrases.*

Search Phrase	Will Find
Greenwald	All summaries that contain "Greenwald."
"Michael Green"	Summaries that contain "Michael Green," "Michael Greenwald," "Michael Greenspan," and so on.
" Michael Green "	Summaries that contain the "Michael Green" but not "Michael Greenwald" or Michael Greenspan.
Greenwald;Fisher or Greenwald Fisher	Files that contain both "Greenwald" *and* "Fisher."
Greenwald;-Fisher	Files that contain "Greenwald" *and* do *not* contain "Fisher."
Greenwald,Fisher	Files that contain "Greenwald" *or* "Fisher."

Searching through Document Summaries

1. Select **File/File** Manager to display the File Manager window.

2. To search only certain files, select the files. (Press Shift+F8 to turn on Select, then use the space bar to select and deselect file names. After finishing the search in step 8, press Shift+F8 to turn off Select. See Appendix D for other selection methods.)

3. Select **Search/Advanced** Find or press Ctrl+F2. The Advanced Find dialog box appears, as shown in Figure 15.6.

4. Go to the Word Pattern text box and type the word pattern for which you are searching. You can use only alphabet characters with no punctuation. You can include the special search operators—semicolon, space, comma, dash, and quotation marks—noted in Table 15.1. For example, type **Greenwald;Fisher** to find Greenwald *and* Fisher; type **Greenwald;-Fisher** to find files containing Greenwald but *not* Fisher.

5. Select the Apply Find To pop-up list button and then select an option from the pop-up list. To search only the selected files, select Selected Item(s). To search all files in the current window, select Current Window. If the File List is displayed, the current window is the File List. If the Navigator is displayed, the current window is the one in which a file name is highlighted. (The Navigator lists files in several directories.)

6. Select the Limit Find To pop-up list button and then select Keywords from thc pop-up list.

7. Select Find. WordPerfect for Windows searches the files. The names of files containing the word pattern appear in the Search Results window, as shown in Figure 15.7.

8. You can view the document summary for one of the listed files. (You might have to move or minimize the Search Results window to read the summary.) You can also double-click on a file name to open the file, or press Ctrl+F4 to close the Search Results window.

You can stop searching at any time by selecting Cancel in the Advanced Find dialog box.

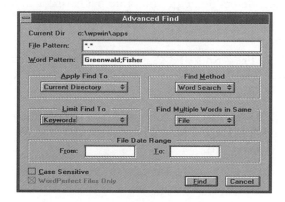

Figure 15.6   The Advanced Find dialog box.

Search results window ——

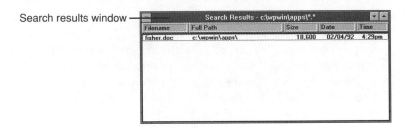

Figure 15.7   Finding the Greenwald/Fisher contract.

Using a Password

Because a contract often contains material that should not be changed by unauthorized or unqualified persons, you may want to use WordPerfect for Windows' Password feature to protect the file. When anyone attempts to open the file, WordPerfect for Windows will not open the file unless the user enters the correct password.

Adding a Password

1. Open the document you want to protect.

2. Select **File/Password**. The Password dialog box appears, prompting you to type the password.

3. Type the password (up to 23 characters). The password does not appear in the text box as you type; instead, WordPerfect for Windows enters asterisks to protect your password from anyone who may be watching.

4. Select **Set**, type the same password again, and again select **Set**. WordPerfect for Windows forces you to enter the password twice to make sure you type it correctly.

5. Press Shift+F3 (Save) or select **File/Save** to save the file under its original name. WordPerfect for Windows saves the file with the password.

The next time you try to open the file, print it from disk, or search or view it in the File Manager, WordPerfect for Windows prompts you to enter the password.

Removing a Password

1. Open the password-protected document.

2. Select **F**ile/**P**assword. The Password dialog box appears.

3. Select **R**emove.

4. Press Shift+F3 (Save) or select **F**ile/**S**ave to save the file under its original name.

By replacing the password-protected version with the new version, which has no password, you remove the password from the file.

Using passwords can be a bit tricky. Because you use them to secure your files, use a password that is easy for you to remember but difficult for someone else to guess. Don't use common passwords, such as your name, age, street address, or birthday or child's name. Use something more cryptic, and follow these guidelines:

- Change your password every few weeks.

- Select a password that is unique and not easily associated with the document you are trying to protect.

- Write down the password for each file and keep your passwords in a safe place away from your computer. Don't store them on the computer, where they are easily found.

- Unless you absolutely need to, don't assign a password to every file you create. Otherwise, you might have difficulty remembering the passwords.

Summary

With this chapter and the real estate contract that accompanies it, you can create customized contracts for any exchange of real estate. More importantly, you can now use WordPerfect for Windows' document management tools to take control of your documents.

With Document Compare, you can follow the development of a contract from its initial stages to its final form. You can use document comments to add nonprinting comments to the document to voice your concerns and ideas to colleagues and others involved in the revision process. Also, you can use document summaries and passwords to help you organize, locate, and protect your contracts. By using these tools, you can ensure that the final contract will contain no surprises for you.

Real Estate Contract

(Page 1 of 2)

Contract

Sale of Real Estate

I, *Joan Fisher*, seller, have sold and agree to convey to *Michael Greenwald* (in joint tenancy) purchaser, upon the terms hereinafter set forth, the following described real estate, situated in *Wilson* County, namely: *#418* according to the plat thereof, subject however, to any change in the size of said property caused by the vacating, opening, widening, narrowing or grading of any street or alley, said property being also known as number *734 Indiana Street* in *Carmel*.

I, *Joan Fisher*, have viewed, examined and purchased said real estate and agree to pay therefor the total purchase price of *eighty-nine thousand two hundred-fifty* Dollars (*$89,250*) of which *five thousand* Dollars (*$5,000*) have been paid at the date hereof, the receipt of which is hereby acknowledged, and the further sum of *eighty-four thousand two hundred-fifty* Dollars (*$84,250*) is to be paid by said purchaser to said seller as follows: *five thousand* Dollars (*$5,000*) in cash on execution and delivery of a deed. *Seventy-nine thousand two hundred-fifty* Dollars (*$79,250*) by assuming and agreeing to pay one certain-proposed mortgage, now-to become a lien against said property, same bearing interest at *10.25%* per annum, interest and principal being payable as *$710.16* monthly.

It is understood and agreed that this sale is made subject to the approval within *30* days by the owner of said premises in writing, and that the undersigned agent is in no manner liable or responsible on account of this agreement, except to return or account for any of the purchase money paid to him under this contract.

Said purchaser agrees to pay the purchase price in the manner and at the times aforesaid, and further to pay all taxes and assessments on said premises, commencing with those assessed thereon for the present year, but not payable until the first Monday in January next, together with assessments and deferred installments thereof, if any, heretofore levied against said land, the payment of which is not yet enforceable.

Said seller shall, within fifteen days inclusive from the date hereof deliver to said purchaser a property certified to date abstract of title or Abstractor's Registered Property Certificate to said land. Said purchaser shall be allowed ten days after delivery of said Abstract or Certificate for examination of title and report in writing to seller and within which to perform this contract, provided that, if the title to said real estate, or any part thereof shall be found to be unmarketable, and can be made marketable in said seller within ninety days after the delivery of said abstract or certificate, said purchaser shall be allowed ten days after he shall have been notified in writing of the correcting of such title, to perform this contract on his part, and payments falling due before the time allowed for the correction of such title shall be postponed until such title is corrected, if corrected within the time specified.

If such title is found to be unmarketable in said seller and cannot be made marketable within ninety days, or said purchaser does not waive the same, then this contract shall be void, and neither party shall be liable for damages hereunder, and earnest money shall be refunded forthwith.

Upon the performance of this contract by said purchaser, said seller shall deliver to said purchaser an Abstract of Title or the owner's duplicate Torrens Certificate of Title, and a duly acknowledged Contract for Deed entitled to record of said land and all thereof, free from dower or statutory rights, taxes, assessments, mortgages and all other adverse claims or liens, except as stated above.

The purchaser agrees that Abstract of Title or Torrens Certificate of Title and fire, windstorm and other hazard insurance policies shall remain in possession of mortgage and or contract seller until all said indebtedness is paid in full.

Real Estate Contract

(Page 2 of 2)

If said purchaser agrees in this contract to assume or join in a mortgage, said purchaser and seller and their respective spouses, if any, shall join in executing the necessary paper for renewing said mortgage or placing a new mortgage for any sum not to exceed *$50,000* so as to keep a mortgage of not to exceed *$50,000* in effect until the property herein described is conveyed in accordance with terms of this contract and said purchaser agrees to pay all usual and reasonable expenses for the renewing of the present mortgages or the making of a new one.

All storm sheds, sash and doors; screens, awnings, shades and venetian blinds; all porch windows and doors; gas or electric fixtures, oil burners, stokers, air conditioners and motors pertaining to the same; drapes and carpets in public halls; radiators and all other like appliances and betterments, plants and shrubbery (if any) which are now provided for or used in or on said premises; and,except in single residences, stoves, ranges and refrigerator units, plant or system; and, except such as are the property of the tenants, are included in this sale.

All papers shall bear even date herewith, and liability as between the parties hereto to pay taxes and assessments on said property shall be determined as of the date hereof. The policies of insurance shall on final closing of this sale so be written or endorsed as to protect the interests of seller, purchaser and mortgagee, and shall be taken by said purchaser at their pro rata value from the date hereof. Rentals and interest shall be adjusted as follows:

Possession of the property herein described shall be given *November 15, 1992* subject however to the rights of the tenants in possession.

All tenders and delivery of papers hereunder shall be made at the office of *the agent* in *Carmel*.

Time is of the essence hereof, and if such purchaser shall fail to perform this contract within the time herein limited, said seller or his agent shall retain the earnest money hereof as a part of his just compensation for such failure, and may declare this contract terminated and proceed for damages, or specific performance against such purchaser. Action to enforce this contract shall be commenced within ninety (90) days from the date of forfeiture of this contract.

Dated at *2:30 p.m.*, on *October 31, 1992*

Signed, Sealed and Delivered in Presence of

Agent *Robert Sheeland*

Seller *Joan Fisher*

Purchaser *Michael Greenwald*

Draw a line

1. Place the cursor where you want the line to begin.

2. Press Ctrl+D or select **Tools/Line Draw**.

3. Select a line-draw character.

4. Select **Draw**.

5. Use the arrow keys to draw the line.

6. Select Close or press Esc.

Compose a line-draw character

1. Press Ctrl+D or select **Tools/Line Draw**.

2. Select **Character**.

3. Press Ctrl+W or select **Font/WP Characters**.

4. Select a character; or type the character set number, type a comma, and type the number of the character from that set.

5. Select Insert and Close.

6. Select OK.

Move the cursor while in line draw

1. Select **Move** from Line Draw dialog box.

2. Press the arrow keys to move the cursor.

3. Select **Draw** to resume drawing.

Erase a line

1. Place the cursor on the line.

2. Press Ctrl+D or select **Tools/Line Draw**.

3. Select **Erase**.

4. Press the arrow keys to erase line.

Change to draft viewing mode

1. Select View/**Draft** Mode.

BUSINESS
SHORTCUTS

Organization Charts

Most businesses and organizations have a chain of command. The Board of Directors may run the company through a Chief Executive Officer, who controls operations through several managers. In larger companies, this chain of command can be complex and cause some confusion. To clearly illustrate its management structure, the company can distribute an organization chart. The organization chart described in this chapter and included on disk will get you started on creating your own chart. You'll use WordPerfect for Windows' Line Draw tool to create boxes and lines; you'll use Typeover mode to type text in boxes; and you'll create a macro that draws a box automatically.

About the Application

The application consists of several boxes connected with lines, as illustrated by the example at the end of the chapter. The boxes and lines were created with WordPerfect for Windows' Line Draw tool, using a single-line character. A 20-cpi (character per inch) font was used (approximately equivalent to a 6-point font), and the left and right margins were reduced to .5" to fit as much text within the margins as possible. In the example at the end of the chapter, text was typed in the boxes in Typeover mode to prevent the boxes and lines from breaking apart.

If you have no need to create an organization chart, you may find this application useful for creating flow charts instead. For example, you can use a flow chart to illustrate the flow of materials through the company. You can also use flow charts in procedures manuals to illustrate the steps required to complete a task.

Opening the Application

To start working with the organization chart, open the file *ORGCHRT.APP*. When you open the file, WordPerfect for Windows automatically reformats it for the selected printer, choosing the closest available font. To view the chart in the document window, you might have to display it in Draft viewing mode. To do so, select View/**D**raft Mode. To see how the chart will appear in print, display it in the Print Preview window (select **F**ile/Print Preview or press Shift+F5).

Draft mode is a viewing mode in which characters in the document window appear in a monospaced font (such as Courier), regardless of the actual font selected. Most graphics do not appear in draft mode. Working in Draft mode is often faster than working in the normal viewing mode, especially if the document contains graphics or complicated formatting.

The viewing mode does not affect how the text appears when printed.

If your printer cannot support a 20-cpi font, the lines in the application might not align. In that case, you should create the application from scratch, using the Line Draw tool as explained in this chapter. Don't try to adjust the lines; that will take more time than starting over.

Customizing the Application

If everything aligns correctly in the Print Preview window and the structure of your company fits the layout of the boxes, you can use the template as is, by typing text in each box. Press the Insert key to change to Typeover mode, position the cursor in the appropriate box, and type your text. If you need to add or delete boxes, however, you'll have to use WordPerfect for Windows' Line Draw tool, as explained in the following sections.

Giving Your Chart Enough Space

Once you've drawn lines and boxes, moving them is difficult. So before you start creating your organization chart, sketch it on graph paper. This will give you a clear idea of relative positions of boxes and relative lengths of lines. If the chart looks wide, you have two options: You can use a smaller font for the document initial font (as explained in Chapter 17), or you can choose to spread the chart across the wide edge of the page—in landscape orientation. Figures 16.1 and 16.2 show the difference between landscape orientation and "normal" portrait orientation, as seen from Print Preview.

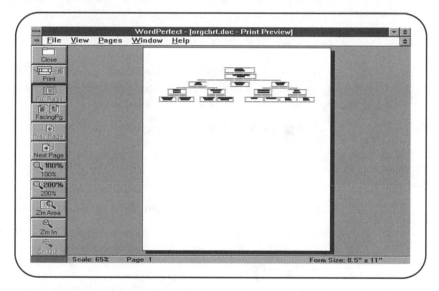

Figure 16.1   The chart application in portrait orientation.

The procedure for using landscape orientation differs depending on whether your printer can rotate fonts. If your printer can rotate fonts, you simply tell WordPerfect for Windows that you want the fonts rotated. WordPerfect for Windows will then rotate the print 90 degrees to print it along the wide edge of the page. If your printer cannot rotate fonts, you can tell WordPerfect for Windows to print the text as usual but on a wider sheet of paper. Then, when you print the page, you insert the paper into the printer wide edge first.

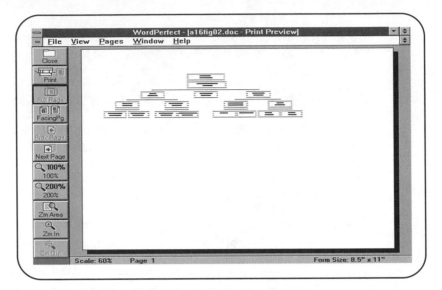

Figure 16.2   The chart application in landscape orientation.

The following directions explain how to print in landscape orientation if you are using a WordPerfect printer driver. If you are using a Windows printer driver, see your Windows manual.

To change to WordPerfect printer drivers, select **F**ile/**S**elect/Printer to display the Select Printer dialog box. In the dialog box, select **W**ordPerfect for the Printer Drivers option, and then choose **S**elect.

Printing in Landscape Orientation With Rotated Fonts

1. Move the cursor to the page where you want to begin printing in landscape. (If Auto Code Placement is off, move the cursor to the top of the page.)

2. Select **L**ayout/**P**age/Paper **S**ize, or press Alt+F9 (Page) and type **s**. The Paper Size dialog box appears, as shown in Figure 16.3.

3. If a landscape paper size appears (for example, 11"× 8.5"), select it by double-clicking on it, or highlighting it and choosing **S**elect; you can skip the remaining step. If no landscape size is listed, select **A**dd to define a size.

4. If you selected **A**dd, WordPerfect for Windows displays the Add Paper Size dialog box shown in Figure 16.4. Select the Paper **T**ype pop-up list button, and then select the paper type or choose **O**ther.

If you choose **Other**, go to the Ot**h**er text box and type a name for the paper type. (You can type any name you want.)

5. Select the Paper Size pop-up list button, and then select St**a**nd Land (standard landscape: 11" × 8.5"), Legal La**n**d (legal landscape: 14" × 11"), A**4** Land (A4 landscape), or Other.

6. If you selected **Other** in Step 5, type the height and width dimensions in the **By** text boxes. Enter the larger measurement first; for example, **11 × 8.5.** Also, select the Rotated Font check box. (If in Step 5 you selected Stand Land, Legal Land, or A4 Land, the Rotated Font check box is automatically selected.) When you select the check box, the lower left icon in the Paper Orientation group is highlighted, indicating the orientation of the paper being fed into the printer and the orientation of the text on the paper.

7. Select any other options you want. (See Chapter 9 for information on these options.)

8. Select OK. WordPerfect for Windows returns to the Paper Size dialog box.

9. Select the landscape paper definition by double-clicking on it, or by highlighting it and choosing Select. WordPerfect for Windows returns to the document and inserts a [Paper Sz/Typ] code at the top of the document.

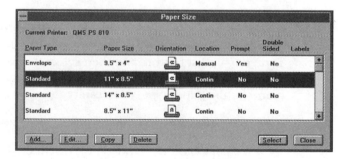

Figure 16.3   The Paper Size dialog box.

 Using Landscape Without Rotating Fonts

1. Move the cursor to the page where you want to begin printing in landscape. (If Auto Code Placement is off, move the cursor to the top of the page.)

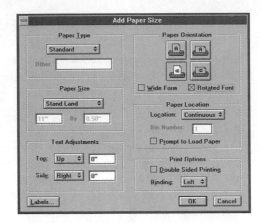

Figure 16.4   The Add Paper Size dialog box.

2. Select Layout/Page/Paper Size, or press Alt+F9 (Page) and type s. The Paper Size dialog box appears, as shown in Figure 16.3.

3. If the dialog box lists a paper definition with the correct paper size and a wide orientation, select the definition by double-clicking on it or by highlighting it and choosing Select; you can then skip the remaining steps. (The wide orientation is shown by an icon depicting a form with the wide edge being fed into the printer, as shown in Figure 16.5). If no such definition exists, select Add to create one.

4. If you selected Add, WordPerfect for Windows displays the Add Paper Size dialog box, as shown in Figure 16.4. Select the Paper Type pop-up list button, and then select the paper type or choose Other. If you choose Other, go to the Other text box and type a name for the paper type. (You can type any name you want.)

5. Select the Paper Size pop-up list button, and then select Stand Land (standard landscape: 11" × 8.5"), Legal Land (legal landscape: 14" × 11"), A4 Land (A4 landscape), or Other.

6. If you selected Other in Step 5, type the height and width dimensions in the By text boxes. Enter the larger measurement first; for example, 11 × 8.5.

7. If the Rotated Font check box is selected, deselect it.

8. Select the Wide Form check box. When you select the check box, the upper right icon in the Paper Orientation group should be highlighted.

9. Select any other options you want. (See Chapter 9 for information on these options.)

10. Select OK. WordPerfect for Windows returns to the Paper Size dialog box.

11. Select the wide-form paper definition by double-clicking on it or by highlighting it and choosing Select. WordPerfect for Windows returns to the document and inserts a [Paper Sz/Typ] code at the top of the document.

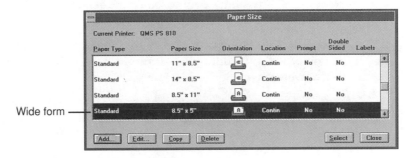

Figure 16.5   A wide form is depicted by an icon showing the wide paper edge being fed into the printer.

Adding Lines and Boxes

Once you have sketched how the chart should look and you have created the necessary space for it, you can start drawing. When you choose the Line Draw tool to start drawing, WordPerfect for Windows does the following:

• Changes the viewing mode to Draft mode.

• Changes the typing mode to Typeover mode. (In Line Draw, the status bar does not indicate that you are in Typeover mode.)

• Displays the Line Draw dialog box at the bottom of the screen.

The Line Draw dialog box, shown in Figure 16.6, provides the following options:

Characters group and the Character button: The Characters group displays 11 common line-draw characters that you can select. You are not limited to these characters; however, you can use any character from the WordPerfect for Windows character sets in Line Draw. To use a character not shown in the Characters group, select the Character button. The Line Draw Character dialog box appears, with a highlighted asterisk in the Character text box. Enter a new character and select OK. (To enter the character, you can press Ctrl+W to display the WordPerfect Characters dialog box, select a character, and then select Insert and Close.) Choose characters carefully. Most line-draw characters change position when they turn corners. But some, such as the third character from the left, do not rotate when they turn.

Draw: Select this to enter Draw mode. In Draw mode, pressing the arrows keys draws lines composed of the selected character. You cannot use a mouse to draw.

Move: Selecting this puts you in Move mode, which lets you move the cursor without adding line-draw characters. To resume drawing after moving the cursor, select **Draw**.

Erase: Selecting this puts you in Erase mode. When you move the cursor over a line in Erase mode, the cursor erases the line-draw characters from the line. To resume drawing after erasing characters, select **Draw**.

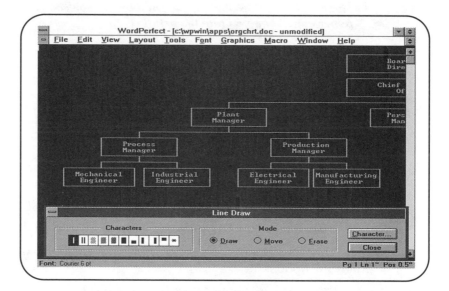

Figure 16.6   The Line Draw dialog box.

Drawing Lines

1. Place the cursor where you want the line drawing to begin.

2. Press Ctrl+D or select **T**ools/Line Draw. The window changes to Draft viewing mode and the Line Draw dialog box appears at the bottom of the window, as shown in Figure 16.6.

3. Select a line-draw character; or select Character, enter a character in the Line Draw Character dialog box, and select OK.

4. If **D**raw is not selected, select it.

5. Use the arrow keys to draw the line up, down, left, or right from the cursor position.

6. To move the cursor without drawing, select **M**ove and then use the arrow keys to move the cursor. Reselect **D**raw when you want to resume drawing.

7. To return to the normal document window, select Close or press Esc.

Erasing Lines

1. Move the cursor before or after the line-draw character you want to erase.

2. Press Ctrl+D or select **T**ools/Line Draw. The Line Draw dialog box appears.

3. Select **E**rase in the Line Draw dialog box. The cursor is now in Erase mode until you select **M**ove or **D**raw.

4. Move the cursor toward the character you want to erase. For example, if the cursor is below the character you want to erase, press the Up Arrow key.

Creating Identical Boxes Fast

For the chart to look professional, the lines and boxes should be uniform. To use several identical boxes in your chart, you can create a macro that draws all four sides of the box. The following steps explain how to create such a macro. When you play the macro in the normal document window, it will automatically select Line Draw and draw the box. When you're done creating the boxes, connect them with lines and enter your text.

Creating a Box Macro

1. Select **M**acro/**R**ecord, or press Ctrl+F10 (Macro Record).

2. Enter a name for your macro (up to eight characters). If desired, enter a description and abstract for the macro.

3. Select **Record**.

4. Press Ctrl+D or select **Tools/Line** Draw to select Line Draw.

5. Select a line-draw character.

6. If **Draw** is not selected, select it.

7. Press the Right Arrow key *x* number of times, where *x* is the number of characters you want in the top line of the box. You might want to write down the number of characters, since you'll need to remember that number in Step 9.

8. Press the Down Arrow key *y* number of times, where *y* is the number of characters you want to use for the right side of the box. You might want to write down the number of characters, since you'll need to remember that number in Step 10.

9. Press the Left Arrow key *x* number of times, where *x* is the number of characters you want in the bottom line of the box. Use the same number you used to draw the top of the box.

10. Press the Up Arrow key *y* number of times, where *y* is the number of characters you want to use for the left side of the box. Use the same number you used to draw the right side of the box.

11. Select Close to return to the normal document window.

12. Select **Macro/Stop** or press Ctrl+Shift+F10 (Macro Stop) to stop recording your macro.

Typing Text in Boxes

When you type text in a box that's been created with the Line Draw feature, you have to be careful. Keep in mind that the lines are created by characters that act the same as any other characters in WordPerfect for Windows. Here are some basic rules to follow:

- If possible, use 10-point Courier. Line Draw works best with monospaced fonts—characters that are all equally spaced. Proportional fonts may insert space between line-draw characters or overlap the characters.

- Always type text within boxes in Typeover mode. Press the Insert key to switch between Typeover mode and Insert mode. If you type in Insert mode, the line-draw character on the right side of the box will shift to the right, as shown in Figure 16.7. You'll then have to delete spaces after your entry to restore alignment.

- Do not use different fonts for the text inside the boxes. Change the font once—for the entire document (see Chapter 17)—and use this font in all boxes. If you change fonts for the text, the box may break up.

- Do not change margins or justification or insert tabs. Such changes may cause alignment problems.

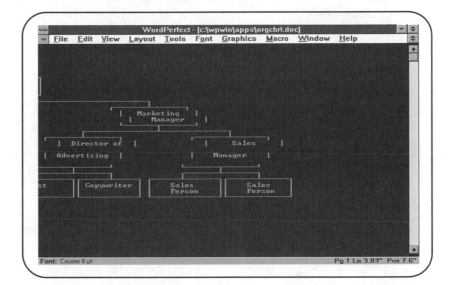

Figure 16.7   Typing in Insert mode throws off the alignment of the box.

 Using the Line Draw tool to create a chart requires you to make numerous adjustments. So save your work frequently to protect it against accidents.

Summary

Although the Line Draw tool is a little difficult to manipulate, it does provide the line-drawing capabilities you need to create organization charts, flow charts, and other documents that require basic lines. By combining this tool with macros, you can create uniform shapes and balanced charts to give your presentations, manuals, and memos a professional look.

The Organization Chart

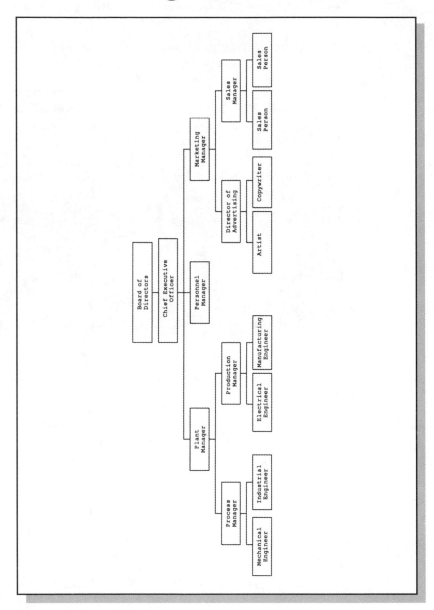

Change the printer initial font

1. Select File/Select Printer.

2. Select WordPerfect as the Printer Driver's option.

3. Highlight the printer and select Setup.

4. Select Initial Font.

5. Select the font and then select OK.

Change the document initial font

1. Open the document.

2. Select Layout/Document/Initial Font, or press Ctrl+Shift+F9 and type **f**.

3. Select the font and then select OK.

Change font within a document

1. Place the cursor where you want the font to change.

2. Press F9 or select Font/Font.

3. Select the font and then select OK.

Change the size attribute

1. Highlight text.

2. Press F9 or select Font/Font.

3. Select the size attribute and then select OK.

Change the type style

1. Highlight text.

2. Press F9 or select Font/Font.

3. Select the appearance attribute and then select OK.

Convert case

1. Highlight the text.

2. Select Edit/Convert Case.

3. Select Uppercase or Lowercase.

BUSINESS SHORTCUTS

Power of Attorney

In many business matters, you may want to assign the legal responsibilities for certain affairs to an attorney who is more capable of handling the specific transactions. To transfer legal responsibility in this manner, you must complete a general Power of Attorney statement, such as the one described in this chapter, and have it signed and notarized. This application is only an example of such a document; do not rely on it to be a binding contract, because laws vary greatly from state to state. Be sure to consult your attorney before signing or using this form.

About the Application

The Power of Attorney application consists of several paragraphs of text. The base font for the document is 11-point Palatino. The heading (POWER OF ATTORNEY) is set in 18-point New Century Schoolbook, and the subheading (General Form) is set in 14-point New Century Schoolbook. In customizing the Power of Attorney application, you'll learn how to change the base font for the document, change fonts for sections of text, and change the size and appearance of blocks of text.

A *font* is a set of characters that has the same typeface and type size. For example, 18-point New Century Schoolbook is a font. Eighteen-point is the size, and New Century Schoolbook is the typeface. For reference, 72 points equals approximately one inch. The fonts for your printer may be measured in points or in cpi (characters per inch).

Opening the Application

To customize the Power of Attorney application, first open the file *POWER.APP*. The template is similar to the example shown at the end of this chapter, but the specific information is not supplied.

Customizing the Application

You can use this application as is by replacing each asterisk with information specific to your Power of Attorney agreement. When you're done, the application should appear similar to the application at the end of the chapter.

Replacing Asterisks with Text

1. Select Edit/Search or press F2 (Search). The Search dialog box appears.

2. In the Search For text box, type * and then select Search. WordPerfect for Windows searches for an asterisk and stops to the right of the first asterisk it finds.

3. Press Backspace to delete the asterisk, and type the required information. Whatever you type appears in italics.

4. Press Shift+F2 (Search Next) to search for the next asterisk.

5. Repeat Steps 3 and 4 until you've replaced all the asterisks with the required information.

To search backwards through a document, press Alt+F2 (Search Previous).

Save your Power of Attorney statement under a different file name, so that you still have the original application. You can then print the file and use it for your agreement.

Changing Fonts

When you installed WordPerfect for Windows, you may have selected a WordPerfect printer driver and a default printer font. If you did, WordPerfect for Windows sets the type for all new documents in this *printer initial font*. You can override this font setting for any one document by changing the *document initial font*. You can override the document initial font anywhere within a document by inserting a [Font] code. The [Font] code affects all subsequent text until the next [Font] code or until the end of the document. The following instructions explain how to change or select a printer initial font. Note that the directions assume you want to use a WordPerfect printer driver.

Changing the Printer Initial Font

1. Select **File/Select** Printer. The Select Printer dialog box appears, as shown in Figure 17.1.

2. If it is not yet selected, select **W**ordPerfect as the Printer Driver's option.

3. Highlight the printer for which you want to change the initial font.

4. Select S**e**tup. The Printer Setup dialog box appears, as shown in Figure 17.2.

5. Select Initial **F**ont. The Printer Initial Font dialog box appears. As shown in Figure 17.3, it lists available fonts.

6. Select the font you want. If you are using a PostScript printer or scalable fonts, also enter the point size.

7. Select OK.

The font you just selected for your printer will be used for all new documents. The setting does not affect fonts for existing documents. You can override this font by selecting a different document initial font or by inserting a [Font] code.

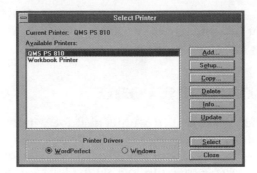

Figure 17.1   The Select Printer dialog box.

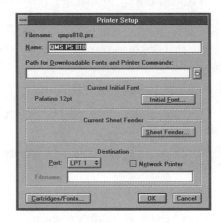

Figure 17.2   The Printer Setup dialog box.

If you have an existing document, such as *POWER.APP,* changes to the printer initial font won't affect that document. To change an existing document's font, change the document initial font.

Changing the Document Initial Font

1. With *POWER.APP* displayed in the window, select **L**ayout/ **D**ocument/Initial **F**ont, or press Ctrl+Shift+F9 (Document) and type **f**. WordPerfect for Windows displays the Document Initial Font dialog box, which is similar to the dialog box shown in Figure 17.3.

2. Select the font you want. If you are using a PostScript printer or scalable fonts, also enter the point size.

3. Select OK.

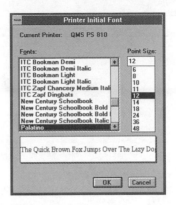

Figure 17.3   The Printer Initial Font dialog box.

Within the document, you can override the document initial font as follows.

Changing Fonts within a Document

1. Position the cursor where you want to change the font.

2. Press F9 (Font) or select Font/Font. The Font dialog box appears, as shown in Figure 17.4. The current font is highlighted in the Font list box.

3. Select the font you want in the Font list box. If you are using a PostScript printer or scalable fonts, enter a type size in the Point Size text box.

4. Select OK. WordPerfect for Windows inserts a [Font] code at the cursor location. You can see the code in the Reveal Codes screen, as shown in Figure 17.5.

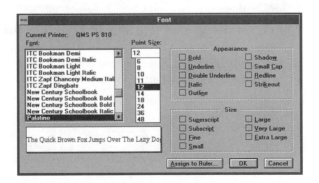

Figure 17.4   The Font dialog box.

[Font] code ──

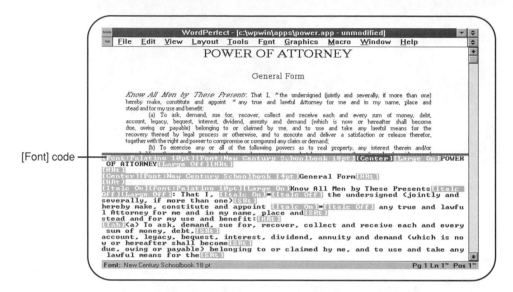

Figure 17.5   The [Font] code changes the font within a document.

You can use different fonts for graphic box captions, headers, footers, footnotes, and endnotes by inserting a [Font] code when you create or edit one. The change affects only that specific feature, not the text within the document itself.

If you often switch fonts, consider assigning the most frequently used fonts to the Font button on the Ruler. If you leave the Ruler displayed while you work, you can quickly select a font from the list that appears when you select the Font button, as illustrated in Figure 17.6. Fonts added to the Ruler remain there until you delete them from the Ruler. If you close the current document and open a different file or a new window, the Ruler retains the list of fonts.

In most documents, you should keep font changes to a minimum. Select one font for the body text and a different font for the headings. If you use 12-point Times Roman for the body text, for example, you might use 14-point Times Roman Bold for the headings.

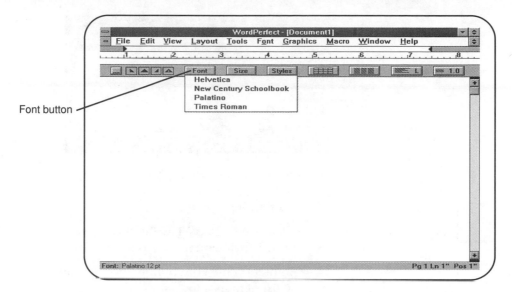

Font button

Figure 17.6   You can use the Font button on the Ruler to change the font within a document.

Assigning Fonts to the Ruler

1. Select Font/Font or press F9 (Font). The Font dialog box appears.

2. Select Assign to Ruler. The Ruler Fonts Menu dialog box appears, as shown in Figure 17.7. The Font List box lists available fonts, and the Fonts on Ruler box lists fonts assigned to the Ruler. Notice that the printer initial font is automatically assigned.

3. To add a font to the Ruler, double-click on the font name in the Font List box, or highlight the name and select Add. The font name appears in the Fonts on Ruler box. (To delete a name from that box, double-click on the name, or highlight the name and select Clear.)

4. Repeat Step 3 to add other fonts.

5. When you finish adding fonts, select OK. WordPerfect for Windows returns to the Font dialog box.

6. Select OK. WordPerfect for Windows returns to the document window. The next time you select the Font button on the Ruler, the pop-up list will display the fonts you selected.

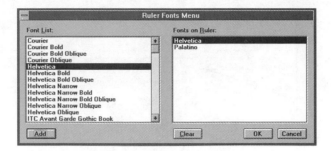

Figure 17.7   The Ruler Fonts Menu dialog box.

Selecting a Font from the Ruler

1. If the Ruler is not displayed, select **View/Ruler** or press
   Alt+Shift+F3 (Ruler). The Ruler appears, as shown in Figure 17.6.

2. Place the mouse pointer on the Font button and press and hold the
   mouse button. The list of fonts appears.

3. Drag the mouse pointer to highlight the font you want.

4. Release the mouse button. WordPerfect for Windows inserts a
   [Font] Code at the cursor location.

The Ruler also contains the Size button. If you use scalable fonts, you
can select this button to display and select from a list of font sizes. (The
selection method is the same as that used for the Font button.) Often
you'll use the Size button and the Font button together. To change a
heading to 14-point Helvetica, for example, you might select Helvetica
from the Font button list and 14 from the Size button list. WordPerfect
for Windows would then insert the code [Font:Helvetica 14pt].

Converting Case

Although changing fonts is one of the best ways to emphasize a heading or
a block of text, you can also use uppercase characters. The heading of the
Power of Attorney application, for example, is set in all uppercase characters. You can change text to uppercase or lowercase, deleting the text and
retyping it, but it is easier to change from lowercase to uppercase (and vice
versa) through WordPerfect for Windows' Convert Case feature.

Converting Case

1. Highlight the block of text whose case you want to change.

2. Select Edit/Convert Case and then select Uppercase or Lowercase. The highlighted text changes case.

Changing Size Attributes

When you change fonts, you change the base font: size and typeface. You can then use size and appearance attributes to modify the base font. For example, you can change the size of type to large, small, extra large, or fine. When you add an attribute in this way, WordPerfect for Windows inserts two codes: one that turns the attribute on and one that turns it off. WordPerfect for Windows then automatically selects a font from the list of installed fonts that reflects the specified attribute. If you select large for the size, for example, WordPerfect for Windows selects a font that is 120% of the base font. If your base font is 10-point, then the large font will be 12-point. Table 17.1 lists the default percentages of base font for each attribute. You can change the default percentages by entering new ones in the Print Settings dialog box. See "Print" in Appendix C for additional information.

Table 17.1   Size Attributes

Size Attribute	Percentage of Base Font
Fine	60%
Small	80%
Large	120%
Very Large	150%
Extra Large	200%
Super/Subscript	60%

Changing Size Attributes

1. Highlight the block of text whose size you want to change.

2. Press F9 (Font) or select Font/Font. The Font dialog box appears, as shown in Figure 17.4.

3. Select one of the Size check boxes: Superscript, Subscript, Fine, Small, Large, Very Large, or Extra Large.

4. Select OK. The highlighted text is now formatted with the size attribute. To see the new format, particularly if you selected a smaller size, you might need to display the text in the Print Preview window (press Shift+F5).

To type new text using a different size attribute, press F9 or select Font/ Font, select the size attribute, and then select OK. WordPerfect for Windows inserts the On and Off codes for the attribute and positions the cursor between the codes. Whatever you type is inserted between the two codes and appears in the selected attribute. When you're done, press the Right Arrow key to move the cursor past the Attribute Off code. This essentially turns the attribute off.

You can select subscript and superscript directly from the Font menu: Select Font and then select Subscript or Superscript. You can select the other size attributes by selecting Font/Size or pressing Ctrl+S (Size), and then selecting Fine, Small, Large, Very Large, or Extra Large.

Use different fonts, type sizes, and attributes to draw the reader's attention to important parts of the document, but don't get carried away. Too many changes can detract from the content of your document.

Changing the Appearance of Text

You can emphasize text by changing its appearance attributes—for example, making the text bold, italic, or shadowed. The font remains the same, but the text *appears* different on screen and when printed. In other words, if you are using Times Roman 12-point as the initial font, and you select italics, the printed text will be Times Roman 12-point italic—a variation of the base font.

Changing Text Appearance

1. Highlight the block of text whose appearance you want to change.

2. Press F9 (Font) or select Font/Font. The Font dialog box appears, as shown in Figure 17.4.

3. Select one or more of the Appearance check boxes: **Bold**, **Underline**, **Double** Underline, **Italic**, Outline, Shadow, Small **Cap**, **Redline**, or Stri**k**eout.

4. Select OK. The highlighted text is now formatted with the selected attribute. To see the new format, you might need to display the text in the Print Preview window (press Shift+F5).

A faster way to select bold, underline, or italics is to highlight the text and press Ctrl+B (Bold), Ctrl+U (Underline), or Ctrl+I (Italic). You can also select some appearance attributes directly from the Font menu: Select F**o**nt and then select **Bold**, **Italic**, **Underline**, **Double** Underline, **Redline**, or Strikeout. For other attributes, you must use the Font dialog box as explained above.

To type new text using a different appearance attribute, use any of the methods described above to select the attribute. WordPerfect for Windows inserts the On and Off codes for the attribute and positions the cursor between the codes. Whatever you type is inserted between the two codes and appears in the selected attribute. When you're done, press the Right Arrow key to move the cursor past the Attribute Off code.

Restoring Text to Its Normal Size and Appearance

You may decide that you prefer the text to have its normal size or appearance. In that case, you can remove the size and appearance attributes for all text between the attribute On and Off codes or for only part of the text between the codes.

Removing Attributes for All Text

1. Press Alt+F3 (Reveal Codes) or select View/Reveal Codes.

2. Highlight the On or Off code for the appearance or size attribute you want to remove.

3. Press Delete. The highlighted code and the other member of its pair (the On or Off code) are deleted. The text no longer has the attribute.

4. Repeat steps 2 and 3 for all size and appearance attributes you want to remove.

You can use the Replace feature to quickly remove all codes for a particular attribute. Just search for the code and replace it with nothing. See Chapter 15.

Restoring Part of the Text to Its Normal Appearance

1. Position the cursor where you want the text to revert to its normal appearance.

2. Select Font/Normal or press Ctrl+N (Normal). WordPerfect for Windows inserts an Off code for *all* size and appearance attributes that applied at the cursor location. Text following the cursor no longer has those attributes.

Summary

You can manipulate the appearance of the Power of Attorney application by changing the look of the type. You can change the font for the document by changing the printer initial font or the document initial font. To emphasize text within the document, you can change the text font or its size and appearance attributes. You can apply these same tools to change the look of any WordPerfect for Windows document.

The Power of Attorney Application

(Part 1 of 2)

POWER OF ATTORNEY

General Form

Know All Men by These Presents: That I, *Mary Howard* the undersigned (jointly and severally, if more than one) hereby make, constitute and appoint *Frank Howard* any true and lawful Attorney for me and in my name, place and stead and for my use and benefit:

(a) To ask, demand, sue for, recover, collect and receive each and every sum of money, debt, account, legacy, bequest, interest, dividend, annuity and demand (which is now or hereafter shall become due, owing or payable) belonging to or claimed by me, and to use and take any lawful means for the recovery thereof by legal process or otherwise, and to execute and deliver a satisfaction or release therefor, together with the right and power to compromise or compound any claim or demand;

(b) To exercise any or all of the following powers as to real property, any interest therein and/or any building thereon: To contract for, purchase, receive and take possession thereof and of evidence of title thereto; to lease the same for any term or purpose, including leases for business, residence, and oil and/or mineral development; to sell, exchange, grant or convey the same with or without warranty; and to mortgage, transfer in trust, or otherwise encumber or hypothecate to secure payment of a negotiable or non-negotiable note or performance of any obligation or agreement;

(c) To exercise any or all of the following powers as to all kinds of personal property and goods, wares and merchandise, chooses in action and other property in possession or in action: To contract for, buy, sell, exchange, transfer and in any legal manner deal in and with the same, and to mortgage, transfer in trust, or otherwise encumber or hypothecate the same to secure payment of a negotiable or non-negotiable note or performance of any obligation or agreement;

(d) To borrow money and to execute and deliver negotiable or non-negotiable notes therefor with or without security; and to loan money and receive negotiable or non-negotiable notes therefor with such security as he shall deem proper;

(e) To create, amend, supplement and terminate any trust and to instruct and advise the trustee of any trust wherein I am or may be trustor or beneficiary; to represent and vote stock, exercise stock rights, accept and deal with any dividend, distribution or bonus, join in any corporate financing, reorganization, merger, liquidation, consolidation or other action and the extension, compromise, conversion, adjustment, enforcement or foreclosure, singly or in conjunction with others of any corporate stock, bond, note, debenture or other security; to compound, compromise, adjust, settle and satisfy any obligation, secured or unsecured, owing by or to me and to give or accept any property and/or money whether or not equal to or less in value than the amount owing in payment, settlement or satisfaction thereof;

(f) To transact business of any kind or class as my act and deed to sign, execute, acknowledge and deliver any deed, lease, assignment of lease, covenant, indenture, indemnity, agreement, mortgage, deed of trust, assignment of mortgage or of the beneficial interest under deed of trust, extension or renewal of any obligation, subordination or waiver of priority, hypothecation, bottomry, charter-party, bill of lading, bill of sale, bill, bond, note, whether negotiable or non-negotiable receipt, evidence of debt, full or partial release or satisfaction of mortgage, judgement and other debt, request for partial or full reconveyance of deed of trust and such other instruments in writing of any kind or class as may be necessary or proper in the premises.

Giving and Granting unto my said Attorney full power and authority to do and perform all and every act and thing whatsoever requisite, necessary or appropriate to be done in and about the premises as fully to all intents and purposes as I might or could do if personally present, hereby ratifying all that my said Attorney shall lawfully do or cause to be done by virtue of these presents. The powers and said authority hereby conferred upon my said Attorney shall be applicable to all real and personal property or interests therein now owned or hereafter acquired by me and wherever situate.

My said Attorney is empowered hereby to determine on his sole discretion the time when, purpose for and manner in which any power herein conferred upon him shall be exercised, and the

The Power of Attorney Application

(Part 2 of 2)

conditions, provisions and covenants of any instrument or document which may be executed by him pursuant hereto; and in the acquisition or disposition of real or personal property, my said Attorney shall have exclusive power to fix the terms thereof for cash, credit and/or property, and if on credit with or without security.

The undersigned, if a married woman, hereby further authorizes and empowers my said Attorney, as my duly authorized agent, to join in my behalf, in the execution of any instrument by which any community real property or interest therein, now owned or hereafter acquired by my spouse and myself, or either of us, is sold, leased, encumbered, or conveyed.

When the context so requires, the masculine gender includes the feminine and/or neuter, and the singular number includes the plural.

WITNESS my hand this 20 day of *December*, 1992

Signed_____

State of *Texas*

County of *Dallas*

Signed_____
Notary Public in and for said State
Witness my hand and official seal.

Create a header or footer

1. Place the cursor on the first page on which you want the header or footer.

2. Select **Layout/Page** or press Alt+F9.

3. Select **Headers** or **Footers**.

4. Select **A** or **B** and then select **Create**.

5. Select **Placement**, select a placement option, and then select OK.

6. Type the header or footer text.

7. Select the **Close** button or press Ctrl+F4.

Edit a header or footer

1. Move the cursor just past the [Header] or [Footer] code.

2. Select **Layout/Page** or press Alt+F9.

3. Select **Headers** or **Footers**.

4. Select **A** or **B** and then select **Edit**.

5. Edit the header or footer.

6. Select the **Close** button or press Ctrl+F4.

Discontinue a header or footer

1. Move the cursor to the first page on which you want to discontinue the header or footer.

2. Select **Layout/Page** or press Alt+F9.

3. Select **Headers** or **Footers**.

4. Select **A** or **B** and then select **Discontinue**.

Suppress a header or footer

1. Move the cursor to the page on which you want the header or footer suppressed.

2. Select **Layout/Page** or press Alt+F9.

3. Select **Suppress**.

4. Select what you want to suppress.

5. Select OK.

Number pages

1. Select **Layout/Page/Numbering**, or press Alt+F9 and type **n**.

2. Enter settings and select OK.

Create a footnote or endnote

1. Select **Layout/Footnote/Create** or **Layout/Endnote/Create**.

2. Type the note text.

3. Select the **Close** button or press Ctrl+F4.

Edit a footnote or endnote

1. Select **Layout/Footnote/Edit** or **Layout/Endnote/Edit**.

2. Type the footnote or endnote number and select OK.

3. Enter your changes.

4. Select the **Close** button or press Ctrl+F4.

Change footnote or endnote options

1. Move the cursor to the top of the first page you want the changes to affect.

2. Select **Layout/Footnote/Options** or **Layout/Endnote/Options**.

3. Select the options you want.

4. Select OK.

BUSINESS
SHORTCUTS

Annual Report

A company's management team is accountable to the groups of people who have an interest in the company, including employees, board members, and stockholders. To keep all interested parties informed, many companies develop and publish an annual report. The report may include the management's philosophy, information concerning expansion and new products, and tables that compare this year's net profit to last year's. The page layout of such a report includes headers and footers, and possibly endnotes or footnotes. In this chapter, you'll work with these tools and others to create an annual report for your own use.

About the Application

The annual report application, shown at the end of this chapter, contains a table of contents that you can use as an outline for your annual report. Following this table are several pages, each containing a heading from the table. The headings were entered first on each page, and then the Table of Contents feature was used to generate the table of contents from the headings. If you add, delete, or change the headings, you can regenerate the table; WordPerfect for Windows will update the table of contents to reflect your changes and incorporate any changes to the page numbers. For more information about the Table of Contents feature, refer to Chapter 5.

The Header/Footer feature was used to create the header MD&E Industries, Inc., which appears in the upper left corner of each even-numbered page, and Annual Report 1991, which appears in the upper right corner of each odd-numbered page. On Pages 7, 9, and 11, the right header changes to reflect a change in sections: New Ventures, Consolidated Fiscal Information, and Directors and Officers. A [Force:Odd] code before each of these sections ensures that each section starts on an odd-numbered, right-hand page.

The Page Numbering feature was used to insert page numbers in the lower left corner of left-hand pages, and in the lower right corner of right-hand pages. The table of contents is numbered with lowercase Roman numerals (i, ii, iii). Following the table of contents, the page numbering changes: Numbering restarts at 1 and the numbering style changes to Arabic numerals (1, 2, 3).

Opening the Application

To customize the annual report application, open the file *ANNUAL.APP*. WordPerfect for Windows automatically formats the document for the printer installed on your system. The document that appears on screen should look similar to the one at the end of this chapter. However, you won't see the header, the footnote, or the page numbers unless you display the document in the Print Preview window.

Customizing the Application

The most basic way to customize this application is to revise the section headings and change the headers. You can then add text after each heading as needed. Don't edit the headings in the table of contents. After you change the headings in the application, you can regenerate the table to reflect your changes.

Don't confuse headings with headers. A *heading* acts as the title of a subject or topic. *Headers* appear at the top of every page, providing a convenient way to reference chapters and sections throughout the document.

Adding and Deleting Headings

You can delete any heading in the application by highlighting the heading and then pressing Delete. When highlighting the heading, however, be careful that you don't highlight hidden format codes that are used to format the rest of the document. Before you delete a heading, turn on Reveal Codes (press Alt+F3 or select View/Reveal Codes), so you can see what you're about to delete.

Adding headings is a little more complicated, because you must format the heading. To set the heading in 12-point Palatino italic type, for example, you must select that type size and font in the Font dialog box, as explained in Chapter 17. After you have formatted the new heading, mark the heading to be included in the table of contents, as shown in the steps that follow.

Marking a Heading for the Table of Contents

1. Select the heading you want to mark. If the selected text includes paired appearance or size attribute codes (for example, [Italc On] and [Italc Off], [Large On] and [Large Off]), the heading will have that attribute in the table of contents.

2. Select Tools/Mark Text/Table of Contents, or press F12 (Mark Text) and type **c**. The Mark Table of Contents dialog box appears, as shown in Figure 18.1.

3. In the Level text box, type the heading level (a number between 1 and 5) or use the increment buttons to enter a level.

4. Select OK. WordPerfect for Windows inserts a [Mark:ToC,n] code at the beginning of the heading and an [End Mark:ToC,n] following the heading. The number n in the codes indicates the level of the heading.

Once all your headings are in place, you can type text under each heading to create your report. If you put a [Font] code before the heading to set it in a larger point size than the rest of the text, make sure you insert another [Font] code after the heading, before the text you type, to use a smaller font. Otherwise, everything will appear the same size as the heading.

When you have finished writing your annual report, you'll have to regenerate the table of contents to update it. Any headings you deleted in the document will be removed from the table of contents, and any headings you added and marked for the table of contents will appear in the table. WordPerfect for Windows will then change the page numbers to reflect the new page numbering.

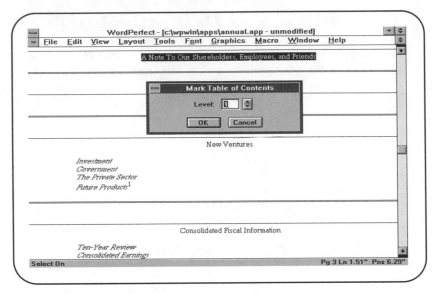

Figure 18.1 The Mark Table of Contents dialog box.

Generating a Table of Contents

1. Place the cursor anywhere in the document.

2. Select **T**ools/**G**enerate or press Alt+F12 (Generate). The Generate dialog box appears, warning that you are about to update the existing table of contents and other lists, and asking you to confirm that you want to continue.

3. Select **Y**es to continue or **N**o to cancel. If you continue, Word-Perfect for Windows begins generating the table of contents. A counter in the status bar shows the progress of the operation. When WordPerfect for Windows has finished, the table of contents appears, replacing the old table of contents.

Editing Header A and Header B

The annual report application contains five different headers: four header A's, and one header B. Header B, MD&E Industries, Inc., appears on all even-numbered (left-hand) pages. The first header A, Annual Report 1991, appears on all odd-numbered (right-hand) pages up to the New Ventures section, where the header changes to New Ventures. It then changes to Consolidated Fiscal Information and Directors and Officers at the beginning of each of those sections. This was done so that anyone paging through the report could easily reference the sections.

You can have a maximum of two headers (A and B) and two footers (A and B) on each page. Different pages can have different header A's and B's and different footer A's and B's. Just create the new header or footer on the page where you want the new header or footer to begin.

You can edit these headers by following these steps.

Editing a Header or Footer

1. Move the cursor just past the [Header] or [Footer] code for the header or footer you want to edit. When you choose to edit a header or footer, WordPerfect for Windows searches backward from the cursor position and displays the first header or footer of the type specified (A or B).

2. Select **Layout/Page** or press Alt+F9 (Page).

3. Select **Headers** or **Footers**. The Headers or Footers dialog box appears, as shown in Figure 18.2.

4. Select **A** or **B**, and then select **Edit**. WordPerfect for Windows searches backward through the document for the header or footer you specified, then displays the header or footer in the Header or Footer window, as shown in Figure 18.3.

5. Edit the header or footer. You can change fonts or add any other formatting. In the application, we even added a horizontal line to clearly separate the header from the rest of the text.

6. Select the **Close** button or press Ctrl+F4 (Close).

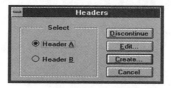

Figure 18.2   The Headers dialog box. The Footers dialog box is similar.

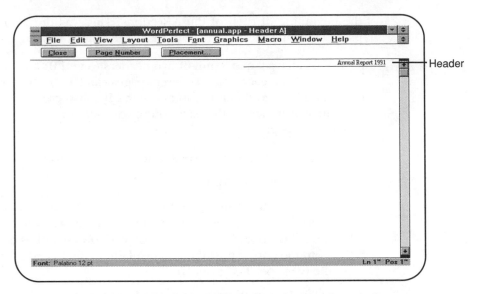

Figure 18.3   A sample header displayed in the Header window.

Shortcut

You can have page numbers appear in your header by selecting the Page **N**umber button in the Header or Footer window. This inserts the code [Insert Pg Num: ^B], which enters the correct page number on each page. You can enter the date from your system by pressing Ctrl+F5 or selecting **T**ools/**D**ate/**T**ext. You can insert a [Date] code, which automatically enters the current date whenever you open or print the document, by pressing Ctrl+Shift+F5 or selecting **T**ools/**D**ate/**C**ode.

Creating a Header or Footer

If you add a section to the application, you may want to add a header or footer. To do so, the [Header] or [Footer] code must be entered *at the top* of the first page on which you want the header or footer to appear. If the code is not at the top of the page, the header or footer will not appear on the first page; it will first appear on the next page.

If Auto Code Placement is off, the [Header] or [Footer] code will appear at the cursor location, so you must move the cursor to the top of the page before creating the header or footer.

If Auto Code Placement is turned on ("on" is the default setting), you don't have to worry about placing the cursor at the top of the page. Just place the cursor somewhere on the page and create the header or footer; WordPerfect for Windows will automatically place the [Header] or [Footer] code at the top of the page, replacing any existing [Header] or [Footer] code of the same type. See Chapter 2 for more information about Auto Code Placement.

To ensure that the [Header] or [Footer] code stays at the top of the page as you edit the document, you may want to insert a hard page break (Ctrl+Enter) before the code.

Creating a Header or Footer

1. Place the cursor on the first page on which you want the header or footer. (If Auto Code Placement is off, move the cursor to the top of the first page.)

2. Select **Layout/Page** or press Alt+F9 (Page).

3. Select **Headers** or **Footers**. The Headers or Footers dialog box appears, as shown in Figure 18.2.

4. Select **A** or **B** and then select **Create**. A Header or Footer window appears.

5. Select the **Placement** button to display the Placement dialog box; then select the pages on which you want the header or footer to appear: **Every** Page, **Odd** Pages, or **Even** Pages. Select OK to close this dialog box.

6. Type the text for your header or footer, adding any desired format. For example, you can change fonts, add enhancements such as bold and italic, and change the size of type. Format you add here has no effect on text in the body of the document.

7. To include page numbers in the header or footer, select the Page **Number** button. The [Insert Pg Num: ^B] code appears at the cursor location.

8. Select the **Close** button or press Ctrl+F4 (Close). WordPerfect for Windows returns to the document window and inserts a [Header] or [Footer] code at the top of the page. The code has the form

```
[Header A:Odd pages;[Flsh Rgt]Annual Report 1991]
```

Discontinuing and Suppressing Headers and Footers

You can *discontinue* a header or footer at any point in the document to prevent the header or footer from appearing on all subsequent pages in the document. These steps show you how.

Discontinuing a Header or Footer

1. Move the cursor to the first page on which you want to discontinue the header or footer. (If Auto Code Placement is off, move the cursor to the top of that page.)

2. Select **Layout/Page** or press Alt+F9 (Page).

3. Select **Headers** or **Footers**. The Headers or Footers dialog box appears, as shown in Figure 18.2.

4. Select **A** or **B** and then select **D**iscontinue. WordPerfect for Windows inserts a [Discontinue] code at the top of the page. This cancels the selected header or footer from this point to the end of the document.

You can also *suppress* the header or footer on a single page in the document. For example, you can suppress the header on the Table of Contents page. Follow these steps:

Suppressing a Header or Footer

1. Move the cursor to the page on which you want the header or footer suppressed. (If Auto Code Placement is off, move the cursor to the top of the page.)

2. Select **Layout/Page** or press Alt+F9 (Page).

3. Select S**u**ppress. The Suppress dialog box appears, as shown in Figure 18.4.

4. Select the check box for the header or footer you want to suppress. You can select more than one check box. To suppress all headers, footers, and page numbering on the page, for example, select all the check boxes.

5. Select OK. WordPerfect for Windows returns to the document window and inserts a [Suppress] code at the top of the page. If Auto Code Placement is on, the code replaces any existing [Suppress] code.

Figure 18.4 The Suppress dialog box.

Forcing Odd or Even Pages

In any document that has facing pages, the common practice is to use odd numbers for right-hand pages and even numbers for left-hand pages. It is also common practice to start each section on an odd-numbered, right-hand page. When you edit a document, however, sections are likely to move at least one or two pages. To make sure your section starts on the desired page, you can insert a [Force] code at the top of the page, forcing the section to start on an odd or even page.

Forcing an Odd or Even Page

1. Move the cursor to the page on which you want to force an odd or even page break. (If Auto Code Placement is off, move the cursor to the top of the page.)

2. Select **Layout/Page/Numbering**, or press Alt+F9 (Page) and type **n**. The Page Numbering dialog box appears, as shown in Figure 18.5.

3. Go to the Force Current Page check boxes and select Odd or Even.

4. Select OK. WordPerfect for Windows inserts a [Force:Odd] or [Force:Even] code at the beginning of the page, and if necessary, inserts a page break to force the page to begin on the specified page.

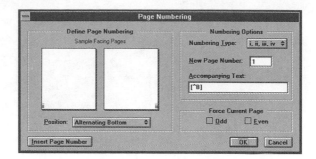

Figure 18.5   The Page Numbering dialog box.

Starting a New Page Numbering Sequence

In any document that contains multiple sections, you may want to use a different type of page numbering for each section. In the application, for example, we numbered the table of contents with lowercase Roman numerals and the rest of the document with Arabic numerals. You might also want to number each section independently. For example, the first section might be numbered 1-1, 1-2, 1-3, and so on; and the second section might be numbered 2-1, 2-2, 2-3, and so on.

To start page numbering at a new number, use the Page Numbering dialog box. The steps are as follows:

Starting at a New Page Number

1. Move the cursor to the page where you want the new page numbering to begin. (If Auto Code Placement is off, move the cursor to the top of the page.)

2. Select **Layout/P**age/**N**umbering, or press Alt+F9 (Page) and type **n**. The Page Numbering dialog box appears, as shown in Figure 18.5.

3. Go to the **N**ew Page Number text box and type the new starting page number. Type an Arabic numeral even if the numbering type is Roman numerals.

4. Select OK. WordPerfect for Windows inserts a [Pg Num] code at the top of the page. The new page numbering continues from this point to the next [Pg Num] code, or to the end of the document if there is no other [Pg Num] code.

You also use the Page Numbering dialog box to precede the page number with a section number (for example, 2-1, 2-2, and so on) or other text, as described in the following steps.

Adding Text to the Page Number

1. Move the cursor to the page where you want the new page numbering style to begin. (If Auto Code Placement is off, move the cursor to the top of the page.)

2. Select Layout/Page/Numbering, or press Alt+F9 (Page) and type **n**. The Page Numbering dialog box appears, as shown in Figure 18.5.

3. Go to the Accompanying Text text box, and type the text you want to accompany the page number. Notice that the text box contains the code [^B], which represents the page number. Text you insert before this code will precede the page number; text you insert after the code will follow the page number. Also notice that the Sample Facing Pages in the dialog box display the new numbering style, as illustrated in Figure 18.6.

4. Select OK. WordPerfect for Windows inserts a [Pg Num Style] code at the top of the page. The new style continues from this point to the next [Pg Num Style] code, or to the end of the document if there is no other [Pg Num Style] code.

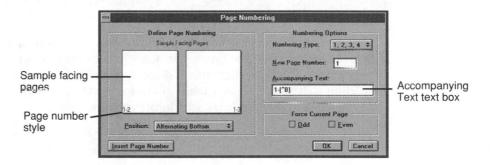

Figure 18.6 The Sample Facing Pages display the Page Number style you entered in the Accompanying Text text box.

The Page Numbering dialog box also includes options that let you control the page numbering type and the page number position. The default numbering type is Arabic numerals. To change this, select the Numbering Type pop-up list button and then select the new type. (You can choose Arabic numerals or uppercase or lowercase Roman numerals.) To choose the position for the page number, select the **P**osition pop-up list button and then select the position. The new position will be illustrated in the Sample Facing Pages.

If you entered an [Insert Pg Num: ⌃ B] code in a header or footer, do not also select a page number position in the Page Numbering dialog box. If you do, two page numbers will appear on the pages. To prevent this, select **N**o Page Numbering for **P**osition in the Page Numbering dialog box.

The dialog box also contains the Insert Page Number option. If you select this option, WordPerfect for Windows inserts the current page number (including any accompanying text) at the cursor position. In the document window, the page number is represented by ⌃ B. To see the actual number, display the page in the Print Preview window.

Creating Footnotes and Endnotes

The annual report application includes a footnote on Page 7. As you can see, the footnote appears at the bottom of the page to which it pertains. Endnotes have a similar format, but they appear at the end of a chapter, section, or book, or wherever you choose to define the endnote list. WordPerfect for Windows automatically numbers the footnotes and endnotes for you and updates the numbers whenever necessary to keep them in the proper sequence.

To create footnotes or endnotes, follow the same basic steps. The only difference is that when you create endnotes, you can define the location of the endnotes. If you decide to use endnotes, you cannot use an endnote in a heading that's marked as a table of contents entry, as was the sample footnote. If you do, you may run into problems when you attempt to generate the list.

Creating a Footnote or Endnote

1. Move the cursor after the word or phrase for which you want to create a footnote or endnote.

2. Select **L**ayout/**F**ootnote/**C**reate or **L**ayout/**E**ndnote/**C**reate. The Footnote or Endnote window appears, as shown in Figure 18.7. Notice that the window contains the note number. If you display the Reveal Codes screen, you will see that the note number is represented by the [Note Num] code.

3. Press F7 (Indent) if you want to indent the note to the right of the note number.

4. Type the note text and add any formatting. (Formatting affects only that note.)

5. If you accidentally delete the note number, place the cursor where you want the number and select the Note Number button. (Do not enter a number from the keyboard. If you do so, the note will not be automatically renumbered if the sequence of notes changes.)

6. Select the Close button or press Ctrl+F4 (Close) to return to your document. A [Footnote] or [Endnote] code appears at the cursor location.

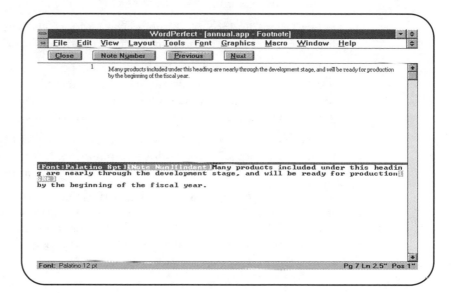

Figure 18.7   The Footnote window. The Endnote window is similar.

The Footnote and Endnote windows contain the Previous and Next buttons, which allow you to cycle through the footnotes or endnotes. Selecting Previous displays the preceding note in the window; selecting Next displays the next note. Any changes you made to the current note are saved when you display the new note.

If you created a footnote, you're done. You can view it by selecting File/Print Preview or by pressing Shift+F5 (Print Preview). If you created an endnote, you can view it by displaying the last page of your document; by default, that is where WordPerfect for Windows displays endnotes. You can change the placement of the list or even define several lists within the document, choosing to number the lists sequentially or to restart numbering after each list.

Placing the Endnote List

1. Move the cursor where you want your endnotes to appear.

2. To place the endnotes on a separate page, press Ctrl+Enter to insert a hard page break. You can also type a title for the endnotes section. For example, type **Endnotes**.

3. Select **Layout/Endnote/Placement**. The Endnote Placement dialog box appears, asking if you want to restart endnote numbering.

4. Select **Yes** to insert the [Endnote Placement] code at the cursor location and to restart endnote numbering at 1 after this endnote list. (If you have a separate endnote list at the end of each section, you can answer **Yes** to number each section separately.)

5. Answer **No** to insert the [Endnote Placement] code at the cursor location without affecting endnote numbering. Notes in subsequent lists will be numbered sequentially with the notes in this list.

When you select **Yes** or **No**, WordPerfect for Windows inserts an [Endnote Placement] comment box at the cursor location (see Figure 18.8) and automatically inserts a hard page break after the code. To view the endnotes, display in the Print Preview window the page containing the [Endnote Placement] code.

Editing a Footnote or Endnote

You can edit a footnote or endnote just as you edit any text. However, before you can edit the note, you must first display it in the Footnote or Endnote window.

Editing a Footnote or Endnote

1. Select **Layout/Footnote/Edit** or **Layout/Endnote/Edit**. The Edit Footnote or Edit Endnote dialog box appears, asking you to specify the number of the footnote or endnote you want to edit.

2. Type the number of the footnote or endnote, and select OK. The specified footnote or endnote appears in the Footnote or Endnote window.

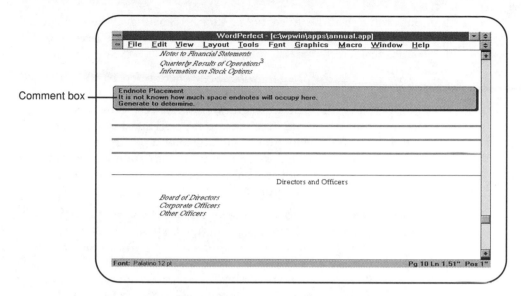

Comment box ——

Figure 18.8   The Endnote Placement comment box.

3. Enter your changes. When finished, select the Close button or press Ctrl+F4 (Close).

Changing Footnote and Endnote Options

You have already seen that you can control character formatting in endnotes and footnotes by adding formatting codes in the Footnote or Endnote window. You can also control more general formatting specifications through the Footnote Options dialog box, shown in Figure 18.9, and the Endnote Options dialog box. Both dialog boxes offer the following options:

Numbering Method: By default, WordPerfect for Windows uses numbers to reference the notes. The Numbering Method pop-up-list button lets you change the numbering method to Letters or Characters.

Beginner's Tip

If you select Characters, enter the note characters in the Characters text box, with no spaces in between them. You can enter any characters from a WordPerfect for Windows character set. WordPerfect for Windows uses the first character for the first note, the second character for the second note, and so on. If you type * , for example, WordPerfect for Windows uses * for the first note, _ for the second note, and _ for the third note. After exhausting all the selected characters, WordPerfect for Windows continues numbering with double characters (for example, **).

Style in Text and Style in Note: "Style" here refers to Number style. By default, footnote and endnote numbers in the text are superscripts—the numbers are slightly above the rest of the text. In the actual notes, footnote numbers are superscripts and endnote numbers are normal numerals followed by a period. You can change this formatting or add to it to have the numbers appear bold, italic, or another style. You can enter separate styles for the number in the text and the number in the note.

Line Spacing in Notes and Spacing Between Notes: The default line spacing in notes is 1 (single spacing), with 0.167" separating the notes. The Line Spacing in Notes text box lets you change the line spacing within a note. For example, type **1.5** to specify one-and-one-half line spacing. You can change the amount of space between footnotes by typing a new distance in the Spacing Between Notes text box.

Minimum Note Height: If a note must continue to the next page, WordPerfect for Windows automatically keeps 0.5" of the note together (on either the first or next page). Say a note is 0.7" high and the first page can accommodate only 0.4" of the note; then WordPerfect for Windows will place about 0.2" of the note on the first page, and continue the remaining 0.5" (the minimum height) on the next page. To specify a different minimum note height, type a new height in the Minimum Note Height text box.

The Footnote Options dialog box contains the following additional options:

Print (Continued) Message: If a footnote continues to the next page, you can select this check box to have WordPerfect for Windows automatically insert "(continued)..." after the last footnote line on the first page, and insert "...(continued)" before the first footnote line on the next page.

Restart Numbering on Each Page: To number footnotes separately on each page, select this check box. Otherwise, WordPerfect for Windows numbers the footnotes sequentially throughout the document.

Separator: WordPerfect for Windows automatically inserts a 2" line between the text on the page and the footnotes at the bottom of the page. This option lets you choose no line or a line that runs from margin to margin instead.

Position: By default, WordPerfect for Windows prints footnotes at the bottom of the page, even if the main text does not fill the page. To have the footnotes immediately follow the last line of text instead, select the **P**osition pop-up list button and then select **A**fter Text.

Figure 18.9   The Footnote Options dialog box. The Endnote Options dialog box is similar, but has fewer options.

Changing Footnote/Endnote Options

1. Move the cursor to the top of the first page you want the changes to affect.

2. Select **L**ayout/**F**ootnote/**O**ptions or **L**ayout/**E**ndnote/**O**ptions. The Footnote Options or Endnote Options dialog box appears, as shown in Figure 18.9.

3. Select the options you want.

4. Select OK. WordPerfect for Windows inserts a [Ftn Opt] or [End Opt] code at the cursor location.

Summary

Annual reports are complex documents that may require sophisticated formatting. With the formatting techniques you learned in this chapter and the application included on disk, you can set up the overall structure of such a document. Combine these tools with the graphics features explained in Chapter 3, with the Tables feature in Chapter 6, and with other tools described throughout this book, and you should be able to lay out and print a most impressive annual report.

The Annual Report Application

(page 1 of 13)

Annual Report 1991

Table of Contents

i

The Annual Report
Application

(page 2 of 13)

MD&E Industries

ii

The Annual Report Application

(page 3 of 13)

Financial Highlights

1

389

The Annual Report Application

(page 4 of 13)

MD&E Industries

2

The Annual Report Application

(page 5 of 13)

Annual Report 1991

A Note To Our Shareholders, Employees, and Friends

3

The Annual Report Application

(page 6 of 13)

MD&E Industries

4

The Annual Report Application

(page 7 of 13)

Annual Report 1991

An Interview with the CEO

5

The Annual Report Application

(page 8 of 13)

MD&E Industries

6

The Annual Report
Application

(page 9 of 13)

New Ventures

New Ventures

Investment
Government
The Private Sector
Future Products[1]

---

[1]   Many products included under this heading are nearly through the development stage, and will be ready for production by the beginning of the fiscal year.

7

The Annual Report Application

(page 10 of 13)

MD&E Industries

8

The Annual Report
Application

(page 11 of 13)

Consolidated Fiscal Information

Ten-Year Review
Consolidated Earnings
Results of Operations
Costs and Expenses
Liquidity and Sources of Capital
Consolidated Balance Sheets
Statement of Consolidated Cash Flows
Changes in Consolidated Stockholder's Equity
Notes to Financial Statements
Quarterly Results of Operations
Information on Stock Options

9

The Annual Report Application

(page 12 of 13)

MD&E Industries

10

The Annual Report Application

(page 13 of 13)

Directors and Officers

Directors and Officers

Board of Directors
Corporate Officers
Other Officers

11

399

Retrieve résumé styles

1. Select **Layout/Styles** or press Alt+F8.
2. Select **Retrieve**.
3. Type **resume** and select **Retrieve**.

Select default style file

1. Select **File/Preferences/Location of Files**, or press Ctrl+Shift+F1 and type L.
2. Type **resume.sty** in the Styles Filename text box.
3. Select OK.

Edit styles

1. Select **Layout/Styles** or press Alt+F8.
2. Highlight the style name and select **Edit**.
3. Edit the style.
4. Select the **Close** button or press Ctrl+F4.

Save styles

1. Select **Layout/Styles** or press Alt+F8.
2. Select Save **As**.
3. Type the name of the style file and select **Save**.

Turn on a style

1. Select **Layout/Styles** or press Alt+F8.
2. Double-click on the style name, or highlight the style name and select **On**.

Create a style

1. Select **Layout/Styles** or press Alt+F8.
2. Select **Create**.
3. Type a style name in the **Name** text box.
4. Type a description in the **Description** text box.
5. Select **Type**, and then select **Paired** or **Open**.
6. Select **Enter Key Inserts**, and then select **Hard Return, Style Off**, or **Style Off/On**.
7. Select OK.
8. Enter the formatting codes and text for the style.
9. Select the **Close** button or press Ctrl+F4.

BUSINESS
SHORTCUTS

Résumé

Every professional should keep an updated resume on hand. If the opportunity arises to improve your position, or if you must seek another position, you don't want to be fumbling around, trying to put together a makeshift résumé. You should be able to add slight changes to your résumé at any time, and print a polished résumé quickly and easily. After working through this chapter and using the Résumé style file included on disk, you'll be able to quickly produce a detailed, professional-looking résumé, like the one shown at the end of this chapter. And you'll be able to change the formatting for all your résumés by changing the format in a single file.

About the Application

The résumé application differs a great deal from the other applications included with this book. The biggest difference is that the résumé application is not a document file; it's a style file, as its name (*RESUME.STY*) suggests. A style file consists of a set of styles, often called a *stylesheet*. Each style contains one or more formatting codes, and some styles also include text. Instead of having to insert several formatting codes whenever you want to format a section of text in a particular manner, you can select a style that inserts all the formatting codes and text required.

You can use two types of styles: *Open* and *Paired*. Open styles insert a set of formatting codes that turn a style on. That style remains in effect until you enter a formatting code that changes the formatting of one of the codes contained in the style. Paired codes turn a style on and off. These codes are similar to those used for character attributes, such as bold and italic.

Using RESUME.STY

Because RESUME.STY is not a document file, you cannot open it as you can open the other application (.APP) files. To use the styles, you must first copy RESUME.STY from the disk that came with this book to the directory that contains your style files. If you aren't sure which directory this is, select **F**ile/ **P**references/Location of Files, or press Ctrl+Shift+F1 (Preferences) and type **L**. The directory containing the style files is named in the Styles Directory text box. Press Esc to return to the document window.

Once RESUME.STY is in the directory you use for your style files, you can use the stylesheet for an individual document or you can use it as the default stylesheet.

Retrieving RESUME.STY for a Single Document

1. Open the document that you want RESUME.STY to affect.

2. Select **L**ayout/**S**tyles or press Alt+F8 (Styles). The Styles dialog box appears. If you have specified a default style sheet, the dialog box lists the name of styles in the default stylesheet.

If you want to clear out the default styles, so they won't clutter the Styles list when you retrieve RESUME.STY in styles, follow these steps for each style: Highlight the style name and select **D**elete; in the Delete Style dialog box, select Delete Definition **O**nly; and then select OK. Clearing the style names from the screen, does not affect the entries in the style file. It also does not affect any style codes you might have entered in the document. (If you scroll past one of those style codes, the style will be relisted in the Styles dialog box.)

3. Select **R**etrieve. The Retrieve Styles dialog box appears, listing style files in the default style directory.

4. Type **resume** in the Filename text box. If RESUME.STY is not in the default styles directory, also type the directory path and the file extension .sty (for example, **c:\wpwin\resume.sty**). Because RESUME.STY has the default file extension .STY and is in the default styles directory, you don't need to type the file extension.

5. Select Retrieve. The résumé stylesheet now appears in the Styles dialog box, as shown in Figure 19.1. When you save the document file, these styles will be saved with the document.

6. Select the Close button or press Esc to exit the Styles dialog box.

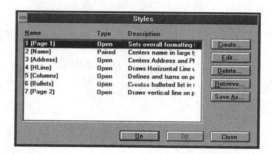

Figure 19.1   The Styles dialog box, displaying the list of styles in RESUME.STY.

Selecting RESUME.STY as the Default Style File

1. Select File/Preferences/Location of Files, or press Ctrl+Shift+F1 (Preferences) and type **L**. The Location of Files dialog box appears, as shown in Figure 19.2.

2. Type **resume.sty** in the Styles Filename text box. Note that in this case, you must type the file extension **.sty**, too. If RESUME.STY is not in the default styles directory, then you must also type the directory path before the filename, for example, **c:\wpwin\resume.sty**.

3. Select OK. WordPerfect for Windows returns to the document window. The résumé styles will now be available in the Styles dialog box whenever you select Layout/Style or press Alt+F8 (Styles) in a document that doesn't already have styles.

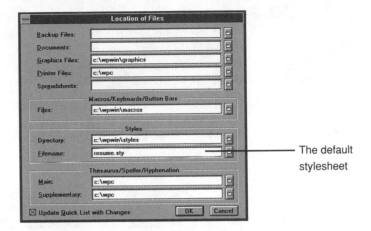

Figure 19.2   Specifying RESUME.STY as the default stylesheet.

Customizing RESUME.STY

Now that RESUME.STY is active for this document, you can view its contents and edit the styles. Select **L**ayout/**S**tyles or press Alt+F8 (Styles) to view the list of styles shown in Figure 19.1. As you can see, RESUME.STY contains seven styles. We numbered the styles in the order in which you are most likely to use them.

To customize this application for your own use, you must edit at least two of the styles included in the list: Name and Address. You can also edit the other styles. For now, edit only the name and address. You can edit the other styles *after* you use them to create your résumé. By using the styles first, you'll see how they look in print.

Editing the Name and Address Styles

Style 2 (Name) inserts the text `Michael Pause, MBA`, centers it, and sets it in a large font size. Style 3 (Address) inserts the address shown in the example at the end of this chapter. Before you use either of these styles, you will want to delete Michael Pause's name and address, and enter your own name and address.

Editing Styles 2 and 3

1. Select **L**ayout/**S**tyles or press Alt+F8 (Styles). The Styles dialog box appears.

2. If the dialog box does not list the Résumé styles, retrieve RESUME.STY. (See "Retrieving RESUME.STY for a Single Document," earlier in this chapter.)

3. Highlight Style 2 (Name) and select **E**dit. The Style Editor window appears, as shown in Figure 19.3, displaying the codes and text in the Name style. (The Reveal Codes screen appears automatically in the Style Editor window.)

4. Highlight Michael Pause, MBA, and then press Delete to delete the text. Be careful not to delete formatting codes.

5. Place the cursor just after the [Bold On] code and type your name. (If you didn't move the cursor after step 5, the cursor should already follow the [Bold On] code.)

6. To change the name, description, or type of style (Open or Paired), select **P**roperties. Enter the changes in the Style Properties dialog box and then select OK.

7. Select the **C**lose button or press Ctrl+F4 (Close).

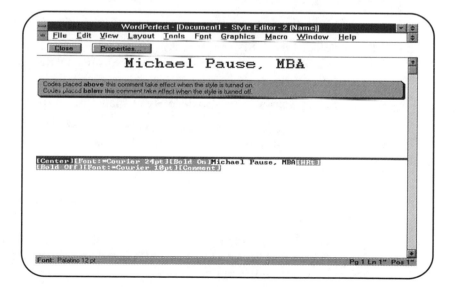

Figure 19.3   The Style Editor window.

Repeat these steps to change the address and phone numbers in Style 3 (Address). These changes are now in effect, but only for this document. If you save the document, the changes you just made will be saved for this file, but will not affect the RESUME.STY file in your styles directory. If you want to save the changes to disk, to update RESUME.STY, perform the following steps.

Saving Style Changes

1. If you closed the Styles dialog box, select Layout/Styles or press Alt+F8 (Styles) to display it.

2. Select Save As. The Save Styles dialog box appears.

3. Type **resume** in the Save As text box. (If you don't include the file extension **.sty**, WordPerfect for Windows automatically adds it.) To save the style file in a directory other than the default styles directory, also type a directory path (for example, **c:\wpwin\resume**).

4. Select Save. The changes are now saved in the RESUME.STY.

The changes will affect the current document and any new documents that use this as their style file. To have the changes affect existing documents that used an older version of RESUME.STY, follow these steps.

Updating the Style in Existing Documents

1. Open the document that you want the revised style sheet to affect.

2. Select Layout/Styles or press Alt+F8 (Styles). The Styles dialog box appears, displaying the version of RESUME.STY that was saved with the document.

3. Select Retrieve. The Retrieve Styles dialog box appears.

4. Type **resume** in the Filename text box. If RESUME.STY is not in the default styles directory, also type the directory path (for example, **c:\wpwin\resume**).

5. Select Retrieve. WordPerfect for Windows displays a dialog box notifying you that styles already exist and asking you whether you want to replace those styles.

6. Select Yes to update the old résumé stylesheet with the latest version (the version most recently saved as RESUME.STY). Select No to cancel the operation.

7. Select the Close button or press Exc to exit the dialog box.

Using the Styles to Create a Résumé

You can now use the styles in RESUME.STY to assemble your résumé. Start with a new WordPerfect for Windows document window. To create your résumé, you will turn on each style in the order in which the styles are listed. Whenever you turn a style on, WordPerfect for Windows inserts a code or a pair of codes at the cursor location. The code consists of the style's name enclosed in square brackets, []. (If you use a Paired style, two codes appear.) If you highlight the code in Reveal Codes, WordPerfect for Windows displays all the formatting codes that make up the style.

Tailor your résumé to the job for which you're applying and to the person who will read the résumé. Call the company first and ask it to send you information about the company's products or services. If you're applying for a particular position, get as much information about that position as possible. Revise the résumé to show how your qualifications can specifically help the company or how they fulfill the advertised requirements. Don't rely solely on a cover letter to accomplish this task. Form résumés are almost as ineffective as form cover letters.

Creating a Résumé

1. Select **Layout/Styles** or press Alt+F8 (Styles). The Styles dialog box appears.

2. If the dialog box does not list the Résumé styles, retrieve RESUME.STY. (See "Retrieving RESUME.STY for a Single Document," earlier in this chapter.)

3. Turn on Style 1 (Page 1) by double-clicking on it, or by highlighting it and selecting **On**. This style sets the top and bottom margins to 0.5", the left margin to 0.9", and the right margin to 0.75". It specifies a paper size of 8.5" by 11", and it draws a vertical line at the left margin. It also creates a footer that inserts a 3.5" right-justified, horizontal line at the bottom of the page, followed by the page number.

4. Select **Layout/Styles** or press Alt+F8 (Styles) to redisplay the Styles dialog box.

5. Turn on Style 2 (Name) by double-clicking on it, or by highlighting it and selecting **On**. Your name appears centered at the top of the page. (To see the text, you might have to press the Left Arrow key or Ctrl+Home to move the cursor across the hidden [Style On] code.)

6. Since Name is a Paired style, move the cursor past the [Style Off] code to turn off the style before selecting the next style.

7. Select **L**ayout/**S**tyles or press Alt+F8 (Styles) to redisplay the Styles dialog box.

8. Turn on Style 3 (Address) by double-clicking on it, or by highlighting it and selecting **O**n. This centers your address one line below your name.

9. To underscore the address with a horizontal line having 30% gray shading, press Alt+F8 to redisplay the Styles dialog box; then turn on Style 4 (HLine) by double-clicking on it, or by highlighting it and selecting **O**n. (You can edit this style to change the line length, position, or gray shading. Refer to Chapter 8 for more information about editing graphic lines.)

10. Select **L**ayout/**S**tyles or press Alt+F8 (Styles) to redisplay the Styles dialog box.

11. Turn on Style 5 (Columns) by double-clicking on it, or by highlighting it and selecting **O**n. This style inserts a [Col:Def] code, which defines parallel columns, the number of columns, column margins, and space between columns. It also enters a [Col On] code, turning the Columns feature on. For more information about parallel columns, refer to Chapter 11.

Shortcut

The styles on the current stylesheet are automatically assigned to the Styles button on the Ruler. If you frequently use styles, you can save many steps by selecting the styles directly from the Ruler. Display the Ruler by selecting **V**iew/**R**uler or by pressing Alt+Shift+F3 (Ruler). To select a style, place the mouse pointer on the Styles button and press and hold the mouse button. The list of current styles appears below the button, as shown in Figure 19.4. Drag the mouse pointer to highlight the style you want, and then release the mouse button to select it.

To see how the résumé will appear in print up to this point, select **F**ile/ **P**rint Preview or press Shift+F5 (Print Preview) to display the document in the Print Preview window, as shown in Figure 19.5.

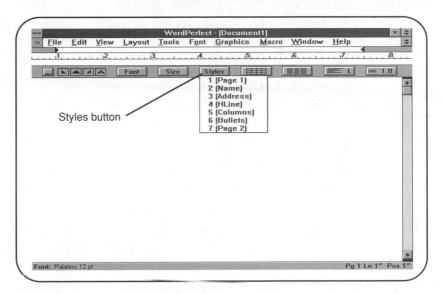

Figure 19.4 *You can choose styles from the list that appears when you select the Styles button on the Ruler.*

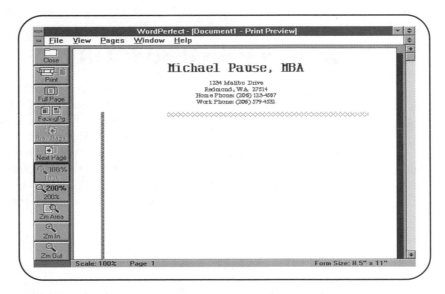

Figure 19.5 *The top of the résumé displayed in the Print Preview window.*

You can now type whatever text you want to use for your résumé. Type an entry for the left column first. For example, type **CAREER OBJECTIVE:**. Press Ctrl+Enter to end this column entry and move the cursor to the right column. Type text in this column as you normally would. WordPerfect for Windows automatically wraps the text to keep it in a column format. When you want to type another entry in the left column, press Ctrl+Enter again.

To create a bulleted list in the right column, move the cursor to the line where you want the list to begin, and select **L**ayout/**S**tyles or press Alt+F8 (Styles). Turn on Style 6 (Bullets) by double-clicking on it, or by highlighting it and selecting **On**. This style creates an indent and inserts a bullet character (4,0) from WordPerfect for Windows' character set number 4. Type the text for the bulleted list.

If your résumé exceeds a single page in length, use Style 7 (Page 2) at the top of the second page. This style inserts the same horizontal line that appeared on Page 1 of the document, giving the two pages a consistent look.

Although it's tempting to include everything in a résumé, try to limit your résumé to two pages. Personnel departments are often bombarded with résumés and have little time to read excessively long ones.

Turning a Paired Style Off

You can cancel a Paired style by removing it completely or by turning it off. To remove the style completely, highlight either the [Style On] or [Style Off] code in Reveal Codes, and press Delete. Both codes in the pair disappear, and the text that was between the codes is no longer formatted according to that style. To just turn a style off, you have two choices. You can press the Right Arrow key to move the cursor past the [Style Off] code, or you can highlight the style in the Styles dialog box and select Off. The text between the [Style Off] code is formatted according to the style; text outside the codes is not.

Creating Your Own Styles

Although the styles in RESUME.STY are sufficient for creating a professional-looking résumé, you may want to use your own styles to customize the application further. Since you already edited styles, the process will seem familiar.

Create a style for each category you use on your résumé. For example, create one style for Career Objective, one for Education, one for Experience, and so on, including the general text you want to use for each. You can then easily rearrange the items to target a particular job. For example, if the position advertised requires a college degree, and you have a master's degree, you may want to list your education first. Another job may require experience using WordPerfect for Windows. If so, you'll want to list your experience first. After inserting the general text, you can then add details specific to this particular résumé.

Creating a Style

1. Select **Layout/Styles** or press Alt+F8 (Styles). The Styles dialog box appears.

2. Select **Create**. The Style Properties dialog box appears, as shown in Figure 19.6.

3. In the **Name** text box, type a name for your style. You can type up to 20 characters, including spaces.

4. Go to the **Description** text box and type a description to help you remember what this style does. You can type up to 54 characters.

5. Select the **Type** pop-up list button, and then select **Paired** or **Open** from the pop-up list.

6. Select the **Enter Key Inserts** pop-up list button, and then select **Hard Return, Style Off,** or **Style Off/On.** This option affects how the Enter key functions if you press it when the cursor is between the [Style On] and [Style Off] codes of Paired styles; the option has no effect on Open styles. If you select **Hard Return,** pressing the Enter key inserts a hard return. If you select **Style Off,** pressing the Enter key turns the style off, by moving the cursor past the [Style Off] code. If you select **Style Off/On,** pressing the Enter key turns the style off and then on again.

7. Select OK. WordPerfect for Windows displays the Style Editor window. Enter the formatting codes and any text you want to use for this style. If you're creating a Paired style, a comment box appears in the window, indicating that codes placed before the comment take effect when the style is turned on, and that codes placed after the comment take effect when the style is turned off.

8. Select the Close button or press Ctrl+F4 (Close). WordPerfect for Windows returns to the Styles dialog box. The name and description of the style you just created appear in the list of available styles.

9. Repeat Steps 2 through 8 for all the styles you want to create.

10. Select the Close button or press Esc to return to the document window.

Figure 19.6   The Style Properties dialog box.

All the styles you created are saved with the document when you save the document. To use these same styles for other documents without re-creating the styles each time, use the Save **As** option described earlier.

You don't have to create styles from scratch. If you have entered formatting codes or text in the document window, you can convert the codes and text into a style. Select a contiguous block of codes, text, or both, and then select **L**ayout/**S**tyles or press Alt+F8 (Styles) to display the Styles dialog box. Select **C**reate, enter a style name and other information in the Style Properties dialog box, and then select OK. The Style Editor window will appear and will contain the codes and text you selected in the document window.

Summary

No two positions are ever the same. One may require strong writing skills, another may require organizational and management skills, others may require interpersonal communications skills. When you're applying for such a variety of positions, you need a standard résumé that is easily tailored. In this chapter, you customized a style file that will allow you to take control of your résumé and add the detail necessary to dazzle prospective employers.

The Résumé Application

Michael Pause, MBA

1234 Malibu Drive
Redmond, WA 27514
Home Phone: (206) 123-4567
Work Phone: (206) 579-4532

CAREER OBJECTIVE

Division manager in charge of development and manufacturing of new CAD/CAM software products.

EXPERIENCE

1986-Present

Project Manager, CAD Mfg., Inc.: Coordinated development for Computer-Aided Design software used in aeronautical engineering plants.
- Manager of the year, 1989 and 1990.
- Elected Chairman of The Software Group, a group of software design and troubleshooting specialists.

1980-85

Production Manager, Orthco Corporation: Acted as interface between Computer-Aided Design department and Computer-Sided Manufacturing department, to ensure quality-control of products.
- After assuming position, I cut the system's down time by over 50% in less than 6 months.
- Percentage of rejected parts dropped by 15% in the same time period.

EDUCATION

1979

MBA, University of Chicago: While working toward degree, worked part time as Controller at nearby manufacturing plant.
- Helped school install and implement a new course about using computers in business.
- Dean's list, 1978 and 1979.

1975

BS in Computer Science, Purdue University: Over 30 hours in programming classes, including experience in co-op program specializing in Software design.

REFERENCES

Available on request.

1

Retrieve equation

1. Select **Graphics/Equation/Create**.

2. Select the Retrieve button or **File/Retrieve**.

3. Type the *drive:\directory \filename.ext* for the equation file you want to retrieve.

4. Select **Retrieve**.

5. Select **File/Close**, the Close button, or press Ctrl+F4.

Edit equation

1. Select **Graphics/Equation/Edit**.

2. Type the number of the Equation box and select OK.

3. Edit the equation.

4. Select **File/Close**, the Close button, or press Ctrl+F4.

Create equation

1. Move the cursor to where you want the equation to appear.

2. Select **Graphics/Equation/Create**.

3. Enter the equation.

4. Select **File/Close**, the Close button, or press Ctrl+F4.

Change equation palettes

1. In the Equation Editor, select the equation palette pop-up list button.

2. Select a palette from the pop-up list.

**BUSINESS
SHORTCUTS**

The Buying Power Index

*Being able to accurately estimate sales is an important part of a
business's success. And, while there are many different models for
evaluating the buying power of a target population, the buying power
index is one of the most widely accepted. In this chapter, you'll learn
how to use the WordPerfect for Windows' Equation feature to customize
this equation for your own use, and how to create other equations to
include in reports and documents. Although the Equation feature does
not let you perform the actual calculations, it does give you the power
to create and print complex formulas that give your reports a professional look.*

About the Application

The *Buying Power Index* (BPI) equation that follows uses a combination of
disposable income, retail sales, and population in a particular area to
estimate the buying power or sales potential for that particular area:

$$BPI = \frac{AI_i + BR_i + CP_i}{10}$$

415

where:

I_i = percentage of disposable income in area i
R_i = percentage of retail sales in area i
P_i = percentage of population in area i

The letters A, B, and C represent the relative importance placed on the three variables in the equation. For example, if A is 2.5 and B is 5.0, then the percentage of retail sales is deemed to be twice as important as the percentage of disposable income. The sum of A+B+C must always equal 10. The relative weights of variables are assigned in this manner according to the individual circumstances of the retail business in a particular area. The 10 in the denominator is the sum of the weights.

The Equation Editor treats equations as graphic elements, so whenever you create or edit an equation, you'll be using the **Graphics** menu. The BPI equation was created by using the following steps:

1. Select **Graphics/Equation/Create**.

2. Select the EquPos button to center the Equation box between the left and right margins. Select it to size the box to make it proportional to the surrounding text.

3. Enter the commands and characters required to create the equation.

Retrieving the Application

To customize the buying power index for your own use, you must retrieve the application BPI.APP into your document. Since this application is an equation, it is not a regular text file. You must use the WordPerfect for Windows graphic tools, as follows:

Retrieving an Equation

1. Move the cursor to the line where you want the equation to appear.

2. Select **Graphics/Equation/Create**. The Equation Editor window appears, as shown in Figure 20.1.

3. Select the Retrieve button or **File/Retrieve**. The Retrieve Equation Text dialog box appears.

4. Type the path and file name for BPI.APP. For example, if you copied the application files to C:\WPWIN\APPS, type **c:\wpwin\apps\bpi.app**.

5. Select **Retrieve**. The Equation Editor window appears with the BPI.APP equation displayed.

6. Select **File/Close**, the Close button, or press Ctrl+F4. The Equation Editor window closes. An Equation box appears in the document window, showing you where the equation will appear in the document.

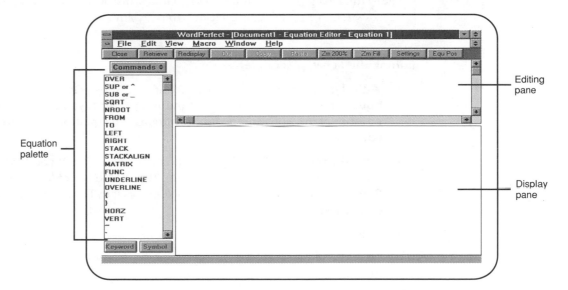

Figure 20.1   The Equation Editor window.

Customizing the BPI Equation

Now that you've retrieved the BPI equation into your document, you can customize the equation by replacing the variables, (BPI, A, B, C, Ii, Ri, and Pi), with whatever values apply. You'll also learn how to manipulate the appearance of the formula by changing its font and its position on the page, and by choosing to print the formula as a graphic image or in text mode.

Editing the BPI Equation

Before you start manipulating the appearance of the formula, you should edit the formula's contents. Editing the formula's contents first ensures that when you view the formula, you're viewing an accurate representation of the formula that will appear in the document.

The Equation Editor window has three panes: the editing pane, the display pane, and the equation palette. (See Figure 20.1.) Press F6 to go to the next pane and Shift+F6 to go to the previous pane. You can also switch to a pane by just clicking in the pane.

Editing the Equation's Contents

1. With the cursor anywhere in the document, select **Graphics/Equation/Edit**. WordPerfect for Windows prompts you to enter the number of the Equation box that contains the equation you want to edit.

2. Type the number of the Equation box and select OK. If you have only one equation in your document, type **1** and select OK. The Equation Editor window appears. (Refer back to Figure 20.1.) The cursor is in the edit pane.

3. Delete BPI.

4. Type the value representing the actual value you calculated as the BPI index.

5. Delete A1 sub i.

6. Type a value for A, and then type an open parenthesis, a value for Ii, and a closed parenthesis.

7. Repeat Steps 5 and 6 for the other two variables, BRi and CPi. (Delete BR sub i and CP sub i.)

8. To update the equation in the display pane, select View/Redisplay, the Redisplay button, or press Ctrl+F3.

Beginner's Tip

If you have a mouse, you can replace the first two steps with the following: Place the mouse pointer within the Equation Box. The status bar displays the prompt: Equ Box - Use right mouse button to display Graphics menu. Click the *right* mouse button, and then place the mouse pointer on Edit Equation and click the *left* mouse button. This procedure works for any graphics box that isn't superimposed on another graphics box. (In that case, you can use this method to select only the underlying box.)

Changing the Equation Options

Whenever you create an equation, WordPerfect for Windows uses a set of default settings to format the graphics box it uses for the formulas. For example, the equation graphics boxes have no border, any captions used are bold, and the graphics boxes are not shaded. If you want to change the default settings for the equation options, you must enter your changes in the Equation Options dialog box, as shown in Figure 20.2. This dialog box offers the following options:

Border Styles: By default, WordPerfect for Windows prints equations in a borderless box. To create a border, select the pop-up list button for each side of the box, (Left, Right, Top, and Bottom), and select a border from the pop-up list that appears. To create a box with a dropped shadow, set the Left and Bottom borders to Double, and the Top and Right borders to Single.

Border Spacing: Lets you control the outside distance between the box and surrounding text, and the distance between the box and the equation inside the box.

Gray Shading: Lets you shade your box. The default, 0%, adds no shading. Entering 100% makes the box completely black.

Minimum Offset from Paragraph: Tells WordPerfect for Windows how close a graphics box can be moved to the top of a paragraph. This option keeps the box on the same page as the paragraph containing the Equation Box code. The default is 0", so the box can be even with the first line of the paragraph.

Caption Numbering: Lets you choose a numbering system for the first and second levels of numbers in captions. For example, if you're numbering equations Formula A-1, Formula A-2, and so on, your **F**irst Level numbering would be **L**etters, and your **S**econd Level numbering would be **N**umbers.

Caption Numbering Style: Lets you set the style for your caption. Type any text you want included with the caption number. Type **1** to indicate where the first level number should appear, and **2** to indicate where the second level number should appear. You can insert codes to make some or all of the caption bold, italics, underline, or small caps. To enter a code, select the pop-up list button to the right of the **S**tyle text box and then select **B**old, **I**talics, **U**nderline, or Small **C**aps. For example, if you want your first caption to appear as *Formula A-1*, select **B**old from the pop-up list, move the cursor between the [Bold On] and [Bold Off] codes, and then type **Formula 1-2**. The **1** represents the first level numbering; the **2** represents the second level.

Caption Position: Select this pop-up list button to control the position of the caption in relation to the box. You can select **B**elow, **A**bove, **L**eft, or **R**ight.

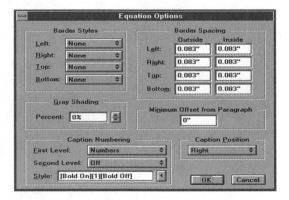

Figure 20.2   The Equation Options dialog box.

Changing Equation Box Options

1. Move the cursor to precede any Equation boxes you want the changes to affect.

2. Select **G**raphics/**E**quation/**O**ptions. The Equation Options dialog box appears.

3. Select the options you want.

4. Select OK. WordPerfect for Windows returns you to the document window and inserts an [Equ Opt] code at the cursor location. This code controls the appearance of Equation boxes until the program encounters a different [Equ Opt] code or until the end of the document.

Changing the Equation's Position and Appearance

In the previous section, you changed the appearance of the Equation boxes throughout your document. In this section, you'll manipulate the appearance of individual equations. You can enter your changes in two places: in the Box Position and Size dialog box and in the Caption Editor window. The Box Position and Size dialog box, shown in Figure 20.3, offers the following options that allow you to define the Equation box:

Box Type: WordPerfect for Windows allows the following graphic box types: Figure, Table, Text, User, and Equation. Each box type is numbered separately from the other types. You also can set different options for each box type. To have the Equation box be numbered with and have the same options as a different box type, select the **B**ox Type pop-up list button and then select a new box type. To have an Equation box be numbered with Text boxes, for example, change **B**ox Type to Text **B**ox. The box will have the characteristics set by the last [Txt Opt] code.

Changing the box type doesn't affect the box contents or the editor window for the box. If you later edit the box in the example just given, you will still use the Equation Editor window, not the Text Box Editor window.

Anchor To: This pop-up list button gives you a choice of where to anchor a box. **P**aragraph anchors the box to the paragraph the cursor was in when you created the box, (in other words, the box moves with the paragraph). P**a**ge anchors the box to the page. **C**haracter treats the box as a single character inserted at the cursor position. (Text leads into the left side of the box and out the right side on the same line.)

Size: If you select this pop-up list button, WordPerfect for Windows presents a list of sizing methods. To have WordPerfect for Windows automatically size the graphics box, select **Auto Both**. To enter your own dimensions, select **Set Both** and enter dimensions for the box in the **Width** and **Height** text boxes. To set one dimension and have WordPerfect for Windows set the other, select Auto **Width**, (you set the height), or Auto **Height**, (you set the width). Enter the dimension you want to set in the appropriate text box below the **Size** button. (It will be the only available text box; the other will be dimmed.)

Vertical Position: Select this pop-up list button to display options for positioning the box vertically on the page. Your options depend on the anchor type. If you anchored the box to the page, select **Full** Page to extend the box from the top to bottom margin. Select **Top** to place it at the top of the page. Select **Center** to center it between the top and bottom margins. Select **Bottom** to place it at the bottom of the page. Or, select **Set** Position to specify an exact location. If you select **Set** Position, enter the distance between the top of the page and the top of the box in the **Position** text box.

If you anchored the box to a paragraph, **Set** Position is automatically selected. You can use the **Position** text box to specify a distance between the top edge of the paragraph and the top of the box, (including outside border space).

If you anchored the box to a character, select **Top** to align the top of the box with the surrounding text. Select **Center** to align the center of the box with the surrounding text. Or, select **Bottom** to align the bottom of the box with the surrounding text. Select **B**aseline to align the baseline of the graphics box contents with the baseline of the surrounding text.

Horizontal Position: Select this pop-up list button to display options for positioning the box horizontally on the page. As with **V**ertical Position, your options depend on the anchor type. If you anchored the box to the page, you can align it with the left or right margins, (Margin, **Left** or Margin, **Right**), center it between the left and right margins, (Margin, **Center**), extend it from the left to the right margin, (Margin, **Full**), or set an exact position, (**Set** Position). You specify the exact position in the **Position** text box. If you have columns, you also can align the box with or between one or more columns; specify the column or range of columns in the text box below the pop-up list button.

If you anchored the box to a paragraph, you can align it with the left or right edge of the paragraph, (Margin, **L**eft or Margin, **R**ight), center it between the left and right edges, (Margin, **C**enter), extend it from the left to the right edge, (Margin, **F**ull), or set an exact position from the left edge of the paragraph, (**S**et Position). You specify an exact position in the **P**osition text box. If you indented the paragraph, the edge depends on where the [Indent] code is. If the [Indent] code precedes the [Box] code, the left edge is the indent position. If you are using columns, you can also align the Equation box with respect to the column margins.

If you anchored the box to a character, you cannot set a horizontal position.

Wrap Text Around Box: If you deselect this check box to prevent the text from wrapping around the box, text may be printed over the box. Deselect this check box only if you want to superimpose text over the box.

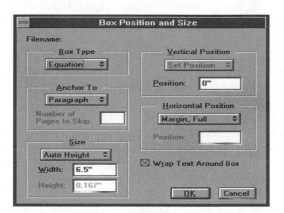

Figure 20.3   The Box Position and Size dialog box.

 Changing the Box Position and Size

1. With the cursor anywhere in the document, select **G**raphics/ **E**quation/**P**osition. WordPerfect for Windows prompts you to enter the number of the Equation box that contains the equation you want to edit.

2. Type the number of the Equation box and select OK. If you have only one equation in your document, type **1** and select OK. The Box Position and Size dialog box appears. (Refer back to Figure 20.3).

3. Select the options you want, and then select OK.

You can also display the Box Position and Size dialog box by placing the mouse pointer within the Equation box and pressing the right mouse button. In the pop-up list that appears, select Box Position. Within the Equation Editor window, you can select the dialog box by selecting File/Box **P**osition or the Equ Pos button.

You can also enter captions for each Equation box. For example, you may want to enter a caption explaining the function of each variable. You enter the caption in the Caption Editor window.

Entering a Caption

1. With the cursor anywhere in the document, select **Graphics/ Equation/Ca**ption. WordPerfect for Windows prompts you to enter the number of the Equation box.

2. Type the number of the Equation box and select OK. If you have only one equation in your document, type **1** and select OK. The Caption Editor window appears, as shown in Figure 20.4. The Equation box number is automatically entered in the format selected in the Box Position and Size dialog box.

3. Type the caption.

4. Select **F**ile/**C**lose, the **C**lose button, or press Ctrl+F4. WordPerfect for Windows closes the Caption Editor window and saves the caption.

You can also display the Caption Editor window by placing the mouse pointer within the Equation box and pressing the right mouse button. In the pop-up list that appears, select Edit **Ca**ption. For more information about captions, see Chapter 3.

When you have changed the settings, select **Graphics/Equation/E**dit to return to the Equation Editor window for this formula. Next, select **F**ile/ **S**ettings or select the Settings button to view the Equation Settings dialog box, shown in Figure 20.5. This screen presents a list of additional options that you can use to customize the appearance of the formula *within* the box:

Print as Graphics: By default this check box is selected, meaning that the equation will print as a graphic image. The formula will appear in print very similar to the way it appears in the Equation Editor. Most printers are capable of printing formulas in this way. You can improve the appearance of the formula significantly by printing it as text. If your printer can print formulas as text, using the selected font, clear the check box. The effects of the two settings are shown in Figure 20.6.

Graphic Font Size: WordPerfect for Windows will print the formula in **D**efault Font, the same size as the default setting for your base font. Use the **P**oint Size option if you want the equation to appear in a different size font, *and* if you choose to print the formula as a graphic image. If you choose to print the formula as text, you must change the font size as discussed in the following section. This option differs from the **S**ize options in the Box Position and Size dialog box, in that it controls the size of the equation rather than the size of the box that surrounds it.

Horizontal Alignment: This option lets you control the horizontal position of the equation *inside* the box that contains the equation. For example, you can center the Equation box and then push the equation to the left side of the box to indent the equation from the left margin.

Vertical Alignment: This option lets you control the vertical position of the equation inside the box that contains the equation.

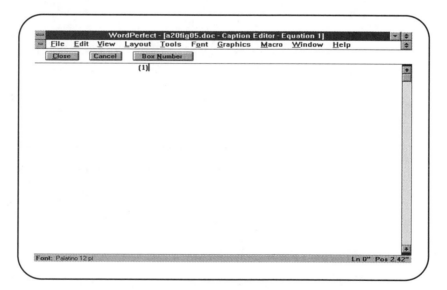

Figure 20.4   The Caption Editor window.

425

Figure 20.5   The Equation Settings dialog box.

This equation is printed in graphic mode:

$$BPI = \frac{AI_i + BR_i + CP_i}{10}$$

This equation is printed in text mode:

$$BPI = \frac{AI_i + BR_i + CP_i}{10}$$

Figure 20.6   The BPI equation printed in graphic and text mode.

Changing Font Size for a Text Equation

If you choose to print the formula as text rather than graphics, WordPerfect for Windows assumes you want to print the formula in the font that is in effect at the location of the Equation box. To make the formula's appearance different from the surrounding text, you must enter codes to make the change and codes to return to the style of the text. If you want to make the font larger or smaller than the text, or to make it bold or italic, you must enter a [Font] code or an attribute code before the Equation box. Specify the font or attribute for the equation. Then, enter a [Font] or attribute code after the Equation box to return to the original font for subsequent text.

Changing Fonts for a Text Equation

1. Select View/Reveal Codes, or press Alt+F3 to display the Reveal Codes screen.

2. Move the cursor so that the highlight in the Reveal Codes screen is on the [Equ Box] code.

3. Select Graphics/Equation/Options, and then select OK. This inserts an [Equ Opt] code at the cursor location, but uses the same Equation options as those specified earlier.

4. Move the cursor so the highlight is on the [Equ Opt] code.

5. Select Font/Font or press F9. The Font dialog box appears, listing available fonts.

6. Enter the new font, (and point size if you are using scalable fonts), or select the appearance and size attributes.

7. Select OK. WordPerfect for Windows inserts a [Font] or attribute On code at the cursor location.

8. Move the cursor to the space after the [Equ Box] code and repeat Step 5 to display the Font dialog box.

9. Enter the original font, (and point size, if necessary), or clear the appearance and size attribute check boxes. Select OK.

10. To view the equation with the new font, select File/Print Preview, or press Shift+F5.

Whenever you enter a [Font] code to change fonts within a document, be sure to enter another [Font] code where you want the font to change back to the original. Otherwise, the rest of your document will be printed in the new font.

At this point, you have all the tools you need to edit and manipulate the BPI equation. However, you may need to create and use other equations for your reports. The following section explains how to use the Equation Editor's Equation Palette to create your own equations.

Creating Equations

Every equation consists of two basic elements: variables, (or values), and mathematical operators. Creating an equation consists of entering the variables or values specific to your application and selecting WordPerfect for Windows' mathematical symbols to act as the operators. But before you can begin creating the equation, you must define the graphics box that will hold the equation.

Defining an Equation Box

1. Move the cursor to the line where you want the equation to appear.

2. Select **Graphics/Equation/Create**. The Equation Editor window appears. (Refer back to Figure 20.1.)

If you were to select **File/Close** to exit the Equation Editor window at this point, the graphics box would be defined. WordPerfect for Windows would return you to the document window and insert an [Equ Box] code at the cursor location. But instead of doing that, we will remain in the Equation Editor to create the following equation for determining the arithmetic mean:

$$\overline{X} = \sum \frac{x_i}{n}$$

You could use this equation to illustrate how you arrived at an average—for example, average retail sales or average overtime hours.

Beginner's Tip

Always use left and right braces {} to enclose a quantity that you want to be treated as a single value. For example, if you want to average A + B + C, type {A+B+C} over 3. If you used parentheses instead, WordPerfect for Windows would put C) over the 3, but (A+B+ would be separated off to the left.

Creating an Equation for the Arithmetic Mean

1. If necessary, press F6, (Next Pane), or Shift+F6, (Previous Pane), to place the cursor in the edit pane.

2. Type **overline**, or press F6 to go to the equation palette, highlight OVERLINE, and press Enter. You can also enter **overline** by just

double-clicking on OVERLINE in the equation palette. This command puts a line over the character that follows it.

3. Type **{vert -20 X}** = and press the space bar. The braces {} group what's between them so the Equation Editor will treat the contents as a single value. The *vert -20* moves the *X* 20/1200ths of an inch down, to create space between the X and the line above it. You can also select the vert command from the equation palette by pressing F6, highlighting VERT, and pressing Enter, or by double-clicking on VERT.

4. Type **sum**, or select the small sigma, (summation symbol), from the equation palette. This inserts a sigma. (To choose it from the palette, select the pop-up list button, and then select **Large**. A new list of commands will appear, one of which will be a small sigma.) If you select sigma by pressing Ctrl+Enter instead of Enter, the symbol, (instead of the word), appears in the edit pane. There will be no difference in how the sigma appears in the formula.

5. Press the space bar, type **x**, and then press the space bar.

6. Type **sub**, or select the pop-up list button in the equation palette, reselect Commands to display the Commands equation palette, and then select SUB from the palette.

7. Press the space bar, type **i**, and then press the space bar.

8. Type **over**, or select OVER from the equation palette, and then press the space bar.

9. Type **n**.

10. Select **View/Redisplay** or the Redisplay button, or press Ctrl+F3, to see the equation displayed. The equation should appear as shown in Figure 20.7.

11. Select **File/Save As**, or press F3, type a file name for the equation, and then select OK.

12. Select **File/Close**, the Close button, or press Ctrl+F4, to close the Equation Editor window. WordPerfect for Windows returns to the document window, where the equation is now displayed.

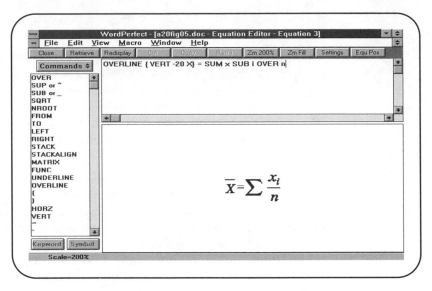

Figure 20.7   The equation displayed in the Equation Editor window.

The Equation Palette

In the previous section, you used the equation palette to enter mathematical symbols in the equation. The more common mathematical functions are displayed when you call up the Equation Editor. However, the palette offers many more commands than those initially shown. In fact, it offers more than seven screens that come under the following categories:

Commands: Contains regularly used equation operations such as SQRT, (for square root), and OVER, (for building fractions).

Large: Contains symbols that can be used in either small or large sizes, such as the summation symbol (sigma).

Symbols: Contains miscellaneous mathematical and scientific symbols, such as the following: /, //,

Greek: Contains the upper- and lowercase Greek alphabet.

Arrows: Contains arrows, triangles, and other symbols.

Sets: Contains mathematical set symbols.

Other: Contains diacritical marks and ellipses.

Function: Contains mathematical functions such as sine, cosine, maximum, minimum, and log.

You can use these other palettes by selecting the pop-up list button in the equation palette and then selecting a symbol from the palette. If you would rather enter the word for the symbol, rather than the symbol itself, highlight the symbol, (click on it or use the arrow keys), and then select the Keyword button.

Using the EQUATION.WPK Keyboard

If you do not find any keyboard alternatives when you look on the Setup menu, it is probably because you elected not to install them. To install alternative keyboard layouts, you must exit WordPerfect for Windows, run the Installation program again to update the installation, and select to install the keyboard layouts.

WordPerfect for Windows comes with several different keyboard layouts, including one for the Equation Editor that lets you increase your editing speed. For example, if you select the keyboard layout for the Equation Editor, you can enter the Overline command simply by pressing Ctrl+Shift+L. Refer to Table 20.1 for a complete list of the keystrokes you can use and the symbols that those keystrokes insert.

Selecting the EQUATION.WPK Keyboard

1. Select **File/Preferences/Keyboard**, or press Ctrl+Shift+F1 and type **k**. The Keyboard dialog box appears.

2. Choose **Select**. WordPerfect for Windows displays the Select Keyboard File dialog box, which lists installed keyboard layouts. If no keyboard layouts are listed, you did not install them.

3. Select equation.wwk.

4. Choose **Select**, and then choose OK. The new keyboard is now in effect.

Table 20.1   The Equation Keyboard Keystrokes and Results

Press	*To Insert*
Ctrl+E	ε
Ctrl+R	ρ
Ctrl+T	θ

continues

Table 20.1   Continued.

Press	To Insert
Ctrl+I	INF
Ctrl+O	Ω
Ctrl+P	π
Ctrl+A	α
Ctrl+S	Σ
Ctrl+D	Δ
Ctrl+F	ϕ
Ctrl+G	Γ
Ctrl+L	λ
Ctrl+B	β
Ctrl+M	μ
Ctrl+N	η
Ctrl+Shift+Tab	$\leftarrow$
Ctrl+Tab	$\rightarrow$
Ctrl+Shift+A	SUP
Ctrl+Shift+B	BAR
Ctrl+Shift+D	Δ
Ctrl+Shift+E	IN (member or element symbol)
Ctrl+Shift+F	FROM TO (runs FROM-TO macro)
Ctrl+Shift+G	GRAD
Ctrl+Shift+I	INT
Ctrl+Shift+L	OVERLINE
Ctrl+Shift+N	GRAD
Ctrl+Shift+O	OVER
Ctrl+Shift+P	PARTIAL
Ctrl+Shift+Q	SQRT
Ctrl+Shift+S	SUM
Ctrl+Shift+Z	SUB

For example, if you want to type the equation shown in Figure 20.7, enter the following sequence of commands in the editing window: `Ctrl+Shift+L {vert -20 X} = Ctrl+Shift+S X Ctrl+Shift+Z i Ctrl+Shift+O n`.

Equation Keyboard Macro

On the disk you received with this book is a macro that switches from the original keyboard to the equation keyboard. To run the macro, select **Macro/Play**, or press Alt+F10, type **ek**, and then select **Play**. The macro performs the following steps:

Keystroke	Function
Alt, **f**, **e**, **k**	Displays the Keyboard dialog box.
Alt+S	Chooses Select.
`equation.wwk`	Enters the name of the keyboard.
Alt+S	Selects the Equation keyboard.
Enter	Closes the Keyboard dialog box.

When you're done using the Equation keyboard, return to the Keyboard dialog box and switch back to the original keyboard. Otherwise, various keystrokes you use in the normal document window may not work as expected.

Additional Business Equations

The following sections provide several equations that are commonly used in business applications. Since the Equation feature does not perform the actual calculations, you cannot use the feature to compute results. However, you may wish to include the formulas in reports to illustrate the methods you used to determine your results. In Chapters 6 and 13, you can see how to use such equations.

Shortcut

Create a directory called EQUATION, and store all the equations you frequently use in this new directory. When you want to use the equation, simply retrieve it into an Equation Box, instead of re-creating the equation from scratch.

Chain Method of Estimating Sales

The following equation uses various parameters to estimate sales potential for individual products.

$$SP = P \times PCE \times PP \times PSP$$

where:

SP = Sales Potential
P = Population of target area
PCE = Per Capita Expenditure
PP = Proportion spent on Product
PSP = Proportion spent on Specific Product

Moving Averages Forecasting

This equation computes the moving average for a set of sales figures which can be used to predict sales for the upcoming sales period.

$$FP = \frac{S_1 + S_2 + S_3}{n}$$

where:

FP = Forecasted Period
S1 = Sales in period 1
S2 = Sales in period 2
S3 = Sales in period 3
n = number of periods included in the estimate (3, in this example)

Compound Interest

The following equation computes the amount of interest earned on an investment when the interest is compounded.

$$S = P \,(1+i)^n$$

where
S = Sum of principal
P = Principal
i = interest rate
n = number of periods p has been at current interest rate

Interest Discounting

This equation computes the present value of an amount, given its future value and the associated discount rate.

$$PV = \frac{FV}{(1+i)^n}$$

where:

PV = Present Value
FV = Future Value
i = discount rate
n = number of years until funds are received

Marginal Revenue

This equation computes marginal revenue, which is the change in total revenue that results from the selling of one additional unit.

$$MR = \frac{TR_1 - TR_2}{A}$$

where:

MR = Marginal Revenue
TR1 = Total Revenues after increase
TR2 = Total Revenues before increase
A = unit increase (or increase in quantity sold)

Summary

The Equation Editor allows you to create any equation, from the simplest to the most complex, and edit it using a wide variety of commands. While you cannot use the Equation Editor to actually compute values, it is an invaluable feature for incorporating mathematical, scientific, or business information in your document that illustrates your methods and results.

The Buying Power Index Equation

$$BPI = \frac{AI_i + BR_i + CP_i}{10}$$

Installing WordPerfect

You must install WordPerfect for Windows onto a hard disk. To do so, use the WordPerfect for Windows installation program. You cannot simply copy the files from the WordPerfect for Windows disks, because the disk files are in a compressed format. The installation program expands the files so your computer can use them. But before you install the program, you should make copies of the program disks as explained in the following section.

Making Backup Copies of the WordPerfect Program Disks

Before you begin making backup copies of the program disks, obtain the following number of blank, formatted disks:

- If you have a 5.25" drive, obtain six new 5.25" high-density disks.

- If you have a 3.25" drive, obtain six new 3.25" high-density disks.

Label each of the new disks to correspond to each of the original WordPerfect for Windows disks. You don't need to format them—DOS will format them automatically when it copies the WordPerfect for Windows files. Now you're ready to copy the program disks.

Making Backup Copies

1. Insert the original WordPerfect for Windows disk you want to copy into the floppy drive.

2. Type **diskcopy drive: drive:** and press Enter, where *drive* is the letter of the floppy drive. If your floppy drive is drive A:, for example, type **diskcopy a: a:** and press Enter. A prompt appears, asking you to insert the Source diskette into the floppy drive and press Enter.

3. Since you already inscrted the source diskette in step 1, just press Enter. DOS starts to copy the files from the disk to your computer's memory. A prompt appears on screen when you need to switch disks.

4. When the `Insert Target Disk` prompt appears, replace the program disk with the blank disk and press Enter. DOS copies the files from your computer's memory to the disk in the floppy drive. You might be prompted to swap disks during the copying. A message will appear telling you when the copying is complete.

5. Remove the disk from the floppy drive, and repeat steps 1-4 until all the program disks are copied.

6. Store the original WordPerfect for Windows disks in a safe place that's free from heat and moisture. Use the copies you just made to install WordPerfect for Windows.

Starting the Installation Process

The first WordPerfect for Windows disk, titled "Install/Program 1," contains an installation program that leads you through the installation process.

Running the Installation Program

1. Turn on your computer, and, if necessary, return to the DOS prompt. C: (or some variant of C) should be displayed.

2. Insert your copy of the Install/Program 1 disk in the A: or B: floppy drive.

3. Type **a:install** or **b:install**, depending on which floppy drive contains the Install/Program 1 disk, and press Enter. The Welcome to WordPerfect 5.1 for Windows screen appears, asking if you want to continue with the installation.

4. Type **y** to continue with the installation or **n** to cancel the procedure. If you type **y**, the WordPerfect Installation Options screen
   appears, as shown in Figure A.1.

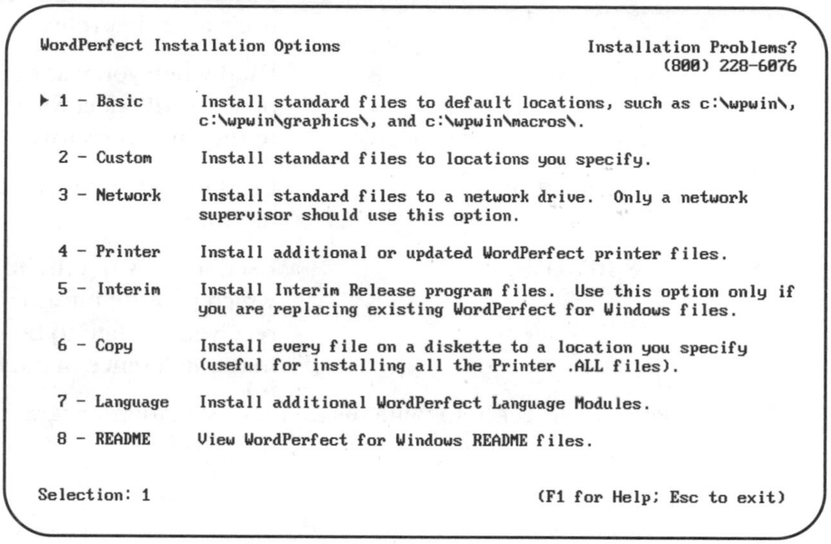

```
WordPerfect Installation Options                    Installation Problems?
                                                          (800) 228-6076

▶ 1 - Basic        Install standard files to default locations, such as c:\wpwin\,
                   c:\wpwin\graphics\, and c:\wpwin\macros\.

  2 - Custom       Install standard files to locations you specify.

  3 - Network      Install standard files to a network drive.  Only a network
                   supervisor should use this option.

  4 - Printer      Install additional or updated WordPerfect printer files.

  5 - Interim      Install Interim Release program files.  Use this option only if
                   you are replacing existing WordPerfect for Windows files.

  6 - Copy         Install every file on a diskette to a location you specify
                   (useful for installing all the Printer .ALL files).

  7 - Language     Install additional WordPerfect Language Modules.

  8 - README       View WordPerfect for Windows README files.


Selection: 1                                        (F1 for Help; Esc to exit)
```

Figure A.1   *The WordPerfect Installation Options screen.*

The WordPerfect Installation Options screen offers the following
choices that let you install WordPerfect in a variety of ways.

Installation Option	*Function*
1 Basic	Used to install WordPerfect for Windows files to predefined default directories, for example, C:\WPWIN and C:\WPWIN\GRAPHICS.
2 Custom	Used when you want to specify different directories for categories of WordPerfect for Windows files.
3 Network	Used for installing WordPerfect for Windows on a network—a group of computers that are all connected to each other and share applications.
4 Printer	Used to install new printer files.

Installation Option	Function
5 Interim	Used to install any updates that you might receive from WordPerfect containing new features or corrections to earlier releases.
6 Copy	Used when you want to copy all files on a WordPerfect for Windows disk to the same directory.
7 Language	Used to install new language modules.
8 README	Used for viewing the README files, which provide information that was received too late to be incorporated in the Reference manual.

| Press F1 to get help while using the Installation program.

Selecting the Basic Installation

Select **B**asic to have WordPerfect install the files to the following directories. If the directories do not exist, WordPerfect creates them.

Files	Directory
Program files	C:\WPWIN
Graphics files	C:\WPWIN\GRAPHICS
Learning files (used with WordPerfect for Windows workbook)	C:\WPWIN\LEARN
Macro files	C:\WPWIN\MACROS
Keyboard files	C:\WPWIN\MACROS
Speller, Thesaurus, File Manager, Macro Facility, and other utilities	C:\WPC
Printer files	C:\WPC

When you select **B**asic, WordPerfect asks from where you are installing the program. If the displayed drive (A:\ or B:\) is correct, press Enter. Otherwise, type **a:** or **b:**, depending on which drive contains the Install/ Program 1 disk, and press Enter.

WordPerfect next displays information about your system, including how much space WordPerfect for Windows will occupy. If this is acceptable and you want to continue installation, type **y**. WordPerfect begins installing the files, prompting you to insert other floppy disks as necessary.

Near the end of the basic installation, WordPerfect asks you to select the CUA keyboard or the WP 5.1 for DOS keyboard. Unless you are familiar with the WP 5.1 for DOS keyboard and don't want to change, we recommend that you use the CUA keyboard, which is similar to keyboards used in other Windows applications.

WordPerfect also asks you whether you want to install WordPerfect printer drivers. You should do so, because this will allow you more flexibility in formatting your documents (see Chapter 1). WordPerfect printer drivers do not allow you to access Windows fonts that you may have installed on your system. However, you can switch back and forth between Windows and WordPerfect drivers at any time. To install one or more WordPerfect printer drivers, type **y** and follow the prompts.

Performing a Custom Installation

If you prefer to copy the WordPerfect files to directories that you specify, perform a custom installation by selecting **2** Custom in the WordPerfect Installation Options screen. WordPerfect starts the custom installation process, displaying the Custom Installation screen shown in Figure A.2. This screen leads you through the process for installing the WordPerfect for Windows files.

During the custom installation process, you can choose to install or not install several types of files. The following list explains the types of files that you can choose. If you have enough room on your hard drive, it's best to install all the files, but the only mandatory files are the WordPerfect program files.

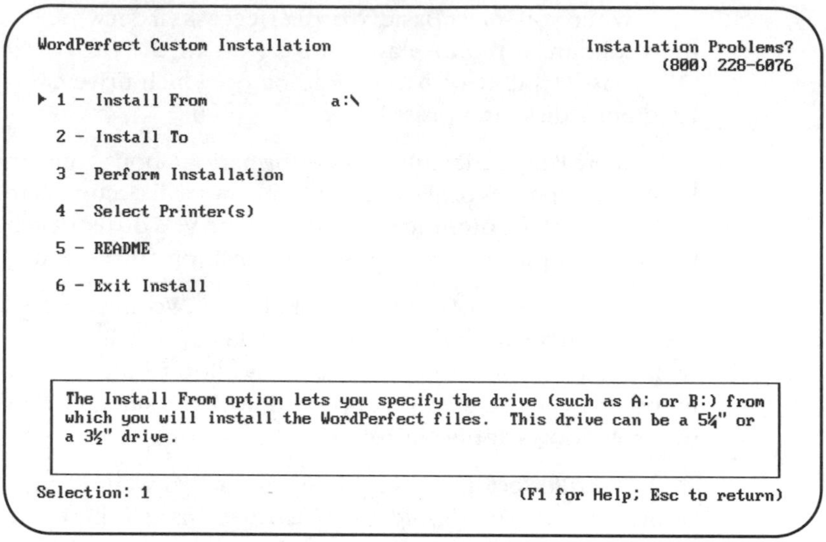

```
WordPerfect Custom Installation                    Installation Problems?
                                                        (800) 228-6076

▶ 1 - Install From                  a:\

  2 - Install To

  3 - Perform Installation

  4 - Select Printer(s)

  5 - README

  6 - Exit Install




  ┌──────────────────────────────────────────────────────────────────┐
  │ The Install From option lets you specify the drive (such as A: or B:) from │
  │ which you will install the WordPerfect files.  This drive can be a 5¼" or  │
  │ a 3½" drive.                                                       │
  └──────────────────────────────────────────────────────────────────┘

  Selection: 1                                    (F1 for Help; Esc to return)
```

Figure A.2   The Custom Installation screen.

Files	*Description*
WordPerfect Program	Files that WordPerfect needs in order to operate.
Documents	Text files included with WordPerfect.
Graphics Files	Sample WordPerfect graphic images with a .WPG extension. You can import these images directly into your WordPerfect documents.
Macros/Keyboards	Various macros and keyboard layouts that can help you use specific features more efficiently.
Styles Files	Preformatted style files that you can use to format your documents.
Learning	A set of WordPerfect tutorials.
WPCorp Shared Products	Files that are shared by more than one WordPerfect Corporation program.
Printer Files	WordPerfect printer drivers and the WordPerfect Printer program.

Performing a Custom Installation

1. Select **1**-Install **F**rom, type the letter of the floppy drive you'll be using, followed by a colon, and press Enter, or just press Enter to accept the default, A:.

2. Press Enter to select **2**-Install **T**o. The Installation: Location of Files screen appears, as shown in Figure A.3. The screen shows the default directories where WordPerfect Windows files will be installed.

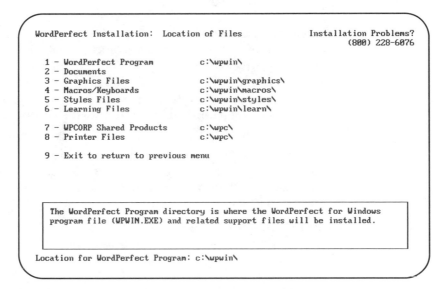

```
WordPerfect Installation:  Location of Files          Installation Problems?
                                                          (800) 228-6076

        1 - WordPerfect Program      c:\wpwin\
        2 - Documents
        3 - Graphics Files           c:\wpwin\graphics\
        4 - Macros/Keyboards         c:\wpwin\macros\
        5 - Styles Files             c:\wpwin\styles\
        6 - Learning Files           c:\wpwin\learn\

        7 - WPCORP Shared Products   c:\wpc\
        8 - Printer Files            c:\wpc\

        9 - Exit to return to previous menu



     ┌──────────────────────────────────────────────────────────────────┐
     │ The WordPerfect Program directory is where the WordPerfect for Windows │
     │ program file (WPWIN.EXE) and related support files will be installed.  │
     └──────────────────────────────────────────────────────────────────┘

  Location for WordPerfect Program: c:\wpwin\
```

Figure A.3   Use the Installation: Location of Files screen to install groups of files in separate directories.

3. To change the default directory for any group of files, select the group name, for example, **1**-WordPerfect Program. A prompt appears at the bottom of the screen, showing the default directory (for example, C:\WPWIN). Press Enter to accept the default; or type a different path and press Enter. If the directory does not exist, type **y** when prompted to have it created.

4. Select **9**-Exit. This returns you to the Custom Installation screen.

5. Press Enter to select **3**-Perform Installation. WordPerfect displays information about your system, including how much space WordPerfect for Windows will occupy. If this is acceptable and you want to continue installation, type **y**. WordPerfect begins installing

the files, prompting you to insert other floppy disks as necessary. When the files are installed, WordPerfect for Windows queries you about the next group of files.

6. Near the end of the installation, WordPerfect asks you to select the CUA keyboard or the WP 5.1 for DOS keyboard. Unless you are familiar with the WP 5.1 for DOS keyboard and don't want to change, we recommend that you use the CUA keyboard, which is similar to keyboards used in other Windows applications. After you select a keyboard, you return to the Custom Installation screen (see Figure A.2)

7. To install a WordPerfect printer driver for your printer, select **4**-Select **P**rinter(s). WordPerfect also asks you whether you want to install WordPerfect printer drivers. (We discussed the merits of WordPerfect and Windows drivers earlier in this appendix.) To install one or more WordPerfect printer drivers, type **y** and follow the prompts. When finished, you return to the Custom Installation screen (see Figure A.2).

8. Select **5**-**R**EADME to display recent WordPerfect for Windows information that supercedes or amplifies information in the WordPerfect for Windows manual. Press Esc one or more times to return to the Custom Installation screen.

9. Select **6**-**E**xit Install to exit the Installation program and return to the DOS prompt. You are now ready to run WordPerfect for Windows. See Chapter 1 for details.

BUSINESS
SHORTCUTS

Windows Primer

When you use software, you don't actually see the software code; rather, the picture you see on your screen is an interface *between you and the software. The interface allows you to more easily use the application: Instead of reading and entering code, you just select from a menu or press a function key. Windows is a Microsoft product that provides an easy-to-use graphic interface between the user and other applications. Because it is a graphic interface, text and graphics you enter on screen closely resemble the actual text and graphics that will print out. Windows also allows you to use a mouse or the keyboard to select options in an application.*

WordPerfect for Windows is a Windows application—that is, it uses the Windows graphic interface to display WordPerfect's features to you. When you use WordPerfect for Windows, therefore, you are using many Windows features, too. The design and use of menus, dialog boxes, and windows all conform to Windows standards. If WordPerfect for Windows is your first Windows application, you might want to review this appendix to learn Windows features that you will frequently use in WordPerfect for Windows.

Windows Features in WordPerfect for Windows

In WordPerfect for Windows, you use the following Windows features:

windows: The Windows interface displays your applications and documents in rectangular boxes called *windows*. When you start an application or retrieve a document, you are *opening* the application or document window. When you exit the application or document, you are *closing* that window. You can have several windows open at once and arrange them on your computer screen. For additional information, see "Windows" later in this appendix.

menus: Menus are lists of options that you can select. For additional information, see "Menus" later in this appendix.

dialog boxes: Some menu options cannot be implemented until you provide additional information. If you select such a menu option, the application displays a dialog box, in which you enter the required information. For additional information, see "Dialog Boxes" later in this appendix.

Using the Mouse

In Windows, you can use a mouse to complete most tasks. Although a mouse is not necessary (tasks can also be completed from the keyboard), you will find in some cases that using the mouse is more convenient than using the keyboard. If you have never used a mouse, the following terms might be new to you:

mouse pointer	The pointer that appears on screen and moves as you move your mouse.
point at an object	Move the mouse pointer so that the arrow points at the desired object.
click the mouse button	Press and release the mouse button. To "click on" an object means to point at it and click.
double-click the mouse button	Click the mouse button twice in quick succession. To "double-click on" an object means to point at it and double-click.

drag the mouse pointer	Press and hold the mouse button while moving the mouse.
drag an object	Point at the object, and then press and hold the mouse button while moving the object.

If your mouse has more than one button, the action refers to the *left* mouse button unless otherwise stated. (If you use a left-handed mouse, the action refers to the right mouse button.)

Menus

Windows applications typically display a menu bar at the top of the application window, as shown in Figure B.1 for WordPerfect for Windows. The menu bar lists the names of menus you can display. Figure B.2, for example, shows a menu displayed from the WordPerfect for Windows menu bar.

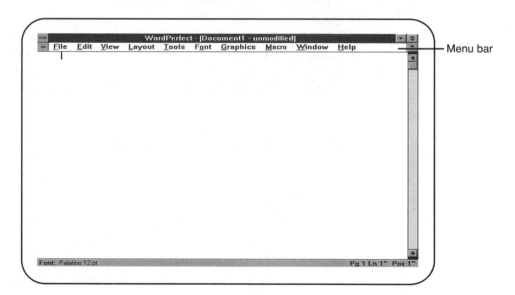

Figure B.1   The menu bar in WordPerfect for Windows.

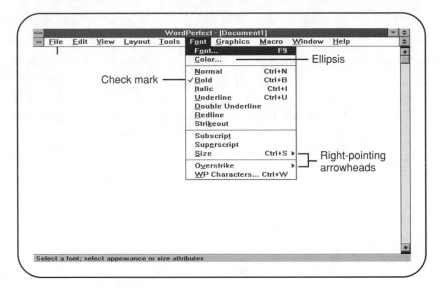

Figure B.2   *The Font menu, an example of a menu displayed from the menu bar.*

Menus have the following characteristics:

- Every menu name and menu option name contains an underlined character. In this book, the underlined characters are shown in bold. When you are in the menu bar, you can choose the menu or option by typing that character. After you enter the menu bar, for example, you can select the F**o**nt menu by typing **o**. (See "Selecting With the Keyboard" later in this section.)

- A right-pointing arrowhead follows some menu items, such as the **S**ize option on the F**o**nt menu, shown in Figure B.2. If you select such an item, WordPerfect displays a *cascading* menu, offering a list of additional, more specific options, as shown in Figure B.3.

- An ellipsis (...) follows some menu items, such as the F**o**nt option on the Font menu, shown in Figure B.2. If you select one of these items, WordPerfect displays a *dialog box*, such as the Font dialog box shown in Figure B.4. You use the dialog box to provide WordPerfect with information it needs to implement the option. For information on dialog boxes, see "Dialog Boxes" later in this appendix.

- If an item is not followed by an arrowhead or an ellipsis, selecting the item executes a function or command.

- Some selections toggle between turning a feature on and off. A check mark before a menu item indicates that feature is turned on. In the Font menu in Figure B.2, for example, the check mark before **Bold** indicates bold is turned on. If you select **Bold** again, you turn off bold and the check mark disappears.

- If a menu item is dimmed, it is unavailable to you. Cut, on the Edit menu, for example, is dim unless you have selected text. (See Figure B.5.)

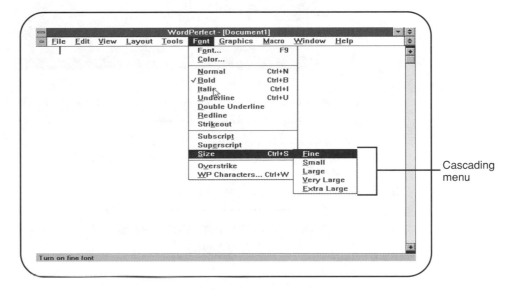

Figure B.3 *The cascading menu that appears when you select Size on the Font menu.*

To use menus, first select a menu from the menu bar and then select an option from the menu. You can use the mouse or the keyboard to make your selections.

Selecting with the Mouse

The mouse is a simple, intuitive way to select items from a menu: You just point to the item you want and click the mouse button to select it, as follows:

1. Click on the name of the menu you want to display. The menu appears below the menu name.

2. Click on the menu item you want to select.

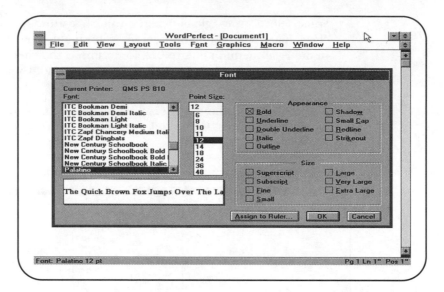

Figure B.4   Dialog boxes, such as the Font dialog box, appear when WordPerfect needs additional information before it can execute an option.

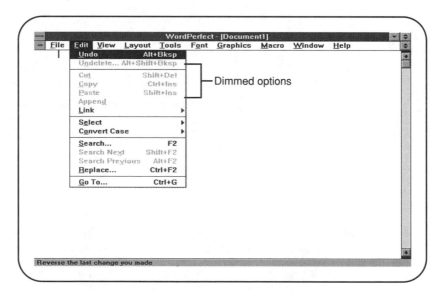

Figure B.5   Menu options that aren't available are dimmed.

3. If the menu item has an arrow to the right of it, Step 2 opens a cascading menu. Repeat Step 2 until you execute a command. If a menu item is followed by an ellipsis, selecting the item opens a dialog box. Fill in the dialog box to execute the command. (For information about completing dialog boxes, see "Dialog Boxes" later in this appendix.)

To leave a menu without executing a command, move the mouse pointer off the menu bar and click the mouse button.

To move through a series of cascading menus quickly, place the mouse pointer on the name of the menu you want to open and hold down the mouse button. Drag the mouse pointer through the cascading menus until you reach the menu item you want. Release the mouse button to select the item. To leave a menu without selecting an item, just drag the mouse pointer off the menu bar and menus and then release the mouse button.

You can also use the keyboard to select from menus. To enter the menu bar, press Alt. You can then select any menu and any option from a menu by typing the underlined character in the menu or option name. You can also use the arrow keys to move among options and then press Enter to select the option.

Selecting with the Keyboard

1. Press the Alt key.

2. Type the underlined letter in the name of the menu you want to display. Or, use the Right and Left Arrow keys to move to the name of the menu you want to display and press Enter. The menu appears below the menu name.

3. Type the underlined letter in the name of the menu item you want to select. Or, press the Up and Down Arrow keys to highlight the item and press Enter.

4. If the menu item has an arrow to the right of it, Step 3 opens a cascading menu. Repeat Step 3 until you execute a command. If a menu item is followed by an ellipsis, selecting the item opens a dialog box. Fill in the dialog box to execute the command. (For information about completing dialog boxes, see "Dialog Boxes" later in this appendix.)

To leave a menu without executing a command, press the Alt key or the Esc key. Pressing the Alt key returns you to the typing area. Pressing the Esc key returns you to the previous menu or, if you are at the menu bar, to the typing area.

Dialog Boxes

When you select a menu option that is followed by an ellipsis (...), a dialog box appears. You need to enter information in the dialog box to implement the option you selected.

A dialog box can contain one or more areas with any of the following items, illustrated in Figures B.6 through B.9:

- *List boxes* from which you can select items. List boxes are frequently used to display lists of file names and directory names.

- *Text boxes* in which you can type information. Text boxes are often used in conjunction with lists. Note, for example, the Save As dialog box shown in Figure B.8. In this dialog box, you can type a file name in the Save **As** text box or you can select a file name from the Files list. As you move the highlight among the names in the Files list, the highlighted name appears in the text box.

- *Radio buttons*, denoted by open circles. Radio buttons are a group of two or more mutually exclusive options from which you can select only one option. The selected option is shown by a "bullet" within the circle.

- *Check boxes*, which are square boxes that contain an X when selected. Check boxes are a group of two or more options from which you can select more than one option.

- *Pop-up list buttons,* denoted by a double or single arrowhead. When you select a pop-up list button, you display a list of mutually exclusive options from which you can select one option.

- *Drop-down list buttons,* denoted by a down arrow pointing to a horizontal line. When you select a drop-down list button, you display a list from which you can select an item. If the list is long, it contains a scroll bar you can use to display more options. (For information on using a scroll bar, see "Moving Within a Document" in Chapter 1.)

- *Increment buttons,* denoted by up and down arrowheads separated by a line. Associated with text boxes, these buttons aid in entering values in text boxes by allowing you to increase or decrease values by preset increments.

- *List buttons,* denoted by an icon that looks like a document folder. Like increment buttons, list buttons are associated with text boxes. Selecting one of these buttons opens a dialog box that displays a list of files or directories that you can select. The Windows program itself does not use this type of list button, although many Windows-based applications do.

- Command buttons, such as **P**rint and Cancel in Figure B.6, apply to the whole dialog box. Selecting a command button executes that command unless the command name is followed by an ellipsis. In that case, selecting the button opens a dialog box.

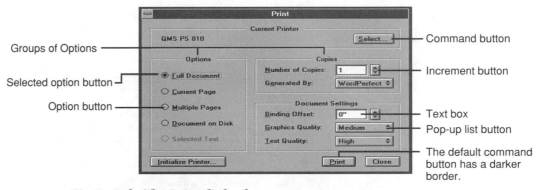

Figure B.6   The Print dialog box.

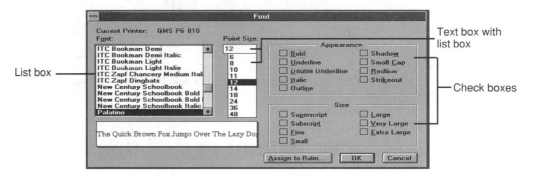

Figure B.7   The Font dialog box.

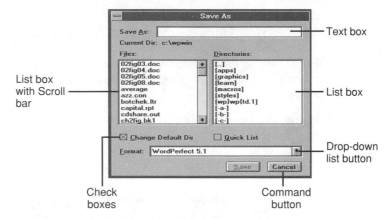

Figure B.8   The Save As dialog box.

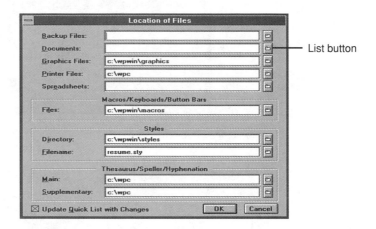

Figure B.9   The Location of Files dialog box contains List Buttons that you can select to display the Select Directory dialog box.

Moving Around in a Dialog Box

Dialog boxes are usually organized into groups of options. The Print dialog box shown in Figure B.6, for example, has the following groups: Current Printer, Options, Copies, and Document Settings. Each group consists of one or more options.

If you are using a mouse, you can move to an option by just clicking on it. This also selects the options if it is a radio button, check box, or command button.

If you are using the keyboard, you move between groups in a dialog box as follows:

- Press Tab to move to the next group.

- Press Shift+Tab to move to the previous group.

To move among the options in a group, use the arrow keys. As you move among options, a dotted rectangle, or *marquis*, functions as a highlight bar to help you keep your bearings (see Figure B.10).

Marquis —

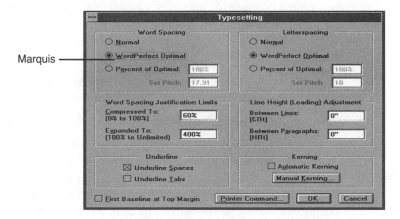

Figure B.10   A marquis highlights the current option being set.

Command buttons are not part of a group. You can reach command buttons with the Tab key.

Most dialog box options have an underlined character in their name. (In this book, the underlined characters are shown in bold.) You can quickly move to an option by pressing Alt while typing the underlined character. This also selects the option if it is a radio button, check box, or command button.

Selecting Dialog Box Options

If you use a mouse, you can select dialog box options as follows:

List boxes: Click on the list item you want selected. If necessary, use the scroll bars to view additional list entries. Double-clicking on an item selects the item *and* executes the function. For example, when opening a file, double-clicking on the file name chooses the file and opens it, just as if you had selected the file and clicked on the Open command button.

Text boxes, increment buttons, and list buttons: Click in the text box and type the entry. If the text box has an increment button to its right, click on the button to increase or decrease the text box value by a preset increment. If the text box has a List Button to its right, click on the button to display a dialog box from which you can select an entry for the text box.

Radio buttons, check boxes, and command buttons: Click on the button or box.

Pop-up list buttons: Point to the pop-up list button, press and hold the mouse button to open the list of options, and drag the mouse pointer to highlight the option you want. Release the mouse button to select the option.

Drop-down list buttons: Click on the drop-down list button to open the list, and then click on the option you want.

If you prefer using the keyboard, you can select dialog box options as follows:

List boxes: Enter the list by pressing Alt while typing the underlined character in the list box name, or by pressing Tab or Shift+Tab. Press the arrow keys to move through the list until the item is highlighted, and then press Tab or Shift+Tab to select the item and exit the list.

To return to the beginning of a list, press the Home key. To jump to the end of the list, press the End key. To skip quickly to a particular item, type the first few letters of its name.

Text boxes, increment buttons, and list buttons: Enter the box by pressing Alt while typing the underlined character in the list box name, or by pressing Tab or Shift+Tab. Type the entry. If the text box has an increment button to its right, you can press the Up- or Down-Arrow keys to increase or decrease the text box value by a pre-set increment. If the text box has a list button to its right, you can press F4 (Open) to open a dialog box from which you can select the text box entry.

In a text box, you can select from a character to the end of the text box by placing the cursor before the character and pressing Shift+End. Press Shift+Home to select to the beginning of the text box.

Radio buttons: Press Alt while typing the underlined character in the radio button name. You can also select a button by pressing Tab or Shift+Tab to place the marquis in the radio-button group, pressing the arrow keys until the marquis in on the button, and then pressing Tab or Shift+Tab to select the button and exit the group.

Check boxes: Press Alt while typing the underlined character in the check box name. You can also select a check box by pressing Tab or Shift+Tab to place the marquis on the check box, and then pressing the space bar to select the check box. To deselect a check box, repeat the selection procedure.

Pop-up list buttons: Place the marquis on the button by pressing Alt while typing the underlined character in the button name, or by pressing Tab and Shift+Tab. (The name of a pop-up list button appears to the left of the button. The name on the button itself is the name of the option currently selected for that button.) Press the space bar to open the list, press the arrow keys to highlight the option you want, and then press the space bar quickly to close the list. If you don't press the space bar quickly enough, the highlight moves to the top of the list and the list remains open.

Drop-down list buttons: Place the marquis on the button by pressing Alt while typing the underlined character in the button name, or by pressing Tab and Shift+Tab. (The name of the drop-down list button appears to the left of the button.) Press Alt+Down Arrow to open the list; press the arrow keys to highlight the option you want; and then press Alt to close the list.

Command buttons: Press Alt while typing the underlined character in the command name. You can also select a command button by pressing Tab or Shift+Tab to place the marquis on the button, and then pressing Enter.

Beginner's Tip

The default command button is pre-selected when you open a dialog box. It has a darker border than the other command buttons. (See, for example, the **P**rint button in Figure B.6.) You can execute this command at any time by pressing Enter, or deselect it by choosing one of the other command buttons instead.

If a dialog box has a Cancel button, you can select it to leave the dialog box without saving any changes you made in the dialog box. You can also press Esc to exit a dialog box without saving changes.

Windows

When you start WordPerfect for Windows, the first screen you see is the WordPerfect applications window, shown in Figure B.11. The features of this window are described in Chapter 1. When you open a document in WordPerfect for Windows, you open a document window that initially occupies the entire application window. You can resize the document window and move it within the applications window. If you have more than one document open in WordPerfect, you can size and move each document window so that you can display them simultaneously. To manipulate the windows, you can use the Control-menu box and the Minimize, Maximize, and Restore buttons. You can also use the mouse.

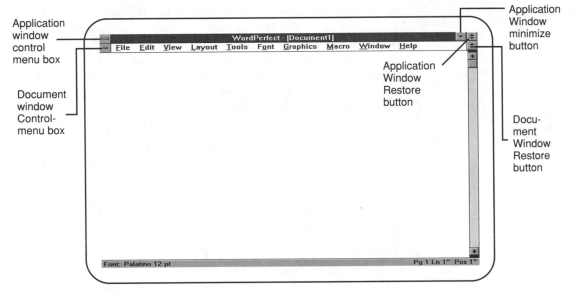

Figure B.11   The WordPerfect for Windows application window.

Using the Control Menu to Manipulate a Window

The Control-menu box is in the upper left corner of dialog boxes, which are special types of applications and document windows. Figure B.11 shows the Control-menu box in the WordPerfect for Windows applications window. The box appears the same in document windows and dialog boxes.

If you select the Control-menu box for an application or document window, you display the Control menu, shown in Figure B.12. This menu has the following options:

Restore: If you resize a window by selecting Minimize or Maximize, you can select Restore to return the window to its original size.

Move: This option lets you use the keyboard to move a window. After you select Move, you can use the arrow keys to move the window.

Size: This option lets you use the keyboard to size a window. After you select Size, you can use the arrow keys to size the window.

Minimize: Select this option to shrink an application or document window to an icon or a document.

Maximize: Select this option to expand the window to its largest possible size.

Close: This option closes the window.

Next: Select this option to go to the next document window. This option appears only on the Control menu for document windows.

Switch To: Select this to start Task List, which lets you switch to another application and rearrange the application windows and icons on your screen. Switch To appears only on the Control menu for applications.

The Control menu for dialog boxes has the options Move and Close. Use Move to move the dialog box, as described above. Use Close to close the dialog box.

You can display a Control menu by clicking on the Control-menu box. You can also use the keyboard to display the menu. The keyboard method depends on the window type:

Application windows and dialog boxes: Press Alt and then press the space bar. To close the Control menu without selecting an option, press Alt.

Document windows: Press Alt and then type a hyphen (-). To close the Control menu without selecting an option, press Alt.

Document Window Control menu

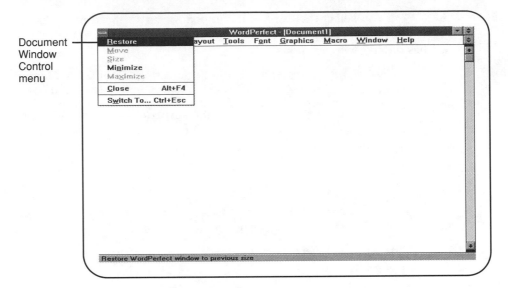

Figure B.12   The Control menu.

Using the Minimize and Maximize Buttons to Manipulate a Window

Each applications window and document window has a Minimize button, as shown in Figure B.13. Selecting the Minimize button shrinks the window to an icon. You can restore a minimized application window to its former size by double-clicking on it.

To select the Minimize, Maximize, and Restore buttons, click on them; you cannot select them with the keyboard. If you don't have a mouse, you can use the Control menu to minimize, maximize, and restore windows. (See "Using the Control Menu" earlier in this section.)

If a window does not fill the whole screen, it also has a Maximize button, as shown in Figure B.13. Selecting the Maximize button enlarges the window to fill the screen.

When a window is at its maximum size, the Maximize button changes to a Restore button, denoted by up- and down-pointing arrows (refer back to Figure B.11). If you select this button, the window shrinks so that it no longer fills the screen, but remains open. The smaller window has the Maximize and Minimize buttons, which function as described previously.

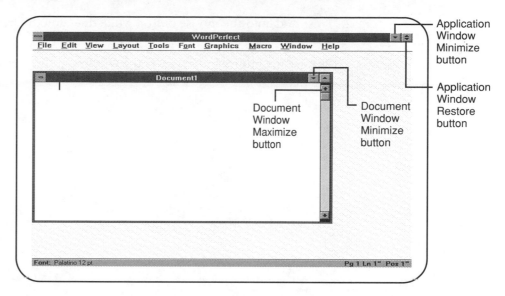

Figure B.13   Windows that aren't at their maximum size have Mini-mize and Maximize buttons.

Using the Mouse to Manipulate a Window

Perhaps the easiest method of moving and sizing a window is to use the mouse to drag it to a new position or size.

Using the Mouse to Move a Window

1. Place the mouse pointer inside the title bar of the window. (The title bar, at the top of the window, displays the title of the application, document, or dialog box. Refer back to Figure B.11.) If the pointer changes to a two-directional arrow, it is on the border of the title bar; move the pointer down so it is *within* the title bar.

2. Press and hold the mouse button while dragging the mouse pointer and window to a new location.

3. Release the mouse button to fix the window in the new location.

Using the Mouse to Size a Window

1. Point to the window border or corner that you want to drag outward or inward. The pointer should change to a two-directional arrow.

461

2. Press and hold the mouse button while dragging the window to a new size.

3. Release the mouse button to fix the window at the new size.

Setting Up WordPerfect for Windows

When you first install WordPerfect for Windows, it uses a set of default options to function. For example, columns are displayed side-by-side, the menus display the shortcut keys next to the menu items, and all your measurements are specified in inches. The Preferences feature lets you change many of these default settings to customize the way in which WordPerfect operates. When you select File/Preferences or Ctrl+Shift+F1 (Preferences), a cascading menu appears, as shown in Figure C.1. Selecting any item from this menu displays a dialog box that allows you to specify details about WordPerfect's setup.

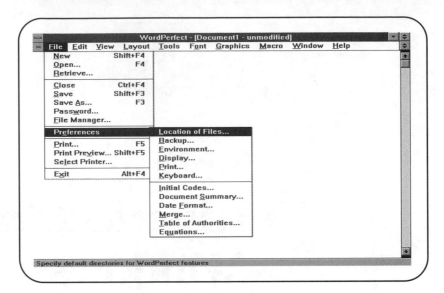

Figure C.1   The cascading menu that appears when you select Preferences.

Location of Files

To use separate directories for related files, such as backup files, document files, or style files, use the Location of Files dialog box to tell WordPerfect where these files are located. If WordPerfect does not know where to find the files, it cannot locate them when needed.

To display the Location of Files dialog box, shown in Figure C.2, select File/Preferences/Location of Files. To specify a default directory, you can type the name of the directory in the appropriate text box; or you can select the list button to the right of the text box, displaying the Select Directory dialog box, and then select a directory from the list that appears in that dialog box.

If you change the default directory for the macro, graphics, or printer directories, you can update the Quick List to reflect the changes. To update the Quick List, select the Update Quick List with Changes check box before you select OK. Updating the Quick List doesn't change any descriptive names you assigned to your default directories; it just maps the descriptive name to the new default directory.

When you have finished changing the directories, select OK to save the changes and close the dialog box.

You can also use the Location of Files dialog box to create default directories. Enter the directory name in the appropriate text box, and then select OK. If the default directory you entered doesn't exist, WordPerfect asks you if you want to create it. Select OK to create the directory, enter the directory name in the dialog box, and close the dialog box.

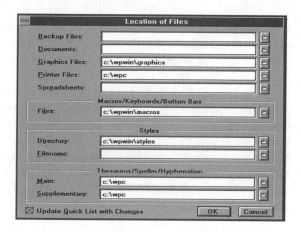

Figure C.2   The Location of Files dialog box, showing the default settings.

Backup

You can use the Backup dialog box to specify whether you want WordPerfect to automatically back up your documents. To display the dialog box, shown in Figure C.3, select File/Preferences/Backup. To create a backup copy of a document file whenever you save the file, select the Original Document Backup check box. To have WordPerfect automatically save your file to disk every few minutes, select the Timed Document Backup check box, and then enter the interval at which you want WordPerfect to save a backup file. The default interval is 20 minutes.

Figure C.3   The Backup dialog box, showing the default settings.

Backups of original files have the same file name as the original file, but have the extension BK!. A backup is stored in whatever directory contains the original file. To recover a .BK! backup file, open it in the WordPerfect window and save it with a name that doesn't have the .BK! extension. If you leave the .BK! extension, the file might be replaced by another backup file.

Backups saved by the Timed Backup feature are stored in the default backup directory named in the Location of Files dialog box. If no default directory is named, the files are saved in the directory containing the WordPerfect for Windows program files. The backup files have names such as WP{WP}.BK1. If you have a second document open, its timed backup file name is WP{WP}.BK2. If you exit WordPerfect for Windows normally (by selecting File/Exit or pressing Alt+F4), the timed backups are automatically deleted from the system. If you exit any other way (for instance, if the power fails), the timed backups remain. The next time you start WordPerfect for Windows, it will inform you that a backup document exists and ask you to rename it, open it, or delete it. If you aren't sure whether you'll need the backup, choose to open or rename the file. If you delete it, you cannot recover it in WordPerfect.

Environment

When you select File/Preferences/Environment, WordPerfect displays the Environment Settings dialog box, shown in Figure C.4. This dialog box lets you change defaults that control the working environment. The following options are listed:

Auto Code Placement: When this check box is selected, formatting codes that normally affect paragraphs are automatically placed at the beginning of the paragraph; and those that normally affect whole pages are placed at the top of the page. See Chapter 2 for more information on the codes affected by this feature.

Confirm on Code Deletion: If you normally don't work with the Reveal Codes area displayed, you can select this check box to have WordPerfect prompt you to confirm whenever you try to delete a code in the document. This feature has no effect if the Reveal Codes area is displayed.

Fast Save: With this check box selected, WordPerfect saves documents without formatting them for the printer. If you clear the check box, saving a file takes longer because WordPerfect formats the file before saving it; but if you print the file from disk, it will print more quickly because it's already formatted.

Allow Undo: When selected, this option enables the Undo feature, which allows you to reverse the last editing change you made (see Chapter 1). When you install WordPerfect for Windows, this option is selected.

Allow Graphics Boxes to Bump to Next Page: Selecting this check box allows WordPerfect to move a page-anchored graphics box to the next page if the box cannot fit on the current page.

Format Retrieved Documents for Default Printer: Select this check box to have WordPerfect automatically reformat opened documents for the currently active printer, changing fonts if necessary.

Beep On: This is a group of check boxes: Error, Hyphenation, Search Failure. If you don't want your computer to beep at you, turn off the beep for these features.

Menu: This group has the check boxes Display Shortcut Keys and Display Last Open Filenames. Select Display Shortcut Keys to have the menus display the keystroke shortcuts for menu items, for example, Ctrl+F4 for Close. If you select Display Last Open Filenames, the File menu displays the names of the last four files you opened. You can then open these files by selecting them from the File menu.

Ruler: This group of check boxes controls the Ruler display and Ruler tab settings. Select Tabs Snap to Ruler Grid to have tabs automatically snap to the nearest 1/16". When this option is selected, you can override the snap feature by holding down Shift while dragging the tab marker. Select Show Ruler Guides to display a guideline when you change margins or tabs on the Ruler. Select Ruler Buttons on Top to display the Font, Styles, and other Ruler buttons at the top of the Ruler. When this option is not selected, the Ruler buttons appear on the bottom of the Ruler. Select Automatic Ruler Display to display the Ruler whenever you open a document.

Prompt for Hyphenation: Use this group of radio buttons to specify when you want WordPerfect to prompt you during hyphenation. Select Never to suppress all prompts. This causes WordPerfect to hyphenate all words according to the selected hyphenation dictionary (see the next list item); words not listed in the dictionary are wrapped to the next line. Select When Required to have Word-Perfect hyphenate words according to the selected dictionary, and to prompt you to hyphenate words not listed in that dictionary. Select Always to have WordPerfect stop at every word that requires hyphenating and prompt you to position the hyphen.

Hyphenation: Choose radio button **E**xternal or **I**nternal to tell WordPerfect which of two hyphenation dictionaries to use. External selects the external dictionary, which is the larger and more accurate dictionary. Internal selects the internal dictionary, which you might consider using if you have limited disk space.

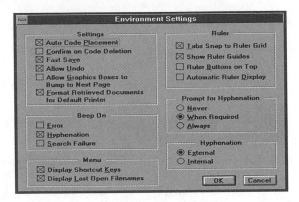

Figure C.4 **The Environment Settings dialog box, showing the default settings.**

Display

The Display settings affect how features appear in your documents. To change the settings, select **File/Preferences/Display**. The Display Settings dialog box appears, as shown in Figure C.5. It has the following options:

Document Window: This group of check boxes controls how text, graphics, columns, merge codes, and dialog boxes appear; and whether WordPerfect automatically reformats text when you edit it in Draft mode.

Scroll Bar: These check boxes let you display a vertical scroll bar or horizontal scroll bar or both.

Hard Return Character: To have a character denote a hard return, enter the character in this text box. You can press Ctrl+W to display the WordPerfect Characters dialog box and select a character from the dialog box.

Units of Measure: These check boxes let you specify the units of measure you want to use when entering measurements and when viewing measurements in the status bar. The default for both is inches.

Draft Mode Colors and Reveal Codes Colors: Select these buttons to display dialog boxes that let you choose display colors for appearance and size attributes, such as bold and subscript; and for text, codes, and the cursor in the Reveal Codes area.

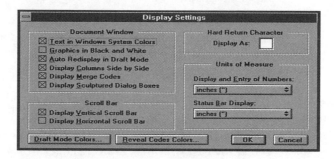

Figure C.5   The Display Settings dialog box, showing the default settings.

Print

The Print Settings dialog box lets you change printing options, the redline method, and the ratio WordPerfect uses to calculate the size of superscripts, subscripts, and fine, small, large, very large, and extra large text. To display the dialog box, shown in Figure C.6, select File/Preferences/Print. You can change the following options:

Multiple Copies: This group of options lets you specify how many copies to print and whether to collate them. Enter the number of copies in the Number of Copies text box. To collate the copies, select WordPerfect file Generated **By** pop-up list button, and then select from the pop-up list. WordPerfect will create the number of copies and then send them, collated, to the printer. If you select **Printer,** WordPerfect generates only one copy of the document and the printer prints the number of copies you specify. In this case the copies are not collated. It is faster to have the printer generate the copies especially with complex graphics. When printing any document, you can override the Multiple Copies settings by selecting different options in the Print dialog box (refer to Chapter 1).

Document Settings: Use the Binding **O**ffset option to specify the amount of space you need to allot for the binding; the printed text will be shifted the amount you specify from the left margin (odd-numbered pages) or the right margin (even-numbered pages).

Select the **G**raphics Quality and **T**ext Quality buttons to specify the print quality or whether to suppress printing graphics or text. When printing any document, you can override the Document Setting defaults by selecting different options in the Print dialog box (see Chapter 1).

Redline Method: Select from this group of radio buttons to specify the redline method. For more information about choosing a redline method, see Chapter 15.

Size Attribute Ratio: Use these text boxes to specify the size of superscripts, subscripts, and fine, small, large, very large, and extra large text. Enter the size as a percentage of the base font.

Windows Print Drivers: If you are using a Windows printer driver, select the Fast Graphics Printing check box to increase the printing speed for graphics. This should not affect the print quality. If you have problems printing graphics, however, try deselecting this check box.

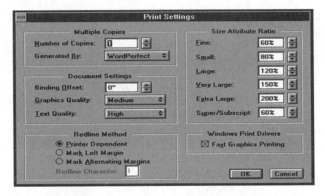

Figure C.6   The Print Settings dialog box, showing default settings.

Keyboard Layout

When you select **F**ile/**P**references/**K**eyboard, the Keyboard dialog box appears, as shown in Figure C.7. This dialog box lets you select a different keyboard, for example, the WP 5.1 DOS keyboard or the equation keyboard (see Chapters 1 and 20). It also lets you create and edit your own keyboards by assigning different functions and macros to various keys. If you select a new keyboard, you can return to the default keyboard, the CUA keyboard, by selecting **D**efault (CUA) in the Keyboard dialog box.

Figure C.7   The Keyboard dialog box.

Initial Codes

Select File/Preferences/Initial Codes to display the Default Initial Codes window, shown in Figure C.8. This window is similar to a normal document window. Enter in this window all formatting codes that you want to apply to new documents. For example, you might enter codes for margins, line spacing, and justification. Select File/Close or the Close button to save the initial codes and close the window. Formatting changes that you enter here affect all new documents, but do not affect previously created documents. You can override the default initial codes for any document by opening the document and selecting Layout/Document/Initial Codes. The Initial Codes window appears, displaying the defaults. Edit the codes, deleting or adding codes as necessary, and then select the Close button (or File/Close). The changes override the defaults for that document only.

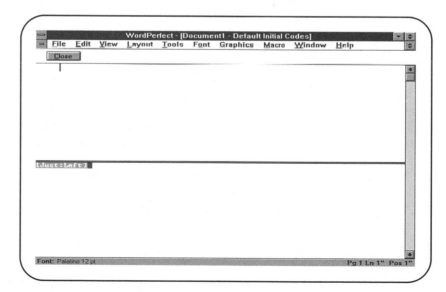

Figure C.8   The Default Initial Codes window.

Document Summary

To specify default settings for document summaries, select File/Preferences/ Document Summary. The Document Summary Preferences dialog box appears, as shown in Figure C.9. In this dialog box, you can specify the text string for which WordPerfect searches when it is looking for a subject statement in a document. The default is *RE:*. You can also specify a default descriptive type, for example, *contract* or *report*. To have WordPerfect create a document summary whenever you save or exit a document that does not have a summary, select the Create Summary on Save/Exit check box. For more information on document summaries and this dialog box, see Chapter 15.

Figure C.9   The Document Summary Preferences dialog box, showing the default settings.

Date Format

WordPerfect's Date feature allows you to insert the date text or a date code that automatically enters the current date when you open the document. By default, the date has the format Month Day, Year, for example, February 14, 1992. To change the date format or to include the time, select File/ Preferences/Date Format. The Date/Time Preferences dialog box appears, as shown in Figure C.10. Edit the spaces and punctuation in the Edit Date Format text box, and insert codes for the date and time. Refer to Chapter 2 for more information about editing the date format and inserting date and time codes (for information on time codes, also see Chapter 12).

Merge

When you select File/Preferences/Merge, WordPerfect displays the Merge Preferences dialog box, shown in Figure C.11. Use this dialog box to specify the characters or codes that indicate where fields or records end in ASCII text files. You can select the pop-up list buttons to display and select from a list of codes commonly used for this purpose.

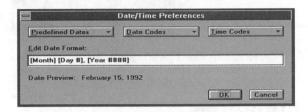

Figure C.10   The Date/Time Preferences dialog box, showing the default settings.

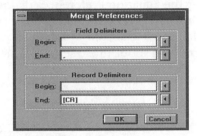

Figure C.11   The Merge Preferences dialog box, showing the default settings.

Table of Authorities

If you often use the same format for tables of authorities, you can specify that format as the default format. Select **File/Preferences/Table** of Authorities to display the ToA Preferences dialog box, shown in Figure C.12. In that dialog box, select **Dot Leaders** to precede right-aligned page numbers with dot leaders. Select **Underlining Allowed** to keep underline codes ([Und]) in the table of authorities entries (if this option isn't selected, those codes are removed). Select **Blank Line Between Authorities** to use double-spacing between entries; otherwise, they are single-spaced.

The settings you enter in this dialog box will become the default settings in the Define Table of Authorities dialog box, which appears when you select **Tools/Define/Table of Authorities**. You can override the default settings by specifying new ones in the Define Table of Authorities dialog box.

Figure C.12   The ToA Preferences dialog box, showing default settings.

Equations

If you use the same printing and alignment options for most equations, you can specify these options as the defaults. Select File/Preferences/Equations to display the Equation Preferences dialog box, shown in Figure C.13. The options in this dialog box are similar to those in the Equation Settings dialog box, which you select from within the Equation Editor. Refer to Chapter 20 for information about those settings.

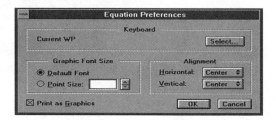

Figure C.13   The Equation Preferences dialog box, showing the default settings.

The Equation Preferences dialog box has an additional option that allows you to select a keyboard that will be active when you are in the Equation Editor. To select a keyboard, choose Select to display the Keyboard dialog box, and then choose Select again. In the Select Keyboard File dialog box that appears, select a keyboard, for example, `equation.wwk`, and then choose Select. Choose OK to return to the Equation Preferences dialog box.

Settings you enter in the Equation Preferences dialog box appear as the defaults in the Equation Settings dialog box. For individual equations, you can override the defaults (except the keyboard selection) by changing the settings in the Equation Settings dialog box.

Setting Up WordPerfect

You can change your setup preferences at any time, even while you're working on a document. Simply display the dialog box for the settings you want to change, enter your changes, and select OK.

Changing the Setup Options

1. Select File/Preferences or press Ctrl+Shift+F1 (Preferences).

2. Select one of the options listed. This displays a dialog box for the selected option.

3. Enter your changes.

4. Select OK. WordPerfect returns you to the document window and saves any changes you made.

BUSINESS
SHORTCUTS

Managing
WordPerfect Files

WordPerfect File Manager allows you to perform all your file-management tasks. To display the File Manager window, select File/File Manager. The first time you open the window, it appears as shown in Figure D.1. The File Manager menu bar and the Button Bar are at the top; in the center, the Navigator window displays files in all directories in the current directory path; and at the bottom, the View window lets you view the contents of any file you select. You can use the File Manager to view a file, open a file, copy files from one drive or directory to another, delete selected files, move or rename files, and more, all without having to leave WordPerfect! It's like having a full-featured file manager within WordPerfect. Because File Manager is a stand-alone program, you can also run it outside WordPerfect. Just select the WordPerfect File Manager program item in the Windows Program Manager.

The File Manager can display several different windows, each of which displays information about files in a different way. The Navigator window, shown in Figure D.1, lists the files in each directory in the current directory path. The File List window, shown in Figure D.2, displays more detailed information for files in a single directory. The Viewer window, shown in both Figures D.1 and D.2, displays the contents of any file you select in the Navigator or File List windows. The options on the View menu let you select which windows are displayed in the File Manager window. See the next section for more information on the View menu.

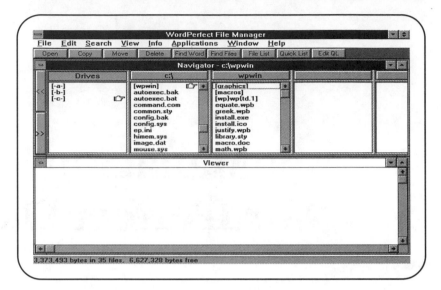

Figure D.1   The File Manager Window when you open it the first time.

File Manager Menu Bar

The File Manager menu bar lists the following menu names, which you can select to display a menu of options:

File: Lets you open, retrieve, print, delete, copy, and move/rename one or more selected files. This menu also has options for creating directories, changing to a different directory, printing a window, running an application, specifying your preferences for file-management activities, and setting up a printer using Windows printer drivers.

Edit: Lets you select all files or deselect all files. Other options on this menu allow you to copy and append to the clipboard selected files and text.

Search: Use this menu to search through directories to find specific files, and through files to find specific words or word patterns.

View: Lets you change what is displayed in the File Manager window. You can choose options to display the Navigator window, File List window, Viewer, or Quick List (a list of directories you frequently use) or you can select from several layouts that display two or more of these windows in various formats. You can also use the View menu to edit a Quick List, adding directories you frequently use to this short list of directories, to display and edit the File Manager Button Bar, and to change the font for the File Manager window. (The change affects only the display in the File Manager window; it does not affect the font in the files.) A final option lets you select viewing options such as the sort order for file lists and whether to display document summaries in the Viewer window.

Info: Lets you obtain and print information about the system, Windows, the printer, and the disk drives.

Applications: Lists applications that you can run by selecting them from this menu. The WordPerfect applications (WordPerfect, Speller, Thesaurus, and Macro Facility) are automatically assigned to this menu. An option on the Applications menu lets you assign other, non-WordPerfect applications to this menu.

Window: Lets you arrange the windows and icons in the windows and switch between windows.

Help: Provides access to the WordPerfect Help feature, including the Help index, keyboard information, instructions for common File Manager tasks, a glossary of terms, and context-sensitive help. See Chapter 1 for additional information on WordPerfect's Help feature.

Selecting Files

Many File Manager operations require you to select a file or group of files. To delete a file, for instance, you must select it before choosing to delete it. You can select a file in several ways:

- To select a single file, click on its name. You can also press Shift+F8 to turn on Select mode, highlight the file name, and then press the space bar to select it. You can use the keyboard method to select more than one file. (To deselect a file while in Select mode, press the space bar again.)

- To use the mouse to select a group of discontinuous files, hold down the Ctrl key while you are selecting the files.

- To select a continuous group of files, place the mouse pointer on the first file you want to select, drag the mouse pointer to the last file you want to select, and then release the mouse button. You can also press Shift+F8 to turn on Select mode, press and hold the Shift key, and then use the up and down arrow keys to highlight and select the files. Release the Shift key when you are finished selecting the files.

- To select all files, select **Edit/Select All** or press Ctrl+S.

Using the File Manager Menus

If you don't have a separate file-management program, such as PCTools or the Norton Commander, you can use WordPerfect for all your file-management tasks. You are not restricted to using it exclusively for WordPerfect files.

Using the File Manager

1. Select **File/File Manager** to display the File Manager window.

2. Select the drive or directory for which you want to list the files, or select the files on which you want to perform an operation.

3. If you are performing a file operation, such as moving or deleting a file, select the operation from the File menu, Edit menu, or Search menu. WordPerfect will display the dialog box for the operation.

4. Enter the information in the dialog box. WordPerfect carries out the operation.

5. Unless you selected **File/Retrieve** or **File/Open**, exit the File Manager window by selecting **File/Exit** or by pressing Alt+F4. (Within the File Manager window, you can close other windows, such as the File List window, by pressing Ctrl+F4).

Selecting and Managing Files in Dialog Boxes

When you use some features, such as Save As and Open, WordPerfect for Windows displays a dialog box that allows you to select a file name (for example, see Figure D.2). Some of these dialog boxes, such as the Open dialog box, also allow you to perform simple file management tasks, such as deleting a file. This section describes both of these dialog box features.

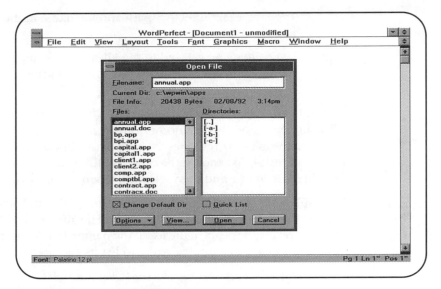

Figure D.2   The Open dialog box.

Selecting Files in Dialog Boxes

When you use Save As, Open, Retrieve, and several other features, WordPerfect for Windows displays a dialog box such as the one shown in Figure D.2. The dialog box contains the following:

Filename text box: If you know the name of the file you want to select, you can enter the file name in this text box.

Files list box: Lists the names of files in the current directory. You can select a file name from this list.

Directories list box: Lists the parent directory (denoted by [..]), the names of subdirectories within the current directory, and the floppy drives (for example, a: and b:). You can select a directory to list the names of files in that directory.

Quick List check box: Select this to list files and directories you commonly use. The list replaces the **Directories** list. To redisplay the **Directories** list, clear this check box.

481

Other features: The dialog box might contain other features, as discussed in following sections.

You can use the dialog box to select a file in any of the following ways:

- Type the exact directory path and file name in the **Filename** text box.

- If the file name is listed in the Files list box, highlight or click on the file name. The name will appear in the **Filename** text box.

The Files list box lists the names of files in the current directory. You can list the names of files in another directory by double-clicking on the directory name in the **Directories** list box. In the Open and Retrieve dialog boxes, you can also list another directory's files by highlighting or clicking on the directory name and then selecting **Open** or **Retrieve**.

To display directories not listed in the **Directories** list box, double-click on the parent directory icon ([..]) until the directory or the parent of that directory appears in the list. If the name of the parent directory appears, double-click on that name to list its subdirectories.

The Quick List feature allows you to list and select the names of files and directories you commonly use. To display the Quick List, select the **Quick List** check box. The Quick List replaces the **Directories** list, as shown in Figure D.3. To add the names of files and directories to the Quick List, follow these steps:

Adding to the Quick List

1. If the **Quick List** check box is not selected, select it. The Quick List appears in place of the **Directories** list box, and the additional option **Edit Quick List** appears.

2. Select **Edit Quick List**. The Edit Quick List dialog box appears.

3. Select **Add**. The Add Quick List Item dialog box appears.

4. In the **Directory/Filename** text box, type the exact directory name or file name (including the path to the file).

5. In the Descriptive **Name** text box, type a more descriptive name, if desired. If you enter a descriptive name, it will appear in the Quick List (rather than the exact name you enter in Step 4).

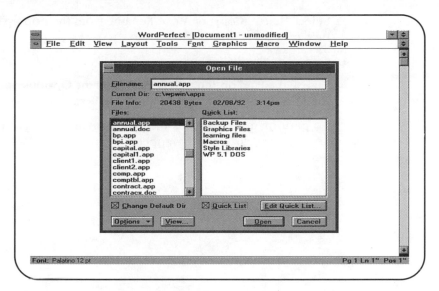

Figure D.3   A Quick List displayed in the Open dialog box.

6. Select OK. The Add Quick List Item dialog box closes. The new item appears in the Edit Quick List dialog box.

7. Select OK. The Edit Quick List dialog box closes.

   To redisplay the **Directories** list box, clear the **Quick List** check box.

Managing Files in Dialog Boxes

Some dialog boxes, notably the Open and Retrieve dialog boxes, allow you to perform simple file management tasks. To see the options available to you, select the Options pop-up list button. The pop-up list displays the following options:

> *Delete:* Delete a file.
>
> *Copy:* Copy a file.
>
> *Move/Rename:* Move or rename a file.
>
> *Find:* Search through files for a file name or word pattern.

To delete, copy, move, or rename a file, follow these steps:

1. Select the file you want to delete, copy, move, or rename.

2. Select the Options pop-up list button.

3. Select **Delete**, **Copy**, or **Move/Rename** from the pop-up list. A dialog box appears.

4. Complete the dialog box.

To use the **Find** option, select **Find** from the Options pop-up list, and then specify the search pattern in the dialog box.

To perform more complex file management tasks, use the File Manager, as discussed earlier in this appendix.

BUSINESS SHORTCUTS

Formatting Codes

[-]	Hyphen Character
-	Soft Hyphen
[Adv]	Advance
[Bline]	Baseline Placement
[Block Pro]	Block Protection
[Bold]	Bold
[Box Num]	Box Number (inserted in captions of graphics boxes)
[Cell]	Table Cell
[Center]	Center
[Center Pg]	Center Page Top to Bottom
[Cndl EOP]	Conditional End of Page
[Cntr Tab]	Centered Tab
[Col Def]	Column Definition
[Col Off]	End of Text Columns
[Col On]	Beginning of Text Columns
[Color]	Text Color
[Comment]	Document Comment
[Date]	Date/Time Function

[Dbl Indent]	Double Indent
[Dbl Und]	Double Underline
[DDE Link Begin]	Beginning of DDE Link
[DDE Link End]	End of DDE Link
[DEC TAB]	Hard Decimal Aligned Tab
[Decml/Algn Char]	Decimal Character/Thousands' Separator
[Def Mark:Index]	Index Definition
[Def Mark:List]	List Definition
[Def Mark:ToA]	Table of Authorities Definition
[Def Mark:ToC]	Table of Contents Definition
[Dorm HRt]	Dormant Hard Return
[DSRt]	Deletable Soft Return
[Embedded]	Embedded Code (Macros)
[End C/A]	End Centering and Alignment
[End Def]	End of Index, List, or Table of Contents
[End Mark]	End of Marked Text
[End Opt]	Endnote Options
[Endnote]	Endnote
[Endnote Placement]	Endnote Placement
[Equ Box]	Equation Box
[Equ Opt]	Equation Box Options
[Ext Large]	Extra Large Print
[Fig Box]	Figure Box
[Fig Opt]	Figure Box Options
[Fine]	Fine Print
[Flsh Rgt]	Flush Right
[Font]	Base Font

[Footer]	Footer
[Footnote]	Footnote
[Force]	Force Odd/Even Page
[Ftn Opt]	Footnote Options
[HdCntrTab]	Hard Center Tab
[HdDecTab]	Hard Decimal-Aligned Tab
[HdRgtTab]	Hard Right-Aligned Tab
[HdSpc]	Hard Space
[HdTab]	Hard Left-Aligned Tab
[Header]	Header
[HLine]	Horizontal Line
[HPg]	Hard Page Break
[Hrd Row]	Hard Row
[HRt]	Hard Return
[HRt-SPg]	Hard Return-Soft Page
[Hyph Ign Wrd]	Ignore Word During Hyphenation
[Hyph Off]	Hyphenation off
[Hyph On]	Hyphenation on
[HyphSRt]	Hyphenation Soft Return
[HZone]	Hyphenation Zone
[Indent]	Indent
[Index]	Index Entry
[Insert Pg Num]	Insert Page Number
[Italc]	Italics
[Just]	Justification
[Just Lim]	Word Spacing Justification Limits
[Kern]	Kerning
[L/R Mar]	Left and Right Margins

[Lang]	Language
[Large]	Large Print
[Line Height Adj]	Line Height Adjustment
[Link]	Spreadsheet Link
[Link End]	Spreadsheet Link End
[Ln Height]	Line Height
[Ln Num]	Line Numbering
[Ln Spacing]	Line Spacing
[Mar Rel]	Margin Release
[Mark:List]	List Entry
[Mark:ToA]	Table of Authorities Entry
[Mark:ToC]	Table of Contents Entry
[New End Num]	New Endnote Number
[New Equ Num]	New Equation Box Number
[New Fig Num]	New Figure Box Number
[New Ftn Num]	New Footnote Number
[New Tbl Num]	New Table Number
[New Txt Num]	New Text Box Number
[New Usr Num]	New User Box Number
[Note Num]	Footnote/Endnote Number
[Open Style]	Open Style
[Outline Lvl]	Outline Style
[Outline Off]	Outline Off
[Outline On]	Outline On
[Outln]	Outline (Attribute)
[Ovrstk]	Overstrike
[Paper Sz/Typ]	Paper Size and Type
[Par Num]	Paragraph Number
[Par Num Def]	Paragraph Numbering Definition

[Pg Num]	New Page Number
[Pg Num Style]	Page Number Style
[Pg Numbering]	Page Numbering
[Ptr Cmnd]	Printer Command
[Redln]	Redline
[Ref]	Reference (Cross-Reference)
[Rgt Tab]	Right Aligned Tab
[Row]	Table Row
[Select]	Select Mode
[Shadw]	Shadow
[Sm Cap]	Small Caps
[Small]	Small Print
[SPg]	Soft Page Break
[SRt]	Soft Return
[Stkout]	Strikeout
[Style Off]	Style Off
[Style On]	Style On
[Subdoc]	Subdocument (Master Documents)
[Subdoc End]	End of Subdocument
[Subdoc Start]	Beginning of Subdocument
[Subscpt]	Subscript
[Suppress]	Suppress Page Format
[Suprscpt]	Superscript
[T/B Mar]	Top and Bottom Margins
[Tab]	Left-Aligned Tab
[Tab Set]	Tab Set
[Target]	Target (Cross-Reference)
[Tbl Box]	Table Box

[Tbl Def]	Table Definition
[Tbl Off]	Table Off
[Tbl Opt]	Table Box Options
[Text Box]	Text Box
[Text Opt]	Text Box Options
[ToA]	Table of Authorites Entry
[Und]	Underlining
[Undrln]	Underline Spaces/Tabs
[Unknown]	Unknown Codes (not a WordPerfect for Windows code)
[Usr Box]	User-Defined Box
[Usr Opt]	User-Defined Box Options
[VLine]	Vertical Line
[Vry Large]	Very Large Print
[W/O Off]	Widow/Orphan Off
[W/O On]	Widow/Orphan On
[Wrd/Ltr Spacing]	Word and Letter Spacing

Index

G

H

W

IF YOUR
COMPUTER USES
3.5" DISKS

While most personal computers use 5.25" disks to store information, some newer computers use 3.5" disks. If your computer uses 3.5" disks, you can return this form to Sams to obtain a 3.5" disk to use with this book.

WordPerfect for Windows Business Shortcuts
Disk Exchange

Sams
11711 N. College Avenue
Carmel, IN 46032

Name: _____

Address: _____

City: _____ State: _____ ZIP: _____

Phone: _____

Special Disk Offer

100 Additional Applications

To receive 100 additional templates plus documentation on how to use them, fill out the order form at the bottom of this page and send the order form and payment to:

WordPerfect for Windows Business Shortcuts
POB 1465
Lawrence, KS 66044

(SAMS assumes no liability regarding the use or accuracy of the information contained on these disks)

WordPerfect for Windows Business Shortcuts
POB 1465
Lawrence, KS 66044

100 Additional Applications   (Please Print All Information)

Name: _____

Company: _____

Address: _____

City: _____ State: _____ ZIP: _____

5.25 360k disk ($20 each) x ___ Number of Sets = $ _____
3.50 720k disk ($20 each) x ___ Number of Sets = $ _____

for overnight delivery add $20 _____   Total _____

Method of Payment:
        ___ Money Order   ___Company Check   ___Personal Check

Please allow three to four weeks for delivery.

WordPerfect for Windows Command Reference Card

Feature	Keystrokes	Pull-Down Menu
Macro, assign to menu	Alt,m,a	Macro/Assign to menu
Macro, cancel playing	Esc	None
Macro, play	Alt+F10	Macro/Play
Macro, record	Ctrl+F10	Macro/Record
Macro, stop recording	Ctrl+Shift+F10	Macro/Stop
Margins	Ctrl+F8	Layout/Margins
Margin Release	Shift+Tab	Layout/Paragraph/Margin Release
Merge files	Ctrl+F12,m	Tools/Merge/Merge
Merge options	Ctrl+F12	Tools/Merge
New document, create	Shift+F4	File/New
New window, open	Shift+F4	File/New
Normal text attributes	Ctrl+N	Font/Normal
Number pages	Alt+F9,n	Layout/Page/Numbering
Outline text attribute	F9, Alt+N	Font/Font, Alt+N
Outlining	Alt,t,o	Tools/Outline
Page numbering	Alt+F9,n	Layout/Page/Numbering
Paragraph number, insert	Alt+F5	Tools/Outline/Paragraph Number
Paragraph numbering, define	Alt+Shift+F5	Tools/Outline/Define
Paste cut/copied block	Shift+Insert	Edit/Paste
Preferences, setup	Ctrl+Shift+F1	File/Preferences
Print	F5	File/Print
Print full document	Ctrl+P	File/Print, Alt+F
Quit	Alt+F4	File/Exit
Redline text	Alt,o,r	Font/Redline
Replace	Ctrl+F2	Edit/Replace
Restore deletions	Alt+Shift+Backspace	Edit/Undelete
Retrieve cut/copied block	Shift+Insert	Edit/Paste
Retrieve file	Alt,f,r	File/Retrieve
Reveal Codes, view	Alt+F3	View/Reveal Codes
Ruler, view	Alt+Shift+F3	View/Ruler
Save file	Shift+F3	File/Save
Save as new file	F3	File/Save As
Search	F2	Edit/Search
Search next	Shift+F2	Edit/Search Next
Search previous	Alt+F2	Edit/Search Previous
Select printer	Alt,f,l	File/Select Printer
Shadow text	F9,Alt+w	Font/Font, Alt+W
Short menus, view	Alt,v,m	View/Short Menus
Small caps text	F9, Alt+C	Font/Font, Alt+C

WordPerfect for Windows Command Reference Card

Feature	Keystrokes	Pull-Down Menu
Small text	Ctrl+S,s	Font/Size/Small
Sort text	Ctrl+Shift+F12	Tools/Sort
Space lines	Shift+F9,s	Layout/Line/Spacing
Spell check	Ctrl+F!	Tools/Speller
Strikeout text	Alt,o,k	Font/Strikeout
Subscript text	Alt,o,t	Font/Subscript
Superscript	Alt,o,e	Font/Superscript
Switch to next document	Ctrl+F6	Window
Switch to previous document	Ctrl+Shift+F6	Window
Switch to next pane	F6	None
Switch to previous pane	Shift+F6	None
Tab set	Shift+F9,t	Layout/Line/Tab Set
Table, create	Ctrl+F9,c	Layout/Tables/Create
Table Box, caption	Alt,g,t,a	Graphics/Table Box/Caption
Table Box, create	Alt,g,t,c	Graphics/Table Box/Create
Table Box, edit	Alt,g,t,e	Graphics/Table Box/Edit
Table Box, new number	Alt,g,t,n	Graphics/Table Box/New Number
Table Box, options	Alt,g,t,o	Graphics/Table Box/Options
Table Box, position/size	Alt,g,t,p	Graphics/Table Box/Position
Text Box, caption	Alt,g,b,a	Graphics/Text Box/Caption
Text Box, create	Alt+F11	Graphics/Text Box/Create
Text Box, edit	Alt+Shift+F11	Graphics/Text Box/Edit
Text Box, new number	Alt,g,b,n	Graphics/Text Box/New Number
Text Box, options	Alt,g,b,o	Graphics/Text Box/Options
Text Box, position/size	Alt,g,b,p	Graphics/Text Box/Position
Thesaurus	Alt+F1	Tools/Thesaurus
Underline text	Ctrl+U	Font/Underline
Underline, double	Alt,o,d	Font/Double Underline
Undo last edit	Alt+Backspace	Edit/Undo
User Box, caption	Alt,g,u,a	Graphics/User Box/Caption
User Box, create	Alt,g,u,c	Graphics/User Box/Create
User Box, edit	Alt,g,u,e	Graphics/User Box/Edit
User Box, new number	Alt,g,u,n	Graphics/User Box/New Number
User Box, options	Alt,g,u,o	Graphics/User Box/Options
User Box, position/size	Alt,g,u,p	Graphics/User Box/Position
Very large text	Ctrl+S,v	Font/Size/Very Large
Preview document	Shift+F5	File/Print Preview
WordPerfect setup	Ctrl+Shift+F1	File/Preferences